MW01492545

ENS RATIONIS FROM

Medieval Philosophy
TEXTS AND STUDIES

Ens rationis from Suárez to Caramuel

A Study in Scholasticism of the Baroque Era

DANIEL D. NOVOTNÝ

Fordham University Press · New York · 2013

Library of Congress Cataloging-in-Publication Data
Novotný, Daniel.
  Ens rationis from Suárez to Caramuel : a study
in scholasticism of the Baroque Era / Daniel D.
Novotný — 1st ed.
      p. cm. — (Medieval philosophy)
  Includes bibliographical references (p.   ) and
index.
  ISBN 978-0-8232-4476-8 (cloth : alk. paper)
  1. Suárez, Francisco, 1548–1617. De entibus
rationis. 2. Metaphysics. 3. Ontology. I. Title.
BD111.N68 2013
111—dc23

                          2012031309

CONTENTS

ILLUSTRATIONS

PREFACE

Famously, within the tradition of twentieth-century analytic philosophy, Bertrand Russell's elimination of apparent ontological commitments to nonexisting objects was for decades thought to be the definitive answer to the question of nonbeing/intentional-being. Perhaps equally famously, however, a number of contemporary logicians and ontologists, drawing especially on the work of Alexius Meinong, showed that this is not the case. But Meinong was not the only traditional philosopher who was preoccupied with the theory of nonbeing/intentional-being. This tangled problem, or rather family of problems, has attracted philosophers since the very beginnings of philosophical ontology. True, as Quine has observed, the problem can be put in three Anglo-Saxon monosyllables, "What is there?"—but to answer it with the word 'Everything' is not acceptable to everyone. There are hobbits and elves that live only in fairy tales, states of affairs that fail to become facts, and events that never occur. There are doughnut holes and quasi-properties, such as being non-smart or blind or sick. There are powerful political and economic institutions that seem to be nothing outside of our minds. There are linguistic expressions and their meanings, numbers in mathematics, and theoretical entities in physics. There are abstract entities, universals, sets of all sets, and—the list could go on. Many would like to say that some or all of the items on the list do not exist, but still they are something, and, perhaps, they are somehow "out there."

It would be useful for us to have a comprehensive study of the historical development of this perennial problem of nonbeing/intentional-being that would range from ancient philosophy through Plotinus up to Jacques Derrida and Graham Priest for the West and from Daoist and Buddhist canons through Nāgārjuna up to Nishida Kitarō and the Kyoto School for the East. The present book can offer nothing but a small contribution to some such future comprehensive history that one day may be undertaken.[1] The chapter that I have picked is one of the least examined and understood: It concerns the thought of seventeenth-century European and colonial universities, the period I call "Baroque scholasticism." It is well known that the scholastic tradition flourished in the West in the Middle Ages, but it also flourished in the Renaissance and the Baroque period. In the minds of many contemporary philosophers this tradition is linked with Platonists (Ficino, Pico della Mirandola) for the Renaissance and with rationalists (Descartes, Spinoza, Leibniz) and empiricists (Locke, Berkeley, Hume) for the Baroque. Yet, according to the estimate of Charles B. Schmitt, there were fewer than five hundred editions of Plato before 1600, whereas there were an astonishing three to four thousand editions of Aristotle (1983, 14). The situation was no different in the seventeenth century, except for the growing influence of Descartes and British empiricism toward its end. Hence, in the minds of historically informed philosophers, the sixteenth and seventeenth centuries no less than the thirteenth and fourteenth centuries should be linked with the overwhelming reality of scholastic philosophy and its predominant, although not exclusive, Aristotelian basis.

It seems to be already an acknowledged fact that the *Metaphysical Disputations*, the paradigmatic Baroque scholastic work published in 1597 by the Spanish Jesuit Francisco Suárez, should be counted among the classics of Western philosophy. Disputation 54, the last disputation of this work, is explicitly devoted to the problem of necessarily nonexistent intentional beings, so-called beings of reason (*entia rationis*). Although this disputation is not "the most comprehensive exposition of the problem," as has been claimed (Oeing-Hanhoff 1974, 56), it is a densely argued text of eighteen thousand words and deserves close scholarly attention.

Suárez's ontology of beings of reason was brought into the landscape of contemporary Anglo-American historiography by John P. Doyle. His first article (1967) dealt with beings of reason only incidentally, in the context of a debate over the reality of non-actualized possibles. Beings of reason were later given explicit and focused attention in Doyle (1987) and (1988). Doyle's work on Suárez's theory of beings of reason culminated in the translation of Disputation 54 into English in 1995. Further systematic, albeit incidental, treatment was given to beings of reason by Gracia (1991b, 1992). Then, *The Theory of the Pure Object* (1990/1996), a work on nonreality by the Spanish phenomenologist Antonio Millán-Puelles, appeared in English in 1996. Millán-Puelles is a systematic author with sound knowledge of texts of several Baroque scholastics, beginning with Suárez's Disputation 54. Most recently, Bernardo J. Canteñs published two papers (2000, 2003).[2]

Thanks to the work of Doyle, Gracia, Millán-Puelles, Canteñs, and others, we have an accurate understanding of Suárez's theory of beings of reason.[3] So what is the rationale for the present study? In this book I try to go beyond what has been reached so far by the aforementioned historians, both historically and systematically. I argue, among other things, that, in the end, Suárez's theory is confused at best and incoherent at worst. Furthermore, I also show that the problems of Suárez's theory were picked up and extensively dealt with by contemporaneous and subsequent scholastic authors of the early Baroque era. Suárez is presented in context as just one of many noteworthy scholastics of the Baroque era.[4]

To the best of my knowledge, the claim that Suárez's theory of beings of reason is incoherent has not been made before. Concerning the claim that Suárez is just one of many excellent philosophers of the time, Doyle made pioneering work by introducing not just Suárez's theory of beings of reason but also the theories of several other post-Suárezian scholastic philosophers into contemporary historiography. One of the objectives of the present study is to continue Doyle's work by fleshing out more detail and providing more rigorous formulation to the theses and arguments presented by Baroque authors.[5]

Up to now, with the exception of Suárez (and perhaps John of St. Thomas), seventeenth-century scholasticism has been a virtually uncharted territory. Maurice Grajewski said sixty years ago: "Seventeenth century scholastic philosophy has suffered at the hands of historians. Not only is there a painful lack of histories of philosophy treating the Scholasticism of this period, but the few historians that mention it usually present an incomplete and distorted view" (1946, 54). Unfortunately, these words are as true today as they were then.

This book is divided into eight chapters. The first chapter provides some information on Baroque scholastic culture and makes a plea for paying more scholarly attention to it. Although this book is primarily concerned with content-analysis of several Baroque philosophical texts and not with the historical and socio-anthropological aspects of Baroque philosophical "industry," I wrote this chapter for those who would like to get at least some context for the authors whose works are being studied. The second chapter introduces the problem of nonbeing/intentional-being ("beings of reason") from a systematic point of view. The chapter should be of interest even to those philosophers who are not particularly interested in the history of scholastic philosophy. At the end is a brief summary of the main results of this book. The next three chapters provide an exegesis of Suárez's main text about beings of reason. The last part of the fifth chapter provides an evaluation and criticism of Suárez's theory of beings of reason. This part serves as a bridge to the chapters that follow: In a philosophically advanced culture, the critique of Suárez's theory was to be expected and, indeed, the three post-Suárezian authors that I discuss provide alternatives to Suárez's theory. The sixth chapter deals with Hurtado's radically different account of beings of reason as mistakes, and the seventh with Mastri/Belluto's improved version of Suárez's view. The eighth chapter takes a look beyond Hurtado and Mastri/Belluto to Caramuel and his linguistic eliminativist approach to scholastic debates over beings of reason. The book concludes with a short reflection on the significance of the results of this study. In the appendix I provide outlines of the Baroque treatises on beings of reason treated here. The core chapters of this book may be naturally divided into two parts—three chapters are concerned with Suárez's theory (chapters 3–5), and three deal with Baroque reactions to this theory (6–8).

I had a hard time maintaining the distinction between mention and use. In theory, Baroque authors distinguished between linguistic terms (spoken and written), concepts (objective and formal), and real beings. In practice they only sometimes expressed these distinctions by using italics or 'ly' to indicate that they were referring to linguistic terms; in general they did not use any tool to explicitly indicate referring to concepts. In my translations of Baroque authors and in the main text I have followed modern usage by using single quotation marks for linguistic terms and double quotation marks for the names of concepts, both formal and objective. (I also occasionally use double quotation marks as "scare-quotes" and italics for emphasis.) If I want to stress that in the given context we speak about something in reality, I use italics. There are various complications with these rules: Some Baroque authors take objective concepts as the (known) reality itself; hence, in translating passages from these authors I often use italics when speaking about objective concepts, in order to indicate that we speak of reality. Sometimes, however, it is not easy to decide what the particular author holds with respect to the doctrine of formal/objective concepts and what exactly he has in mind. So I do not distinguish between italics and double quotation marks too strictly.[6]

In writing this book I had two kinds of readers in mind. First, all those who are not fluent in Latin but still are curious about what was going on philosophically in Baroque texts. These readers may skip most of the endnotes of chapters 3 through 8 that contain Latin quotes and occasional discussions of secondary literature. Second, those who are fluent in Latin and specialize in medieval, postmedieval, or early modern history of philosophy. For them the endnotes with extensive Latin quotes are intended to serve as a convenient and quick way to check the translations and interpretations I give.[7]

For the most part, the book was written between July 2006 and July 2008. It was generously supported by the Mark Diamond Research Fund (SUNY at Buffalo, 2006–7) and College of Arts and Sciences Fellowship (SUNY at Buffalo, 2007–8). It was later awarded the Thomas D. Perry Memorial Prize. For this and for other support, I am truly grateful to the University of Buffalo and its Department of Philosophy, which I will always remember as my formative "philosophical home." Whatever philosophical τέχνη I may have comes from the interaction with its faculty and graduate students at the time of my study there. I would like to name especially John T. Kearns, Barry Smith, John Corcoran, and Jiyuan Yu. Last but most important, let me mention Jorge J. E. Gracia, who has read the entire manuscript and suggested countless corrections and improvements (though, needless to say, he is not to blame for whatever mistakes remain). Also a great help has been Světla Jarošová, who has read the entire manuscript, spared me of many mistakes, posed some probing questions, and rekindled my interest in this abstruse topic by her own contemplative vision of it. Nicholas Frankovich of Fordham University Press provided excellent copyediting, which made my final review of the manuscript a pleasurable experience in spite of time constraints. I would also like to express my gratitude to the parents of my wife for providing me with an excellent working environment during the two years of my research for the book, to my parents for their interest in my work, and to my colleagues and employer—a small regional museum, Mountain Synagogue Hartmanice, located at the foothills of the Bohemian Forest—for tolerating my scholarly work during the less busy working hours at the museum.

During 2011 and 2012, I revised the manuscript of the book, updated the bibliography and made various corrections and additions. I wish I had another year to make more thorough revisions, but then, it would probably become another book and double the size. The work on the revision was generously supported by a postdoctoral grant from the Czech Science Foundation (P401/11/P020). I thank Gyula Klima and the editors of Fordham University

Press for their encouragement and belief in this project. The book appears in the series Medieval Texts and Translations. As I argue in chapter 1, this book does not exactly fit into this category. Nevertheless, as there is so far no series for Baroque texts and translations, I am very grateful that this study was given a warm welcome in the Middle Ages. I also thank my colleagues on the editorial board of *Studia Neoaristotelica: A Journal of Analytical Scholasticism* and in the Department of Philosophy of the Faculty of Theology at the University of South Bohemia for their interest in my work. In particular I would like to mention Paul Richard Blum, Petr Dvořák, James Franklin, Daniel Heider, Sven Knebel, Tomáš Machula, Lukáš Novák, David Oderberg, Jan Palkoska, David Peroutka, Peter Volek, and Vlastimil Vohánka. The interest in Baroque scholasticism among the younger generation of Czech scholars is owing to Stanislav Sousedík (Charles University Prague) and his deep conviction that Renaissance and Baroque scholasticism is relevant even for contemporary philosophy and theology. It was Sousedík who several years ago advised me to take up the topic of beings of reason. I am also obliged to thank the libraries of the University of Buffalo, of the Theological Faculty of the University of South Bohemia, and of the Strahov Monastery in Prague for their invaluable help. Recently, several libraries have started to collaborate with Google Books in digitization of their Renaissance and Baroque collections and making them available online; this effort creates exciting opportunities for more thorough investigation of these long-forgotten volumes.

Portions of this book have been published in various forms and read at various conferences, workshops, and symposia. Chapter 1 appeared as "In Defense of Baroque Scholasticism" (2009). Chapter 2 appeared as "Scholastic Debates about Beings of Reason and Contemporary Analytical Metaphysics" (2012). Some material from chapters 3, 4, and 5 appears in "Suárez on Beings of Reason" (forthcoming-d). Chapter 6 mostly overlaps with the paper "The Historical Non-Significance of Suárez's Theory of Beings of Reason: A Lesson From Hurtado" (forthcoming-c). An abbreviated version of chapter 7 appeared as the article "Forty-Two Years after Suárez: Mastri and Belluto's Development of the 'Classical' Theory of Entia Rationis" (2008). Some material in chapter 8 was published in a short paper, "*Ens rationis* in Caramuel" (2008). I would like to thank the publishers of these papers and book chapters (Studia Neoaristotelica, Ontos Verlag, Brill, Brepols, Filosofia) for their kind permission to reuse them. Papers related to this book were read in Steubenville, Ohio (Suárez Conference, March 26, 2006); Prague, Czech Republic (Bohemia Jesuitica Conference, April 27, 2006; Caramuel Conference, October 12, 2006; Suárez's Metaphysics Conference, March 10, 2008; Metaphysics: Aristotelian, Scholastic, Analytic Conference, June 2, 2010); Sázava, Czech Republic (Aristotelian Society Workshop, April 21, 2007); Bonn, Germany (Workshop on Medieval and Modern Applied Logic, June 30, 2007); Buffalo, N.Y. (University at Buffalo philosophy colloquium, December 3, 2008); Leeds, England (International Medieval Congress, July 9, 2008); and New York , N.Y. (APA meeting Philosophy of Mind in Historical Perspective, December 29, 2009).

The work is dedicated to my wife, Magdalena, with gratitude for her patience and support.

是以無有為有

無有為有　雖有神禹

且不能知吾獨且奈何哉

Zhuangzi, Inner Chapters, 2, 4

τὸ γὰρ αὐτὸ νοεῖν ἐστίν τε καὶ εἶναι

Parmenides, B3

1

Scholasticism of the Baroque Era

In this chapter I briefly discuss the broader historical context of the texts analyzed in this book. Although the chapter provides some information on Baroque scholastic culture, which these texts belong to, it is by no means intended to be a short history of Baroque scholasticism. The chapter offers only preliminary and general considerations with elementary bio-bibliographical data. The focus of the chapter is not to provide details of Baroque scholasticism but rather to answer the question of why to study it. I shall argue, first, that seventeenth-century scholasticism is best labeled 'Baroque scholasticism' and should not be subsumed under the headings 'Renaissance' or 'late medieval scholasticism' (section A). Second, I give a sketch of its emergence (B). Third, I argue that Baroque scholasticism should be viewed as a sui generis chapter in the history of ideas (C). Fourth, I give some reasons for investing more scholarly effort into its investigation (D). Finally, I provide some biographical information about the Baroque authors treated in this book (E).[1]

A. Labels

Seventeenth-century philosophy has often been presented simplistically "as a contest between two philosophies—Cartesian rationalism and British empiricism" (Popkin 1992, 90). But it is now generally accepted by the historians of philosophy that in the seventeenth century many diverse thinkers and philosophical movements flourished. Yet one significant philosophical culture—namely, scholasticism—running parallel to, and often in isolation from, the well-known culture of so-called "modern philosophy" has until recently been until almost utterly forgotten. The scholastic culture of the seventeenth-century had its own agenda (which was, however, not entirely dissimilar from the agenda of "modern philosophy"), a common set of as-sumptions, and its own technical language and methods. In both Protestant and Catholic parts of Europe and the Americas, it was at home at universities, seminaries, and other institutions of higher learning. In fact, this culture had reached as far as the Orthodox Kyiv-Mohyla Academy in Ukraine, and through the works of Catholic missionaries and their converts it was brought into dialogue with the philosophical and religious cultures of the Far East.[2] Although it is now a well-established fact that the "two-party view" of seventeenth-century philosophy (rationalism versus empiricism) is inadequate,[3] the sociological and intellectual importance of seventeenth-century scholasticism is still rather underestimated.[4]

Some of the roots and traditions of seventeenth-century scholastic culture lie in the Middle Ages, but many new elements had been integrated into it during the Renaissance, and some features of it emerged in the Baroque period. This culture seems to have reached its peak between 1630 and 1680, but it was still alive in the mid-eighteenth century, in the works of authors such as Luis de Losada (1681–1748). There are probably only two philosophers of this tradition whose names might be occasionally heard outside of the small circle of experts: the Spanish Jesuit Francisco Suárez (1548–1617) and the Portuguese Dominican John of St. Thomas (1589–1644, also known as João Poinsot). The two are paradigmatic representatives of this culture but by far not the only interesting ones.

Historians of philosophy use several labels to refer to this culture. Some of these labels—such as 'late medieval', 'Renaissance', 'early modern Aristotelianism/scholasticism'—are inaccurate, whereas others—'Second scholastic', 'Counter-Reformation philosophy'—might carry unwelcome connotations.[5] My suggestion is to call this culture *Baroque scholasticism* and take it to be the successor of *Renaissance scholasticism*, both being phases of *post-medieval scholasticism*. Let me discuss these labels. The appropriateness or inappropriateness of a label for a historical culture is an important factor influencing our decision of whether we pay attention to it or not. I shall take up the inaccurate labels first. The main problem with the term 'late medieval scholasticism' is that, in spite of the well-known difficulties with establishing the boundaries of the Middle Ages, it is too far-fetched to call any seventeenth-century philosophers "medieval." And to mean by 'medieval' merely "being inspired by medieval thinking" would not do, for many contemporary thinkers, such as Norman Kretzmann or Peter Geach, would have to be turned into "very late medievals" as well. Some have suggested that the distinguishing feature of medieval philosophers is their concern to "measure their philosophical speculation against the requirements of Christian doctrine" (Spade 2004). This would, however, turn into medieval figures not just Justin Martyr (mid-second century) and Suárez, who is anyway considered by some to be "the last chapter in the history of medieval philosophy," but even some contemporary thinkers such as Elizabeth Anscombe or Karol Wojtyła. This would make the term not useful.[6]

What about the terms 'early modern' and 'Renaissance'? Historians of philosophy commonly use 'modern' or 'early modern' for philosophers from Descartes onward.[7] According to this usage, the history of philosophy between antiquity and the Enlightenment is divided into medieval, Renaissance, and early modern. This language, however, is at odds with the practice of general historians who by 'modern period' mean the times since the end of the Middle Ages. According to their convention, whatever the end of the Middle Ages is, the seventeenth century is by no means *early* modern times; rather it overlaps with what art historians call 'the Renaissance'. But suppose that we disregard the other conventions and stick to the practice of historians of philosophy. Should we call the scholasticism of the seventeenth century 'early modern' or 'Renaissance scholasticism'? The latter option has been more common. Frederick Copleston (1953), for instance, deals with Suárez and a few post-Suárezians under the heading 'the Scholasticism of the Renaissance'. The same is true of Charles H. Lohr, who published his bibliography of the Aristotelian commentaries from 1500 to 1650 under the title 'Renaissance Latin Aristotle Commentaries'. Yet Renaissance scholasticism is supposed to end with the Renaissance, isn't it?[8] Consequently, it is somewhat awkward to say that Rodrigo Arriaga published "a Renaissance scholastic work" (namely, the newly revised *Cursus philosophicus*) in 1666, almost fifteen years after Lorenzo Bernini's *The Ecstasy of St. Theresa* (1652) and more than sixty years after Claudio Monteverdi's *Vespers for the Blessed Virgin* (1610). It would have been hard for Renaissance scholastics to flourish in the midst of burgeoning Baroque architecture, sculpture, music, painting, literature, and drama. Moreover, "Renaissance scholastic works," such as Lossada's three-volume *Cursus philosophicus*, were published in the eighteenth century (1724–35) too. Hence, if we want to use the terminology of art history, we should adopt the term 'Baroque' and drop 'Renaissance'.

But let us go back to the term 'modern'. We need to distinguish a culturally laden and a culturally neutral meaning of the term. The latter designates a historical period that simply starts at a certain point in time. As mentioned above, there is a discrepancy between what historians in general and what historians of philosophy take as the beginning of modern times, but, whatever it is, Descartes and Bacon are modern philosophers. Hence their contemporaneous colleagues, such as Suárez or John of St. Thomas, must also be modern philosophers—in this culturally neutral sense.

In the culturally laden sense, 'modern' designates the familiar assumptions, goals, methods, and terminology that have progressively gained importance in the Western history of philosophy. Modern philosophical culture in this sense has a certain "physiognomy" that sets it apart from premodern medieval philosophical culture.[9] Suárez and most of the seventeenth-century scholastics (*pace* Ferrater Mora, as we shall see) do not belong to modern philosophy in this culturally laden sense of 'modern'. For one thing, modern philosophy is epistemology-driven, whereas the *standard* seventeenth century scholasticism is metaphysics-driven. For another, modern philosophy is science-driven, whereas the standard seventeenth-century scholasticism is theology-driven. I say "standard" because it is wrong to consider seventeenth-century scholasticism a philosophical monolith. There were even self-professed scholastics who combined scholasticism with Cartesianism, such as the French Franciscan Antoine Le Grand (1629–99) in his *Institutio philosophiae secundum principia Renati Descartes* (1672/1679), or with a sort of Baconism, such as the Spanish Jesuit, working in Rome, Sebastian Izquierdo (1601–81) in his *Pharus scientiarum* (1659).[10] Such "modern scholastics" or "semi-modern scholastics" in the culturally laden sense were perhaps a minority against the background of mainstream scholastic Aristotelians of the Baroque era, but they existed as well.

At this point one could object that 'scholasticism' implies Aristotelianism and that therefore there cannot be such a thing as *modern scholasticism* in the culturally laden sense of 'modern'. In other words, the objection would argue that if Le Grand and Izquierdo are moderns, they are no longer scholastics. So let us consider the term 'scholasticism'. As in the case of 'modern', one should distinguish among various meanings. In a narrow sense, scholasticism is a philosophical method and a system of thought, rooted in Aristotle and Aquinas, with close ties to the Catholic Church of the Latin West.[11] In this historically laden sense, someone may wish to disqualify Le Grand, Izquierdo, and others from being scholastics, because, in spite of their impeccable Catholic credentials, they were not faithful Aristotelians. There is, however, a broader sense according to which scholasticism is any professional institutionally based philosophical culture that is characterized, at least in times of health, by comprehensiveness, teamwork, rigor, systematicity, and friendliness to an organized religion.[12] Le Grand, Izquierdo, and many others were clearly scholastics in this broader sense.[13] This means that scholastic culture taken in its broader sense should not be called *Aristotelianism*, because this downplays the significant role that Plato and, later, Descartes and Bacon had for some philosophers *within* this culture. It is true that Aristotle plays *by far* the greatest role for these philosophers, but to be an Aristotelian requires a more sincere commitment to Aristotle's views than just "taking Aristotle into account."[14]

The meaning and usefulness of the term 'Counter-Reformation philosophy' has been explored by José Ferrater Mora in "Suárez and the Modern Philosophy" (1953). He asks whether there is such a thing as modern philosophy in opposition to Counter-Reformation philosophy. While there may be differences in stress between the two traditions, such as the attempt to start from scratch versus rootedness in tradition, or this-worldliness versus the existential priority of Christian faith, there are also fundamental similarities:

> The interest in philosophy, and in philosophy capable of affording a complete explanation of the world and of the human person in *rational* terms, is common alike to modern philosophy, to Protestants since Melanchthon, and to the so-called Counter-Reformation philosophers. (1953, 531)

Ferrater Mora suggests that "Counter-Reformation philosophers are *to a certain extent* 'modern' philosophers" and so their scholasticism is something that belongs to the "modern spirit." Without explicitly acknowledging this fact, Ferrater Mora continues, we cannot explain why the paradigmatic philosophers of modernity, such as Descartes or Leibniz, take seriously the scholasticism of the time, and why only a few years after the anti-scholastic flames of the Reformation scholasticism à la Suárez became unprecedentedly popular all over Europe, including the Protestant countries:

> The outstanding importance of Suárez was really due to the fact that he was the first to erect a systematic body of consistent metaphysics at a time when people seemed to want something more than a series of Aristotelian commentaries, or than a rhetorical philosophy like Peter Ramus's, or even than a vague skeptical philosophy. (1953, 531)

Now it cannot be denied that Suárez, John of St. Thomas, and others qualify as 'Counter-Reformation philosophers'. Nevertheless, this term gives an impression that these thinkers *reacted* against the Reformation. And although it is true that they wrote occasional polemical works against one aspect of the Reformation or another, their main *philosophical* works, such as Suárez's *Metaphysical Disputations*, have nothing to do with the Reformation; in fact, most of these works were equally regarded in both Protestant and Catholic countries.[15] Furthermore, the term 'Counter-Reformation philosophy' undermines the very thesis Ferrater Mora himself defends— namely, that the philosophy of Suárez and the likes is *almost* as modern as the philosophy of Descartes and the likes. (I disagree here with Ferrater Mora, so I am not worried about this point, but Ferrater Mora should have been.)

Finally, we come to the term 'Second scholastic'. This term was proposed by the Italian confrère of Suárez, Carlo Giacon (1946). The term originally presupposed the Thomistic picture, according to which the history of scholasticism can be divided into the *First scholastic* (the Golden Age) in the thirteenth century, reaching its apex in Aquinas and starting its decline with Scotus and Ockham, and the *Second scholastic* (the Silver Age) in the sixteenth century, reaching its apex in Suárez (counted a fellow Thomist for the purposes of this classification) and starting its decline under the influence of Descartes and Bacon.[16] I am somewhat skeptical about this picture, for scholasticism seems to be a multifaceted, continuous movement with various peaks and dips for various "schools" and regions. A Thomistic decline may coincide with a nominalistic revival, or vice versa. A decline in one country may coincide with revival in another. On the other hand, the Black Death in the mid-fourteenth century does seem to be a significant blow to the thriving scholastic culture, and mid-sixteenth-century Spain does seem to be the beginning of a spectacular scholastic revival (lasting, as I would say, at least until the 1680s). Thus, although I do not share the preference for Aquinas over other scholastic authors, the intuitions about the Golden and Silver Ages might prove to be roughly correct in the end. If we avoid a priori Thomistic criteria of evaluation, the term 'Second scholastic' may be a good term for the entire period of postmedieval scholasticism (hence its meaning is broader than that of 'Baroque scholasticism').[17]

At this point it might be objected that I merely indulge in tedious verbalism here. My answer is that labels have power. If something is called 'middle age' and lies between 'classical age' and 'revival age', then only a few will spend their time investigating it. Similarly, if something is called 'Renaissance scholasticism', the humanist criteria of evaluation tend to be applied (and if something fails to satisfy such criteria, it is bad for that something). Again, if we label some period 'late medieval' and a book chapter appears with the subtitle "From the Rediscovery of Aristotle to the Disintegration of Scholasticism, 1100–1600," we will probably not spend much time reading anything later than Suárez's *Metaphysical Disputations*. A good and accurate label is needed in order to motivate and facilitate unbiased and thorough research.[18]

B. Emergence

It is not uncommon to speak of Renaissance scholasticism as a philosophical movement coinciding with what is generally called Renaissance art. Why is it then that almost nobody speaks of Baroque scholasticism during the period when Baroque art flourished?[19] There are at least three reasons. First, the term has bad connotations. As *Merriam-Webster* puts it, the Baroque is "a style characterized by grotesqueness, extravagance, complexity, or flamboyance." Hence, out of respect, those who are sympathetic to authors such as Suárez or John of St. Thomas do not call them "Baroque." Second, it is generally assumed that scholasticism died with Suárez, so that, properly speaking, there is no scholastic philosophy after him—the Baroque era has art but no philosophy. Third, the few who do acknowledge the existence of the scholastic tradition in the Baroque era assume that it had no "distinct physiognomy"—scholasticism lived in the Baroque but only under a thoughtlessly conserved facade inherited from a glorious past.

This study does not address these three reasons in general, for such task would have been too large. It simply takes up one of the many "hot issues,"— namely, beings of reason, dealt with by Suárez and a few subsequent scholastic philosophers, to reconstruct the argumentative structure of their discussions. Nevertheless, this study shows that what seems to be "extravagant complexity" is rather an admirable accomplishment required by the difficulty of the problems involved; that there is nothing wrong with being 'Baroque' (just as, in art, we no longer take this term to be derogatory); and that scholasticism after Suárez has features that justify distinguishing the Renaissance and Baroque phases of postmedieval scholasticism.

I discuss the differences between Renaissance and Baroque scholasticisms in the next section. Let me now turn to some similarities between them. A major transformation of the scholastic tradition occurred during the Renaissance, so that both Renaissance and Baroque scholasticisms resemble each other more than they resemble medieval scholasticism.

In a very simplified way, one could argue that the Renaissance revival of scholasticism was initiated by Dominicans and transformed into the Baroque by Jesuits, with the addition of a strong voice of Franciscans later on. Dominicans were committed to Aquinas, Jesuits had nominalist and empiricist tendencies, and Franciscans were committed to Scotus.

The Dominican initiators of the Renaissance revival of scholasticism were first French and Italian, and later also German and then, Hispanic. The latter played a major role in the formation of Baroque scholasticism.[20] This was quite opportune, for Spain was in its Golden Age, and its cultural and political power spread from Bohemia to Peru. Spanish culture became relatively isolated from the "disturbing" influence of anti-Christian humanism, the Reformation, and skepticism, and this isolation, together with good economic conditions and the commitment both of the elite and of ordinary people to Catholicism, created an excellent niche for scholastic philosophy.[21] The seminal figure in the formation of Renaissance scholasticism was Francisco de Vitoria (1492–1546), a charismatic teacher, deeply influential even though he published little during his lifetime (Reichberg 2003). Vitoria studied at the University of Paris, which was predominantly nominalist. He creatively enriched his Thomistic synthesis with elements of nominalism and humanism without compromising the fundamental Thomistic tenets. Today he is known primarily for his landmark work on the ethics of war, but the case could be made that his circle also prepared the way for modern economics (Rothbard 1976). Vitoria had several outstanding Dominican students and colleagues who spread their version of intellectually vigorous scholasticism from their headquarters in Salamanca to other places within the reach of Hispanic power.[22] Thomism during the Renaissance was also on the rise in Italy, where the major figure is the Dominican Tommaso de Vio, known as Cajetan (1469–1534). Cajetan is known especially for his commentaries (written between 1507 and 1522) on the *Summa theologiae* in which he deals especially with Scotus's criticisms of Aquinas.

A major event of the sixteenth century, which in fact contributed to its transformation into the Baroque, was the founding of the Society of Jesus in 1534, by the Basque soldier Ignatius of Loyola (1491–1556). From his original group of six companions, one of the greatest cultural forces of the sixteenth and seventeenth centuries quickly developed. The Jesuit activity had two priorities: missions and education. By the time of Ignatius's death, there were already seventy-four Jesuit colleges in Europe and the Americas, with growing missionary, scientific, and intellectual networks in Asia. Owing to the tireless work of the Jesuits, an ingenious blend of medieval systematic thought, humanist scholarship, natural science, mathematics, and technology spread from Europe to the Americas and Asia. The Jesuits were by no means the only actors in this drama, but they were clearly one of its main intellectual motors. The two major Jesuit philosophers of the sixteenth century were the Spanish Francisco Toledo (1532–96), who wrote many commentaries on Aristotle, such as *De anima*, and Pedro da Fonseca (1528–99), dubbed "the Portugese Aristotle," who wrote *Institutionum dialecticarum* (Elementary dialectics,1564), which would be widely reprinted, and a commentary on Aristotle's *Metaphysics* (1577). The commentary is a beautifully done work, which includes not only the Greek text, a Latin translation, and detailed exegetical discussions but also a systematic treatment of topics that, inspired by Aristotle's work, go well beyond it. In a sense, Fonseca's commentary stands even today as a model of good philosophy done historically. Fonseca also supervised the writing and the publication of the *Coimbra Commentaries on Aristotle* (five quarto volumes, first published between 1591 and 1606). The Jesuits were influential not because of a number of great personalities but institutionally as well: In 1599, they published *Ratio atque institutio studiorum Societatis Iesu* (The official plan for Jesuit education), which was a product of eighteen years of labor, debates and experimentation. This plan gave an institutionally codified position to philosophy as an autonomous discipline for the first time since antiquity.[23]

The Scotistic school of the Franciscans underwent a great revival later, beginning in the seventeenth century. The landmark event for them was the first splendid edition of Scotus's *Opera omnia* in 1639. The first students of Scotus were heterogeneously-minded thinkers: Some tried to follow Scotus strictly; others, such as the French Franciscus Mayronis (d. 1325) or the Italian Nicholas Bonetus (d. 1344), only loosely. The Scotistic school in the narrower sense of involving an agreement on some fundamental doctrinal and methodological points emerges only during the fifteenth century. The two peaks of Scotism come around 1500 and in 1650. With a few exceptions, all major Scotists were members of the Franciscan order, in particular the Conventuals, which was the parent stem founded by St. Francis in 1209, and the Observants, which were constituted in 1517. The Capuchins, constituted in 1619, were not very active as scholars and adopted as their master not Scotus but Bonaventure. The influence of Scotism, however, extends far beyond the Franciscan family, and some argue that it is the dominant force in seventeenth-century scholasticism.[24]

For the most part, Baroque scholasticism had a Catholic and Hispanic character. Nevertheless, in German Protestant countries there was a revival of scholasticism too, starting with the work of Cornelius Martini (1568–1621), in Lutheran universities, and of Clemens Timpler (1567/8–1624) in Reformed institutions. Cornelius Martini published his *Metaphysica commentatio* in 1605, Clemens Timpler his *Metaphysicae systema methodicum* in 1604. It seems that Baroque Protestant scholasticism emerged independently of Suárez, since the *Metaphysical Disputations* became known in Germany only in the Mainz edition (1600). Timpler explicitly points out that in writing his book he could take Suárez into account only too late.[25]

As pointed out earlier, Baroque scholasticism recognized the autonomy of philosophy, but it was predominantly "theology-driven." This means that it still saw theology as the discipline of highest authority and the object of final ambition for the most talented. Hence, even though philosophical arguments were never compromised by theological intrusions, the selection of philosophical problems was motivated primarily by their applications in theology. Beside this theological scholasticism, there was also scholasticism driven by mathematics, science, and technology, especially at Jesuit colleges, but this type of scholasticism is more practical than speculative.[26] Interestingly, for a long time, the "standard," theologically oriented scholastics were biased against their scientific colleagues—the work of the latter was considered unscientific. Mathematics was looked down on in that it did not involve syllogisms but "imagination," and only syllogisms were believed to constitute real proofs. The crucial person in dispelling some of the bias against mathematics, at least among the Jesuits, was the German Christopher Clavius (1538–1612), called "the Euclid of his century" (Lattis 1995). For many years, the mathematical and the conceptual-theological traditions within the Jesuit order lived side by side, without much intellectual interaction.[27] This seems to have been in part in order to prevent intra-Jesuit controversies concerning the question of whether mathematics is a proper science in the sense of

Aristotle's *Posterior Analytics*. The charges against the scientificity of mathematics (and, hence, also of mathematical physics) were leveled by some Jesuit natural philosophers such as Benito Pereyra (1535–1610) in *De communibus omnium rerum naturalium principiis et affectionibus* (1562).[28] These attacks were politically and institutionally neutralized owing to the influence of Clavius, who found them detrimental for motivating students to study mathematics. It seems to have been only in the latter part of the seventeenth century that some authors, such as Juan Caramuel y Lobkowitz and Sebastián Izquierdo in his *Pharus scientiarum* (1659), began to apply mathematical methods to philosophical and theological problems.[29]

C. Distinctive Character

Whereas the basic history of Renaissance scholasticism is more or less known, our knowledge of Baroque scholasticism is much more rudimentary.[30] In fact, with some exaggeration, we may say that historians of philosophy (especially Anglo-American) know *nothing* about it. One of the reasons for this is that the differences between Renaissance and Baroque scholasticisms are not sufficiently understood. This section highlights some of these differences.

One important feature of Baroque scholasticism has already been noted in the previous section. Baroque scholasticism is a blend of three philosophical schools—Jesuit, Scotist, and Thomist. Whereas sixteenth-century (Renaissance) scholasticism was characterized by Dominican and Jesuit exegesis of Aristotle, the seventeenth century is dominated by the more progressive and diverse schools of the Jesuits and the Scotists.[31]

A second feature of Baroque scholasticism is a great concern for systematic thought (Pereira 2007). Although Copleston (1953) assumes the standard view of "Renaissance" scholasticism being dead by mid-seventeenth century, he notes some changes in this respect around the time of Suárez:

Both Dominicans and Jesuits looked on St. Thomas as their Doctor. Aristotle was still regarded as 'the Philosopher'; and we have seen that Renaissance Scholastics continued to publish commentaries on his works. At the same time there was gradually effected a separation of philosophy from theology, more systematic and methodic than what had been generally obtained in the medieval Schools. . . . We find, then, the gradual substitution of philosophical courses for commentaries on Aristotle. (Copleston 1953, 344)

This leads to a third feature, namely, a much looser attitude toward Aristotle (and thus toward Aquinas). Suárez routinely complains about how disorganized the *corpus Aristotelicum* is; others, such as Caramuel, even cease to be soi-disant Aristotelians. We may observe progressively freer attitudes toward the philosophical authority of Aristotle, Aquinas, or Scotus.

A last feature has to do with individualism versus community attitudes (Blum 1998). Modern non-scholastic philosophers developed their views with little regard for what the larger philosophical community thought and wrote; their argumentation took into account views of only a handful of authors. Also, their treatises often take up particular issues without intending to develop a comprehensive, all-embracing philosophical system. And even if they do intend to develop such a system, its drift may be original but it often lacks precision. In contrast, scholastic philosophers (both Renaissance and Baroque) took into account a large number of works, arguments, and positions; their aim was usually to classify and present all possible answers to a question before answering it in their own way. Moreover, they shared a terminology, agenda, and training, and this enabled them to reach a level of detail in their discussions unparalleled in non-scholastic philosophy at the time. The scholastics—in contrast to modern individualists—regarded themselves as workers in a large network. But there is a difference between Renaissance and Baroque scholastics: In the Renaissance, the convention was not to name living adversaries, and most authors shied away from originality. In the Baroque, individual personalities came much more clearly to the fore. Baroque authors engaged in extensive polemics with each other and, despite "obligatory" references to some past philosophers (e.g., Aquinas and Scotus), they seem progressively less concerned with history—this is true especially of the Jesuits. It was the current state of the debate that most concerned them. In many respects Baroque culture resembles contemporary "English philosophy" as described by Scruton:

> Let us say merely that contemporary English philosophy is modern in the true sense of the word. . . . It attempts to build on past results and, where they are inadequate, to supersede them. Hence English philosophy pays scrupulous attention to arguments, the validity of which it is constantly assessing; it is like science, a collective endeavor, recognizing and

absorbing the contributions of many different workers in the field; its problems and solutions too are collective, emerging often 'by an invisible hand' from the process of debate and scholarship. (Scruton 1994, 1)[32]

This is not to deny that there are dissimilarities between the two cultures as well:

Modern philosophers are not system-builders in general: or, at least, their systems are peculiarly bare and unconsoling, in a manner foretold in the title of a work by the influential logical positivist Rudolf Carnap: *The Logical Construction of the World*. Since the turn of the century, philosophical problems and arguments have usually been introduced through articles, often devoted to some minute work of logical analysis, and sparking debates which to an outsider may seem extremely arid and in any case pointless when set beside the aching questions of the human spirit. Learning to take an insider's view of the debates, and to discover that they are not arid at all but, on the contrary, addressed to the most important human questions, is an exciting intellectual adventure. But it is hard work, and nothing can be learned without the patient study of difficult texts. The only mercy is that—with few exceptions—the greatest works of modern philosophy are short. (Scruton 1994, 2–3)

Unlike contemporary Anglo-American philosophers, Baroque scholastics were system builders par excellence. Every Baroque philosopher aspired to write a complete cursus, comprehending "all of philosophy." No one was considered an accomplished philosopher without having a comprehensive philosophical system, going from logic though natural philosophy to metaphysics and ethics. There was no division of labor within philosophy. Hence, "hot" philosophical problems and arguments were discussed through various editions of huge volumes. Within these mammoth works, dozens of parallel discussions were going on. This means, sadly for us, that there is no mercy in Baroque scholasticism; none of their major works is short.

D. Why Study Baroque Scholasticism?

Contemporary Anglo-American historians of philosophy either completely overlook scholastic philosophy of the Baroque or their description of it is quite inadequate. Let me justify this claim with the example of three major synthetic works that have attempted to cover seventeenth-century scholas-tics: *The Cambridge History of Later Medieval Philosophy* (Kretzmann et al. 1982/1988), *The Cambridge History of Renaissance Philosophy* (Schmitt, Skinner, et al. 1988/1991), and *The Cambridge History of Seventeenth-Century Philosophy* (Garber and Ayers 1998/2003). Each of these otherwise outstanding works fails completely when it comes to Baroque scholasticism. The faults of these works are not by commission but by omission. When something is said, it is usually correct but it is almost nothing. These works do not relate basic facts of seventeenth-century scholasticism; they show no knowledge of major Jesuit or Scotistic philosophers of the time; and they do not gather a proper bibliography in English, let alone in other languages. At the deepest level the problem with the current state of Anglo-American knowledge of Baroque scholasticism is not just ignorance of elementary facts but the second-order ignorance of its own ignorance, ignorance of a lack of knowledge in this area. Perhaps this is a phenomenon of Everybody's Land = Nobody's Land: Scholars of the Renaissance and late Middle Ages do not treat the seventeenth century, and scholars of the seventeenth century focus primarily on non-scholastic authors.[33]

Why do so few seventeenth-century scholars pay attention to Baroque philosophy? There are probably many reasons, one of them being that Ba-roque scholastic works are long and highly complex taken individually—and also collectively, given the amount of literature produced during this period. Also, they are linked to each other by innumerous references, sometimes explicit but mostly implicit. Scholastic authors freely borrowed from each other, and what seems to be an original argument might be in fact just a currently fashionable topos. Most controversies of the time have to do with disagreements about the analysis of some traditional slogan that they all accept as a platitude. Hence, the real disagreements of Baroque authors are often hidden to the eye of superficial readers, and the only adequate way to understand them is through patient and in-depth comparative research.

Another reason why Baroque scholasticism gets so little attention has to do with its sui generis philosophical culture and the need to approach it without prejudice and a priori evaluations in terms of standards foreign to it. The prejudice against the Baroque comes from at least three sources. The first is inherited from the fathers of modern philosophy and their superficial, outsider knowledge of the scholastic culture of their time. Descartes, for example, disliked scholastic authors such as Toletus, Rubio, and the Coimbrans

(AT 3, 185) whom he learned from in La Flèche. On the other hand, he praised Eustache de Saint Paul (1573–1640). Anybody who has ever looked into the works of the four mentioned authors will agree with Dennis Des Chene:

> Eustachius's *Summa quadripartita,* which Descartes called "the best book ever written on this matter," is, to put it bluntly, *not.* It is a kind of *Cliff's Notes* condensation, mainly of the Coimbrans, from whom Eustachius sometimes takes whole sentences verbatim. It is extremely sparing in its citations of authorities . . . , it often gives no arguments for its conclusions, and it rarely considers alternatives or objections. I am inclined to think that Descartes, who had no patience for details, little regard for authority, and an aversion to dialectic, liked it because it was unequivocal, comprehensive, and short. (Des Chene 1996, 11)

Modern non-scholastic philosophers were for the most part *dilettantes,* whereas scholastic philosophers were *professionals.* Their perspectives differ, and hence we should not take the judgment of Descartes and Locke as the last word.[34] It is, of course, an interesting question why in the end the moderns won over the scholastics, but we should not presume that this has anything to do with winning a fair philosophical dispute.[35]

The second source of prejudice against Baroque scholasticism comes from the Thomistic historiography of the nineteenth and twentieth century. John of St. Thomas was considered to be the best Thomistic author and Suárez the best non-Thomistic author. Other Baroque authors were believed to be inferior and sometimes even "decadent." Hence they did not deserve to be carefully studied. Some historians went even further and stressed the gap between the medieval genius (Aquinas, Scotus, Ockham) and the second-rate and derivative nature of the Renaissance and Baroque scholastics.[36]

The third source of prejudice comes from experts on Renaissance philosophy (both scholastic and non-scholastic). For instance, Charles H. Lohr, a confrère of Suárez and a great pioneer of Renaissance Aristotelian research, says:

> *Cursus philosophicus* . . . was meant to be an answer to the syncretism, skepticism and new encyclopedism which threatened the scholastic view of the world. . . . An increasing narrowness was consequently a second characteristic of the *cursus.* Whereas writers like Pereira and Suárez had

still attempted to master the entire tradition, the philosophy professors of post-Tridentine Catholic schools had less and less direct knowledge of Greek and Arabic sources and even a very limited acquaintance with their own medieval Latin authorities. (Lohr 1988b, 619)

Lohr assumes that since "post-Tridentine professors" had less direct knowledge of Greek and Arabic sources, they were "increasingly narrow." In fact, most of these professors *did not care* for the Greeks and the Arabs. They were interested in issues and arguments, not so much in commentaries on past texts or in history as such.[37] They are less accomplished as historians of philosophy, but this does not mean that they make no progress from the systematical, problem-solving point of view. Lohr continues:

> Because their teaching was directed in each case to the members of a specific religious community, they stressed the importance of its uniformity. Disturbed by the doctrinal confusion which marked the Renaissance period, they tended increasingly to return to the teaching of one of the great thirteenth-century doctors. . . . Summaries of scholastic philosophy were composed in Spain by the Jesuits Pedro Hurtado de Mendoza and Francisco de Oviedo, the Dominican John of St. Thomas and the Carmelite college of Alcalà; in France by the Cistercian Eustachius a S. Paulo (who is said to have an influence on Descartes); in Italy by the Jesuit Cosma Alamanni and the Franciscans Bartholomeus Mastrius and Bonaventura Bellutus; and for use in Germany and Eastern Europe by the Jesuit Roderigo de Arriaga. (Lohr 1988b, 619)

It is true that most of the scholastic philosophical literature was directed to a specific religious community, but it is wrong to think that such literature was "uniform"—even *within* a given community.[38] The Baroque period (especially from 1620 until 1680) was marked by great controversies both across and within the divides of the philosophical schools. Controversies are mostly recorded in subsequent revisions of various *cursus*, and they are constant and explicit. Also, as already indicated above, Baroque professors did not care that much for the thirteenth and fourteenth centuries. It was common practice to enlist Aquinas as an authority, but he could very much look in their works as a Scotus or an Ockham. It should be also pointed out that it is strange to list Eustachius's little pocket book next to the great works of Mastri, Arriaga, and others. (The list also has important omissions.)

Eustachius's work is truly a mere "summary of scholastic philosophy." Other works on the list, however, are "summaries" only in the sense in which, for instance, David Armstrong's *Universals and Scientific Realism* (1978) is a "summary of analytic metaphysics." As I shall try to show with the example of one of the topics discussed in Baroque scholasticism—namely, beings of reason—if one studies exemplary Baroque works patiently and in depth, one can discover quite complex and ingenious argumentation addressing deep and important metaphysical issues.

E. Authors

Before we open the systematic part of this book, let me say a few words about the thinkers discussed: Francisco Suárez, Bartolomeo Mastri, Pedro Hurtado de Mendoza, and Juan Caramuel y Lobkowitz. The choice of Suárez for this book needs no justification. Mastri is a major representative of Baroque Scotism, Hurtado de Mendoza of a rather peculiar form of Jesuit scholasticism, and Caramuel is an example of an original "independent" scholastic author. There are hundreds of other Baroque authors writing about beings of reason, some of whom deserve detailed analysis of what they have to say. Unfortunately, on this occasion it is not possible for me to give an account of all major scholastic theories of beings of reason. The representative sample of authors selected for this study needs to do. In what follows I provide brief bio-bibliographical data about these authors and also add information about a few other Baroque thinkers whom I have come across during my research on beings of reason. The authors are listed chronologically according to the year of their birth.

Francisco Suárez, S.J. (1548–1617)

Francisco Suárez was born in Granada, Spain, in 1548. From the age of thirteen (not unusual at the time) he studied law at the University of Salamanca. He entered the Jesuit order at the age of sixteen but only after an appeal, since out of fifty students he was the only one rejected for not being "bright enough." This rejection may have to do with Suárez's Jewish origin (Maryks 2010), though traditionally it is also explained as a miracle. Suárez studied in Salamanca under the Dominican Juan Mancio (1497–1576), who was a student of the famous Dominican Francisco de Vitoria (1492/3–1546). Suárez started to teach in Salamanca in 1570. Then he taught at various

Jesuit colleges in Segovia, Valladolid, Rome, and Alcalá. In 1597, at the request of the Spanish king Philip II, Suárez moved to the chair of theology at the University of Coimbra, which he held until his retirement in 1615. Suárez died in Lisbon in 1617, while on a church-political mission.[39]

Suárez's first book was theological: *Commentariorum ac disputationum in tertiam partem divi Thomae: Tomus primus* (1590). This book began an astonishing publication record, which ended only with his death, with many works published posthumously. Suárez's literary output is estimated to be twenty-one million words (Fichter 1940, 327). His contribution lies in the fields of theology, philosophy, and law. In philosophy, Suárez's most famous work is his *Metaphysical Disputations* (1597).[40]

Antonio Rubio, S.J. (1548–1615)

Rubio, known under the Latinized name "Ruvius," was born in La Roda in Albacete, Spain in 1548 and died in Alcalá in 1615. He entered the Jesuit order at twenty-one and studied philosophy and theology at Alcalá. In 1576 he came to New Spain (today's Mexico), where he taught philosophy and theology for twenty-two years. In 1599/1600 he returned to Alcalá in Spain in order—among other things—to publish his works. There he died in 1615. Apart from *Logica mexicana*, the subject of a monograph by contemporary logicians (Redmond and Beuchot 1985), Rubio published a few enormously successful commentaries on Aristotle. His textbooks became obligatory material at the University of Alcalá, but they were read all over Europe and America. Descartes, for instance, recalls Rubio in his letter to Mersenne (AT 3, 185). Rubio probably exercised more direct influence on the birth of early modern philosophy than did Suárez or medieval authors such as Aquinas (Ashworth 1999). Rubio is considered to be "the most important Spanish Jesuit logician" (Risse 1970, 399). One may even speak of a pan-European "Rubio vogue" in the first quarter of the seventeenth century (Redmond 1998, 330). Rubio's *Treatise on the Nature of Being of Reason* in his *Logica mexicana* is roughly half the length of Suárez's Metaphysical Disputation 54. Rubio agrees with Suárez on all major issues, and he does not notice any problems in Suárez's synthesis. His theory of second intensions, however, is more developed, which is not surprising, given that Rubio was interested primarily in logic, and Suárez, in metaphysics.[41]

Marcin Smiglecki, S.J. (1564–1618)

Smiglecki, known under the Latinized name "Smiglecius," was born in Lvov in 1564 and died in Kalisz in 1618. He entered the Jesuit order at seventeen and studied philosophy and theology in Rome. In 1586 he came back to his native Poland and taught philosophy and theology at the Academy of Vilnius for fourteen years. Smiglecki published twenty-three works on various subjects, including apologetics and economics. His *Logica*, his last book, was published in 1618. "This is interesting, since the study of logic was . . . chronologically the first in the university *curriculum* of the time. . . . The *Logica* should therefore be regarded as a mature work, probably composed over a long period of time and resulting from the author's lasting interest in the subject" (Roncaglia 1995, 29–30). *Logica* became an influential textbook especially in England, where it went through three editions from 1634 to 1658, even giving rise to a circle of "Smiglecians." Smiglecki deals with beings of reason in Logical Disputation 1, a piece of about twenty-four thousand words long. It is interesting that in the context of beings of reason Smiglecki is never mentioned by other Baroque scholastic authors known to me, not even by Mastri, who is quite thorough in his references. Smiglecki's views seem to be similar to the views of Suárez, Rubio, Mastri, and others, developing what I consider to be the classical paradigm of Objectualism.[42]

Pedro Hurtado de Mendoza, S.J. (1578–1641)

Hurtado entered the Jesuit order in 1595 in Salamanca, where he studied and later taught (from 1611 until his death; previously he taught in Valladolid). He is less known than Suárez, but his influence might have been equal or greater . Much of what passes under the label of "Suárezianism" is rather "Hurtadism." He influenced many Jesuit authors, such as Rodrigo de Arriaga. Hurtado is considered to be the main force of the renewal of nominalism in Baroque scholasticism (Caruso 1979). In philosophy, Hurtado produced one of the first textbooks covering not only metaphysics (which defines the scope of Suárez's *Metaphysical Disputations*) but the "whole" of philosophy. His textbook, called *Disputationes in universam philosophiam a summulis ad metaphysicam*, was published five times between 1615 and 1619; after 1624 it was substantially recast and extended and its title changed to *Universa philosophia*.[43] As we shall see in chapter

6, Hurtado's account of beings of reason, Fallibilism, is radically at odds with Suárez's theory.

Francisco de Araújo, O.P. (1580–1664)

Araújo was born in Verín, Spain, near the border of Portugal, in 1580. He joined the Dominicans in Salamanca, where he also studied and taught philosophy and theology. His main works include the multivolume *Commentariorum in universam Aristotelis Metaphysicam* (1617–31) and commentaries on Aquinas's *Summa Theologica* (1635–47). Araújo died in Madrid in 1664.[44] He was an original thinker and an explicit but respectful and perceptive critic of Suárez (whom he calls "Magister Suárez"). Araújo openly rejects some of Suárez's claims about beings of reason.[45]

John of St. Thomas, O.P. (1589–1644)

John of St. Thomas was a Portuguese Dominican, today also known under his civil name, João Poinsot. He considered himself to be a "strict Thomist" in the tradition of Cajetan. Poinsot's *Cursus philosophicus Thomisticus* (1631–35) is the only Baroque scholastic work that has inspired a score of systematically oriented followers in the twentieth century.[46] Poinsot's *Treatise on Beings of Reason* is part of his *Cursus*. It is relatively brief and has been translated into English twice (Poinsot 1631/1949, Deely 1985). In spite of the relatively great interest that contemporary philosophers take in Poinsot, he did not advance the theory of beings of reason beyond Suárez.[47] Within the culture of Baroque scholasticism, Poinsot seems to be just one of the many able thinkers, and the relatively high contemporary appreciation of his work is owing only to the widespread ignorance of other Baroque authors.

Rodrigo de Arriaga, S.J. (1592–1667)

Arriaga was born in Logroño, Spain. In 1606 he entered the Jesuit order and studied in Valladolid under Hurtado. Like Hurtado, he is mistakenly considered to be a Suárezian (e.g., by Eschweiler 1931, 275). In 1625 he settled in Prague, where he spent the rest of his life. For many years he was the rector of the Charles-Ferdinand University in Prague. There he died in 1667. Owing to his brilliance, he instigated an extraordinary development of philosophy in Bohemia—not so much because he had many followers but because he had many critics who were challenged by his bold and original views (Sousedík 1997). He is considered to be the most important of the many Spanish philosophers who worked in Germany and Austria. His works were discussed in Europe and South America. Arriaga's theory of beings of reason seems to follow Hurtado's Fallibilism.[48]

Bartolomeo Mastri, O.F.M. (1602–73), and Bonaventura Belluto, O.F.M. (1600–76)

Both Bartolomeo Mastri (Mastrius) and Bonaventura Belluto (Bellutus) were Italian Franciscan Conventuals. Mastri was born in Meldola, Italy, in 1602, where he also died in 1673. He joined the Franciscan Conventuals at the age of fifteen. He studied in Bologna, Parma, Naples, and finally at the prestigious St. Bonaventura College in Rome. There he met his lifelong friend Bonaventura Belluto from Catania, Sicily. Mastri was generally recognized as one of the most accomplished Scotistic philosophers of the seventeenth century, so that he is even given the honorific title *Princeps Scotistarum*. It is noteworthy that Mastri/Belluto exceed Suárez in the number of authors they take into account, and so they are a gold mine of information for anybody who studies postmedieval scholasticism.[49] From a systematic point of view, their modification of Objectualism seems to me the most plausible of all scholastic theories. (For more, see chapter 7.)

John Punch, O.F.M.Obs. (1603–72/3)

Punch (Pontius) was born in Cork, Ireland, in 1603. He joined the Irish Observants (Franciscans) in Louvain, Belgium. He taught philosophy and theology, mainly at St. Isidor's College in Rome, founded by Luke Wadding. In 1643 he published in Rome his major philosophical work, *Philosophiae ad mentem Scoti Cursus integer*, which was republished at least five times. He also published philosophical commentaries on Scotus as part of Wadding's *Opera omnia* edition of Scotus. Punch's theory of beings of reason seems to be quite novel, perhaps going as far as claiming mind-independency of the essences of beings of reason.[50]

Juan Caramuel y Lobkowitz, O.Cist. (1606–82)

Caramuel was born in Madrid in 1606 to a Czech father and a Luxemburgian mother. After studying at the University of Alcalá and Salamanca, he entered the Cistercian order. He pursued the doctorate of theology in Louvain in

1638. Throughout his adventurous life he served in various ecclesiastical and state missions, lastly as a bishop of Vigevano (near Milan), where he died in 1682. He was an extremely prolific author. He produced two hundred sixty works, out of which only sixty were published. The manuscripts in his archive are divided into nine categories: *liberalis, mathematicus, musicus, chirosophicus, philosophicus, theologicus, philosophiae moralis, theologiae moralis, scripturarius* (Velázquez Campo 1654/2000, 11). As we see, besides philosophy, Caramuel contributed to several disciplines, including music, physics, mathematics, linguistics, and architecture. He was in contact with many of his contemporaries, including Descartes and Gassendi. Posthumously a detailed criticism of Descartes's *Meditationes* was published, entitled *Notes on Cartesian Meditations in Which It Is Very Clearly Proven That Nothing Was Proven by Descartes* (Pastine 1972). We could mention among his works at least *Theologia regularis* (1646, Lyons 1665), *Theologia rationalis* (Frankfurt 1654–55), *Metametrica* (Rome 1663), *Mathesis biceps* (Lyon 1670), *Theologia moralis fundamentalis* (1652, Lyons 1675–76), and *Leptotatos latine subtilissimus* (Vigevano 1681).[51] Caramuel's theory of beings of reason takes self-contradictions within beings of reason as the point of departure and then argues for their elimination. (For more, see chapter 8.)

2

Problems Posed by Beings of Reason

Having discussed the historical context of the scholasticism of the Baroque era and the motivation for investigating it, I introduce in this chapter the main philosophical target of my study, namely *ens rationis* (being of reason). I will do so from a systematic point of view, attempting to make this chapter accessible even to those who are not interested too much in philosophical historiography. The chapter provides a broad conceptual framework within which the various elements of the theories of Suárez, Hurtado, Mastri/Belluto, and Caramuel, dealt with in later chapters, may be located. The chapter is divided into three parts. First, I make an attempt to draw an absolutely general map of scholastic ontology (section A). Then, I turn to the question of what sort of roles beings of reason were supposed to fulfill in scholastic ontologies (B). Finally, I summarize the plan for the following chapters of this book and the main results of it (C).[1]

A. Super-Categories of Scholastic Ontology

Traditional Western metaphysics is centered on the question of what really exists.[2] The Baroque scholastic authors studied in this book, however, were intensely preoccupied not just with what really exists but also with what is *beyond* the margins of reality. There are various nonreal items that one may encounter when browsing through their huge folio books. Let me provide a scheme that attempts to capture in one classification all such nonreal items together with the real ones. The scheme will be explained below, but throughout this book it should be taken as a guide, up for further clarification. If we reserve the word 'category' to refer to classifications of real things in the world, then the list below amounts to a list of "super-categories (see figure 2.1)."

At the very top of our classification we see the term 'item'. By this term I mean anything to which one can refer and of which one can say that "it is (in some sense) there" (*datur*)—regardless of such issues as whether it exists

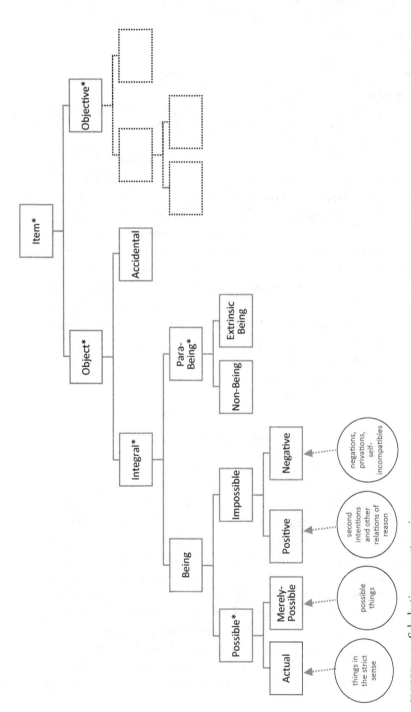

FIGURE 2.1. Scholastic super-categories

Note: An asterisk indicates a non-scholastic term.

or whether it is real. (The term was not used by the scholastics themselves, but it is useful for us to talk about their views; all such terms are indicated in the scheme by the asterisk placed next to them.) For comparison, Bertrand Russell tried to capture this broad meaning of 'item' by the term 'term':

> Whatever may be an object of thought, or may occur in any true or false proposition, or can be counted as *one*, I call a *term*. This, then, is the widest word in the philosophical vocabulary. I shall use as synonymous with it the words unit, individual, and entity. The first two emphasize the fact that every term has being, i.e. *is* in some sense. A man, a moment, a number, a class, a relation, a chimaera, or anything else that can be mentioned, is sure to be a term. (Russell 1903/1938, §48)

And Peter Strawson, to take another example, also acknowledged the possibility of having such a "widest word in philosophical vocabulary":

> Anything whatever can be introduced into discussion by means of a singular, definitely identifying substantival expression. . . . Since anything whatever can be identifyingly referred to, being a possible object of identifying reference does not distinguish any class or type of items or entities from any other. (Strawson 1953, 137)

Contemporary logicians discuss such an all-encompassing domain and the problems linked with it, under the heading of 'absolute generality' (Rayo and Uzquiano 2006).

Items are divided into objects and what Meinong calls "objectives" (*Objektive*), by which I mean things and propositions/states-of-affairs, respectively.[3] Let me explain a bit. Etymologically, the word 'object' means "thrown in the way;" a stone, for instance, could be an object. The stone is something that catches our attention—it becomes an *object of perception* and *thought*. But 'object of thought', as Prior says, is ambiguous:

> The phrase 'object of thought' may be used in two very different ways. An object of thought may be (1) what we think, or (2) what we think *about*; e.g., if we think that grass is green, (1) what we think is *that grass is green*, and (2) what we think about is *grass*. 'Objects of thought' . . . are sometimes called 'propositions', not in the sense of sentences, but in the sense of what sentences mean. . . . *What we think*, may be *false*; and what we think *about* may be *non-existent*. These are quite different

defects, though philosophers have sometimes slipped into treating them as if they were the same. (Prior 1971, 3–4; italics in original)

Prior's propositions are claimed by some philosophers to be primary truth-bearers, corresponding or failing to correspond to facts or obtaining states of affairs as truth-makers. I lump into the category of *objectives* both truth-bearers and truth-makers, because the Baroque scholastics in the texts I deal with in this study pay almost no attention either to truth-bearers or to truth-makers—with the exception of Hurtado, as we shall see in chapter 6. For Baroque scholastics, the world is the totality of *things* and not of *facts* (pace Wittgenstein 1922/2009, proposition 1.1).

Next comes the division into *per accidens* objects (accidental, loosely united objects, aggregates) and *per se* objects ("innerly integrated," tightly/ naturally united objects). The *per accidens* objects include artifacts, heaps, and any kind of arbitrary wholes.

The following division, the division of *per se* objects, is of crucial importance, for many scholastic authors simply identify *per se* objects with beings (*entia*). As we shall see, however, there are texts in which Suárez acknowledges categories of nonbeings and extrinsic beings (see chapter 4, section B.2.1). These, for the lack of a better term, I call "para-beings," a term that I have made up but that captures the idea of a category of objects *para*sitic on beings in the strict sense. The term is mine, but it is inspired by Caramuel's 'παρα-οντα'.

Then we get to the division of beings into possible in the broad sense (the scholastics did not have a term for this notion) and impossible (*impossibilia*). Broadly, possible beings are divided into actual (*entia actu, vera entia*) and merely possible (*possibilia*). Actual beings, i.e., beings in the narrowest sense of the word, make up the world/reality of the scholastics.[4] They are ontologically prior to everything else. Beings divide into substances, such as people, animals, plants, or stones, and their various accidents, and are typically classified into nine structured groups, called 'categories'. Merely possible beings are enormously controversial among the scholastics.[5]

Impossible beings cannot exist in actual reality. According to a fundamental scholastic assumption, every impossible being is mind-dependent and vice versa, so impossible beings are called '*entia rationis*', which means "beings of reason" (i.e., "beings from reason" or "beings made up by reason"). There are at least three other translations of this term in use:

'mental being' (Gracia 1991), 'rationate being' (Schmidt 1963), and 'intentional being' (Sousedík 2004). I use 'being of reason', not only because it is most common (Doyle 1987, Canteñs 2003) but also because its oddity highlights that we speak about a kind of item within a specifically scholastic context.

Now the surprising fact: Suárez and most other Baroque scholastics considered merely possible beings to be *real*, and hence they were not classified as beings of reason. This fact is often overlooked by contemporary metaphysicians (who care to read scholastic texts). Nicholas Rescher, for instance, writes:

> With regard to nonexistents, the medieval mainstream thus sought to effect a compromise. On the one hand, their lack of reality, of actual existence, deprived nonentities of a self-sustaining ontological footing and made them into mind-artifacts, *entia rationis*. On the other hand, their footing in the mind of God endowed them with a certain objectivity and quasi-reality that precluded them from being mere *flatus vocis* fictions, mere verbalisms that represent creatures of human fancy. (Rescher 2003, 362)[6]

Hence, to use non-scholastic terminology, beings of reason might be best described as intentional or mind-dependent impossible objects. This mind-dependency of beings of reason, however, is more precisely characterized by the scholastics as merely objective mind-dependency. This sort of mind-dependency is contrasted by them with subjective mind-dependency, which is the real relation of mental accidents—such as sensations, emotions, thoughts, and volitions—to the mind. There are two sorts of objective mind-dependency. First, there is the case of a person p who apprehends a real being x. In this case x is not *merely* objectively in the intellect of p, for x also has real being in itself. Second, there is the case of a person p who apprehends x when x has no other being besides the being it has in the intellect of p. It is only in this last sense, of 'mind-dependent being', that the term '*ens rationis*' is appropriately used among the scholastics. Hence, the standard scholastic definition of beings of reason is "what has merely objective existence in the intellect." (See chapter 3, section C.2.1.)[7]

Impossible beings (beings of reason, necessarily mind-dependent) divide into negative beings (*negativa*) and positive beings (*positiva*). The former are further divided into negations (*negationes*) and privations (*privationes*), and the latter are typically identified with relations of reason (*relationes rationis*). Impossible beings should be understood as objects for which it is impossible to exist in actual reality, and hence they need to be distinguished from what I call "self-contradictory beings," which are objects, such as square circles or goat stags, that contain explicit contradictions.[8] Although many later Baroque authors reduced impossible beings to self-contradictory objects, this is not a trivial move. For there seem to be objects that cannot exist in actual reality but still are not self-contradictory (for instance, the universal *human being* or *blindness*). As we shall see in chapter 5, section B, Suárez argues that self-contradictory beings are a special kind of negation.

So far for the explanation of the above schematic classification of scholastic super-categories.[9] Before we move on to the second part of the chapter, let me make three clarificatory observations about this classification.

Observation 1: Classifications and Natural Classes

The classification of super-categories (if I am right) provides an overview of the various ontological items one can encounter in scholastic texts. But why did the scholastics themselves not formulate such a classification? I can only speculate. First of all, many elements of the classification I give were controversial among them. Not all scholastics agreed, for instance, that extrinsic beings or nonbeings were in some sense real and therefore a special "genus" of items. Hence, since there was no agreement on these issues, they did not feel the need to provide an explicit classification of the items they talked about. Second, the hesitancy to formulate such a classification might be due to their assumption that "good" concepts *must* delimit natural classes (members of which are at least analogically related). And since there is no natural class, for instance, of existing and nonexisting beings, the two should not be lumped under one label. Today, however, we feel free to draw such classifications, provided that we keep in mind that some of the "fields" of our classification may represent just arbitrarily united classes. That x and y belong to a class C does not imply that x and y share some common (intrinsic) feature. Later Baroque scholastics seem to have been going in this direction in that they started to acknowledge "extrinsic thinkability," i.e., the possibility of subsuming x and y under a common concept, without implying that they share anything intrinsically in common—except for the extrinsic feature of *belonging to the same class*.[10] The notion of extrinsic thinkability gave rise to the idea that there are super-transcendental terms, such as 'thinkable' or 'something', which are applicable to both real and nonreal objects.[11]

Observation 2: Existence and Being

One of the presuppositions of any classification of nonexisting items is the distinction between the meanings of 'there is' and 'exists'. Many analytical philosophers, notably those in the Frege–Quine tradition, like to treat the expression 'there is' with metaphysical seriousness. In their view, 'there is' and 'exists' are synonymous—they both have "ontological import." The scholastics would disagree.[12] According to them one needs to make a distinction between 'there is' (*datur*, "is given"), which is meant to be as neutral and broad as possible, and narrower predicates, such as 'exists', which express a first-order non-trivial feature of individuals.[13]

Observation 3: Categories and Transcendentals

There is another group of terms one may encounter in scholastic texts, the so-called transcendentals ("one," "true," "good," etc.) that apply to every being. Besides these, there are also other terms—such as "actual/potential" and "real/nonreal," and perhaps "whole/part," "one/many," etc.—that apply to beings from various categories but not to everything. Although one could perhaps subsume these trans-categorial terms (and whatever they express) under "item," it is more convenient and closer to scholastic usage of the words to keep the super-categories and the super-transcendentals separate, to not include them in the same classification. To put the difference between the two in a rather simplistic way, one could say that the aim of the categories and the super-categories is a general *division* of what there is and is not, whereas the aim of the transcendentals and super-transcendentals is a general *characterization* of what there is and is not.[14]

B. Problems of Beings of Reason

Having classified the nonexisting items discussed by the scholastics into super-categories, and having identified the position of beings of reason within this classification, let us take a look now at the roles they played in scholastic ontology. Why did scholastic authors feel the need to talk about them? They used them to address various philosophical puzzles, most conspicuously the problem of nonbeing/intentionality. Hence we start with the latter issue (section B.1) and then discuss several other problems related to beings of reason (B.2).

1. The Problem of Nonbeing

Thought and language direct our attention to various sorts of objects that either clearly do not exist or whose existence is questionable. This fact is the main source of the problem (or the family of problems) addressed first by Parmenides and discussed by philosophers ever since. From one point of view, the problem concerns nonbeing including questions such as "What is the status of nonbeing?" Is it in some sense real and mind-independent? What belongs to its domain: past, future, potential, merely possible, impossible, fictitious, and so on? From another point of view, the problem concerns intentionality and intentional being. The pertinent questions in this case include: "What is an intentional object, if any?" "Does a category of intentional objects help to explain our thinking of nonbeing?"

Several basic strategies are used to deal with the problem of nonbeing. First, however, we need to note that the problem of nonbeing divides into the problem of nonexisting objects and the problem of negative facts (also referred to as negative truths). The question whether there are negative facts is more fundamental than the question whether there are nonexisting objects. Indeed, negative facts are sometimes taken as evidence that there are nonexisting objects but not vice versa. And it is possible to hold that there are negative facts and no nonexisting objects, but not vice versa.[15]

With respect to nonbeing, one may adopt views of various sorts. The most radical one holds that there are no negative facts and consequently no nonexisting objects. A less radical view acknowledges negative facts but rejects nonexisting objects. The least radical position acknowledges both. These views might be further subdivided according to the account they give of negative facts and of nonexisting objects.

With respect to nonexisting objects, drawing on Meinong and Findlay, I would distinguish three accounts: intentional, quasi-being, and *Ausser*-being views (Findlay 1933/1995, 42–58). The intentional view explains nonexisting objects in terms of mind-made, intentional being. Quine ascribes a version of the intentional view to (the fictional philosopher) McX and dismisses it as a deception "by the crudest and most flagrant counterfeit." Quine asks, What can be more dissimilar and unlike than, for instance, Pegasus (an alleged nonexisting object) and the Pegasus-idea (the intentional object)? If it comes to real objects, Quine contends, such as the Parthenon and the Parthenon-idea, we would never be deceived, but when it comes to Pegasus, somehow, confusion sets in (Quine 1948/1980, 2). Meinong also rejects the intentional view, for "with regard to an innumerable multitude of non-existent objects it may be the case that no one thinks of them or needs to think of them" (Findlay 1933/1995, 45).

The quasi-being view explains nonexisting objects in terms of some peculiar sort of being that pertains to everything. Every object, whether existing or not, whether nonexisting contingently or necessarily, has it. As the early Russell puts it, "being is a general attribute of everything, and to mention anything is to show that it is" (Russell 1903/1938, 449). Meinong suggests calling this sort of being "quasi-being," for it has no contrary and so it is a very unusual sort of being. Quine ascribes a version of the quasi-being view to Wymen and dismisses it, as it offends his "aesthetic . . . taste for desert landscapes" and is to him "a breeding ground of disorderly elements," in the case of unactualized possibles, and something contradictory in the case of unactualizable impossibles (Quine 1948/1980, 2–5). In the end, Meinong also rejects the quasi-being view, although for some time he was, as he confesses, tempted by it (Findlay 1933/1995, 48).

The *Ausser*-being view is Meinong's own child, although in a different context an analogy to it might be seen in Aquinas's notion of *natura absoluta*. Findlay summarizes the *Ausser*-being view as follows:

> The pure object stands beyond being and non-being; both alike are external to it. Whether an object is or not, makes no difference to *what* the object is. The pure object is said to be *außerseiend* or to have *Außersein*: it lies 'outside'. What the object is . . . consists in a number of determinations of so-being. . . . Such determinations are genuinely possessed by an object whether it exists or not. . . . This does not mean that any objects are exempt from being or non-being; the law of excluded middle lays it down that every object necessarily stands in a fact of being or a fact of non-being. . . . [but] being and non-being have nothing to do with the object as object. (Findlay 1933/1995, 49)

This view and its distinctive thesis was dubbed by Ernst Mally "the principle of the independence of so-being from being." It has been the main source of the attraction to Meinong in contemporary philosophy.[16]

The classical scholastic view is a version of the intentional view: Nonexistent objects are immanent to (=staying within) our mental/intentional activity and "exist" only as long as somebody is actually thinking of them.[17] For the most part, however, this was the view that was simply assumed and not argued for, because no alternative was seriously entertained by them.[18]

2. Other Problems

Although beings of reason have to do primarily with nonbeing and intentional being, the scholastics used the theory of beings of reason for various purposes, two of which stand out. First, to account for higher-order predicates—so-called second intentions (=objective concepts), which do not apply to real things but to other intentions. Second, to account for self-contradictory objects, such as square circles or chimeras.[19] Second intentions do not receive adequate treatment in this study, for this would presuppose a detailed explanation of such major scholastic topics as predication, relations, and concepts. Each of these would require a study of its own.[20]

Several kinds of questions in standard philosophical works of Baroque scholasticism were posed with respect to beings of reason. The issues can be divided into three areas (Roncaglia 1995; Novotný 2006):

> NATURE: What is a being of reason? Do beings of reason exist? Are they to be identified with extrinsic denominations? Why do we construct beings of reason? In what sense do beings of reason exist? Is there a sense of 'being' that is common to real beings and beings of reason? Is there a science that studies beings of reason?
>
> CAUSES: What mental powers are involved in conceiving beings of reason? Intellect, will, sense, imagination?
>
> DIVISION: What is the division of beings of reason (negation, privation, relation, . . .)? What is negation? What is privation? What is a relation of reason?

Various "additional" issues, which perhaps could be subsumed under "nature," were also treated. For instance: motivation (Why do we need beings of reason?) and methodology (Does their study belong to the domain of logic, or of metaphysics?). Baroque scholastics did not seem to care much for semantic problems (the meaning of being-of-reason terms, the truth-value of sentences with such terms, etc.).[21]

Besides nonbeing, higher-order predication, and self-contradiction, there are many other issues that are related to beings of reason. Here is a list:

(1) Nonbeing (in thought): nonexistent objects, negative facts
(2) Nonbeing (in perception): vacuums, holes
(3) Intentionality: mental objects, objects of thoughts, semantic content
(4) Modality 1: possible (i.e., contingently nonexisting) objects
(5) Modality 2: impossible (i.e., necessarily nonexisting) objects
(6) Temporality: past or future (i.e., now nonexisting) objects
(7) Fictitiousness: texts, objects of literary fictions
(8) Fallibility: objects of errors, misrepresentations, illusions
(9) Ontologically suspicious items 1: abstract entities (universals, sets, numbers, etc.)
(10) Ontologically suspicious items 2: extrinsic properties, logical, semantic, social relations, etc.
(11) Methodology: fictionalism, ontological commitments, paraphrases

The scholastics have much to say about all of these matters, perhaps with the exception of (7), which is astonishing, given the extent and detail of Baroque scholastic works.[22] In the treatises on beings of reason, the scholastics were concerned mainly with (1), (3), (5), (9), (10), and (11), although some authors discussed (8). The remaining issues—(2), (4), and (6)—were extensively treated elsewhere, but not under the heading 'beings of reason'.[23] Accordingly, these issues will not be discussed in this study.[24]

C. Summary of the Plan for this Study

Having finished a brief description of the ontological framework presupposed by the scholastic debates about beings of reason, let me now summarize the plan for this book. It concerns beings of reason, which, as we have seen, are impossible intentional objects, such as—on the usual account—blindness (privation), genus-relation (second intention), or square circle (self-contradictory object). The first three chapters (3–5) that follow are structured around a close reading of Suárez's main text on the subject, namely Disputation 54. The next three chapters (6–8) center on other texts of three outstanding philosophers of the time, namely, Hurtado, Mastri/Belluto, and Caramuel. Two overall theses are defended, one concerning systematic philosophy, and another, philosophical historiography. First, I argue that Suárez's theory of beings of reason is beset by various philosophical problems. Second, I argue that Suárez stands at the beginning and not at the end of a series of first-rate scholastic philosophers of the Baroque era. These two theses are related: I show by way of detailed analytical reconstructions of the main arguments and theses pulled out from the relevant texts that post-Suárezian philosophers attempted to improve on the standard Suárezian account of beings of reason either by (1) modifying his theory, working out further details, and/or resolving the objections against it, or (2) coming up with altogether different theories. This shows that post-Suárezian Baroque scholastic culture was lively and from the philosophical point of view quite advanced.

We shall see that Suárez's theory of beings of reason is a version of the traditional or "classical" view, which might be called *Objectualism*. According to this view, beings of reason are "pure objects" of thinking, essentially dependent on our actual thinking about them. The core ideas of this view can be captured by the following five theses:

> Beings of reason cannot exist in actual reality (in the ordinary sense of 'exist').
> There are beings of reason—in an analogical sense of 'are'.
> Beings of reason are merely objectively in the intellect.
> Beings of reason are thought of in the manner of (real) being.
> Beings of reason are totally dependent on actual mental acts.

Suárez is the paradigmatic representative of Objectualism, although he introduces into it various elements that may not have been present in the Renaissance scholastic tradition before him. Thinkers such as Mastri/Belluto revised Objectualism in several ways but remained faithful to it (see chapter 7). A quite different path was taken by some Jesuit authors, such as Hurtado, who considers beings of reason to be mere mistakes that happen, for instance, when we (mistakenly) think of a substance as a quantity. This is the view I call *Fallibilism* (see chapter 6). Still other Jesuit authors reduce beings of reason to explicitly self-contradictory objects, such as square circles—the view I call *Self-Contradictorism*. Caramuel takes Self-Contradictorism one step further and completely denies that beings of reason are something nonreal, i.e., he eliminates them from his ontology. (And hence I call this view *Eliminativism*; see chapter 8). I also need to report that there might have been at least one more paradigmatic view present in the Baroque period, namely, *Potentialism*, according to which beings of reason are (partially) mind-independent: Before we actually think of them, they are potentially out there as thinkable. Potentialism seems to have been formulated and defended by Punch.[25] One of his intriguing arguments for the (partial) mind-independence of beings of reason goes as follows: Suppose Peter thinks of a chimera and Paul thinks of a chimera; the two chimeras are similar; is this similarity mind-dependent or mind-independent? It seems that it is mind-independent, for it is "out there" even if nobody is actually thinking of it; hence we have a mind-independent relation of reason.[26] Potentialism is dealt with in this study only insofar as Mastri/Belluto argue against it (chapter 7). Unfortunately, a more thorough and adequate investigation of Punch's defense of Potentialism needs to be left for another occasion.[27]

It seems that Objectualism, Fallibilism, Self-Contradictorism (with the more radical Eliminativism as a special case), and Potentialism are the main Baroque paradigms of how to think about beings of reason. Each of the paradigms comes in countless versions, differentiated by various details, and defended by individual authors. In the next chapter we begin our discussion of Suárez's version of Objectualism. As far as convenient I shall follow Suárez's own structure of argumentation embodied in his main text dealing with beings of reason (Disputation 54), since his sense for systematicity and synoptic vision is one his greatest intellectual virtues; by following the original structure I hope to convey at least some of its beauty. In the same way I shall closely follow the structure of the texts of Mastri/Belluto and Hurtado. Caramuel's text, in contrast, is organized rather haphazardly, and so in this case I do not follow its structure.

3

Suárez's Objectualism: The Nature of Beings of Reason

The aim of the following three chapters (3–5) is to provide the reader with a thorough understanding of Suárez's theory of beings of reason, a peculiar version of Objectualism. The present chapter deals with a somewhat broad range of issues centered on the question of what beings of reason are. I have subsumed these issues under the heading "nature." The chapter is divided into three parts. First, I deal with Suárez's metatheoretical claim that, although the proper task of metaphysics is to study real beings, beings of reason also belong to metaphysics. Second, I discuss what Suárez has to say about beings of reason in the *Metaphysical Disputations* prior to Disputation 54. (From the elucidation of the notion of real being, we shall see that in his view beings of reason *cannot* be actualized in reality. In this sense they are *impossibilia*, although this does not imply that they contain inner self-contradictions.) Third, I analyze section 1 of Disputation 54. The section deals with several interrelated issues concerning the nature of beings of reason. I begin by discussing the definition and existence of beings of reason (sections C.1 and C.2)—in Suárez's view, the clarification of the term 'being of reason' as something merely objectively in the intellect is sufficient to make its existence evident (albeit in a sense different from the usual sense in which real beings exist). Then, I briefly show Suárez's motivation for postulating beings of reason and the roles they are supposed to play in his ontology (C.3). Finally, I turn to the sense in which beings of reason are said to be *beings* (C.4).

A. Beings of Reason and Metaphysics

The aim of an Aristotelian-scholastic science is the possession of certain knowledge of truth, which is acquired by demonstration. In demonstrations, *something* (*x*) is shown about *something* (*o*) from *something* (*p*).[1] Since for

Suárez metaphysics is the science about "being as real being" (*ens inquantum ens reale; ens qua ens reale*), beings of reason are excluded from the *direct* concern of this science.[2] In Disputation 1 (On the Nature of Metaphysics or the First Philosophy), he explains why this is so: "Beings of reason . . . are neither true beings (but rather almost in name only), nor do they share a common concept with real beings (only through a certain imperfect analogy of proportionality)."[3]

Nevertheless, even though beings of reason are excluded from the *direct* concern of metaphysics, they do have *some* place in it:

> It is not necessary for everything that is somehow dealt with in a science to be directly contained under its proper [*adaequatus*] object, for many things are dealt with . . . [just] in order to elucidate the [proper] object itself. . . . Hence, although this science [i.e., metaphysics] deals with many things concerning beings of reason, it is correct to exclude them from the directly intended object of metaphysics as such [*per se*]—unless somebody wants to argue about words. . . . Beings of reason are dealt with . . . but not for their own sake (*per se*) but because of some similarity [*proportionalitas*] that they have with real beings, so that the latter are distinguished from them and so that one can see in a better way and more clearly what, among entities, has being [*entitas*] and reality [*realitas*] and what has merely the appearance [*species*] of it.[4]

Suárez claims that metaphysicians need beings of reason because they may help us see more clearly the reality of real beings. It would seem, based on this passage, that beings of reason are useful for nothing else but this. However, when the discussion of beings of reason is taken up in the introduction to Disputation 54, Suárez's tone toward beings of reason gets much friendlier, and we are presented with other roles in which beings of reason may serve:

> Although we did say in the first disputation of this work that being of reason is not included under the proper and direct object of metaphysics . . . nevertheless I believe that [1] it belongs to the completion of this doctrine and [thus] it is the metaphysician's task to treat its common and general characteristics. [2] For the knowledge and science of beings of reason is necessary for our theories. Indeed, without them we can hardly speak either in metaphysics itself, or in [natural] philosophy, much less

in logic, and (what is more) even in theology. [3a] Moreover, this task [of investigating beings of reason] cannot in fact belong to anybody else but to the metaphysician. [3b] For, first of all, since beings of reason are not true beings but, as it were, "shadows" of being, they are not intelligible by themselves but by some analogy and conjunction with true beings. [3c] Consequently, they cannot be, as such, objects of some science [*scibilia*], nor is there a science that has been instituted directly and primarily in order to know them alone. [3d] Indeed, the fact that some [authors] ascribe this task to dialectics is a dialectical error, since the purpose of dialectics is only to direct human rational operations and to reduce them to an art. And these operations are real beings—not beings of reason in the relevant sense. [3e] Thus, no craftsman [*artifex*] and no science directly and primarily aims at the knowledge of beings of reason; they must be treated only insofar as they are joined with knowledge of some real being.[5]

In this passage we see that Suárez remains committed to the view that beings of reason are merely "shadows" of true beings and can be treated only derivatively (3b) (3e), but he is quick to point out that for at least two additional positive reasons metaphysicians should have a general theory of beings of reason. First, to make the metaphysical doctrine complete (1), and second, because beings of reason are indispensable in other sciences as well (2). Suárez's discussion suggests a tension between the proper object of metaphysics, which he claims is real being, and the need for metaphysics to include a discussion of beings of reason. Whereas the "science" of shadows clearly needs a science of light, it is not so obvious why the science of light would need to deal with shadows. Suárez explains the need to treat beings of reason in metaphysics by appealing to the fact that there is no other science that can carry on this task (3a) (3c). Specifically, it cannot be dialectics/logic (3d), and there is no other candidate (3e).[6] So what is the task of metaphysics with regard to beings of reason? Suárez describes it as follows:

[1] It is proper to metaphysics to deal with being of reason as such—its common character, properties, and divisions. [2] For in their own way the features [*rationes*] of beings of reason are quasi-transcendental and cannot be understood except by comparison to true and real features of beings (whether transcendental or so general that they belong to metaphysics). The reason is that what is fictitious or apparent must be understood by comparison to what truly is. Hence, although other disciplines, like physics

or dialectics, sometimes touch upon some beings of reason that are linked with their objects . . . nevertheless, they cannot out of their own resources explicate the quasi-essential features of beings of reason. . . . Hence, we must deal with them in the present disputation. [3] We will first address the nature and causes of being of reason. Then, we add [a discussion of] their division and take up various genera of these beings.[7]

The job to be done with respect to beings of reason mirrors the metaphysician's task with respect to real beings: to investigate their nature, causes, and divisions (1) (3). Moreover, Suárez suggests that just as metaphysics is the science of the transcendentals, so the study of beings of reason is the study of quasi-transcendentals (2).[8] This suggestion, however, is not developed and, as we shall see in chapter 7, among Baroque authors it is developed only by Mastri/Belluto.

We may summarize Suárez's views as follows:[9]

SM1: The proper objects of metaphysics are real beings, and beings of reason are studied in metaphysics only in order to facilitate the understanding of real beings.

SM2: The study of beings of reason that metaphysics undertakes is useful in various ways.

SM3: The study of beings of reason involves their nature, causes, division, and attributes (quasi-transcendentals).

SM4: Real beings are both ontologically and epistemically prior to beings of reason.

The first three claims are metatheoretical, the fourth is metaphysical. Note the tension between SM1 and SM2: On the one hand, it is claimed that beings of reason are just incidental objects of metaphysics studied merely for the sake of real beings; on the other hand, it is claimed that the knowledge of beings of reason is useful in various ways. It seems that we should either acknowledge a new science dealing with nonreal beings or extend metaphysics to include all being, whether real or of reason. Suárez implicitly rejects both of these options (perhaps out of fear that the realism captured by SM4 would be endangered), but this refusal to face the choice cannot do. Once nonreal beings are taken seriously, one needs to find a good place for their investigation. (See also chapter 5, section E.1.)

Since beings of reason are contrasted by Suárez to *real* beings, we now need to discuss real beings in order to understand what beings of reason are *not*.

B. Beings of Reason in Disputation 2

It has been noted already by Gracia that Suárez uses the word 'real' in more than one sense.[10] In its broadest sense, 'real' seems to mean anything independent of human mental activity. Unfortunately, he never explicitly elucidates this broadest sense but includes it only within a discussion of other complex notions, such as "real being," "real essence," "real extrinsic being," and "real nonbeing."

The most extensive discussion concerning "real" can be found in section 4 of Disputation 2 (On the Concept of Being). There Suárez first distinguishes two senses of 'being': as a participle of the verb 'to be' and as a name.[11] In the first sense, 'being' refers to now-actually-existing objects. The second sense of 'being' ("being" as a name) is explained by him via the notion of *real essence*:

> Since essence is that from which a thing is called or denominated 'a being' [*ens*], . . . one cannot explain the notion of "real being," unless one understands the notion of "real essence." Two things may be asked here . . . : first, what the notion of "essence" involves; second, what it is for an essence to be real.[12]

Suárez proposes to explain the notion of "real essence" in two phases: first, in terms of *essence*, and second, in terms of *real* essence. Concerning the first, he notes:

> Essence cannot be explained by us otherwise than either with respect to effects or attributes of things, or with respect to our way of thinking and speaking. [1] With respect to the former, the essence of a thing is the first basic and intimate principle of all its actions and attributes; [2] here we mean "the nature of the thing." [3] With respect to the latter, the essence of a thing is made explicit by its definition. . . . [4] Here also the essence is what is known first about a thing. I say "first" not in temporal sense (for we usually begin to know a thing from what is external to its essence) but rather in the sense in which essence is the "fundamental" [*notabilis*] and primary object [of our intellect]. [5] For the essence of a thing . . .

primarily and intrinsically constitutes its being [*esse*]; [6] in this sense we also refer to essences by the expression 'whatness', since the essence gives the answer to the question "What is it?"[13]

Suárez ascribes to essences multiple roles. *Within* a given being, the essence is a principle of its actions and attributes (1) and even of its very being (5). *With respect to us*, essences are grasped by definitions (3) and are somehow "fundamental" and primary (4). Essences may also be called "natures" (2), or "whatnesses" (6), from the functions they have. Each of these claims would require further explanation, but since this is not a study of essence in Suárez we do not need to discuss them further here. We rather turn our attention to the second phase of Suárez's analysis, namely, what it is for an essence to be real:

> What it is for an essence to be real can be explained either in a negative or in an affirmative way. In the former way we say that an essence is real because [1] it does not involve "resistance" [*repugnantia*], [2] nor is it merely made up [*conficta*] by the intellect. (In the latter way, we may either proceed in our explanation from effects [*a posteriori*] or from causes [*a priori*].) [3] Concerning effects, we say that a real essence is a principle or a root of real operations and effects; . . . there cannot be any real essence that could not have real effects or real properties. [4] Concerning extrinsic causes, a real essence can be really produced by God and thus constituted in the being [*esse*] of an actual being [*ens*]. [5] Concerning intrinsic causes, we cannot give an explanation in the proper sense, for the notion of essence is . . . the most primitive [*simplicissima*]. Thus, we may merely say that a real essence is an essence that is as such [*ex se*] apt to be [*esse*], i.e., to really exist.[14]

This rich passage is of crucial importance for us. In Suárez's view, real essences do not involve "resistance" (1), and they are not made up (2). Furthermore, they are causally efficacious (3), producible by God (4), and apt to really (i.e., actually) exist (5). Let us briefly comment on these conditions:

1. Real essences do not "resist" existence.

"Resistance" (*repugnantia*) does not mean simple *self-contradiction*, incompatibility, or inconsistency.[15] For as we shall see in later chapters, for Suárez, many beings of reason, such as privations and logical relations, "resist real actual existence," but taken as such they are free of any inconsistency or incompatibility.[16]

2. Real essences are not "made up" (*confictae*).

What does this mean? Unfortunately, neither Suárez (nor Aquinas) makes it explicit.[17] All we can say is based on linguistic considerations: The adjective '*confictae*' (feminine plural.) is a derivative from the verbs '*confingere*', or '*fingere*'; both verbs were commonly used in classical Latin, where they meant "to make or form something," physically or mentally.

3. Real essences are principles of real effects.

Real essences are principles of real operations and effects, so that "there cannot be any real essence that could not have real effects or real properties." Presumably, this is intended to mean not that every real essence does have real effects (for some are nonexisting) but merely that they *would* have them *if* they actually existed.

4. Real essences are producible by God.

This is to be expected, for God is omnipotent, and therefore he should be able to produce everything that is "apt to exist."

5. Real essences are *apt* to exist actually.

Real beings have real essences and these are apt to exist actually. Some of these real essences do exist, and some of them do not. Both existing and nonexisting essences constitute real beings (in the sense of "being as a name").[18] Hence, beings of reason are not just (actually) non-existent, but are *unfit* for existence—they *cannot* be actualized in reality.[19] Suárez further discusses what real beings are and how God relates to them in Disputation 31 (On the Essence of Finite Being).[20] We do not need to follow the details of these tangled questions, for they do not add to our basic insight into Suárez's notion of being of reason.[21]

The analysis of the notion of real essence and real being determines, by way of negation, the properties of nonreal beings, i.e., beings of reason: (1) resisting existence, (2) being made up, (3) not being a principle of real effects,

(4) not being producible by God, and (5) not being apt to exist. Most importantly, Suárez holds, based on property 5, that:

SN1: A being of reason is what cannot be actualized in reality.

But he also holds, based on property (1), that:

SN2: Not every being of reason is self-contradictory.[22]

In a sense, beings of reason are nothing but impossible beings—provided we understand 'impossible being' broadly, for self-contradictory beings are just a subclass of beings of reason. Let us turn now to Suárez's main text, Disputation 54.

C. Beings of Reason in Disputation 54

After a brief introduction, Disputation 54 turns to the nature and existence of beings of reason in section 1, entitled "Whether there are beings of reason and what essence they could have." Suárez first presents arguments for the view that there are no beings of reason (s1n2) and then for the view that beings of reason are real beings (s1n3). Finally, he defends his own middle-course view, according to which *there are* beings of reason (against the first view) but they do not *exist* in the sense in which ordinary real beings do (against the second view) (s1n4–7). The defense of this view is based on Suarez's discussion of *what* beings of reason are, which involves three phases: first, clarifying the term 'being of reason' (s1n5–6); second, providing a real definition of it (s1n6); and third, suggesting that we speak of beings of reason in a non-usual sense of 'being' (s1n7). Apart from defending the sui generis "there-is-ness" or existence of beings of reason, Suárez discusses the occasion (*occasio*) at which our reason makes them up (s1n8) and the sense of proportional analogy in which they are appropriately called 'beings' (s1n9–10). [23] In Suárez's text, one may also identify a positive "ontological argument" for beings of reason (s1n7). As we see, section 1 is rather tangled, dealing with several interdependent aspects of the issue (intension, extension, ontological status, and "motivation," or *occasio*).

1. Extension of 'Being of Reason'

For Suárez and virtually all later scholastics until Caramuel, there was no doubt as to the question of whether there are beings of reason (see chapter

8). Nevertheless, Suárez does seem to be aware of some controversy going on with respect to whether there are beings of reason, although he does not hide his impression that its source is a verbal misunderstanding:

> Not even this issue lacks contrary views at the opposite extremes, at least in words. For if the authors of these words are more closely examined, perhaps they are arguing only about the words.[24]

What does he mean by this statement? As we shall see, according to the first "extreme" view *there are no beings of reason,* whereas according to the second *they are as other real beings.* Both of these opposite views seem to share the assumption:

R: Every being is a real being.

So, the disagreement would then concern the question whether *some* real beings are *also* beings of reason. Would this be a substantial disagreement? Perhaps it would, but as far as Suárez is concerned, beings of reason in the sense *he* finds relevant *must* be something *nonreal.* Hence Suárez's fundamental assumption involves the qualification of R and the thesis:

R': Every being is a real being in the narrower sense of 'is' and 'being'.
SN3: Not every being is a real being in the broader sense of 'is' and 'being'."

At this point I should state a presupposition that Suárez does not make explicit but that seems to be implied in what he says: Real beings and beings of reason are mutually exclusive and jointly exhaustive (this claim is stronger than SN3, and hence it will serve as its replacement):

SN3': Every being is either a real being or a being of reason but no being is both.

The thesis should not be understood in the stronger sense that every *referable item* is either a real being or a being of reason, for there are many items to which Suárez refers and that are neither (see also 2.A).[25]

The distinction between the two senses of 'being' lies at the heart of Suárez's approach to beings of reason. He appears to believe that nobody

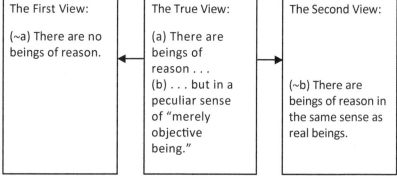

FIGURE 3.1. Argument map of section 1 of Disputation 54

could *seriously* insist on R when confronted with the clarification in terms of R' and SN3. Within the Suarezian framework, one who insisted on R would count as an opponent of beings of reason.[26]

Schematically, we may represent the basic structure of section 1 as shown in Figure 3.1.

Now let us take a closer look at Suárez's text.

1.1. FIRST VIEW: THERE ARE NO BEINGS OF REASON

Concerning the view that there are no beings of reason, which we might call eliminativism, Suárez says:

> Certain people simply deny that there are beings of reason, [maintaining] instead that all that is said of them can very well be understood of [real] things themselves and "preserved" in them. Mayronis . . . and a certain Bernardinus Mirandulanus try to argue for this view, although rather for the sake of controversy than in earnest. The basis [for their view] could be: [1] Something is called 'being of reason' either because it is in reason as in a subject or because it is made by reason. But neither will do, because "to be in" and "to be made by" are properties of real beings (and it is clear that acts [or reason] and [intelligible] species are real beings); [2] something is called 'being of reason' because it is made up [*fictum*] by reason, but since what is merely made up does not exist, to say that it does involves a contradiction. [3] . . . beings of reason are not in any way needed, either for the doctrines or for grasping true things; for intellectual fictions are not necessary for these purposes.[27]

This brief paragraph is insufficient for us to understand clearly the view of the pre-Suarezian opponents of beings of reason. The first sentence almost sounds like a sort of linguistic reductionism, according to which the language of beings of reason ("all that is said of them") can be paraphrased into a language of (real) things themselves. Suárez is obviously unimpressed—"some *try* to argue for this view," as he puts it. As the "basis" (*fundamentum*) of this view, Suárez lists three arguments:

(AR1) Beings of reason have either *being in reason as in a subject* or *being made by reason*. But both are kinds of real being. Thus, there are no true beings of reason.

(AR2) A being of reason is "what is made up by reason." But what is made up does not exist. Thus, it is a contradiction to say that beings of reason exist.

(AR3) Beings of reason are unnecessary.

In light of what Suárez says later on, it is easy to find replies to (Ar1) and (Ar2). The third argument (Ar3) will be taken up below (section C.3). In reply to (Ar1), Suárez would accept the second premise but deny that the first premise exhausts the possibilities—besides the listed two kinds of real being, there is also nonreal being, i.e., being of reason.[28] In reply to (Ar2), Suárez would distinguish two senses of the second premise. It is true that what is made up does not exist in a real sense but it *does* exist in another sense. If we keep in mind that 'exist' (or 'is') is used in different senses, no contradiction arises.

1.2. SECOND VIEW: BEINGS OF REASON ARE REAL BEINGS

Concerning the second (false) view, which might be called ultrarealism, Suárez says the following:

The second view, completely opposite, claims that [1] not only there are beings of reason but they are subsumed under the common appellation 'being' through a single signification or even conception. [2] Indeed, there are those who posit univocal likeness between some beings of reason and some real beings, for example, in the case of relations. (We have refuted their view above). [3] Then there are [even] some who attribute to beings of reason an entity independent of the actual knowing of the intellect.

Their opinion touches upon the question of the manner in which beings of reason arise or are caused (by the intellect), and accordingly we will treat it better in the following section.[29]

The view that beings of reason and real beings share the same concept (1) does not seem to play any role in Suárez's further discussions, and the brevity of its description militates against the need to further engage it here. The view that some beings of reason are "univocally alike" to real beings (2) is discussed and rejected by Suárez in Disputation 47 (On Relation; s3n2–5). Its proponents claim that there is a genus (namely, relation) that is divided into real species and species of reason.[30] Suárez objects that there cannot be any such genus, for real being and being of reason drastically differ: The difference between them is greater than between a living and a dead man.[31]

The third view (3) involves extrinsic denominations—hence Suárez alludes to section 2 of Disputation 54, where he deals with the question of whether extrinsic denominations cause beings of reason. Proponents of (3) argue that if beings of reason are extrinsic denominations and these are mind-independent, then beings of reason are mind-independent. Suárez rejects the antecedent. In his view, to be an extrinsic denomination is not sufficient for something to be a being of reason.[32]

What could be said in favor of ultrarealism? Suárez provides the following:

> The basis of this [second] view could be that [1] we say that blindness and similar such things are said to be in an unqualified way [*absolute*]; thus, they somehow agree with real beings in the character [*ratio*] of being. Likewise, [2] the attributes of being belong to beings of reason [as well], for the latter are also *one* or *many, intelligible,* etc.[33]

This argument poses no serious difficulty for Suárez: Blindness is either a real nonbeing or a being of reason but never a real being (contra [1]). The attributes of being are applied to beings of reason in a metaphorical sense only (contra [2]). The sense in which attributes are applied to beings of reason will be discussed under analogy of proportionality below (C.4.).

2. From Extension to Intension of 'Being of Reason'

After the exposition of what Suárez considers to be opposing false views, he presents his own "true view":

> We hold [1] that there are beings of reason, which are neither true real beings, because they are not capable of true and real existence, [2] nor do they have some true similarity with real beings in virtue of which they would share with them the common concept "being." The first part of this view is standard [*communis*], as is clear from the common usage and the way of speech both in theology and in philosophy.[34]

Under (1), Suárez affirms that there are beings of reason and claims that beings of reason "are not capable of true and real existence." We have already explained the claim above. (2) concerns the ontological status of beings of reason: They are called "beings" but they do not share any similarity with real beings. Nevertheless, as we shall see below, in C.4, there is a kind of analogy between beings of reason and real beings. Hence:

sn4: There are beings of reason—in an analogical sense of 'are'.

Suárez offers a defence of the "true view" via a clarification of what beings of reason are.[35]

2.1 INTENSION OF 'BEING OF REASON'

Suárez elucidates the expression '*ens rationis*' by distinguishing three different relations (*habitudines*) that a being (*ens*) may have to reason (*ratio*):

> The first part [of the true view, namely, that there are beings of reason] cannot be confirmed by argument [*ratio*], unless we first explain what [sort of] being [*esse*] and what [sort of] essence [*essential*] beings of reason have. Since beings of reason, as the term itself indicates, entail a relation to reason, it is right and usual to distinguish a variety of [meanings of] 'being of reason' according to diverse relations. [1] There is a kind of being that is *effected* by reason, with a true and real efficiency. In this sense, all artifacts can be called 'beings of reason'.... This usage, however, is abnormal. [2] Then there is a relation to reason as to a *subject* of inherence; ... And so all perfections [=a kind of act] that inhere *in* the intellect ... can be called 'beings of reason'. We are presently not speaking

of these, for they are true and real beings, included in the previously mentioned categories of accidents [namely, qualities]. This usage of 'being of reason' is also infrequent. [3] Finally, something is said to be in reason [i.e., related to it] by way of being an *object* [for it]. For since knowledge consists in a certain assimilation of the known thing and its being drawn into the knower, the known thing is said to be in the knower not only as inhering through its image but also objectively as it itself is.[36]

We see that in Suárez's view there are three ways for x to be related to the intellect of a person p (henceforth I say elliptically, "related to p") First (1), x is *effectively* related to p if and only if (henceforth "iff") it is an *effect* of the intellect, e.g., in case of an artifact being produced according to a plan. Obviously, such x is a real being. Second (2), x is *subjectively* related to p iff it inheres in p as an accident in its subject, e.g., in case of p's grammatical knowledge inhering in p's intellect. Within the scholastic ontological framework presupposed here, the subjectively related x is a real being as well, namely, a quality. Third (3), x is *objectively* related to p iff p thinks of x. Suárez says here that x is "in reason by way of being an *object*," but he also uses phrases such as "x is *objectively* in p" or "x has *objective being* in p." The idea in the background is that for p to know x or to think of x, x must be somehow "in" p. And since x is a physical thing, x cannot be in the intellect physically but only "objectively."[37]

> SN5: The expression 'being of reason' indicates three different relations to reason: (a) effective, (b) subjective, and (c) objective.

Now there are two ways in which something can be objectively in the intellect:

> [3a] Sometimes, what is . . . objectively in the mind has, or can have, true real being in itself. . . . This is not a genuine being of reason but rather a real being, for true real being belongs to it simply and essentially, whereas to be an object of reason belongs to it extrinsically and accidentally. [3b] Other times, however, something is an object of reason . . . without having in itself any other being, [i.e.,] real and positive, except for this being an object of the intellect.[38]

First, x has both real being in itself and being as an object of the intellect. For instance, *Peter knows Paul*. Paul is a real individual and hence he has real being in himself but also has being as an object of Peter's intellect. Second, *x* has being as an object of the intellect and it has "no other being." For instance, *Peter knows a chimera*. A chimera has no being apart from that in the intellect of Peter. It is only when *x* has no being in itself that we speak of beings of reason in the proper sense:

> It is only in the latter sense [i.e., something is an object of reason without having in itself any other being] that we most appropriately speak of beings of reason. . . . Therefore, what is commonly and rightly defined as a being of reason is *what has only objective being in the intellect*, or, it is *what is thought of by reason as a being, even though it has no entity [being] in itself.*[39]

Suárez does not consider any other definitions. It seems that he adopts a formulation that was universally held in his times. But note that his definition contains in fact two definitions rather than one:

> SN6: A being of reason has only objective being in the intellect.
> SN7: A being of reason is thought of as a being, even though it has no being in itself.

Suárez appears to assume that these two definitions are equivalent, coextensional, but we shall see that they are not in fact equivalent, given what Suárez says later about conceiving something in the manner of a being and in the manner of a nonbeing (see chapter 5, section E).

2.2. EXTENSION OF 'BEING OF REASON'

Now that Suárez has presented a definition of beings of reason, what can be said in favor of their existence? One may distinguish two arguments in Suárez. First, "from experience":

> From this explanation of the [meaning] of the term, which is also a definition of the signified thing (as far as it is definable here), it seems that one may clearly infer that there is something that can be called by the expression 'being of reason'. For many things are thought by our intellect that do not have real being in themselves, although they may be thought of in the manner of beings, as is clear from the examples brought up—of blindness, a relation of reason, etc. Likewise, many things are thought of that are impossible, and fashioned in the manner of possible beings, for

example, a chimera, which does not have any other being besides being thought of.[40]

Suárez believes that once he has clarified what 'being of reason' means, the existence of beings of reason becomes obvious in our experience of thinking about blindness, chimeras, etc.

The second argument for the existence of beings of reason might be called "ontological":

> Again, this very thing we are doing, in disputing about beings of reason, does not come about without some thinking about those [beings]. Therefore, unless one does not know what one is saying, one cannot deny that there is something of this kind contrived by thinking alone, unless perhaps one is laboring under an equivocation in the use of the expressions 'there is' [dari] and 'to be' [esse]. For when we say that there are or that there exist beings of reason, we do not mean that they have real existence in [extra-mental] reality; otherwise, we would be involved in a contradition of terms. Hence, if those who deny that there are beings of reason mean only this, they do not contradict us. But they do not speak here in accord with the subject matter. For beings of this kind are said to be not without qualification [simpliciter] but in a certain respect [secundum quid] . . . namely, objectively in the intellect, and in this way the issue is clear. We will explain the manner of this existence more in the following section.[41]

The argument is that beings of reason are by definition entities that exist as objects of our thought. Hence, their essence includes their being-thought-of or existence-in-thought. Suppose you claim that beings of reason do not exist. You either know what you are talking about or not. If you do not, then your claim is beside the point. If you do, then you claim that the entities that you think about do not exist in the relevant sense, i.e., they do not exist in thought. This is a self-contradiction. Hence, beings of reason exist. (The argument was rejected by Caramuel, as we shall see in chapter 8).

3. Motivation for Beings of Reason

Why do we make up beings of reason? The question concerns the motivation, or, as Suaréz says, "occasion" whereby beings of reason are made up:

> Second, from the previous discussion, we may infer the reason or the occasion for making up or contriving beings of reason. [1] First, it is the

knowledge that our intellect tries to gain even about negations and privations themselves, which are nothing. For since the adequate object of our intellect is being, it can conceive of nothing except in the manner of being. Thus, while it tries to conceive of privations and negations, it conceives of them in the manner of beings, and so it forms beings of reason. St. Thomas touches on this reason [for making up beings of reason] . . . although it does not seem to be applicable to relations of reason. Hence, [2] second, we need to add another reason [causa], which stems from the imperfection of our intellect. For since sometimes our intellect cannot know things as they are in themselves, it conceives of them by comparing them with some other things [per comparationem unius ad aliam], and so it forms relations of reason, where there are no true relations. . . . Both of these reasons or occasions [modi] are in some way grounded in reality [fundantur in re] or they are ordered to what can be truly said of things [de rebus ipsis]. But there is, [3] third, yet another reason [causa], which stems from a certain fecundity of the intellect, which can construct [conficere] fictitious entities from true ones by conjoining parts that cannot be composed in reality, and thereby it makes up a chimera or something like it. In this way the intellect forms beings of reason, which are called 'impossibilia' or, by others, 'entia prohibita'. In these conceptions the intellect does not commit mistakes, because it does not affirm that such beings of reason are so and so in reality as they are conceived by a simple concept. . . . And thus we have sufficiently answered the arguments of the first opinion.[42]

We see that, according to Suárez, there are three reasons or causes for making up beings of reason:

(1) "Filling up" nonbeing: Negations and privations are nothing but we take them as something; hence we make negative beings of reason.
(2) Comparison of nonrelated beings: We sometimes do not know the thing as it is in itself but only as it is compared to other things; hence we make relations of reason.
(3) "Making up": Our intellect is capable of joining together what cannot be joined in reality; hence we make self-contradictory beings of reason. (We would expect consistent fictions to be included here but they are not. Presumably, Suárez counted them as possible—i.e., real—beings).

The first reason

(1) motivates the emergence of beings of reason that are both necessary and useful: We cannot conceive of anything except in the manner of being, because the adequate object of our intellect is being (as Suárez says in the passage above). Hence when we encounter a nonbeing we create a being of reason that enables us somehow to take the nonbeing into account. (But see Suárez's change of mind when he speaks about conceiving in the manner of a nonbeing [chapter 5, section B.3].)

(2) also motivates the emergence of beings of reason that are both necessary and useful: Sometimes we cannot know things as they are in themselves, and hence we need to compare them to other things. What does this mean? Suárez does not say, but he may have had the following in mind: Suppose you mention to me Peter as your friend. I have never met Peter and I know nothing about him except that he is a human being. By knowing that he is a human being I know Peter "comparatively," for I compare Peter to other human beings whom I know individually. Hence, my thinking about Peter qua human being is thinking about a being of reason.

(3) motivates the emergence of beings of reason that are not necessary: We can contrive self-contradictory beings, such as a chimera or a square-circle. Suárez does not say whether such beings of reason could be useful, but they could be, for we use such beings of reason in indirect argumentation. In mathematics, for instance, we often argue by defining a self-contradictory object that is then shown to not "exist."

At this point, referring to the just quoted passage, Millán-Puelles (1990/1996, 785–86) criticizes Suárez for the following reasons: First, not just privation/negation but *every* being of reason is a nonbeing as such. Second, not just privations/negations but *every* being of reason is taken as (= in the manner of) a being. Third, the imperfection of the human understanding is relevant to the origin of *every* being of reason, not just to the relations of reason. Fourth, the fertility of the human understanding is relevant to *every* being of reason, not just to self-contradictory beings. Millán-Puelles correctly observes that what Suárez suggests as a particular "motivation" for particular kinds of beings of reason in fact applies to every being of reason.

In sum, Suárez is commited to the following thesis:

SN8: Beings of reason are needed for three tasks: (a) to know nonbeing, (b) to know things relatively by comparison with other things, (c) to explain the capacity of our intellect to think of self-contradictory beings.

It is surprising that Suárez does not explicitly mention the "truth-making" role of beings of reason—what is it that makes propositions about nonexisting objects true? This oversight, however, does not mean that beings of reason play no role in Suárez's discussion of truth, for they do. Suárez merely does not explicitly take notice of it here.[43]

4. Ontological Status of Beings of Reason

As we saw above, Suárez argued that beings of reason exist but not in the same sense as real beings. So we must ask: In what sense, then, do they exist? In what sense are they beings? Suárez explicitly addresses this issue, which concerns the ontological status of beings of reason:[44]

Although beings of reason share with real beings the *name* 'being' (which is not just an equivocation, as they say, "by chance" but through some analogy and proportionality to true beings), they cannot ever share the same *concept* "being." The first part of this assertion is clear . . . [1] from what has been said: Beings of reason are called 'being' only because they are fashioned and thought of in the manner of being . . . [2] [Also, if] something could not in any way be related or put into proportion with a true being, [then] it could not be called 'a *being* of reason'—there would be no reason to do so. Thus, we speak of beings of reason as beings because of some analogy [with true beings], at least of proportionality.[45]

Beings of reason and real beings are not called 'beings' just by chance. This may be expressed in the statement:

SN9: Beings of reason and real beings are related by an analogy of proportionality.

Nevertheless, there is no univocal concept "covering" both beings of reason and real beings. Why not?

A common concept has no place here, because such a concept requires that the form signified by the term [expressing the concept] is truly and intrinsically participated by its inferiors [i.e., by things to which it applies]. But "being" . . . cannot be intrinsically participated in by beings of reason. For *being only objectively in reason* is not *being* but rather *being thought of* or *being fashioned*. . . . [Hence, beings of reason] cannot be said to have an essence, for this . . . would indicate . . . the capacity for being [*esse*], which beings of reason lack. . . . To confirm this claim: Insofar as being is concerned, beings of reason are further away from real beings than a painted man is from a true one. For in this latter case there is at least some real likeness in accidental features and there is none between real beings and beings of reason.[46]

There cannot be a common concept covering both real beings and beings of reason, because there would have to be something (a form) intrinsic to beings of reason. But beings of reason are only made up, so there cannot be anything *in* them. Note the claim here that beings of reason have no essence: Of course, they have no real essence, but much in the same way as we say that they are sui generis beings, couldn't we say that they have a sui generis essence?

If there is no common concept to real beings and beings of reason, since the latter are such that nothing can be *in* them, there arises an objection: There cannot be any analogy of proportionality between them and real beings. Suárez replies that, although beings of reason do not have a foundation of proportion in themselves (since they are nothing as such), they are *thought to have a foundation* and this is enough—according to Suárez—for the analogy. In order to properly appreciate this claim, we need to know what Suárez means by "analogy of proportionality."[47]

Suárez explains this in Disputation 28 (On the Division of Being into Finite and Infinite).[48] There he distinguishes analogy of proportionality (also called 'of proportion of proportions') and analogy of proportion (also called 'of attribution'). The former is described as follows:

Analogy of proportionality is taken from the proportion of several things. . . . It consists in that the first [or main] analogue is denominated as such from its form considered absolutely, whereas the other analogue . . . [is denominated] in the respect that . . . the first analogue has to its form. For instance, a human being is said to be smiling from the

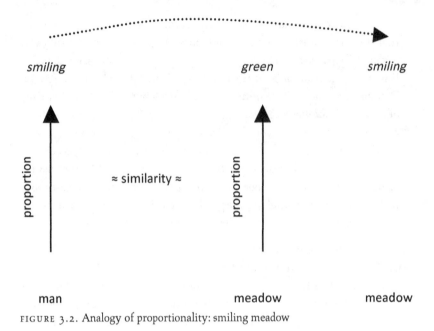

FIGURE 3.2. Analogy of proportionality: smiling meadow

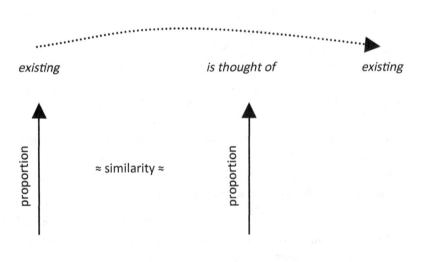

FIGURE 3.3. Analogy of proportionality: existing objects of reason

proper act of smiling . . . whereas a meadow is said to be smiling based on its greenness—not "absolutely" but insofar as it serves for some proportion between the green meadow and the smiling human being. Since this is a proportion between two relations, it is usual to call this analogy 'analogy of proportion of proportions' or 'analogy of proportionality'.[49]

Although this explanation is somewhat tangled, Suárez seems to mean that since a meadow is to *green* as a man is to *smiling* (both proportions indicate a sort of well-being), we have a sufficient ground for the analogical sense in which we can predicate *smiling* of a meadow. This is represented schematically in Figure 3.2.

Similarly, since a real being is to *exists* as an object of reason is to *being thought of*, we can predicate *exists* of an object of reason (and consequently call the latter beings of reason). See Figure 3.3.

An *object of thinking* (which has no extra-mental existence) is to *thinking of it* as an *object* is to *existing*. Hence we may say that an object of thinking is or exists. Since this solution indicates that "exist" for beings of reason involves "to be thought of," it is natural that some scholastics proposed the view that to be a being of reason is an extrinsic denomination: To be is to be thought of. The next chapter explores the causes of beings of reason and deals extensively with this suggestion.

4

Suárez's Objectualism:
The Causes of Beings of Reason

In this chapter I deal with Suarez's views on the causes of beings of reason. Suárez takes up the question of causes in section 2 of Disputation 54. His discussion is divided into three parts; the sections of this chapter are divided accordingly. First, Suárez argues that beings of reason can have only an efficient cause, though he then seems to qualify this claim rather substantially by allowing other types of causes (section A). Second, he argues that only the intellect can be such an efficient cause, though again, he then qualifies this view substantially by stressing the role of the imagination (B.1 and B.3 through B.4). In this context Suárez inserts an extensive and rather complex discussion of extrinsic denominations. He rejects the view that extrinsic denominations are sufficient causes of beings of reason (B.2). Third, Suárez discusses the question of whether and in what sense God knows or makes up beings of reason (C).

A. There Is No Cause but the Efficient Cause

Within the Aristotelian-scholastic framework, four types of causes are distinguished, namely, efficient, final, formal, and material. Hence, the prior question that needs to be asked is whether beings of reason need all four types of Aristotelian-scholastic causes or just some of them. Then, once the types of causes have been identified, we can come to the posterior question, namely, what particular causes of beings of reason there are. Suárez's section 2, entitled "Whether a being of reason has a cause and what it is," deals with these two questions, together with the question of sufficiency of an extrinsic denomination as the cause of beings of reason.

Suárez argues against three false views by claiming that beings of reason have only an efficient cause; that their cause is the intellect only (plus imagination); and that it is only the intellect's reflexive act that makes them (i.e., an extrinsic denomination whereby we think of something, is not sufficient). Schematically we may represent the basic structure of section 2 as shown in Figure 4.1.

Now let's take a closer look at Suárez's text. He first argues that beings of reason have no final causes (1), because "they are not intended by nature or another agent":

> *Whether beings of reason have causes and what they are . . .* —This question needs to be understood only with respect to the efficient cause. For [1] since beings of reason are not . . . directly [*per se*] intended by nature or by an agent, they cannot of themselves [*ex se*] have a proper final cause. [2] And if, on the part of the human being making up beings of reason, it is possible to give some explanation in terms of a final cause . . . this is rather the final cause of that human beings's thinking

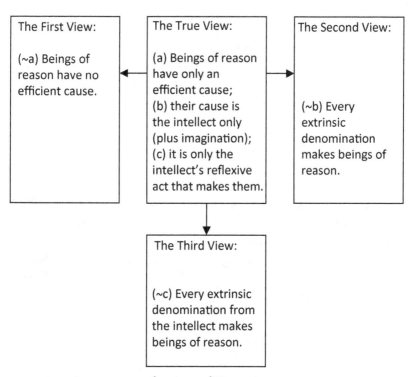

FIGURE 4.1. Argument map of section 2 of Disputation 54

than of the made up object as such. . . . That sort of final cause [*finis*] has been sufficiently explained in the preceding section [i.e., DM d54s1n8; see chapter 3, section C.3].[1]

We see that Suárez is aware that to deny that beings of reason have a final cause sounds odd (2). If beings of reason, as Suárez argues, stem from the imperfection of the human intellect, they would seem to be *intended* by nature (even if imperfect nature). Moreover, beings of reason are often useful and indispensable in science. But if they are indispensable in science, they are *intended* by humans. Hence beings of reason seem to involve both natural and human teleology, i.e., they have a final cause. Suárez addresses this oddity by claiming that the final cause of beings of reason concerns the intellect, which produces them, but not the product, i.e., beings of reason themselves (2). Is this answer convincing? In one sense this claim is right: Beings of reason are not real beings, and as such they cannot have a real final cause. But as Suárez makes clear throughout Disputation 54, we speak about beings of reason in an analogical sense. Hence, I would say, beings of reason have a final cause *in an analogical sense*, otherwise it would be unclear how they could be indispensable and useful.[2]

Suárez then argues that beings of reason have no formal or material causes (1) (2). The exact meaning of this claim, however, is perhaps more obscure than his denial of the final cause:

> Again, [1] since beings of reason are themselves fashioned in the manner of certain forms, e.g., of relation . . . , any other formal cause is unnecessary. [2] . . . [and] since beings of reason are not *in* anything as *in* a subject, but . . . they are mere objects of the intellect, they do not have a material cause either. [3] Although, if a thing denominated as a being of reason is considered in the manner of a subject, it could be called 'matter' or 'quasimatter' . . . Hence . . . [beings of reason] could [also] be said to have a formal cause, namely, the being of reason itself taken abstractly. For example, when "man" is . . . a species . . . the matter is *man* and the form is the relation of species.[3]

When Suárez says that "any *other* formal cause is unnecessary" (1) it sounds as if there is *a* formal cause after all. Moreover, Suárez immediately qualifies his denial of formal and material causes by explaining that in some sense one *could* speak about formal and material causes (3). Unfortunately,

Suárez leaves the discussion at this point, leaving unclear what his real opinion is.

After Suárez argues that beings of reason have no final, material or formal causes—at least in *some sense*, he argues that they have an efficient cause. First, he addresses those who denied this:

> Some simply deny the [efficient] cause of beings of reason. Soncinas held this view . . . although he does not say that beings of reason have abso-lutely no cause, only that they have no cause giving them being (*esse*). He is evidently speaking about existential being (*esse existentiae*), in which sense the matter is most clear, since . . . beings of reason have only objective being [*esse obiectivum*] in the intellect. . . . Thus, it is pointless to seek the cause that gives [real] being [*esse*] to beings of reason through real efficacy, whether mediate or immediate.[4]

Although Soncinas apparently denies that beings of reason have an efficient cause, Suárez takes him to mean "an efficient cause as giving real existence." Suárez, of course, agrees with the so-interpreted-Soncinas. There is no ef-ficient cause of the *real being* of beings of reason because they have no such being. However, this does not mean that there is no efficient cause of their *objective being*:

> Nevertheless, since there is no being of reason that would *always* be [in the sui generis sense of 'be'] but rather every being of reason *begins* to be [at some time], . . . it is not pointless to ask about the cause of this [beginning] to be.[5]

Then Suárez argues that because beings of reason have objective being in the intellect, which they do not have always, there must be a *sufficient reason*, i.e., an efficient cause, for it. The efficient cause, however, does not "work" *directly*, but in some (as we shall see, rather obscure) *indirect* way:

> We need to say that there is an efficient cause from which beings of reason get their own "kind" of being. Yet, the effective causation (*efficiencia*), since it is a real production, does not terminate at the being of reason as at the terminus of the production, but only at the object of this produced terminus. I argue for this: [1] since . . . any given being of reason . . . has objective being, but it does not have it always; thus, that it does have it now and not before, is to be explained in some way by an efficient cause;

otherwise no sufficient reason for this variation could be given. [2] Also, objective being, although it is nothing in beings of reason themselves, necessarily presupposes some real being on which it is founded . . . ; hence the cause of this real being is the cause of the being of reason. [3] From this it is clear that . . . the cause makes something in virtue of real efficacy, for instance, in virtue of an act of thinking or contriving, which is something real. . . . This causal process (*efficientia*) itself terminates in some way at the formal concept of the mind and it stops there. However, it thereby also happens that the formal concept terminates in some way at the being of reason, which is its object . . . Thus, finally, the being of reason itself has objective being in the intellect.[6]

First (1), Suárez points out that, given the principle of sufficient reason, there must be some efficient cause of beings of reason. But now a problem arises: Causality is (supposed to be) a real process, starting with real causes and ending up with real effects; hence it would seem that beings of reason must be real. At this point (2), Suárez shifts his focus from beings of reason to the *foundation* of beings of reason. He declares that the cause of the foundation of a given being of reason is also the cause of this being of reason. However, this is a half-truth at best, because, even though the foundation as such may be *necessary* for beings of reason to emerge, we are in search of a *sufficient* explanation.[7] In the end (3), Suárez does not defend the view that beings of reason *themselves* have an efficient cause, but rather that the mental act that the being of reason is an object of, has it. Beings of reason would then come "for free," and we are back to where we started: There is no sufficient explanation for beings of reason and there should be one.

In sum, what can we make of Suárez's views and arguments? On the most charitable reading Suárez wants to say that there is *some* important difference between the efficient and other causes of beings of reason. It is not clear, however, what this difference supposedly consists in. He does not simply say that:

SC1: Beings of reason have no final, material, or formal cause.

Rather, he qualifies SC1 in such a way that it should be stated as:

SC1'A: Beings of reason have no final, material, or formal cause in the *strict* sense.

sc1'b: Beings of reason have a final, material, and formal cause in *some* sense.

But the same can be said about Suárez's view concerning the efficient cause:

sc2a: Beings of reason have no efficient cause in the *strict* sense.
sc2b: Beings of reason have an efficient cause in *some* sense.

Hence, it is more plausible to say that the causality that leads to beings of reason is: sui generis, i.e., not the usual natural causality but intentional causality; and applicable to all four kinds of causes. This view was explicitly adopted by some post-Suárezian authors, such as Mastri/Belluto (see chapter 7, section C.1).

B. The Intellect as the Efficient Cause of Beings of Reason

Suárez's text on the intellect as the efficient cause of beings of reason can be divided into four parts. First, Suárez states this thesis in a preliminary way (DM d54s2n4–5, B.1). Then he addresses what he sees as the main challenge to this thesis, namely, that beings of reason are nothing but extrinsic denominations (DM d54s2n6–14, B.2). Third, based on the discussion of extrinsic denominations, Suárez determines the kind of mental acts that cause beings of reason (DM d54s2n15–16, B.3). Finally, he takes up again the thesis that only the intellect is capable of the kind of mental acts required for beings of reason but complicates the matter by appearing to hold that the imagination also makes them (DM d54s2n17–18, B.4).

1. Preliminary Formulation of the Thesis

Suárez divides his view about the causes of beings of reason into two parts. The first, which we have just discussed above (chapter 4, section A), states that beings of reason have only an efficient cause. The second part states that:

sc3: The only efficient cause of beings of reason is the human intellect.

This thesis seems obvious to Suárez from his previous discussion:

Secondly, I say: the efficient cause of beings of reason is the intellect. It effects them only by producing some thought or concept, by reason of which a being of reason is said to have objective being in the intellect. This is clear enough from what has been said above. . . . For if a being of reason has only objective being in the intellect, then it has that by means of some act of the intellect for which it is an object. But it has (objective) being through the effective process [that produced] that act. Hence, the effective process of the act is also the effective process of the being of reason itself—in a broad sense. . . . Against this assertion, one might bring the opinion that every extrinsic denomination is a being of reason, even before any consideration of the intellect. About this opinion I will presently speak.[8]

Note that Suárez reaffirms again the problematic claim that beings of reason are *indirectly* caused by the cause of the intellectual act of which they are objects (see IV.A.). But this problem will not be our concern in this section. We shall discuss instead the extrinsic-denomination view, which is, according to Suárez, the only challenge to SC3. The extrinsic-denomination view states that to be denominated extrinsically is sufficient for something to be a being of reason. Suárez distinguishes between two basic versions of this view. According to one, let's call it the *general view*, any extrinsic denomination is sufficient; but according to the other, let's call it the *restricted view*, only an extrinsic denomination from the intellect, such as "being thought of," will do. Suárez argues that although extrinsic denominations are necessary, they are never sufficient conditions for beings of reason.

Before we proceed to Suárez's discussion of extrinsic denominations, let me cite his summary of the questions he wants to address:

Indeed, about this assertion [i.e., that beings of reason are caused efficiently by the intellect] there are many things we need to ask and explain. [1] First, what is that action or thinking of the intellect, from the efficacy of which a being of reason is to result? . . . does it result . . . from any act of the mind or only from certain determinate [sort of] acts . . . ? [2] Then, [we ask]: whether producing beings of reason . . . is proper to the intellect, or whether [this capacity] belongs also to the will or even to the senses and other powers having . . . objects? [3] Finally, [we ask] whether we should discuss only the human intellect or whether beings of reason also result from the divine or angelic intellects?[9]

The first question will reemerge below in section B.3, the second in B.4, and the third in C.

2. Extrinsic Denominations

Let us begin the discussion of extrinsic denominations by asking the more general question "What is a denomination?" Stated simply, 'to denominate' means "to name a thing derivatively." More precisely, a denomination is the substitution of the name N_2 of a thing T_2 for the name N_1 of another thing T_1 to which T_1 is somehow related. We can divide denominations into intrinsic and extrinsic. For instance, Socrates (T_1) is denominated as 'the white' (N_2)—instead of 'Socrates' (N_1)—for he is *intrinsically* related to *whiteness* (T_2). In contrast, Socrates (T_1) is denominated as 'the seen' (N_2)—instead of 'Socrates' (N_1)—for he is merely *extrinsically* related to *being seen* (T_2). What is this *being seen*? It is the "thing" or, as the scholastics put it, the form derived from the founding relation of sight (P) that somebody has toward Socrates (T_1).[10] Hence, we may say that an extrinsic denomination involves four basic elements: the denomination (N_2: 'the seen'), the thing denominated (T_1: Socrates), the denominating form (T_2: *being seen*) and the relation founding the denomination (P: somebody's seeing Socrates).[11]

Central to Suárez's claim is the view that (normally) extrinsic denominations are *real*, hence they are not sufficient conditions of beings of reason.

2.1. GENERAL EXTRINSIC-DENOMINATION VIEW

That beings of reason are somehow related to extrinsic denominations is plausible, for, as we have seen above (chapter 3, section C.4), beings of reason are called "beings" in virtue of the similarity between the two relations ("proportions"), namely, *real-object/exist* and *object-of-thought/being-thought-about*. Hence, beings of reason may be extrinsically denominated as 'being thought of' (or 'being merely thought of'), which means that some extrinsic denomination is *necessary* to them. This is assumed by Suárez and most other Baroque scholastics. But this leads to a controversial question: Is an extrinsic denomination *sufficient* for something to be a being of reason? According to the general denomination view it is:

> It is . . . an opinion of certain people that beings of reason are nothing but extrinsic denominations by which a known thing is denominated from

the act of intellect according to some property or condition belonging to it insofar as it is known. This denomination can be of different sorts. The first denomination . . . seems to be that by which a thing is said to be "known," . . . Then there are denominations taken from various operations of the intellect . . . to be "universal," . . . "affirmed," "an antecedent." . . . For it is the common consensus of everyone that these are all beings of reason (which is obvious because to be so denominated is nothing real in things and, nevertheless, it is conceived and said as if it were something). . . . And thus explained, this opinion is attributed to Durandus . . . we shall see afterwards whether this is what he thought.[12]

Suárez attributes the general denomination view to Durandus and promises to come back to him "afterward." (In reality, however, he forgets to fulfill this promise –the name of Durandus does not appear anymore in the rest of Disputation 54.) His argumentation against the general denomination view is indirect. He draws three unacceptable consequences of it. The first is that God would on this view make up beings of reason:

From this opinion it follows, first, that beings of reason not only result . . . in things known by a human or created intellect, but also [in things known] by the divine intellect. For those things are also denominated as *the known*, inasmuch as they are objects of the divine intellect. Duns Scotus[13] almost embraced this view.[14]

The second consequence is that not only the intellect, but also other mental faculties, would be capable of making up beings of reason:

It follows, secondly . . . that beings of reason result not only from the intellect but also from the will, and indeed from vision and other similar acts as well. For, from these also, objects are denominated according to some being that is nothing in them, e.g., *being willed* or *being seen*.[15]

A similar problem is raised further below (DM d54s2n12; chapter 4, section B.2.2): Suárez argues that if the extrinsic-denomination view is accepted, we should have many more terms, besides 'being of reason', for them in so far as they are also beings of will, beings of sight, beings of imagination, etc. All these beings are nonreal; they are "beings of extrinsic denomination." Hence the proponents of the extrinsic-denomination view should drop the term 'being of reason' and adopt the term 'being of extrinsic denomination', if they want to be consistent.

The third and most undesirable consequence is that items such as "the left" or "the clothed" are beings of reason:

> Third, . . . it follows that there are not only beings of reason because of the acts of vital powers but they can also arise from other things or dispositions of things. . . . For instance, the denomination by which a column is said to be "the left" or "the right" of an animal. . . . Even more, it follows . . . that the denominations "the clothed" from a garment or "the located" from a place . . . are beings of reason . . . For each such denomination posits nothing in the thing denominated; indeed it is on this account that it is called extrinsic and therefore . . . a being of reason.[16]

Suárez takes these three consequences to constitute a clear refutation of the general extrinsic-denomination view. According to him *being seen* or *being clothed* and the like are not mind-dependent beings of reason for they *are* really and mind-independently "out there":

> These consequences, then, make it plain, I think, that this view cannot be true in its unrestricted version, namely, that an extrinsic denomination as such constitutes a being of reason. *For if the denomination is taken from a real form, by this very fact it exists in reality* and, consequently, it does not count as a being of reason. The antecedent is clear: for that form has true real being independently of reason. Therefore, the denomination resulting from that form, although extrinsic, is also, nonetheless, real and not just objectively in the intellect or in virtue of the working or fantasizing of the intellect.[17]

Someone might object, however, that the process of denomination involves an act of the intellect, and hence there *must* be some being of reason involved:

> You may say: By the very fact that it is a denomination, it cannot be more than a being of reason for the denominating is a work of reason. In reply: If by 'denomination' one understands the imposition of the denominating name—that indeed is a work of reason. We are, however, not speaking about the imposition of names now, for in this way . . . even intrinsic denominations are works of reason. We speak [now] of unities and relations among the things themselves in which these denominating names are founded. And these are not works of reason. In an intrinsic denomination

there is a real unity or identity or something like this; in an extrinsic denomination (which is taken from real things themselves), there is a real relation of one thing toward another and based on this [fact] the thing toward which the relation is directed is denominated by the [name] of the other thing.[18]

We see that Suárez's reply involves a distinction between the mental (linguistic) act of imposing a denominating name, and the expressed form or thing itself. If one wishes to argue that extrinsic denominations are beings of reason because they involve the mental act of denominating, then all denominations, even intrinsic ones, would have to be beings of reason. But this is absurd. Hence, the extrinsic things (forms) expressed by extrinsic denominations are real even though in order to express them we need thought and language. The claim that the forms of extrinsic denominations are real means that Suárez's system of super-categories contains *extrinsic beings*. I subsume these, together with *real nonbeings*, under the category of "para-beings" for they are in some sense *parasitic* upon real beings (see also chapter 2, section A).[19]

2.2. RESTRICTED EXTRINSIC-DENOMINATION VIEW

The extrinsic-denomination view may be revised in such a way as to avoid some of the undesirable consequences of the general view. One could say that only an extrinsic denomination derived from (an act of) the intellect is sufficient for something to be a being of reason. But Suárez does not like this restricted view either, for acts of the intellect toward something are just as real as other relations:

> But if the view regarding extrinsic denominations derived from [any] real being is not true in its unrestricted version, neither it is when applied only to acts of the intellect. . . . For an act of the intellect is just as much a true and real form as other forms and it has a real . . . relation to its objects, whence these objects are denominated as "the known."[20]

The fact that not every denomination from the intellect is a being of reason, i.e., that it is not a sufficient condition of beings of reason, does not mean, however, that they cannot *give rise* to beings of reason:

> *You may say:* it is peculiar to denominations taken from acts of the intellect that they can "fall into" beings of reason, and thus . . . be called 'being

of reason'. *But this is not enough,* for we may only infer from this that some extrinsic denominations, even if . . . taken from real forms, can be "extended" to beings of reason. However, we cannot infer conversely that a denomination is *sufficient* to constitute a being of reason. In this context Scotus rightly noted that . . . extrinsic denominations [from acts of the intellect] *can* be the foundation of some beings . . . of reason *if* they are conceived as something *in* the thing denominated. Nevertheless, taken precisely in themselves, these [denominations] are not properly beings of reason.[21]

But the proponents of the restricted extrinsic-denomination view might continue their argumentation by saying that denominations from acts of the intellect differ from other denominations in that (a) the thing so denominated exists only objectively in the intellect; and (b) it is dependent on the actual operation of reason. And *such* denomination is sufficient for a being of reason to arise/emerge:

But it can further be said to be peculiar to denominations taken from acts of the intellect that the being that they confer is only objectively in the intellect, which is characteristic of beings of reason, as we have said above. Thus, although extrinsic denominations taken from other things or acts agree with denominations from the intellect insofar as they posit no real being in the things denominated, they differ, nonetheless, insofar as they do not exist only objectively in the intellect and insofar as they are not dependent upon the actual operation of reason.[22]

Suárez has two things to say in reply. First, he points out that granting this defense of the restricted denomination view we would have to either (1) extend the normal meaning of 'being of reason' to include other beings (that are merely objectively in some mental faculty and dependent on its actual operation) or (2) recognize many other nonreal sorts of being:

In this [defense of the restricted denomination view], two mistakes are committed. The first is that either [1] one twists the [normal] meaning of the term 'being of reason' or [2] one will have to admit other kinds of beings that are neither real nor beings of reason. The latter (i.e., [2]) is explained thus: if a being constituted through an extrinsic denomination from an act of reason has its own character of being, distinct from real being, then the *being seen* or *being loved* and in general any extrinsically denominated being will [also] have . . . a certain [peculiar] character of being. . . . [Hence there are many other kinds of beings beside beings of reason]. Or we twist the meaning of the term "being of reason" (i.e., [1]), which *seems* to signify a peculiar dependence upon *reason*. But why not . . . produce other similar terms . . . such as 'being of imagination', 'being of sense', 'being of will', etc., all of which will be distinct from real being? If we . . . look at reality, [we see] that all [these items] can be called 'being of extrinsic denomination' for . . . all agree in that they signify . . . a being distinct from real being. [Hence we should adopt the term 'being of extrinsic denomination' rather than 'being of reason'].[23]

Both (1) and (2) are unacceptable because they would involve a too drastic revision of the traditional scholastic framework.

Second, Suárez argues that the restricted extrinsic-denomination view confuses two meanings of 'known':

Secondly, the [defense of the restricted denomination view] is mistaken, because it is . . . false [to say] that a denomination taken from a *direct* act of the intellect has being merely *objectively* in the intellect. For, properly speaking, it has being in the intellect *formally* rather than *objectively*. [1] Hence, we must avoid an equivocation when dealing with [the expression] 'being known' [*esse cognitum*] . . . for it can mean either "being that is known" and this is indeed *objectively* in the intellect, or it can mean "being that a thing is said to have from the fact that it is known" and this is not . . . in the intellect not *objectively* but *formally*. [2] The latter is objectively in the intellect [only when] the intellect knows itself to be knowing in reflexive cognition or rather [when] it knows that the thing is known [by it]. [3] Moreover, although the latter cognition *may* be objectively in the intellect, it is not *merely* objectively in the intellect. For the form from which the denomination 'being known' is derived is not *just* objectively in the mind but *also* in reality. To take another example: when the intellect knows of some thing that it is loved, the "being loved" of this thing is indeed objectively in the intellect but this is not its total being. . . . For in reality itself a certain act of love tends to the thing and terminates in it.[24]

What does Suárez mean here? Suppose Peter is thinking of (=knows) Paul. Hence, Paul is the object of Peter's thinking, i.e., he is objectively in Peter's intellect.[25] This is the *objective* sense in which Paul is being known (1). There is, however, yet another meaning of 'being known', which refers not to Paul but to the whole fact of Paul's-being-known-by-Peter. This is the formal sense in which Peter is being known (1). This fact is not the normal object of Peter's thinking. Normally (in direct cognition), Peter is thinking of Paul and not of Paul-as-I-Peter-am-thinking-of-him, although it is possible for Peter to change the object of his thinking from Paul to "my-thinking-of-Paul" (i.e., Peter's-thinking-of-Paul), which is what happens in reflexive cognition (2). Nevertheless, regardless in which sense we take 'being known', it is not sufficient to account for the emergence of a being of reason. In both cases the object of Peter's thinking has not just objective, but also real, being and thus is not a being of reason (3).

Summarizing his position, Suárez says:

> All in all, if we stick . . . to an extrinsic denomination that results from a real form and from a relation that is true and existing in reality and not made up, I do not think it falls under beings of reason. Rather, it belongs to the extension of 'real being'. . . . Hence, the intellect conceives no being of reason if it [gets to] know nothing else than [the fact] that a certain form, for example, sight, has an intrinsic relation to a certain object . . . and that this object is (on this basis) extrinsically denominated as "the seen." For all these [elements of the extrinsic denomination "the seen"] are truly in reality as they are known: namely, the thing denominated, the denominating form, and the union of the two which completes the denomination (and which is rather a real relation). The same argument applies mutatis mutandis to a denomination taken from an act of the intellect as it directly knows a thing, which is thus denominated as "the known." . . . All of this will be more clear from what follows [d54s2nn.15–18].[26]

The claim is that when the intellect simply knows a real object, there is nothing fictitious about the object being known by it: The object, the form of being known, and their extrinsic union are all real. Hence the extrinsic form is also real (a species of what I call "para-being," see chapter 2, section A). Suárez concludes that:

> sc4: Extrinsic denominations are necessary but insufficient conditions of beings of reason.[27]

3. Beings of Reason Are Caused by a Special Mental Act

If an extrinsic denomination as such is not enough to produce a being of reason, what do we need in addition to it? Suárez argues that we need a special sort of act of the intellect:

> SC5: Beings of reason are caused by an act of the intellect that con-
> ceives of something that has no being in the manner of a being.

Suárez offers three reasons in favor SC5:

> We need to say that a being of reason . . . is made [*fieri*] by an act of the
> intellect in which something that has no being [*entitas*] in reality is
> conceived in the manner of a being [*ens*]. [1] This assertion is taken from
> what we have said in the first section. . . . [2] Second, it is proven by what
> has been said against the preceding opinion, for if an extrinsic denomina-
> tion as such is insufficient [to make] a being of reason, there remains no
> other way of explaining the causal emergence [*causalitas*] of beings of
> reason. [3] Third, [the thesis] is made clear by the thing itself, and by a
> certain quasi-induction. Thus, by way of example, blindness . . . can be
> conceived of in two ways. First, negatively only—by conceiving that in
> a certain organ there is no power of sight; in this way there arises no
> being of reason since nothing is conceived of in the manner of a being,
> but only in the manner of a nonbeing. Then, however, the intellect [may
> start to] conceive of blindness as a condition affecting an animal or an
> organ, in order to form a simple concept of it. . . . It is now that the intel-
> lect conceives of something in the manner of a being and since it does
> not conceive of a real being, it is properly forming a certain being of
> reason.[28]

The first two reasons are trivial: (1) SC5 simply follows from the definition of beings of reason given in the first section of Disputation 54; (2)
there is no other explanation available if the extrinsic-denomination view
fails. The third reason is more informative (3). Suárez argues that one
and the same state of affairs (e.g., Homer's not-having-sight) can be
viewed in two ways: either "in the manner of a nonbeing" or "in the
manner of a being." It is only in the latter case that a being of reason
emerges. (In chapter 5 section E.1, I argue that this step is Suárez's crucial
mistake.)

Similarly, as it is possible to conceive of a negative state of affairs in two ways, it is possible to conceive of the situation of extrinsic denominations in two ways:

> Something similar "happens" in case of beings of reason that have a foundation in extrinsic denominations, such as the relation of *the seen* [to the seer], *the known* [to the knower], etc. These denominations can also be conceived of in two ways. [1] First, as mere extrinsic denominations; in this way (insofar as the intellect directly knows that a thing is seen) . . . no being of reason is formed or known. [2] Then, however, . . . correlatively, when something is conceived of in the manner of a relation *in* the denominated thing [and directed *from* the thing back *to* the seer or knower].[29]

We see that extrinsic denominations may give rise to beings of reason when they are believed to be intrinsic to the denominated thing. Also, note that no being of reason emerges when the intellect *directly* knows a thing. Hence it is to be expected that for beings of reason one needs a *reflective* act:

> Secondly I say that the act of intellect by which a being of reason arises is in some way comparative or reflexive. . . . This needs to be proven and explained: the act . . . by which a being of reason is fashioned and emerges, presupposes . . . another concept of a real being in proportion to and in imitation of which the being of reason is conceived of and formed. For example, in a privation such as darkness, there is some knowledge of light presupposed so that its removal or negation may be conceived of as the opposite condition. . . . Thus . . . the [process] of making up beings of reason happens through *reflective* acts of knowing (here we broaden the meaning of 'reflective' to include all acts of knowing presupposing and based on other acts of knowing). . . . This reflection occurs in multiple ways . . . but as soon as something that is not a true being is conceived of as if it were a (true) being, the intellect has [as its object] a made-up-being-of-reason.[30]

Suárez's second thesis concerning the sort of act of the intellect needed for beings of reason is:

sc6: Beings of reason are caused by a reflexive act of the intellect.

However, we should keep in mind that the sense in which Suárez says that the required act of the intellect is reflexive is rather peculiar: If I want to conceive of blindness, I first need to know what sight is. If I want to make up beings of reason, i.e., nonreal entities, I first need to know real entities.

4. The Intellect as the Only Efficient Cause

From what has been said about the cause of beings of reason, it follows that neither the senses, nor the will, are capable of producing beings of reason because these powers are not sufficient to conceive of as a being what is a nonbeing:

> It is, hence, easy to answer the second question as well [see chapter 4, section B.1]. For we need to say that beings of reason are formed neither in the senses nor in the will . . . because . . . [these faculties] do not have the power to form or conceive of what is truly not a being in the manner of a being. Sense is not reflective . . . and being as being is not its proper object . . . and the same is true of the will.[31]

But someone might object that the will is capable of tending toward an *apparent* good. Hence there seems to be also some "nonreal being of the will." Suárez answers that a nonreal good is an object contrived by the intellect, not the will:

> The human will sometimes tends toward what is not good in reality as if it were good. Nevertheless the will does not *fabricate* such good but it presupposes it as apprehended and represented by the intellect. Hence, even this [apparent] good counts as a being of reason—it is not fashioned by the will but by the intellect. True, the will (like the senses) denominates its objects as "loved" or "desired" by a real extrinsic denomination. . . . But it does not further reflect or inquire what "to be loved" and "to be desired" is *in* such objects. . . . This is the task of the intellect. And although the will can . . . reflect upon its own object, by loving love or desire . . . still through this reflection it does not fashion anything that is not good in itself in the manner of a being or a good. The will tends to each thing as it exists in itself or as it is proposed to it by the intellect.[32]

Moving on from the will to the senses, Suárez hesitates on what to think of the imagination (one of the internal senses): It seems that the imagination is capable, by joining together sensual appearances, to make up not only possible nonexisting entities (e.g., a golden mountain) but also impossible entities (e.g., a chimera), i.e., beings of reason. Hence, not only the intellect but also the imagination is capable of making up beings of reason?

> From this general rule [*regula*] an exception should be made for the human imagination, for it sometimes fashions certain beings that in fact never exist nor even can exist, by composing them of beings accessible to the senses. This happens, for instance, in the case of a golden mountain that does not exist, although it is possible [that it exists]. In the same way the imagination may fashion an impossible thing, for instance, a chimera, for it has the power to combine simple appearances [*species*], forming of them an image [*idolum*]; . . . and just as it can combine those that do *not* involve incompatibility [*repugnantia*] . . . it can fabricate a combination of things that cannot cohere. Hence, the dialecticians also say that 'imaginable being' has wider extension [*ampliatio*] than 'possible being'. Thus, we must certainly say that the merely impossible beings of reason, which do not have a foundation in reality . . . can also be made up by the imagination.[33]

But there is a twist, for Suárez appears to revoke immediately what he has just said:

> However, because in this case the human imagination participates somehow in the power of reason, and perhaps it never does this without the cooperation of reason, all these things are said to be beings of *reason*, and the task of their production is (without qualification) attributed to reason.[34]

Suárez claims that the imagination as such is incapable of producing beings of reason; it needs to work in tandem with the intellect. But can the two passages be reconciled? It seems that Suárez is undecided as to what to hold:

> SC3': The efficient cause of beings of reason is either (a) the human intellect alone, or (b) the human intellect together with the imagination.

Perhaps Suárez wants to say that the intellect is the sole necessary and sufficient condition of beings of reason, but, as a matter of fact, it often closely "collaborates" with the imagination. For it appears that we sometimes *imagine* impossible entities such as goat stags; but whatever we imagine is not yet, strictly speaking, impossible. An imagined goat stag is an animal looking partially like a goat and partially like a stag and even though it does not exist actually, it is *possible* for it to exist. A truly impossible-to-exist animal is then one that combines the *essences* of a goat and a stag. Impossible-to-exist entities can be grasped by the intellect-with-imagination, but not by the imagination alone. This phenomenon of our mental life could be perhaps an explanation for Suárez's unclear statements. In chapter 7, section C.1, we shall see that Mastri/Beluto explicitly accuse Suárez of confusion concerning the role of the imagination in the production of beings of reason.[35]

C. Beings of Reason and God

Does God know beings of reason? On the one hand it would seem that he does for he is omniscient.[36] On the other hand this would seem to imply imperfection in him (see chapter 3, section C.3. for the motivation), which is unacceptable for theists such as Suárez. One could defend the former claim by pointing out that the imperfection involved in knowing beings of reason lies on the side of the object in question and not on the side of the knower (God):

> Again, it belongs to the perfection of a knower to know each thing as what it is or how it is. But these beings of reason are such that they are not true beings in themselves, they can be thought of only in the manner of beings. . . . [Accordingly,] although they are not beings, to know them in the manner of beings will not be *an imperfection in the divine intellect* but rather *an imperfection of the objects themselves.*[37]

Suárez disagrees. When an object is thought of in a manner that differs from the way it is, this is not a mere imperfection of the object; it is also an imperfection of the knower:

> Nevertheless, from another standpoint, it seems to contradict the perfection of the divine intellect that it would form beings of reason. For a being of reason is not formed except by conceiving of what is not a being in the manner of a being. . . . Thus, it seems false to assume . . . that the formation of beings of reason does not result from an imperfect way of knowing. . . . For every conception of a thing [object] such that the thing as

known differs from the way it is . . . is imperfect in itself and it does not have that condition by virtue of the object but from the side of the knower. . . . For the perfection of knowledge consists in adequation with the thing known and, consequently, in the representation of that thing as it is in itself.[38]

We see that in Suárez's view, (real) things never force the (perfect) intellect to make up beings of reason, i.e., to know something otherwise than it is in itself. This pertains both to relations of reason and to negations:

> The claim [that to form beings of reason contradicts divine perfection] can be easily proven by looking at particular objects or beings of reason. An absolute being . . . does not demand to be known in the manner of something relative. Indeed, even though two things may *appear* to us connected, if they are not *in fact* related, they will be known . . . without any real or contrived relation more perfectly than if they are known in a relative manner that does not belong to them. . . . [Similarly,] . . . a positive being does not demand to be known in the manner of a negative being, nor conversely a negative being in the manner of a positive being. The latter is, perhaps, hard to accept because a negation has no entity that could be represented through cognition, unless it is fashioned in the manner of a being. But we must observe that perfect knowledge of a negation does not consist in its being represented directly and in the manner of a being. Rather, in clear knowledge . . . we know that one thing is not another thing . . . without some direct representation of the negation . . . itself.[39]

Hence, according to this view, God can know everything without making up beings of reason. This is further explained as follows:

> In this way, God knows negations themselves most perfectly by a positive act and a judgment of the simultaneous intuition of two things and [the fact] that one is not the other. . . . God does not have any other act by which he would know a negation in the way of something positive; for such conception would be neither necessary nor compatible [*spectans*] with his perfection. God is said to know those things that do not exist, as well as those that do exist, not because in order to know these things that do not exist . . . he needs to know the negation in the manner of a positive being, but because he clearly and distinctly knows the things that exist,

as well as the things that do not exist, by knowing and judging about each one what it is or is not. Moreover, God does not receive knowledge from things; in order to know them he does not depend upon their existence, but he equally knows possible things as well as existing things, and future things as well as present things, yet he knows each one to be as it is, or not to be as it is not.[40]

God knows each thing by knowing "what it is" and "what it is not." He does not need to create "proxy" objects (i.e., beings of reason) *in order to* know something else (nonbeings or beings that we know only relatively). Suárez adopts this view, but he adds:

> To me this latter opinion seems true and very much consistent with divine perfection. It occurs to me only to add that, although God does not directly [*per se*] and immediately know beings of reason by forming them, nevertheless he does most perfectly know beings of reason [as formed by us]. For this reason beings of this kind can be said to have some being in virtue of the divine cognition. For their being is objective being in the intellect. If, however, they are known by God, they are objectively in the divine intellect and hence they have being that is proportionate to them from the "force" of the divine intellect.[41]

Suárez makes two points here: (a) Although God does not make up beings of reason "for his own sake," since there are some beings of reason anyway (made by us), he needs to know them; (b) if there are some beings in God's intellect they also *get* some being from his intellect. The former thesis is obvious for Suárez:

> The fact that these beings [of reason] are perfectly known by God can be confirmed because God comprehends all acts of human imagination and reason. Accordingly, he comprehends all "formal fictions" (if I may put it thus) that can exist in these [mental] potencies. Therefore, he also knows "objective fictions" that correspond to or are objects for these mental [potencies and their] acts. And thus he knows all beings of reason, which can in any way arise through the operations of these potencies.[42]

And to this must be added thesis (b), namely, that beings of reason receive some being in virtue of God's knowing them. Suárez even adds that beings of reason in God's intellect are *actually* there:

Someone . . . can say that, even though God . . . knows beings of reason, this is not sufficient for them to be said to be in actual being . . . but only that they are possible, or rather imaginable or able to be fashioned by the human mind. *The answer* is: if this way of speaking is more acceptable to someone, we need not dispute it. . . . However, if we speak more broadly about any objective being they have, just as they are actually known by the divine intellect, so also they can be said actually to be.[43]

Millán-Puelles observes that John of St. Thomas disagrees here with Suárez: "One is not to say that God forms beings of reason on the grounds that He intellectively apprehends them as formed by our understanding. . . . God knows a being of reason formed by me, and yet . . . He knows it as originating from my understanding, not His" (1990/1996, 797). This view, however, assumes that God can know something without *adding* to it the objective-being-in-God's-intellect. This seems, however, logically impossible to be the case.

In conclusion, with respect to God's knowledge of beings of reason, Suárez holds the following two theses:

SC-G1: God does not make up his own beings of reason.
SC-G2: God knows beings of reason that *we* produce.

Suárez also briefly considers whether angels make up or know beings of reason but we may pass over this question because it does not contribute to the overall understanding of Suárez's theory of beings of reason.[44]

Having dealt with Suárez's views on the causes of beings of reason, we proceed to his views on their division.

5

Suárez's Objectualism: The Division of Beings of Reason

In this chapter I deal with Suárez's views on the division of beings of reason and also provide an overview and evaluation of Suárez's entire theory. The chapter is divided into five parts. First, I discuss Suárez's views on whether the traditional division of beings of reason into negation, privation, and relation is exclusive (section A). Second, I turn to his views on whether this division is exhaustive (B). Third, I present his position on the commonalities and differences between negations and privations (C). Fourth, I add a few words about relations of reason (D). And finally, I summarize Suárez's theory of beings of reason in general and identify some problems and objections it faces (E). The question of the division of beings of reason is taken up in sections 3 to 6 of Suárez's Disputation 54.

Suárez pays great attention to the division of beings of reason, although it would seem to be a somewhat less important issue in comparison with the nature and causes of beings of reason. Indeed, in this chapter I leave out many passages of Suárez's text because they seem to be just detailed descriptions without sufficient relevance for the general structure of the theory of beings of reason. Some of Suárez's claims made in sections 3 to 6, however, are fundamental even for the general structure of his theory. For instance, Suárez presents here his doctrine of two types of nonbeings: nonbeings considered in the manner of nonbeings, and nonbeings considered in the manner of beings. I argue that this doctrine is inconsistent with what Suárez says elsewhere about the very nature of beings of reason.

A. Is the Traditional Division of Beings of Reason Mutually Exclusive?

The discussion of the division of beings of reason occupies the largest bulk of Disputation 54. There was a standard scholastic doctrine that said that they are divided into the three highest genera: negations, privations, and relations.[1] Various doubts, however, arise concerning this standard division. Is it mutually exclusive (correct)? Is it exhaustive (sufficient)? In section 3 Suárez takes up the exclusivity of the division and in section 4 its exhaustivity. Sections 5 and 6 are devoted to particular members of this division, namely, negations/privations and relations of reason, respectively.

With respect to exclusivity Suárez identifies four difficulties:

> This division gives rise to difficulties both with respect to its sufficiency [=exhaustivity] and the [proper] distinction of its members [=exclusivity]. We will speak of the first issue in the following section. With regard to the second issue, there are the following reasons for doubt: [1] Negations and privations seem to be incorrectly numbered among beings of reason. For they are not something produced by the mind but truly belong to things themselves, since [e.g.,] air is dark and lacking light in actual reality. . . . [2] If the latter things are said to be beings of reason because they are fashioned in the manner of beings [while they are not], all beings of reason will then be certain negations since none of them are real and true beings. . . . [3] Another problem: It is unclear why negation and privation are counted as diverse [species of] beings of reason. . . . [4] Finally, negations and privations are conceived . . . with relation to something else. Therefore, they are not properly distinguished from relations of reason. The antecedent is evident, for a privation is the privation *of something*.[2]

Let us see how Suárez addresses the difficulties (1) through (4). The first difficulty, (1), states that negations/privations do not seem to be beings of reason. Rather, they seem to be something *really* in things. Suárez concedes that negations and privations taken "precisely" as such are *nonbeings*, i.e., they are not beings of reason (let alone real beings):

> Both negations and privations as such, if they are considered precisely insofar as they are nonbeings, are neither real beings nor beings of reason— they are not beings nor considered as beings but as nonbeings. In this way they are not something made up but they are said to belong to the things themselves—not as putting something into them but as taking something away [from them]. . . . Thus we say that *there are* privations, such as blindness in the eye, darkness in the air, evil in human actions.[3]

Suárez then points out that the intellect may attribute negations/privations to things not only in the proper (negative) way but also in an improper (positive) way:

> Our intellect attributes [negations and privations] to things, not only in negating, but also in affirming, [and so] we conceive of them not only negatively but also in the manner of positive beings. Conceived in this way, they have the character of beings: not of real beings, but of beings of reason. This . . . point is clear because in the affirmation 'A man is blind' the predication of being is virtually included, for the verb 'is' indicates the [present] participle of 'to be'. It is also clear because our intellect does not conceive of anything as existing in reality unless in the manner of a being.[4]

We see that the improper way of attributing negations/privations to things takes negations/privations "in the manner of" positive beings. This "in the manner of" indicates that the character of being that such negations/privations have is not real but merely "of reason." Consider, for instance, the statements 'Socrates does not have sight' and 'Socrates is blind'. Both of these statements are true. However, the former statement is true because that sight (a real entity) is intellectually *removed* from Socrates (another real entity), whereas the latter statement is true because that blindness (a nonreal entity) is *attributed* to Socrates (a real entity). Is the latter, improper, way of thinking, false? Suárez states:

> In this [latter] kind of conception or affirmation [i.e., 'A man is blind' or 'Socrates is blind'], there is no admixture of falsity or deception. For statements of this kind are entirely true. . . . Hence [in these statements] we do not ascribe something real to reality but only [something] of reason.[5]

To affirm that Socrates is blind is an *improper* way of grasping reality but not *false*. It is not false in that we do not ascribe to Socrates blindness-as-real-being but only blindness-as-being-of-reason. Suárez will work out the thesis about the two "kinds" of negations/privations later (see this chapter, section C; for criticism, section E).

The second and the fourth difficulty with the traditional division concerns the issue whether one can reduce all sorts of beings of reason to negations, namely, to negations of true and real existence (2) or to relations of reason (4). In reply Suárez argues that the relation (of reason) needs to be properly distinguished from negation/privation. That there is a distinction becomes clear when one considers the foundations of the negation/privation on the one hand and of the relation on the other:

> That relations are diverse from the other two things [i.e., negations and privations] encompassed within this division is clear from the diversity of their foundations. For the foundation that the intellect has for conceiving a relation of reason is not some negation or removal of an entity. Rather it is some positive entity that is conceived by us imperfectly in the manner of a relation.[6]

Hence, even though every relation of reason involves a lack of something real, namely, of a real relation, this feature itself is not sufficient to turn it into a negation/privation:

> *You may say:* in order to conceive a relation of reason, there is always presupposed a lack of the real relation in reality. For if the real relation were present, the relation of reason would not be made up. *The answer is:* It is true that a lack of this kind is presupposed as a necessary condition, but not, however, as the proper foundation of the relation of reason. For the relation of reason is not made up in order to conceive of the negation or the lack of a relation in the manner of a positive being but in order to conceive of what is positive and absolute [=nonrelative] in reality, as connected to something else, so that it is conceived by us in the manner of something relative.[7]

Hence, neither the relation nor the negation/privation is reducible to the other—in spite of some superficial similarities. Suárez has more to say on the difference between relations of reason and nonrelations of reason (s3n5–7), but the details are not pertinent for us here. We rather note something else: Suárez says that relations of reason are absolute but "conceived in the manner of something relative." But if this is so, then Suárez contradicts his proposed definition of beings of reason as "what is conceived as being when in fact it has no being in itself" (see chapter 3, section C.2.1, thesis SN7). It should rather be: "what is conceived otherwise than it is, namely, as a being, when it is a nonbeing, or as something relative, when it is something nonrelative" (see also this chapter, section E.1)

The third difficulty, (3) concerns the distinction between negations and privations. Suárez says:

> Finally, with regard to the distinction between the two other members, namely, privation and negation, there is no doubt that they are in some

way distinct. For privation expresses a lack in the naturally apt subject, whereas negation expresses a lack in the subject . . . without qualification. Whether this difference is essential, i.e., formal, or not, is a question of little importance and we will answer it more fittingly in section 5. Now I will only note that the expression 'negation' has two senses. . . . Negation in the broad sense is properly distinguished from relation of reason; negation in this sense is then further divided into privation . . . and negation in the narrow sense, where the former expresses a lack in an apt subject and the latter in an inapt subject. . . . Hence, the three-member division . . . contains a pair of two-member divisions: The first is the division of being of reason into positive . . . and negative; [and the second into privation and negation].[8]

We see that at this point Suárez simply *states* his division of beings of reason, postponing the discussion of the proper distinction between negations and privations to section 5 (see section C below). The traditional division that Suárez adopts here contains three members, but negations in the narrower sense (as lacks in an inapt subject) and privations (as lacks in an apt subject) may be both subsumed under negations in the broad sense (as lacks without qualification). This is represented schematically in Figure 5.1.

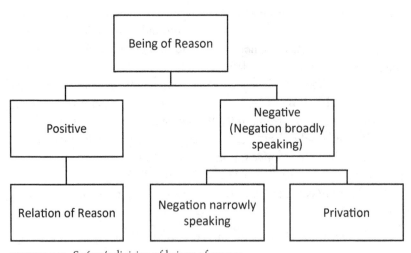

FIGURE 5.1. Suárez's division of beings of reason

Suárez concludes the discussion of section 3 by adding a brief paragraph about whether the traditional division of beings of reason is a univocal division of the generic notion of being of reason into species. He seems to think that it is univocal since "there is no sufficient reason for an analogy." Nevertheless, he does not consider this issue important and leaves it "to the discussion and thinking of the reader."[9]

B. Is the Traditional Division of Beings of Reason Jointly Exhaustive?

In section 4 of Disputation 54, Suárez considers the question of whether the traditional division into negations, privations, and relations of reason is exhaustive, or, as he puts it, "sufficient." Suárez begins with the following objection:

> One reason for doubting [the sufficiency of this division] is that beings of reason can be divided proportionately through all the categories. . . . For, if we review all the categories, in each of them . . . there are some made-up beings-of-reason. . . . For example, in the category of substance, there are . . . chimeras or similar monsters of reason. . . . In the category of quantity . . . there is an imaginary space . . . or the quantity of a chimera. . . . Again, in [the category of] quality, beings of reason seem to be widespread. For example, we conceive of reputation and honor as a disposition belonging to the person who is honored or who has a good reputation, even though in that person [the honor or the reputation] is only a being of reason. . . . Then, just as we make up a chimera, we can imagine its distinctive figure, which . . . is a certain quality of reason . . . [etc.] Therefore, the division of beings of reason is not correctly restricted to the three members.[10]

The objection states that there are as many beings of reason as there are categories (for chimeras are substances, imaginary space is a quantity, fame is a quality, and so on). Hence the traditional division is not exhaustive. But Suárez rejects this idea (embraced by Mastri/Belluto; see chapter 7) and proposes instead two strategies in defense of the traditional three-member division.[11] The first strategy states that the traditional division intentionally leaves out self-contradictory beings of reason, which have no foundation in reality (s4nn2–9). The second strategy argues that self-contradictory beings

are a special case of negation (s4n10). Eventually Suárez expresses a preference for the second strategy, although he does not decisively reject the first.[12]
The first strategy is expressed as follows:

> The proposed [three-member] division can be explained in two ways. The
> first is that it applies not to being of reason taken over its whole extension,
> but only to what has some foundation in reality. For . . . there are certain
> beings of reason that have a foundation in real things, although they are
> "completed" by reason, for example, . . . universals, . . . negations, and
> privations. . . . There are [also] other beings of reason that are totally
> fabricated by the intellect, without any foundation in reality, for example,
> a chimera. Accordingly, the division may be taken to divide only the being
> of reason with a foundation in reality. . . . One can argue for this, inasmuch
> as the being of reason [with a foundation] is somehow of service to sci-
> ences and knowledge . . . [whereas] the other kind of being of reason, i.e.,
> the merely fictitious, is entirely accidental and can be multiplied to infin-
> ity. . . . Hence, according to this interpretation, it can be conceded that the
> beings of reason that are merely fictions range through all the categories—
> unlike beings of reason with a foundation in reality.[13]

The first strategy concedes that beings of reason without a foundation may
indeed be divided into as many categories as real beings. Concerning beings
of reason with a foundation in reality, there still remains a difficulty: The
traditional three-member division includes all positive beings of reason under
the relations of reason. Is this right? Suárez is aware of this problematic claim:

> Following this opinion, however, it remains to be explained why those be-
> ings of reason that have a foundation in reality . . . cannot be at least mul-
> tiplied through several categories of accidents. For as I have said in the
> preceding section, being of reason . . . is first divided into the positive and
> the negative being. . . . It is necessary, therefore, that every positive being
> of reason is relative. Therefore, we are examining the argument for this
> fact. For the discussion at the beginning seems to show that there are many
> beings of reason having a foundation in reality that are thought of in the
> manner of other categories, especially of quality, . . . action, and passion.[14]

Suárez then extensively argues that every positive being of reason is a
relation of reason. The argument is complex and its discussion would presuppose a detailed explanation of the scholastic ontology of relations, an

explanation into which I cannot go here. Let me just register my overall impression that no matter how hard Suárez tries, it is implausible that every positive being of reason could be reduced to a relation. Consider, for instance, the universal "man," which is, on the traditional scholastic view, a relation of reason. Why? Because "man" is *predicable* of individual men; hence, it is a relation. To this I would say that, though "man" as such may be a *potential* relation of reason, this does not make it an *actual* relation. For "man" as such is not thought of *as if* it were a relation. It is rather thought of *as if* it were a kind of substance. One could object that even if I think "man" without its attribute of predictability of individual men, it is "in reality" predicable of individual men, and so even if I forget that it is a relation, it is a relation. Against this objection, I would insist that in order for something to be a relation of reason it must be *actually* thought of as a relation (because objects of reason have only those properties that they are actually thought to have).[15]

The second strategy for defending the traditional three-member division is to take self-contradictory entities as a special case of negation. Suárez says:

> The foregoing explanation of the [traditional three-member] division is suitable enough and it makes the matter sufficiently clear. But we can add another defense in which this division is adequate for every being of reason: we include fictitious and impossible beings, whether they are fashioned in the manner of a substance or of an accident, under negation. For since fictitious beings . . . are simply nonbeings, they are correctly included under negation.[16]

The idea is that self-contradictory beings of reason explain why some negative statements are necessarily false, i.e., it is *impossible* for them to be true:

> Indeed, in order to explain a complex and impossible negation [= negative statement] by a simple concept, impossible beings are sometimes made up. For example, because it is impossible that a horse is a lion, we say that the being conceived simultaneously in the manner of a horse and a lion is a fiction (and we call it a chimera or something like that). Similarly, in order to explain that the negation "An ox cannot fly" is necessary, we conceive of a flying ox as something impossible and a being of reason.[17]

But this explanation seems to be a mere verbal trick: Since self-contradictory beings of reason may serve as truth-makers for negative statements, or *'negationes'* (in Latin), they are included into the species of beings of reason also called '*negationes*'. But *negatio* as a species is supposed to be a lack what is thought of as something positive. Hence, it has nothing to do with explaining the impossibility of some negative statements.[18] Anyway, in the end, Suárez himself prefers the second strategy:

> This [second defense of the division] appears to be more common: All these [self-contradictory] things are included under negation. Hence, when the other points made in the previous discussion have been added, it is clear that the division is sufficient . . . for, besides relations, all [beings of reason] are fashioned in the manner of privations or negations.[19]

To summarize: Suárez makes a considerable effort to show that the traditional division of beings of reason into relations, negations, and privations holds good:

> SD1: Beings of reason have three exclusive and exhaustive species, namely, negation, privation, and relation.

Concerning exhaustivity, Suárez suggests two defensive strategies. Both are based on the view that the problem applies mainly to self-contradictory beings of reason:

> SD2: Self-contradictory beings of reason are either outside of the traditional three-member division or they are a special case of negation.

Concerning the exclusivity of the division, the distinction between relation and negation/privation has been already addressed. (See Suárez's reply to the second and fourth difficulty above in section A.) But the distinction between negation and privation remains to be established.

C. Negations and Privations: Commonalities and Differences

In section 5 of Disputation 54, Suárez takes up detailed comparison of negations and privations. As already indicated above (section A), Suárez acknowledges two ways of considering negations and privations: Insofar as they are real "removals" of a form and insofar as they are beings of reason. The comparison is divided accordingly:

We can treat of negations and privations *either* insofar as they only remove the form or the positive entity *or* insofar as they are beings of
reason. For we have distinguished between these two aspects above and
in accord with them the comparisons of negations and privations
differ.[20]

The thesis captured in this passage may be expressed as follows:

> SN10: There are two "kinds" of negations/privations: as they are in
> things (i.e., "real negations/privations") and as they are beings of
> reason (i.e., "nonreal negations/privations").

We shall see below (in section E) that this thesis does not fit in well with
other elements of Suárez's theory and makes his overall theory
inconsistent.

1. Negations and Privations as They Are in Things

Before Suárez goes into the comparison of negations and privations itself,
he makes the following important point:

> If a negation is true, no fictitious activity of the intellect is involved. If an
> intellect precisely conceives [, for instance,] that a man is not a horse, it
> conceives what truly is in reality . . . for truly and in reality one is not the
> other, even if it is not considered or known by any man. But I have said "if
> it is a true negation," because if a negation is false, [such as, for instance,] if
> someone conceives of a man who is not an animal, then that negation even
> under the character of negation is merely made up by the intellect, and it
> has being only as an object of that intellect. Therefore, it is a being of reason,
> or rather a *negation of reason*. For this negation, precisely conceived under
> the character of negation, is not apprehended in the manner of a being but
> rather in the manner of a nonbeing, and so it is a certain negation made
> up by reason. In contrast, the other negations, i.e., the true ones, may be
> called 'real negations', for they truly remove real forms or natures.[21]

According to Suárez, then, there are not just *true* negations/privations that
are mind-independent and hence real, but also "false negations" or "negations
of reason," such as the *non-animality of a human being*. These are entities
conceived as nonentities and hence they are something like "nonbeings of

reason." This means that Suárez's ontology contains real beings, real nonbe-ings, nonreal beings (=beings of reason), and nonreal nonbeings (=non-beings of reason). This multiplication of items is one of the most troubling features of Suárez's theory (see also below, section E.1).

1.1. WHAT THEY SHARE

Suárez identifies four (or perhaps five) similarities between privations and negations as they are in things. The first (1) is that they both "remove" real forms; the second (2), that they are both in a real opposition with some positive real being:

> Leaving aside false or fictitious negations, since they neither relate to the present consideration nor require a new exposition besides what was said about falsity in Disputation 9 [On Falsity], true and real negations and privations [1] first of all agree in that . . . they both consist only in a "removal." . . . They agree, [2] secondly, because each is an extreme of an opposition that is somehow found in things and not just made up by the intellect . . . They presuppose in objects an opposition that is not made up by the intellect but rather precedes all fiction-producing activity, as has been declared above in Disputation 45 [On the Contrariety of Qualities].[22]

Contrary to what Suárez says here, there is nothing about negations of reason (*negationes rationis*) in Disputation 9. Moreover, if negations of rea-son are to be treated in the context of falsehood, shouldn't beings of reason be as well?[23] Suárez does not do this, which means that his reference is misplaced. Concerning Disputation 45: This Disputation is about the opposi-tion (*contrarietas*) of qualities; but privations and negations are not supposed to be qualities, according to Suárez, and so the reference is again rather misplaced here.[24]

The third similarity between privations and negations is that they both have foundations in reality:

> Third, they agree because they both can have a foundation in the thing to which they are attributed. . . . We call "foundation" not only the subject to which a given privation or negation is attributed (for example, the negation of the capacity to neigh in human beings is founded on the intrinsic differentia of human beings) but also the proximate cause or

root due to which the given privation or negation belongs to the subject.... For example, if a man is blind, that privation is not founded in
the ... nature of man but in some other cause that removes the form
denied by the privation.[25]

(Note that quite diverse things are called 'foundation', namely, the subject
to which a given negation or privation is ascribed and the causes that deprived
the subject of the negated form in question.)

The fourth similarity is that real privation and real negation can both be
predicated of things without any fiction-producing activity of the intellect
(not without *any* activity but without any *fiction-producing* activity):

> Fourth, they agree inasmuch as both negation and privation can be truly
> and absolutely predicated of a thing without any fiction-producing activity
> of the intellect. I am not saying "without any operation of the intellect,"
> since the predication itself is a certain operation of the intellect, but I do
> say "without any fiction-producing activity," because sufficient basis on
> the side of things themselves is presupposed so that the intellect is able
> to deny one thing of another, conceiving of each as it is in itself. Hence,
> just as the divine or angelic intellect knows the negation or privation
> without any fiction (and without composition or division), so does the
> human intellect.... But because of the imperfect way of operating,
> the human intellect does this by means of composition or division. For
> the same reason, it does so indirectly and, as it were, discursively.[26]

We see that human knowledge of negations and privations as they are in
themselves is "by means of composition or division" and that it is indirect
and discursive.

The fifth similarity is stated as follows:

> For this also is common to privations and negations: that they cannot be
> directly represented through their own species [likeness]. Therefore, they
> are known by us indirectly though the species of opposite forms and by
> means of some discursive reasoning. Hence the knowledge of a given
> privation [or negation] necessarily presupposes knowledge of a positive
> thing whereby the intellect comes to know the privation [or negation].[27]

The *indirect* knowledge or representation of real negations or privations
as they are may happen in two ways, namely, through negative and through

affirmative statements. The latter way is *close* to giving rise to beings of reason, but it is still not sufficient to make them:

> We must, however, consider that both privations and negations are known by the intellect in two ways. The first is by division or negation; in this way they are properly known as they are. . . . The second is by composition or affirmation (as when we say 'The man is blind' or 'He is non-white'); in this second way, a certain improper mode of knowing and conceiving seems to be already intermixed, for being itself is somehow included in the word 'is', and hence something is predicated in the manner of being that in fact is not a being. . . . But we must note that in these affirmations only what is conceived, namely, the negation or privation itself, is attributed to the subject . . . not the manner in which the predicate is conceived. (Hence the affirmative statement ['The man is blind'] is actually equivalent to the negative one ['The man does not see'] as far as both remove the predicate.)[28]

In statements such as 'The man is blind', we do not claim that something *real* inheres in the man. Hence, according to Suárez, we are not making up a being of reason. However, it seems that Suárez *should* insist that we are making up a being of reason, even if we do not predicate it "seriously" of the subject. For according to the definition of being of reason as "what is thought of as a being although it is not," it is sufficient that we make up the predicate "blind," which is not a being, though we take it as a being. That we predicate it of the subject mistakenly, believing that something positive inheres in it, should not make the difference.[29]

1.2. HOW THEY DIFFER

Suárez describes with considerable phenomenological detail seven differences between real negations and privations. Let me briefly describe them.

1. Privation is the absence of a form in a subject that is capable of having it, whereas negation is the absence of a form in a subject that is *not* capable of having it. 'Negation' can be also used in a broader sense of the absence of a form in a subject regardless of the subject's capacity of having it. Negation in this sense is a genus that includes privation and negation in the narrower sense as its species (see also

above, section A). This difference is not "essential" but rather "connotative," which is explained by Suárez as follows:

> Privations and negations differ . . . because privation means the lack of a form in a naturally apt subject, whereas negation means a lack without any such . . . aptitude. . . . This diversity, however, is not in the proper and formal character of what privation and negation directly express, but rather in what is connoted. For privation as such does not intrinsically include a subject or its aptitude. Otherwise, a privation would not be distinguished from the deprived subject, which is, as it were, a composite of a subject and a privation. And it would not be a pure real nonbeing but would consist of the reality of a potency and the negation of . . . a form—which contradicts the nature of privation. . . . In this way, privation is said to differ from negation obliquely. . . . This kind of difference is customarily found also among positive forms. . . . Aristotle often says that *snubness* differs from *curvature*, for, although they formally express the same figure, *snubness* signifies it with respect to a certain kind of matter. . . . This is, then, how we should think of the difference between negation and privation.[30]

Suárez continues with a comprehensive description of the varieties of privations (species-relative, genus-relative, time-relative, partial, total, etc.) (s5n8–9). Then he adds the following three differences:

2. privation admits of degrees of more/less, whereas negation does not (s5n10);
3. privation cannot be necessary for a subject, whereas negation can (s5n11);
4. there can be a "medium" between predicating privation and possession, but not between predicating negation and the opposite affirmation (s5n12–13).

The fourth difference is phrased in semantic terms (predication, negation/affirmation). It shows that Suárez was somewhat familiar with the debates about nonexisting objects that had been going on among logicians, although he paid little attention to them. The fourth difference is stated by Suárez as follows:

> Between negation and the opposite affirmation there is no medium, but between privation and possession there is. . . . For negation simply removes the form . . . and requires no special condition in the subject. Therefore, it is necessary that either the form or the negation of the form belongs to the subject. In contrast, in privatively opposed things there is something in between . . . because privation does not mean negation as such but negation with the connotation of an aptitude in the subject. Hence . . . a subject can exist, which lacks this connoted aptitude. . . . For instance, a stone is neither blind nor having-sight, although it is necessarily either having-sight or non-having-sight.[31]

In a pair of propositions where one predicates a privation (*blind*) and the other possession (*able-to-see*), both propositions may be false (hence "in between" or "medium"), whereas in a pair of propositions where one predicates a negation (*not-able-to-see*) and the other an "affirmation" (*able-to-see*), one must be true.

But somebody might object that negations (= negative predicates) also have a medium, namely, in case they are ascribed to things that do not exist—both propositions would be false:

> But an objection may occur: Even between contradictorily opposite terms, there is a medium "by denial," at least with respect to the nonexisting subject. For example, a chimera is neither white nor nonwhite, because each affirmation is false; it concerns a subject without supposition. [1] A first [possible] answer is that only negation taken in the sense of a pure negation does not have a medium. But if something positive is mixed with it, it may have it. For instance, if "A chimera is non-having-sight" is false, it is not simply because having-sight is denied but because some being is [implicitly] affirmed. . . . In this way some proportion is preserved between negations and privations. [2] A second [possible] answer denies the assumption [namely, that both "A chimera is having-sight" and "A chimera is non-having-sight" are false]. For of the two propositions, the one that has the negative predicate is true, even if the subject does not exist, especially if (as the logicians say) that negation is not taken "infinitely" but "negatively."[32]

Suárez offers two solutions to the objection: (1) Both such propositions are false but it is because the negation is not "pure" in that it includes a reference to something positive; (2) one of the propositions is true, namely, the negative one.[33]

The fifth difference is that privations can be predicated only of true entities, whereas negations can also be predicated of fictitious ones: Privations (according to Suárez) require really existing subjects.

> Another difference . . . between privations and pure negations is that the former can be attributed only to true and real beings. For . . . privation means the lack of a form in a naturally apt subject . . . and [such] an aptitude . . . exists only in a real being. . . . A negation, however, can be attributed not only to true and existing beings but also to fictitious and nonexisting beings. . . . For the proposition . . . "A chimera is a nonbeing" is true, since, if it is a fictitious being, it is a nonbeing. . . . But if it is a non-being, it is also a non-man, a non-horse, and any other similar thing contained under nonbeing.[34]

We see here why Suárez has suggested above that predicating negations of chimeras yields true propositions: If something is nothing, then we can truly predicate of it everything prefixed with 'non-'. But because some scholastic authors might have had scruples about the copula "is"—that it expresses (actual) existence—Suárez adds the following:

> The reason for this fact [that the predication of negations of chimeras is true] can be that even though these propositions have an affirmative form, nevertheless, they are equivalent to negations in sense and signification. Hence, although . . . the negation ['non'] is placed *after* the copula, it falls *on* it in its power and sense.[35]

According to scholastic conventions, the Latin sentence 'Chimaera est non videns' means "A chimera is non-having-sight." To say "A chimera is not having-sight," one would need to change the word order to 'Chimaera non est videns'. For scholastics, the latter sentence does not seem to pose a problem. It is construed by them as "A chimera isn't" (i.e., "A chimera doesn't exist"), which is true, and hence (according to them) everything else we say of these nonexisting chimeras is also true. They see a problem with the former, affirmative, sentence, for it seems to require the existence of a chimera. Suárez makes an ad hoc claim that in this case the affirmative sentence should be paraphrased as the negative one. (The idea that the grammatical and the logical structure of a sentence differ, and that we need to paraphrase it, occurs much more prominently in Hurtado; see chapter 6).

In this context Suárez observes that some of the negative predications of chimeras are not only true but even necessarily true:

> The copula can be also taken atemporally. Since the subject is conceived as a fictitious being, the predication of something intrinsic to the nature of the subject is not only true, but necessarily true. And this answer . . . does not displease me.[36]

Suárez, however, goes on to qualify the fifth difference as follows:

> I only note that what has been said [above] about [the difference between] privations [and negations] must be understood as pertaining to true and real privations. For there can be some imaginary and made-up privations in fictitious beings, for example, . . . in a blind chimera or in a dark imaginary space. . . . Indeed, such privations could be attributed to fictitious beings with a copula . . . amplified to fictitious beings. In this way, a negation of a fictitious being can be predicated [or denied] of another fictitious being . . . ; [for instance,] 'A chimera is a not a goat-stag'.[37]

The fifth difference may not be a genuine difference in that it may apply both to privations and negations. For in both cases we *can* make true predications about fictitious subjects. Hence there is no genuine difference between the two.

For the sake of completeness, let me mention the last two differences that Suárez discusses, although they are not pertinent to our main concerns with beings of reason: The sixth difference is that privation is a principle of change, whereas negation is not (s5n17–18); and the seventh is that a privation cannot be naturally restored, whereas a negation can (s5n19).

Having discussed negations/privations as they are really "in things," we come to negations/privations as they are beings of reason.

2. Negations and Privations as Beings of Reason

Suárez's discussion concerning the commonalities and differences between negations and privations as they are beings of reason is considerably shorter. He seems to find only one thing common to all of them, namely that they are absolute, i.e., nonrelative.[38] But there are at least two differences:

(1) Privations are thought of in the manner of qualities, whereas negations are also thought of in the manner of other categories— if we subsume self-contradictory beings under them.[39]

(2) Privations are always (thought of as being) in a subject, whereas negations can be thought of as being "on their own," as is the case with *nothing*.[40]

Suárez's text continues with a discussion of whether negations differ from privations "formally" or whether this difference comes only from a relation to different subjects.[41] We may leave this question aside because it does not affect the general structure of Suárez's theory of beings of reason. Suárez's allusion to propositional beings of reason is more interesting:

> [So far] we have been speaking about negation as it is conceived in the manner of a simple [*incomplexae*] form. For if we speak about complex negations, the diversity [between them and privations] is . . . essential. . . . For the negation "An angel does not have sight" or the affirmation "An angel is non-seeing" are quite different from "A man is blind" or "A man lacks sight." For the former are necessary propositions, whereas the latter contingent. Hence, they differ essentially.[42]

So far in Disputation 54, Suárez has discussed only conceptual beings of reason (non-sight, blind, chimera, etc.). But at this point Suárez seems to be suggesting that there are also propositional beings of reason, for here he talks about 'complex negations'. This is perhaps the only place where Suárez alludes to the possibility of propositional beings of reason.

What is the main point of Suárez's comparison between negations and privations? The particular details of this comparison are not very important with respect to his overall metaphysics. There are two important lessons. The first is that negations/privations are in things and are also beings of reason—SN10. The thesis could be phrased also as: There are real nonbeings and there are nonreal nonbeings (=negative beings of reason). SN10 implies that negations/privations are not one but two (pairs of) distinct supercategories. The second important lesson is:

SN11: We can think not only "in the manner of a being" but also "in the manner of a nonbeing."

Below, in section E.1, I argue that SN10 and SN11 create an inconsistency in Suárez's theory of beings of reason. However, before we go into this topic, let me discuss Suárez's views on relations of reason.

D. Relations of Reason

Suárez deals with relations of reason in section 6. The section is brief, for relations of reason are closely related to relations in general, and Suárez in the long Disputation 47 has devoted to almost fifty-eight thousand words to relations (see Suárez 1597/2006). Much of what he says about relations of reason concerns special issues with little impact on the overall general theory of beings of reason. I provide here only a few selected observations, for the sake of completeness.

For Aristotelian scholastics, relations are monadic accidents that "turn" the subject in which they inhere *toward* something else. There are no genuine polyadic relations in the sense of entities existing somehow "in between" their *relata* (Brower 2003; 2005). This fundamental assumption, which might sound unfamiliar to contemporary post-Fregean logical and philosophical ears, is aptly expressed by Henninger (1989, 4–5):

> Today we might talk of one symmetrical relation R of color similarity between two pieces of white chalk, a and b. But for the medievals, if there are two really distinct substances, there must be two really distinct accidents. Being an accident, a relation is not an entity that somehow hovers between the two things related or, in Aristotelian terms, inheres in both. . . . In the chalk example, one relation of color similarity R of a to b is based on an accident, the quality of whiteness in a. A numerically distinct relation similarity R' of b to a is based on a numerically distinct accident of whiteness inhering in b. There are two relations, one in each of the things related.

In medieval and postmedieval philosophy, this rejection of polyadic relations was almost universal.[43] There are three individually necessary and jointly sufficient conditions for a *real* relation to obtain:

1.   Both the first and the second element ("extreme") of the relation really exist (its subject and term).

2. These two elements are really distinct.

3. There is a (real) fundament *in* one or both of these elements.[44]

Violation of any of these conditions is necessary, and it and the fiction-producing activity of the intellect are jointly sufficient for the emergence of a relation of reason.[45] In Suárez's somewhat uninformative words, relation of reason is "a relation that the intellect contrives in the manner of a form ordered or related to something . . . which in fact is not ordered or related . . . to this something."[46]

Relations of reason may be divided according to their foundation. There are two basic genera. One contains relations of reason that do not have a foundation in reality. This group includes (1) relations between completely made up beings of reason, e.g., the similarity between two chimeras; (2) relations between beings of reason with some foundation in reality, e.g., between two "blindnesses," and (3) relations between unactualized possible entities, e.g., the relation of temporal precedence of Adam to Antichrist.[47] (It is surprising that relations between *possibilia*, which are real, are counted by Suárez as relations of reason.)

The second genus contains relations with a foundation in reality. It includes (1) relations of real entities to nonexistents, whether possible or of reason; (2) relations of real entities to themselves (i.e., the two elements of the relation fail to be really distinct; this group is further subdivided according to the kind of nonreal distinction between the two elements); (3) various semantic, social, economic, and other relations obtaining between really distinct existents but still not satisfying all the conditions for real relations; (4) various logical relations that also fail several conditions for real relations.[48] The last two types of relations of reason are of particular importance, for they may provide the metaphysical foundation for semantic, social, and logical reality (although to my knowledge Suárez did not try to develop this possibility). Schematically, the classification of relations looks as follows:

Relations of Reason
Without a foundation
    ✦ completely made up (e.g., between chimeras)
    ✦ with some remote foundation (e.g., between privations)
    ✦ between nonexistent possible entities

With a foundation
+ relations of real entities to nonexistents
+ relations of real entities to themselves
+ relations that violate conditions other than existence or
  difference
+ logical intentions (relations based on extrinsic denominations
  from the intellect, with some foundation in reality)

Suárez concludes the discussion of relations of reason with a very brief discussion of second intentions, i.e., "higher-order predicates" (Hickman 1980). Unlike other late scholastic authors, Suárez has almost nothing to say about them (only three short paragraphs).

E. Evaluation of Suárez's Objectualism

It is time to pull together the diverse elements of my exegesis of Suárez's texts presented in the previous chapters and to make an overall evaluation of Suárez's theory of beings of reason. Suárez's overall accomplishment is undoubtedly great. He was able to put together many pre-Suárezian scholastic arguments into a unified framework, sufficiently detailed and analytical but properly counterbalanced by being positioned within a synoptic synthesis. Nevertheless, one may notice certain problems or difficulties in this grand system. There remain several questions or objections that one may ask but to which Suárez does not provide answers. Most of these questions or objections have been overlooked by contemporary scholars, but they did not go unnoticed by post-Suárezian scholastics. One can distinguish between two kinds of problems with the Suárezian synthesis. First, Suárez makes assertions (or assumptions) that endanger the consistency of his theory. These are the basis for serious objections against Suárez's views. Second, there are obscurities and questions that Suárez does not address. These represent points that a Suárezian might address without (perhaps) abandoning the fundamentals of Suárez's theory. Most of these problems have already been indicated in previous chapters; here I only put them into relief. [49]

1. Fundamental Problems of Suárez's Theory

Let me start with the metatheory of beings of reason, i.e., with the question concerning the science that studies them. Suárez claims (see chapter 3, section A):

> sm1: The proper objects of metaphysics are real beings, and beings of reason are studied in metaphysics only in order to facilitate the understanding of real beings.
>
> sm2: The study of beings of reason that metaphysics undertakes is useful in various ways.
>
> sm3: The study of beings of reason involves their nature, causes, division, and attributes (quasi-transcendentals).
>
> sm4: Real beings are both ontologically and epistemically prior to beings of reason.

There is a certain tension between SM1 and SM2: On the one hand, beings of reason are just incidental objects of metaphysics; on the other hand, the knowledge of beings of reason is useful in various ways. The question is: "How seriously should we take beings of reason as the subject-matter of scientific investigation?" In my view, we should either acknowledge a new science to deal with nonreal beings or generalize metaphysics to include any being, whether real or of reason. Suárez appears to implicitly reject both of these options, but then we would have no good place for the investigation of beings of reason. For this reason it is not surprising that toward the end of the seventeenth century the majority of Baroque thinkers took beings of reason to be an equally legitimate topic of metaphysics as real beings are. This holds true especially for late Jesuit scholasticism (Doyle 1998a) but also for Protestant scholasticism.[50] Three hundred years after Suárez, Meinong invented a new name for this generalized metaphysics, namely, the 'theory of objects' (*Gegenstandstheorie*). In his terminology, metaphysics deals with existent objects, whereas the theory of objects extends to the study of objects in general, whether existent or not (Meinong 1904; Chisholm 1960). The view that metaphysics deals with both real and nonreal beings might perhaps incline one toward disregarding the existence and primacy of reality (SM4), but this does not seem necessary. (The broader definition of metaphysics is at least prima facie compatible with SM4.)

Concerning the nature of beings of reason, i.e., what beings of reason are, Suárez claims:

> SN1: A being of reason is what cannot be actualized in reality.
>
> SN2: Not every being of reason is self-contradictory.
>
> SN3': Every being is either a real being or a being of reason, but no being is both.
>
> SN4: There are beings of reason—in an analogical sense of 'are'.
>
> SN5: The expression 'being of reason' indicates three different relations to reason: (a) effective, (b) subjective, and (c) objective.

All these five theses, with the exception of SN2, seem to be well explained and justified by Suárez. Concerning SN2, there is an open question: What makes it impossible for beings of reason to exist in actual reality? For Suárez, many beings of reason, for instance, privations or logical relations, "resist their real actual existence," but they are nevertheless free of self-contradiction. Suárez does not (as far as I know) explicitly deal with the question of what makes it impossible for beings of reason to exist if it is not their "inner" self-contradiction, what *absolutely* prevents something from existing if it is not self-contradiction. One such obstacle could be *incompleteness*.[51] For instance, the universal "human being" cannot as such exist in actual reality, for it would have to be neither a man nor a woman, and neither short nor tall. Incomplete objects are impossible-to-exist objects, but they are not self-contradictory objects. However, Suárez does not mention incompleteness.

Here are Suárez's other claims about the nature of beings of reason:

> SN6: A being of reason has only objective being in the intellect.
>
> SN7: A being of reason is thought of as a being, even though it has no being in itself.
>
> SN8: Beings of reason are needed for three tasks: (a) to know nonbeing, (b) to know things relatively by comparison with other things, and (c) to explain the capacity of our intellect to think of self-contradictory beings.
>
> SN9: Beings of reason and real beings are related by an analogy of proportionality.

SN10: There are two "kinds" of negations/privations: as they are in things (i.e., "real negations/privations") and as they are beings of reason (i.e., "nonreal negations/privations").

SN11: We can think not only "in the manner of a being" but also "in the manner of a nonbeing."

From this we see that Suárez has two definitions of beings of reason (captured by SN6 and SN7) that may be expressed by the following formulas:

D1: In order for x to be a being of reason, it is necessary and jointly sufficient for it to have only objective being in p.

D2: In order for x to be a being of reason, it is necessary and jointly sufficient for it to be thought of by p as a being, even though it has no being in itself.

Throughout *Metaphysical Disputations*, Suárez assumes that these two formulas are co-extensional (D2 is probably intended as an explanation of D1). But are they really coextensional? Let me show that they cannot be, based on SN10 and SN11.[52] First we note that in Suárez's ontology it follows from SN11 that there are (P1) beings thought of in the manner of beings, and (P2) nonbeings thought of in the manner of beings. Then, it follows from SN10 that there are also (P3) nonbeings thought of in the manner of nonbeings, and even (P4) beings thought of in the manner of nonbeings. This gives us four possibilities, as shown in Figure 5.2.

Now, D1 requires that a being of reason both have objective being in the intellect of a person p and have *nothing else than that*. This is obviously satisfied by items of P2 (we think of nonbeing as if it were a being) and violated by items of P1 (we think of being as it is, namely, a being) and P4 (we think of being as it is not, namely, a nonbeing). But what about items of P3? Nonbeings thought of in the manner of nonbeings appear to be beings of reason as defined by D1, for they are (a) objectively in the intellect and (b) they have no other being besides the being of objects-in-the-intellect. Hence nonreal beings (items of P2) and real nonbeings (items of P3) are both beings of reason in the sense of D1.

When we come to D2, the latter part of the definition—namely, "to have no being in itself"—is satisfied only by items of P2 and P3. With respect to the former part of the definition, however, D2 states that x is thought of

	REAL	NONREAL
BEING	**(P1) real beings** beings thought of as beings	**(P2) nonreal beings** nonbeings thought of as beings
NONBEING	**(P3) real nonbeings** nonbeings thought of as nonbeings	**(P4) nonreal nonbeings** beings thought of as nonbeings

FIGURE 5.2. Suárez's ontology of beings/nonbeings

Note: In the diagram in chapter 2, figure 2.1, items of P1 are categorized as "possible*
beings," P2 as "negative impossible beings," and P3 as "nonbeings" under "para-
beings"; items of P4 are not there. P2 could also be called "negative beings of reason"
or "nonreal privations/negations" and P3 "real privations/negations." P4 are called by
Suárez "false negations."

in the manner of a being. This excludes items of P3, for they are nonbeings
thought of in the manner of nonbeings. Hence only items of P2 are beings
of reason in the sense of D2.

Concerning the items of P4, in some sense they appear to be beings of
reason. To speak strictly, however, they do not satisfy either D1 or D2. We
might say that, in Suárez's ontology, these become "homeless objects."

If my criticism is cogent, Suárez's theory of beings of reason cannot be
right. The problem seems to sneak in with SN10 and SN11. Although phenomenologically we appear to be able to think of nonbeings in two ways,
namely, in the manner of beings and in the manner of nonbeings, the traditional scholastic (Thomistic) view—explicitly defended, for instance, by
Araújo—was correct in acknowledging only one possibility, namely, to think
of nonbeings in the manner of beings. Why? Because nonbeings do not exist,
and so they are nothing, and so we cannot think of them—there is nothing
to think of. In fact, it is even wrong to speak of them in the plural, for they
are all "confounded in the grave of a common nothingness" (Findlay
1933/1995, 56). Suárez unwittingly ascribed to nonbeings a degree of "ontological density." They can be compared and described as real items in
ontology. But this creates problems, and if Suárezians think the issue
through, they need either to drop one of the definitions (D1 or D2) or to
give up the need to postulate nonreal beings (privations/negations of reason).
For if we can think of nonbeings in the manner of nonbeings, why do we

need to think of them in the manner of beings, i.e., otherwise than they truly are? Nonreal beings become useless theoretical items at best and misleading mistakes at worst.[53] Suárez's view that there are real negations/privations and negations/privations of reason contradicts other elements of his theory, and this makes his views on the nature of beings of reason inconsistent.[54]

Now we turn to Suárez's views about the causes of beings of reason. We have seen that Suárez claims that:

SC1'A: Beings of reason have no final, material, or formal cause in the *strict* sense.

SC1'B: Beings of reason have a final, material, and formal cause in *some* sense.

SC2A: Beings of reason have no efficient cause in the *strict* sense.

SC2B: Beings of reason have an efficient cause in *some* sense.

Suárez holds that beings of reason have no final, formal, and material cause (SC1'a) but that they need to have an efficient cause (SC2b). Since beings of reason do not exist in the strict sense of the word, but only analogically, they cannot have an efficient cause in the strict sense, but only analogically (SC2a). This doctrine, however, is compromised by Suárez when he adds that in *some* sense we could speak of other causes as well (SC1'b). (See also chapter 4, section A.)

With respect to causes, Suárez further claims:

SC3: The only efficient cause of beings of reason is the human intellect.

But then he claims:

SC3': The efficient cause of beings of reason can be either (a) the human intellect alone, or (b) the human intellect together with the imagination.

This is again a troublesome doctrine. First Suárez claims that only the (human) intellect makes up beings of reason (SC3), but then he claims that the imagination is an exception. And he takes this back again to say that the imagination participates in the activity of the intellect so that the intellect remains the sole necessary and sufficient condition for beings of reason (SC3').

At this point we might object that the intellect is the efficient cause of beings of reason but that the intellect is a real being. Hence, shouldn't its products, i.e., beings of reason, also be real? There are three options here: First, we may acknowledge that there is some sort of causality from the act of the intellect to its object. But then we must address a further question, namely, what this causality is. Second, we may deny that there is any causality from a mental act to the object—but in consequence we need to reject the thesis that the intellect is the efficient cause of beings of reason. Third, we may insist that the cause of the object is the same as the cause of the mental act—but then the question remains as to how a real cause can produce nonreal effects. The best way out of this impasse is to acknowledge that, besides the four standard types of Aristotelian causality, there is another type of causality, one that is sui generis and intentional. (This is the view of Mastri/Belluto; see chapter 7, section C.1.)

Finally, Suárez claims with respect to the causes of beings of reason:

SC4: Extrinsic denominations are necessary but insufficient conditions of beings of reason.

SC5: Beings of reason are caused by an act of the intellect that conceives of something that has no being in the manner of a being.

SC6: Beings of reason are caused by a reflexive act of the intellect.

Suárez rejects extrinsic denominations as constitutive of beings of reason (SC4). This seems to be one of the few generally accepted claims in post-Suarezian scholasticism. Suárez also claims that beings of reason are made up by the acts of the intellect in which something that has no being in reality is conceived in the manner of a (real) being (SC5), which is a reflexive act (SC6). The latter two claims are problematic, given what has been said above about the incoherence of Suárez's views about the nature of beings of reason (SN6–SN11).

Finally, Suárez claims that:

SC-G1: God does not make up his own beings of reason.

SC-G2: God knows beings of reason that *we* produce.

These views were also generally accepted among post-Suárezian authors. Now, concerning the division of beings of reason, Suárez claims:

SD1: Beings of reason have three exclusive and exhaustive species, namely, negation, privation, and relation.

SD2: Self-contradictory beings of reason are either outside of the traditional three-member division or they are a special case of negation.

Even though Suárez made an enormous effort to defend SD1 and SD2, neither is defensible, for at least two reasons. First, relations do not seem to be the only positive beings of reason; second, self-contradictory beings of reason are irreducible to negations; they are the fourth species of beings of reason. As we shall see, both SD1 and SD2 were rejected by Mastri/Belluto (see chapter 7, C.4)

2. Unresolved Problems of Suárez's Theory

There are several questions a student of Suárez's theory of beings of reason might ask, to which, however, Suárez does not provide answers. Let me briefly mention some of them.

1. IS IT ESSENTIAL TO BEINGS OF REASON THAT THEY ARE ACTUALLY BEING THOUGHT OF?

Beings of reason must be objects of reason. But do they have to be *actual* objects of reason? In other words, is it essential to them that they are *actually* being thought of? If, for instance, nobody is *actually* thinking of a chimera, is there a chimera? Actualism is the view that denies that there is a chimera or any other being of reason if nobody is thinking of it. The actualist understanding of beings of reason goes against the commonsense principle that in order for something to be actualized, there must be a preceding possibility or potency for it. Hence, if we want to preserve this principle of potency preceding actuality, we should acknowledge beings of reason in potency. I call such a view potentialism. Unfortunately, both actualism and potentialism are linked with serious difficulties. Actualism violates the principle that the actual is brought about into existence from potency, and potentialism seems to imply that beings of reason have mind-independent parts (essences in potency).[55] Actualism versus potentialism is an issue on which Suárez says nothing except by an off-hand remark that shows his unquestioned actualist assumption: "In a proper sense . . . [beings of reason] are said to be only when they are actually being contrived."[56] The issue is taken up by later authors, such as Mastri/Belluto (see chapter 7, section A.3).

2. CAN WE REDUCE CONSISTENT FICTIONS TO *POSSIBILIA*?

Suárez and other Baroque scholastic authors seem to assume without questioning that *consistent fictions*, such as Hamlet, might become real beings. This implies that Hamlet is a possible being and therefore that he is a real being. But is this a valid assumption? For several reasons I do not think that a consistent fiction as such is a real possible being. First, Hamlet has "underdetermined features." Thus, for instance, it *cannot be said* whether he liked ham and eggs for breakfast. Unlike with real people, where we simply do not know many things about them, this is an ontic issue: It is undetermined whether Hamlet liked ham and eggs, because Shakespeare did not make up his mind about this. And even if he had, there are countless other features about which he did not. Second, it seems to be part of Hamlet's identity that he is a fictitious person made up by Shakespeare. If suddenly a person stood in front of us, claiming to be Hamlet, would he be *Shakespeare's* Hamlet? The same holds true of another world in which everything would be as Shakespeare described it. Does Shakespeare's Hamlet live there, or only a Hamlet-counterpart satisfying Shakespeare's description? Third, there is an infinite number of possible Hamlet-like beings satisfying perfectly all of Shakespeare's descriptions. Which one is identical to the "real" Hamlet that Shakespeare and his readers have in mind? These and other puzzles indicate that the problem of fictitious individuals cannot be reduced to the problem of possible individuals.

3. WHAT DOES IT MEAN TO BE "MADE UP" OR "FICTITIOUS"?

According to Suárez "real essences are not made up (*confictae*)" (see chapter 3, section B). But what does this mean? In classical Latin the word could be used more broadly, meaning "to make something up *in whatever way* and *for whatever reason*," or, more narrowly, "to make something up *in a false way* or *in order to deceive*."[57] Unfortunately, the two meanings differ significantly. If I make up something, it may be either out of necessity (of human nature), or by mistake (which can be corrected), or for a reason. The latter may then be a good reason (convenience) or a bad reason (deception).

If real beings are made up in none of these ways, does it mean that beings of reason are made up in any of these ways? These issues are not only left open by Suárez but, more surprisingly, they are not even discussed in association.[58] The question is: Are nonreal entities, i.e., beings of reason, deceptive? Suárez does not answer the question explicitly, although it seems clear that in his view they are not. In this, Hurtado parts company with Suárez (see chapter 6).

4. ARE BEINGS OF REASON INDIVIDUAL OR UNIVERSAL?

It is unclear whether beings of reason are individual or universal, or whether some are individual and other universal. In English this question is forced on us, for we need to decide what article to use. 'Chimera' seems to be often a species for the scholastics, although in mythology it is rather a fictitious individual. Similarly with nonbeings—Socrates' blindness seems to be individual, just like his sight, and it is an instance of a fictitious quality. So are there not just universal but also individual nonbeings? Shall we say 'chimera' or 'a chimera' or 'the chimera'? In Latin there are no articles, and so this question may be left open. It is, for instance, unclear whether two people can think of two chimeras, individually different, but having exactly the same features. It would seem that the answer is positive, for one person can think of two individually different chimeras of exactly the same features. At any rate, Suárez does not address this question.[59]

5. OTHER QUESTIONS

There are still other questions that Suárez does not address. For instance: Are beings of reason *distinct* from the acts directed toward them, or are they parts of them? In other words, are they act-immanent or act-transcendent? What are the synchronic and diachronic criteria of identity for beings of reason? Do two or more people think of the same being of reason, if in each case what they think of shares all the same features? Does one person think of the same being of reason at two or more occasions? How to account for the difference between referring to nonexistent objects and a failure to refer to an object (objects of mistakes)?[60] These and other questions would need to be addressed in any theory of beings of reason that aspires to comprehensiveness.

My criticisms of Suárez should not be viewed as a denigration of Suárez's achievements. As it happens, in the history of thought, philosophers are successful and fruitful according to the measure not only of what they accomplish,but also of what they fail to accomplish. This is true of Suárez too, as I try to demonstrate in the following chapters. Philosophers after Suárez, such as Hurtado, Mastri/Belluto, and Caramuel, attempted either to replace or to improve what Suárez had bequeathed to them. Such efforts motivated an extraordinary development of philosophy in the seventeenth century.

6

Hurtado's Fallibilism

The aim of the following three chapters (6–8) is to provide detailed accounts of some of the theories of beings of reason that emerged in Baroque scholasticism after Suárez. In the present chapter I focus on the theory of beings of reason of Pedro Hurtado de Mendoza (1578–1641) who was a younger Jesuit colleague of Suárez at the Salamanca College. Hurtado takes up beings of reason in Metaphysical Disputation 19 (On Beings of Reason), published in two versions: first in his *Disputations in General Philosophy* (1615/19) and then in his *Universal Philosophy* (1624). Although the two works overlap, they also differ significantly. I discuss both in order to determine the development of Hurtado's thinking. The chapter is divided into three parts: First, I analyze the original version of Metaphysical Disputation 19 (section A); then, its revised version (B); and finally, I summarize the results of these analyses and show that Hurtado's theory essentially differs from that of Suárez (C).[1]

A. The Original Version of Disputation 19

The original version of Metaphysical Disputation 19 (henceforth Disputation 19) is not very long: It has only about five thousand words.[2] The disputation has three sections: (1) What is a being of reason? (2) Does God know beings of reason? (3) Some corollaries.[3] Let me deal with this last section first. Hurtado makes there one important point: He defers to Suárez on the discussion of the division of beings of reason:

> Beings of reason are divided into privations, negations, and relations, i.e. second intentions. [Of course] this needs to be understood [only] when they are apprehended otherwise than they are. . . . Beings of reason are divided on account of the ubiquity of falsehoods. . . . On how they are "detained" within certain "enclosed places," see Fr. Suárez [DM d54s4].[4]

We see that Hurtado claims to endorse Suárez's view here (see SD1):

> H1D1: Beings of reason are divided into privations, negations, and
> relations.

Unlike Suárez, however, Hurtado says nothing about how and why beings of reason are divided in this three-fold way. In fact, as we shall see, on Hurtado's theory this division makes no good sense and it is not surprising that he drops H1D1 in the revised edition.

Now we return to the preceding two sections of Hurtado's Disputation 19. The first section concerns the nature and the causes of beings of reason (section A.1); the second concerns beings of reason and God (A.2).

1. Nature and Causes of Beings of Reason

In section 1 Hurtado discusses several issues concerning the nature and causes of beings of reason.[5] The section is arranged somewhat ad hoc. Five theses (*conclusio*) stand at the center of the section, preceded by a discussion of extrinsic denominations and of the concept "merely objectively in the intellect," and followed by a discussion of simple apprehension and the question of whether senses and will make up beings of reason. In general, my analysis follows the order of Hurtado's text but I further subdivide it into an outline of Hurtado's Fallibilism (section A.1.1), and consequences of Hurtado's Fallibilism (A.1.2).

1.1. AN OUTLINE OF FALLIBILISM

This section is divided into three parts: First, I discuss Hurtado's refutation of the extrinsic-denomination view; second, I propose a preliminary outline of his view; and third, I give a more extensive description of his view, captured in four of Hurtado's five central theses (the last thesis will be discussed in the next section, A.1.2).

Let us begin with extrinsic denominations. The Thomists hold, according to Hurtado, that a being of reason is "what does not posit anything intrinsic into the object," i.e., a being of reason is an extrinsic denomination.[6] Hurtado finds this view totally unjustified:

> The Thomists generally claim that a being of reason is what does not
> posit anything intrinsic into the denominated object. Hence second inten-

tions, such as genus, species, subject, predicate, etc. are beings of reason. . . . Similarly, all other extrinsic denominations will be beings of reason. I have never seen any argument for this claim, but they propose it as a metaphysical principle. I argue against them: everything that has physical being from the side of reality is a real being, not a being of reason . . . [and] an extrinsic denomination is a real concept physically existing at some place; hence it has physical being in reality. I prove the latter premise: *knowing* [*cognitio*] is an extrinsic denomination of the object and an intrinsic one of the intellect; hence an extrinsic denomination has intrinsic being somewhere.[7]

Hurtado argues that even *extrinsic* denominations do exist somewhere *intrinsically*, namely in the intellect, and hence they are real:

> H1N1: In order for something to be a being of reason it is not sufficient that it is an extrinsic denomination.

Given H1N1 Hurtado concludes that the definition "a being of reason is what posits nothing intrinsic into the thing" is wrong. We shall see that in the revised edition Hurtado further explains this argument and suggests a more charitable reading of the definition (see section B.1.2).

Having "refuted" the extrinsic-denomination view, Hurtado makes a preliminary outline of his own view: A being of reason is "what has merely objective being in the intellect" (1). This he explains as follows:

> [1] A being of reason is what has merely objective being in the intellect. . . . [2] Thus two aspects can be distinguished, namely, *the [act of] knowing*, which denominates the thing as known and as objectively existing in the mind, and *the thing itself*, or the object, which is extrinsically denominated from this [act of] knowing. [3] If the [act of] knowing denominates the thing so that it has being as (*sicut*) it is known and denominated, then the thing does not have merely objective being in the intellect. . . . In this situation no being of reason is made up. [4] For instance, if somebody [e.g., Paul] mentally affirms *Peter is a human being*, the identity between Peter and a human being has objective being in the intellect that affirms this . . . [but] beside this objective being there is also a real identity because Peter has identity with a human being also outside of Paul's intellect. . . . [Hence] *Peter is a human being* does not have merely objective being in

the intellect. [5] But if the [act of] knowing does not terminate at the thing as it is or no object corresponds to it ... then a being of reason emerges: For the object is not in reality but merely in [the act of] knowing. Such object is called a 'being of reason', for it has no other being beside the one apprehended by reason. [6] For instance, [suppose] I affirm *Quantity is a substance*, when in reality it is an accident. Hence it *is*, i.e., *is judged to be*, a substance in my intellect and [in my act of] knowing. But it is not a substance in reality. Hence the identity of quantity and substance has no being other than objective being in the intellect.[8]

Hurtado first distinguishes between *the act of knowing* in virtue of which a thing is denominated as "the known thing" and *the denominated thing* [2]. Then he describes two possible scenarios:

(1) The denominated thing has being *as* it is known (3). This 'as' (*sicut*) is understood by Hurtado *propositionally*: Paul's knowledge of Peter as a human being simply means that Paul makes a judgment that Peter is a human being. This situation involves the proposition "Peter is a human being" judged by Paul and the extra-mental fact that Peter is a human being.[9] Since there is the fact corresponding to Paul's judgment, the latter is not *merely* objectively in Paul's intellect and no being of reason arises (4).

(2) The act of knowing does not terminate at the thing *as* it is (5). For instance, Paul makes a judgment that quantity is a substance. This situation involves the proposition *Quantity is a substance* and the lack of the corresponding extra-mental fact in reality. Since there is no fact corresponding to the (false) proposition, judged to be true by Paul, the latter is merely objectively in Paul's intellect and a being of reason arises (6).

> H1N2: A being of reason is what has merely objective being in the intellect.
>
> H1N3: A being of reason is a (false) proposition that is judged to be true.

Note that I say 'proposition', not 'judgment', to indicate that Hurtado's being of reason is not a mental act (event) but a result or product of such act. It is an object of thought in the sense of what we think, not in the sense of what we think of (see section 1.A).

Having drawn a preliminary outline of his view, Hurtado formulates five theses that he probably intends to be a fuller description of his view. The third and fourth thesis collapse into one, and I deal with the fifth in the next section; here are the first three:

H1N4: There are beings of reason.

H1C1: Beings of reason are made up only by false mental acts.

H1N5: Beings of reason are totally dependent on *actual* mental acts.

H1N4 is justified by a trivial appeal to the existence of errors:

> Hence first you can infer that Valles and with him not a few others were hallucinating when they denied beings of reason: For [the fact] that there are beings of reason is so clear that it is obvious that they have been deceived. For there are many things that we affirm or deny that have no being except in our affirmations and negations. The objects are thus denominated or represented in a different manner than they are . . . in the proposition *Peter is a stone*, we represent Peter, a stone, and a unity; the latter, however, has being nowhere, except in the cognition.[10]

H1C1 is justified by H1N2 and H1N3:

> Second, . . . because a being of reason has merely objective being in the intellect . . . necessarily, the act that makes beings of reason is false [=H1N2]. The implication is clear, for there is nothing from the side of the object that is represented by the act [=H1N3] . . . hence this act is inadequate (*difformis*) to the object and hence it is false. . . . This explanation I take not only from Aristotle and St. Thomas . . . but also from Father Suárez himself and from Vázquez, Fonseca and others that deal with beings of reason.[11]

Note Hurtado's claim that he has taken over this view from Suárez. This is, in fact, quite untrue. H1N5 is stated in this passage:

> Third, I claim: some [authors] badly think that there are beings of reason before the actual operation of the intellect . . . I argue against them that beings of reason in themselves have no being, either actual or possible. . . .

[1] You will say: beings of reason *can* be [and hence they are possible before actually thought of]. I answer: yes, but this possibility is [derived] from the possibility of the false acts [of the intellect]. . . . Fourthly, I claim that beings of reason do not precede the acts by which they are made up. . . . [2] Some might say that being comes first before being known. Against: This is true of things that have being distinct from being known. But if in beings of reason to be is to be known, how could their being precede their being known? [12]

Although Hurtado does not use the formulation "a being of reason is *totally* dependent on actual mental acts," this is what he means, for if there is nothing before the actual operation of the intellect, the being of reason that results from that operation is totally dependent on it. Objections (1) and (2) to which Hurtado alludes here were unknown to Suárez but they became progressively more prominent in scholastic discussions (see Mastri/Belluto in chapter 7, section A.3).

1.2. CONSEQUENCES OF FALLIBILISM

In the fifth thesis Hurtado draws some surprising consequences from H1N3 (beings of reason as false propositions) and H1C1 (beings of reason made by false acts). So far Hurtado's examples of beings of reason included only necessarily false judgments ("Peter is a stone," "Quantity is a substance," etc.) but now he considers contingently false judgments [2] and judgments about self-contradictory beings [3]:

> [1] Fifthly I claim that in order to form a being of reason, it is not necessary that the object of the act is impossible; what is required is that the object is not as it is represented by the act, for only in such case it has merely objective being in the intellect. For instance, [2] [suppose that] Peter is not running and I affirm *Peter is running*; the [actually] exercised existence has no being except objectively in my intellect; for although [*Peter is running* as such] has possible being, the act represents it as [having] actually actual being—but this actuality is only objectively in my intellect. [3] Contrariwise, if the act conforms to the object, even if the object at stake is a chimera, with respect to this act there is no being of reason, for this [object] has other being than the being from the act whereby somebody, e.g., I think of it.[13]

We see (in 2) that Hurtado openly acknowledges that:

H1C2: Beings of reason are made up both by necessarily and contingently false judgments.

Hence:

H1N6: Some beings of reason can be actualized in reality.

The claim that not every being is "impossible to exist in reality" contradicts Suárez and is a radical departure from the standard scholastic views
of the time; but Hurtado is even more radical: If a self-contradictory object
is the subject of a true judgment, it is not a being of reason (3):

H1N7: Self-contradictory beings are not beings of reason.

Hence the traditional paradigms of being of reason, namely chimeras and
square circles, are not beings of reason. This prima facie shocking claim is
further explained:

> This act [of truly thinking of a self-contradictory object] does not make
> up anything because its object is not merely objectively in the intellect
> in virtue of [per] this [same] act. For besides the objective being in virtue
> of this act, the [self-contradictory object] has other being, namely the
> merely objective being in the intellect of somebody else or the [merely
> objective being] it had in another act of the same intellect.[14]

Hurtado's idea seems to be that judging *truly* about self-contradictory beings
necessarily presupposes judging *falsely* about them. It is the latter act where
they *get* their being from. For instance, when I make a true judgment about
a square circle, my mental act conforms to the already "existing" square
circle, which is made up by some false judgment (my own in the past or of
other people); the square circle does not receive any being from the true
judgment of mine.

H1N8: True judgments about self-contradictory beings necessarily
presuppose false judgments in virtue of which they are
made up.

But there is another obstacle, for self-contradictory beings to be beings
of reason: The former are objects, whereas the latter are supposed to be

propositions (from H1N3). Hence simple apprehension (the mental power responsible for forming concepts) is incapable of making them:

> You ask whether beings of reason are made up by simple apprehension. [1] I answer that mere apprehension of the subject or the predicate is not sufficient because . . . there is no falsity in them. [2] You say that when a chimera is apprehended as the subject of the proposition *A chimera is a being of reason,* then a being of reason is made, for chimeras have merely objective being in the intellect. [3] I answer that no being of reason is made up here since . . . the object of this act has not merely objective being in the intellect in virtue of this act but it has other being to which the act conforms. [4] No [real] being is attributed to a chimera but rather denied: to say *A chimera is a being of reason* is the same as to say *A chimera is some fictum.* And since [true] being is denied of it, the claim is true. Hence this is a proposition about the object as it is. [5] (The expression 'as it is' does not indicate . . . real being but fictitious being, which indeed, chimeras have).[15]

Simple apprehension is not sufficient for making up a being of reason, since truth/falsity do not apply to concepts (1). In other words:

> H1C3: Simple apprehension of the subject or the predicate is not capable of making up a being of reason.

To the objection that there are true statements about chimeras and hence about non-propositional beings of reason (2), Hurtado replies in two different ways. First, he says that within true statements chimeras *do have some being* to which the statement conforms (3). This being is called "fictitious" but it must be in *some sense* real (otherwise Hurtado would have to give up H1N7) although it is not real in the narrower sense (5). Second, Hurtado says that to predicate 'being of reason' or 'fiction' of a chimera is the same as to deny '(real) being' of it (4). This could, perhaps, be understood to mean that we speak about *nothing*—as we can see in this series of paraphrases: 'A chimera is a being of reason', i.e., 'A chimera is not a real being', i.e., 'There is no such thing as a chimera'. Thus Hurtado seems to offer two possibilities:

> H1N9-A: Self-contradictory beings are pure nothing.

H1N9-B: Self-contradictory beings have a peculiar sort of real being, namely fictitious being.

Hurtado returns to this question at the end of section 1 (now I jump ahead in Hurtado's text):

[1] Notice that with respect to beings of reason two [aspects] need to be considered: the act of contriving and the fictitious object. The act of contriving is real and the denomination of the fictitious and known object is also real. In this there is no difference [between the fictitious] and the real being [or object]. . . . [2] But [if] the fictitious object is nothing and the real denomination "fictitious and known" as a whole falls upon nothing, [3] it is false, for it does not fall on an object that on its part has something that the act of knowing gives it. And this is to be merely objectively in the intellect. [4] . . . and hence [we see that] the distinction [real/of-reason] concerns the objects and not the acts.[16]

That the mental acts, and the denominations derived from them, are real regardless of their objects (1) is clear: The distinction real/of-reason applies to the objects, not to the acts (4). But we want to know what self-contradictory beings, i.e., fictitious objects, are. Hurtado states that a fictitious object is *nothing* (2), which would seem to support H1N9-a. If a mental act *fails* to reach its *proper* object, which happens in the case of errors, we speak of a "fictitious object" (3). But in what sense is this fictitious object 'nothing'? There are two possibilities: Hurtado could mean "pure nothing"—in which case "fictitious object' is just an abbreviation for 'there is no such thing as'; or he could mean "nothing truly real"—in which case "fictitious' would indicate a special sort of real being.[17] Hence the passage as such does not show clearly whether Hurtado holds H1N9-a or H1N9-b (see also section A.2 below).

There are two more consequences of Hurtado's theory that should be mentioned. First, one may not only *create* but also *destroy* a being of reason:

[1] In order for something to be a being of reason it needs to have objective being in the intellect so that it is not known as it is. For if it is known as it is, it is . . . destroyed by this act. [2] For instance, when I say *Quantity is a substance*, I give objective being to the identity of these two things

that they do not have in fact; hence I make up a chimera.[18] [3] However, if I say *A chimera is to say that quantity is a substance*, . . . I do not make up a being of reason but rather destroy . . . [the being of reason] made up by the prior act; the latter act is true, for it conforms to the object (which [already] has being in itself, distinct from the objective being of the latter act).[19]

Every *true* judgment about a chimera presupposes another *false* judgment about it—this we know already from H1N8. Hurtado now adds that whereas the latter gives it some fictitious being (2), the former "destroys" it (3):

H1N10: Beings of reason can be destroyed by true judgments.

The second consequence of Hurtado's view that I would like to mention is:

H1C4: The senses and the will cannot make up beings of reason.

The justification of this thesis is that neither the senses nor the will are directed to something that could be evaluated in terms of truth/falsity.[20]

2. Beings of Reason and God

Since for Hurtado beings of reason are made up by false mental acts (H1C1) and God is perfect, it clearly follows that:[21]

H1CG1: God does not make up his own beings of reason.

There is, however, controversy concerning whether God knows beings of reason as made up by us:

[1] It is more difficult, however, to decide whether God knows beings of reason that we have made up. There is a great controversy between Fr. Francisco Suárez and Fr. Gabriel Vázquez concerning this issue, which I confess I cannot quite easily put together. [2] Suárez [DM d54s2n23] affirms that God undoubtedly knows beings of reason [made up by us,] . . . for he knows human acts . . . and hence also their objects. The implication is obvious since it is not possible to know an act without knowing the object that it concerns. . . . [3] Vázquez replies that God knows the real

"extremes" that are the object of such an act, but not their fictitious unity.[22]

The controversy first arose between Suárez and Vázquez (1). Suárez argues that God must know beings of reason made up by us, for (a) he knows all our mental acts (2), (b) in order to know all our mental acts he needs to know all their objects, including beings of reason. Vázquez agrees with (a) but disagrees with (b): God does not know beings of reason as a whole but only their real "extremes" (components) (3). Hurtado sides with Suárez:

> I do not like [Vázquez's] solution, for [1] [an act of] fiction not only represents the real "extremes" of this chimera, *Human being is irrational,* but also the identity of these "extremes;" in fact this is precisely the reason that makes the proposition false. . . . [2] Second, I say that although it is an imperfection to make up a chimera (for in this way the thing is apprehended otherwise than it is), it is a perfection to know that somebody else "wrongly" knows something; similarly it is a great perfection to know the errors of other people.[23]

We see that Hurtado defends:

H1CG2: God knows beings of reason as made up by us.

First, because a being of reason precisely consists in the mistaken identification of the two real components, God's knowledge should not leave out this identification (1). Second, the knowledge of the errors of others is a perfection that God should have (2).[24]

Vázquez objects to H1CG2: If God knows beings of reason, he makes them up; but if he makes them up, they are eternal:

> Vázquez . . . vehemently attacks this view [that God knows beings of reason as made up by us,] . . . for if God retains in his mind what is not, even if just secondarily, not primarily (primarily these ficta are made up by the human intellect), he really forms in his mind some figment or monster, which is . . . in virtue of his intellect conserved [=kept in being]. . . . This is confirmed: . . . If God knows beings of reason as made up by human beings, he knows these beings of reason from all eternity, hence from all

eternity they have some objective being from God alone, hence God makes up beings of reason.[25]

Such a consequence is acceptable neither to Vázquez nor to Hurtado. But whereas Vázquez rejects H1CG2, Hurtado saves it by invoking his H1N10, namely that God "destroys" these figments of our mistaken minds by knowing them as they are (i.e., as parts of false judgments):

> To [Vazquez's] argument: God neither retains nor conserves "monsters" made up by human beings but rather destroys them by his quite true acts. . . . God does not give being to these figments that human acts give them, he rather destroys them by his knowledge that humans are deceived . . . he can see that the figment are formed by humans and that vision is quite true and expresses these objects as they are.[26]

Hurtado concludes this section with the following clarification:

> Although [beings of reason] have objective being in God, they do not have *merely* objective being in God, for from their object side they are [in the same way] as they are objectively in God . . . and not differently in . . . themselves. A being of reason, although it has in itself no real actual or possible being, has in itself fictitious being (or at least possibly fictitious being) during some temporal interval and as such it is known by God.[27]

When God knows a being of reason, it is not merely objectively in his intellect, for this being of reason has some fictitious being in itself (in virtue of a human mistake "during some temporal interval")—this might perhaps suggest that Hurtado considers fictitious being to be a peculiar kind of real being (H1N9-b); see also section A.1.2 above.

B. The Revised Version of Disputation 19

The revised version of Disputation 19 is much longer than the original one—it has thirteen thousand words. It is divided into six sections: whether extrinsic denominations *are* beings of reason (s1); whether beings of reason *result* from extrinsic denominations (s2); what a being of reason is (s3); some corollaries (s4); causes and division of beings of reason (s5); and whether God knows beings of reason (s6). The first section is divided into two subsections: replies to arguments affirming extrinsic denominations to be sufficient for beings of reason (s1sb1); an attack on this view (s1sb2). The second section is divided into six subsections: discussion of the view that all beings of reason *result* from *some* extrinsic denominations (s2sb1); discussion of the view that beings of reason *result* from *every* extrinsic denomination (s2sb2); first, second and third attack on the latter view (s2sb3, s2sb4, s2sb6); and an intermezzo about moral beings (s2sb5).[28]

When we compare the revised and the original editions of Disputation 19, only section 6 (originally section 2 on God and beings of reason) remains verbatim the same. The introduction and sections 1 and 2 on extrinsic denominations are completely new, except for the first paragraph stating that the treatment of beings of reason belongs to metaphysics (UP-M d19Intr. n1:942); sections 3–5 contain substantially reworked and expanded material of the original sections 1 and 3.

My discussion of the revised version of Disputation 19 is divided into two main parts: First I deal with Hurtado's view on the nature of beings of reason, and second with his view on the causes and the division of beings of reason.

1. Nature of Beings of Reason

In this section I discuss four issues: (section 1.1) intension of 'being of reason', (1.2) extrinsic denominations, (1.3) an outline of Hurtado's revised theory, (1.4) some consequences of this theory. In all four areas Hurtado makes substantial additions (and subtractions) to his original theory.

1.1. INTENSION OF 'BEING OF REASON'

The introduction of Disputation 19 opens with an analysis of what the term 'being of reason' means. This analysis markedly differs from that of Suárez:

> [1] 'Being of reason' in the *effective* and *subjective* sense refers to acts of the intellect that reason produces in itself. [2] In the *denominative sense* it refers to the passive denominations through which the objects are called "known." [3] In the *foundational sense* it refers to those extrinsic denominations that provide a foundation so that they can be conceived by us as intrinsic. [4] In the *most proper sense* it is what is not from the side of reality but is contrived by us as what is [from the side of reality].[29]

We see that Suárez's two meanings (*effective* and *subjective*) are integrated by Hurtado into one (1). Then, two new meanings appeared, namely *denominative*, which includes extrinsic denominations (usually made by grammatically passive verb forms) (2) and *fundamental*, which includes extrinsic denominations with a foundation in reality (3). In its *most proper sense* a being of reason is something that is not in reality but is conceived of as if it were in reality (4)—Hurtado interprets this formula, as we know already from the original edition, as "a false proposition judged to be true." Conspicuously, the *objective* sense of 'being of reason' disappeared, although it is likely that Hurtado would say that the "most proper sense" of 'being of reason' means "merely objective." (See section A.1.1 above.)

> H2N1: The expression 'being of reason' can be used in four senses: (a) effective and subjective; (b) denominative; (c) foundational; and (d) proper.

Hurtado continues:

> [1] Hence it is clear that the name 'being of reason' is ambiguous: it signifies many things as many things and these . . . have nothing in common, for fictitious beings have nothing in common with true beings. What would acts of the intellect have in common with fictitious beings? [2] In the present disputation we do not intend to explicate beings of reason in the first sense, for acts of the intellect are dealt with . . . by the "soul-scholar." Neither have we dealt with beings of reason in the second sense, for these are studied by the logician. The third sense is partially relevant for the metaphysicians, [3] the fourth sense, however, is what really matters: we are treating of beings of reason as they are opposed to real beings. . . . For in the first three senses a being of reason is not distinguished from a real being as such.[30]

We see that according to Hurtado the four senses are quite unrelated (1) and dealt with by different sciences (2). Even more important (3):

> H2N2: Only beings of reason in the proper sense are nonreal.

Beings of reason in the other senses, i.e., extrinsic denominations and beings of reason with a foundation in reality are *real*. Broadly speaking, we may call them beings of reason but properly speaking they are not.

1.2. EXTRINSIC DENOMINATIONS

In the revised edition Hurtado adds an extensive discussion of the extrinsic-denomination view (in sections 1 and 2), which takes up two thirds of the disputation. This, however, should not be taken as indicative of the importance of the view for, as Hurtado acknowledges, some of the versions of the extrinsic-denomination views are held by nobody so that he discusses them only for the sake of argument.[31] Hence, given the lack of historical relevance of these views, I report and discuss Hurtado's arguments in this matter only relatively briefly.[32]

Section 1 deals with the view that identifies beings of reason with extrinsic denominations. This view, known already to Suárez (see chapter 4, section B.2), has two versions, namely, *general*, according to which *every* extrinsic denomination is a being of reason and vice versa, and *restricted*, according to which only *some* extrinsic denominations are beings of reason. Section 2 deals with a new version of the extrinsic-denomination view according to which beings of reason cannot be *reduced to* extrinsic denominations although they somehow (necessarily) *result* from them (henceforth "resultant extrinsic-denomination view").[33]

Let us first consider the general and restricted extrinsic-denomination views discussed by Hurtado in section 1. The section is divided into subsection 1, in which Hurtado *replies* to the arguments of the proponents of these views (in the original edition he claimed that he had never seen any argument in favor of it, see section A.1.1), and subsection 2, in which he positively *argues against* them. I only quote a passage from subsection 1:

[1] The Thomists generally hold that every extrinsic denomination is a being of reason.... [2] I have shown, however, ... that they do not speak about beings of reason as they are opposed to real beings as such, but about beings extrinsic to some objects, intrinsic to others.... [3] For instance, they say that the object known is a being of reason because to be known is not intrinsic to the known object.... But the act of knowing in virtue of which the object is said to be known is intrinsic to the intellect, although it is not intrinsic to the [known] object.... [4] These authors define a being of reason as what posits nothing intrinsic into things. This definition, if it is understood about every thing, is true; if, however, [it is understood] only about some thing, it is false, for a being intrinsic to one thing can be extrinsic to others.[34]

We see that in the same way as in the original edition Hurtado ascribes to Thomists the view that every extrinsic denomination is a being of reason (1) (=a being of reason is what posits nothing intrinsic into a thing). Unlike the original edition, however, Hurtado offers a charitable reading, namely that the Thomists may be using the expression 'being of reason' in a sense compatible with real being (2) (see H2N1 and H2N2). But this remains true even in the revised edition:

H2N3: In order for something to be a being of reason in the *proper sense* it is not sufficient that it is an extrinsic denomination.

There are other senses of 'being of reason' (namely, the *denominative* and *fundamental*) in which it is true that for a being of reason it *is* sufficient to be an extrinsic denomination.[35] In these senses, however, we speak about beings of reason that are just a sort of real beings.

Hurtado also points out that if something is extrinsic to one object it does not mean that it is extrinsic to every object. For instance, if an object x is known by Peter, then "being known" is extrinsic to x but intrinsic to Peter's intellect. And this suffices to make the form "being known" real (3). The only way to save the truth of the Thomistic claim that every extrinsic being is a being of reason, i.e., that a being of reason posits nothing intrinsic into a thing, is (4):

H2N4: A being of reason is what posits nothing intrinsic into *any* one thing.

If, however, the Thomistic claim is interpreted in the (usual Thomistic) sense: "A being of reason is what posits nothing intrinsic into a *given* thing," then it is false.[36]

Now we come to the resultant extrinsic-denomination views, discussed by Hurtado in section 2. The section is divided into six subsections. Subsection 1 deals with the restricted version of the view according to which beings of reason result only from extrinsic denominations derived from the intellect.[37] Subsection 2 deals with the general version of the view according to which beings of reason result from any extrinsic denomination (this is the view that according to Hurtado nobody holds). In subsections 3, 4, and 6, Hurtado positively argues that anything resulting from an extrinsic denomination is real.[38] Subsection 5 contains an interesting mention of moral beings:

What remains is that these authors flee to moral beings that are neither real nor formally of reason: such as the dominion [of *x*], the signification of words, the value [of *x*] . . . and other similar [things]. To those I say in one word that all moral beings are either intrinsic denominations or extrinsic from some real being; . . . the created dominion . . . is an extrinsic denomination from the will of the one declaring the law . . . the signification of words is an extrinsic denomination from the will of the one imposing [the linguistic meaning] similarly as the value of money from the will of the prince. . . . Hence there is no moral being that is not real.[39]

We see that unlike Suárez, who holds that beings of reason include also semantic, social and other institutional relations, Hurtado considers them real. (See also chapter 5, section D).

This is all that needs to be mentioned with respect to Hurtado's discussion of extrinsic denominations and their relation to beings of reason. There is only one last observation I would like to make: The intuition that drives Hurtado's defense of the reality of extrinsic denominations is that statements such as 'Peter can see Paul' or 'Paul is seen by Peter' may be *paraphrased* by each other and still refer to the same reality.[40] This idea, perhaps common today, was novel at the time, for the standard scholastic view distinguishes between predicating something of Peter (he is *seeing Paul*) and predicating something of Paul (he is *seen by Peter*); hence—according to the standard scholastic outlook—the facts to which the two statements "refer" are not *quite* the same.

Having discussed extrinsic denominations, which all Jesuit authors seem to consider a "blind alley" in the account of beings of reason, let us take a look at Hurtado's positive theory, i.e., his revised version of Fallibilism.

1.3. OUTLINE OF REVISED FALLIBILISM

In section 3 of the revised edition of Disputation 19, Hurtado draws again an outline of his theory of beings of reason (Fallibilism). The part of the theory depicted in this section remains the same although it is explained in greater detail. Hurtado begins with what he sees as the standard definition of beings of reason:

It is not possible to effectively discuss whether a being of reason is possible unless we [first] explain its definition. . . . Philosophers and theologians have stated that a being of reason is distinct from every real being both actual and possible, both positive and negative. They have determined the following definition: *A being of reason is* [1] *the whole of which consists in being known,* or [2] *what does not have other being than an objective one in the intellect.* This definition was proposed as standard by Fr. Suárez.[41]

The first part of the definition (1) corresponds (roughly) to H1N5, whereas the second part (2) to H1N2.[42] Note that Suárez in fact did not explicitly state (1), although there are indications that he would probably have agreed with it. Also note that Hurtado leaves out the second part of Suárez's definition, namely, "a being of reason is thought of as a being when in fact it has no being in itself" (SN7).

Hurtado proceeds with an explanation of [2]. The explanation may be divided into three steps:

Step 1: *All* that we directly know are the objects of our minds. These mental objects may represent extra-mental objects similarly as a statue represents a person:

> I explain the definition as follows: *to have objective being in the intellect* means to be known by the intellect. Objects are said to be *in* the intellect, for the cognitions/images of these objects are *in* it, . . . in fact usually we [even] say that the image *is* the thing that it represents. For instance, when we see the statue of Caesar, we say "This is Caesar": Caesar is *intentionally* or *representatively* . . . in the cognition similarly as he is in the image [e.g., in the statue]. ∴ . . [However,] the object is not in its image properly speaking but only metaphorically, for the images are *images of* the objects. Hence I conclude that all the objects of our acts of knowing are objectively in the intellect, i.e., they are represented as the objects of their images.[43]

Step 2: Now it turns out that Hurtado's mental objects are not in fact objects (in the usual sense) but propositions. Some such mental "objects"/ propositions represent mind-independent facts:

> But there is this difference: many objects have in themselves other being that is distinct from their intentional being . . . and representation . . . For instance, I say "Peter is a human being": This object has [not only] intentional and objective being *in my intellect* but also (beside this being-

represented) it has what it is claimed to have *in itself* . . . : for Peter is a human being both inside and outside of my intellect. Thus it is a real being and does not have *merely* objective being in the intellect. For this reason the proposition *Peter is a human being* is true because Peter is a human being. The same I have stated about privation and negation. (For the objects *Antonius is blind, The stone does not see* . . . are not just objectively in the intellect but also outside of it, . . . for . . . they obtain independently of our intellect).[44]

Step 3: Other mental "objects"/propositions do *not* represent mind-independent facts. These and only these are beings of reason:

Other objects are not outside the proposition through which they are affirmed or negated; for instance, *God is not Trinity, Human being is a brute*: These objects are not in themselves as they are conceived by the intellect. The lack of being-Trinity is neither in God . . . nor irrationality in human beings. Behold these objects have objective being in the intellect through these propositions but nowhere else in some other being; hence they are *merely* objectively in the intellect. These propositions do not just represent real "extremes" that have some being outside of the intellect, . . . for the one who says "Human being is a brute" conceives not just a human being and a brute but also their real identity, which is nowhere but in the representation. The proposition is false, for it represents in the object what is not in it.[45]

We see that Hurtado explained but did not modify his original claim H1N3 (A being of reason is a [false] proposition that is judged to be true).[46] Now we look at some of the consequences of Hurtado's Fallibilism.

1.4. CONSEQUENCES OF REVISED FALLIBILISM

In section 4 Hurtado draws six consequences of Fallibilism. The second, fourth and fifth consequences correspond to those mentioned in the original edition:

Extrinsic denominations (derived from real extrinsic forms) are not beings of reason.[47] This is an upshot of the long discussions in sections 1 and 2 (see above H2N3).

Not every mental act about a "chimera" (=false proposition) makes it. Suppose I make up a "chimera" by judging "a human being is a brute." The reflexive judgment "I have judged that a human being is a brute" is true and hence it does not make up a "chimera." The reflexive act "I have falsely judged that a human being is a brute" not only does not make it up but it even "destroys" it.[48] This claim roughly corresponds to H1N10.

There are (dari) beings of reason.[49] This claim corresponds to H1N4.

The first, third and sixth consequences bring up something new: Beings of reason are not correctly divided into 'actually formal' and 'foundational'. By 'actually formal', Hurtado means "without a foundation in reality," for otherwise he would not contrast it with 'foundational'. The foundational beings of reason are not beings of reason in the proper sense, for they are real and they "pop up into existence" mind-independently—at least this is what their proponents say, according to Hurtado (see also H2N1 and H2N2).[50]

H2N5: There are no beings of reason with a foundation in reality.

Privations and negations are mind-independent "foundations of true propositions" and all beings of reason are supposed to be (according to Hurtado) without any proximate or remote foundation in reality (as he stated in H2N5).[51] Hence:

H2D1: Negations and privations are not beings of reason.

Furthermore, the term 'being' is purely equivocal when applied to beings of reason and real beings—not even Suárez's weakest analogy of proportionality applies. Hurtado holds that for this analogy to obtain the referents of the analogical terms must exist. But this is not the case with beings of reason for they are "just nothing." Beings of reason are *thought to exist* but this does not make them exist.[52]

H2N6: There is no analogy between real beings and beings of reason.

Let us proceed now to Hurtado's views on the causes and the division of beings of reason.

2. Causes and Division of Beings of Reason

Hurtado deals with several issues in the context of the causes of beings of reason. First, he claims that beings of reason have all four types of causes; second, that beings of reason are made up by false mental acts (whether contingently or necessarily false acts is a matter of definitional fiat). Third, Hurtado discusses simple apprehension and a few other special questions. Concerning the division of beings of reason, Hurtado is only very brief and merely revokes his support of the traditional three-member division expressed in the first edition of his book.

What sort of causes do beings of reason have? Since beings of reason are not physical entities, they cannot have causes in the usual, physical, sense:[53]

H2C1: Beings of reason have no causes in the *physical* sense.

Nevertheless, since beings of reason are intentional entities, there are various other senses in which beings of reason do have causes:

H2C2: Beings of reason may have a material and a formal cause in a *fictitious* sense.
H2C3: The *intentional* efficient cause of beings of reason is the intellect.
H2C4: Beings of reason have a *nondirect* final cause.

In H2C2 we see again the term 'fictitious'. By 'fictitious', Hurtado probably means "nonexisting but mistakenly thought to be existing" (but see chapter 5, section A.1, for the difficulties with interpreting 'fictitious'). By 'nondirect', Hurtado probably means "somehow directed" but "not naturally," for neither nature nor any person as such *intend* to fall into error. This is all that Hurtado says, referring his readers to Suárez for further elaboration (who holds, however, as we know from previous chapters, a quite different view).

What about the mental acts in virtue of which beings of reason are produced? First Hurtado says:

The greater controversy concerns the acts whereby beings of reason are made up. First I say that beings of reason are made up by false acts whereby we judge that something exists or can exist that in fact cannot exist: For instance, *Human being is brute*. Similarly when we say that something is impossible what in fact is possible.[54]

> H2C5: Beings of reason are made up by false acts by which we claim
> that something exists or can exist that in fact cannot, or vice versa.

From the examples (e.g., "A human being is a brute") we see that so far Hurtado has applied his Fallibilism to necessarily false judgments only.

> H2C6: Beings of reason are made up by necessarily false mental acts.

But now the question is: Do contingently false acts make up beings of reason? We know that Hurtado's original answer was affirmative (H1C2) in spite of the radical consequences (H1N6 and H1N7) that he drew from it. However, here he says:

> [1] The question, however, may be raised whether a being of reason hap-
> pens in virtue of a false judgment representing a possible thing as existing
> when in fact this thing does not exist. For instance, given that Peter is not
> running and somebody says, "Peter is running," is this *Peter's running*
> a being of reason or a real being? [2] I answer that this is a verbal dispute.
> That this being [*esse*] is not a being of reason seems to be apparent from
> [the fact] that this *running* has possible being: hence it is not a being of
> reason (for a being of reason is a chimera and *Peter's running* is not a
> chimera). [3] Against this, in favor of considering it to be a being of reason,
> there is [the fact] that the existence [of *Peter's running*] as actually ex-
> ercised has being nowhere but objectively in the intellect. . . . [4] The reply
> to the first argument [see 2] is that beings of reason are more commonly
> chimeras but that it does not follow from this that no other beings of
> reason happen—[e.g.,] when something does not have what it is claimed
> to have, although it could have it. [5] The reply to the second argument
> [see 3] is that the object [such as in our example] lacks the condition of
> [actually] exercised existence only accidentally and hence the extension
> of 'being of reason' does not have to be extended—for beings of reason
> require absolute impossibility to exist.[55]

Hurtado claims here that the issue of contingently false propositions is just a verbal matter (1). He proposes two arguments to the contrary positions (2) and (3), with replies (4) and (5), so that in the end he does not take a position of his own. Hurtado's agnosticism, however, is illegitimate at this point. For based on his claim that beings of reason are merely objectively in the intellect (H1N2, explicitly accepted in the revised edition as well), one should infer that contingently false propositions judged to be true are beings of reason in the proper sense. The addition that beings of reason require "absolute impossibility to exist" in (5) is not warranted by what Hurtado had said before.[56] Nevertheless, Hurtado's "official" doctrine in the revised edition states:

> H2C7: It is a verbal issue whether the result of a contingently false judgment should be called 'being of reason'.

Hurtado presents four more theses about the acts whereby beings of reason are made up: (a) They are not made up by 'precisive intellection' (this means, roughly, that they are not made up by abstraction);[57] (b) they are not made up by the simple apprehension of the subject and predicate;[58] (c) they may be made up by the apprehension of unity between something incompatible (for instance quantity and substance)—which results in a simple (*incomplex*) being of reason;[59] (d) they are not made up by the external or internal senses.[60] The second and the fourth theses amount to the earlier claims H1C3 and H1C4 respectively. Hence we get only two more new claims:

> H2C8: Beings of reason are not made up by abstraction.
> H2C9: Beings of reason can be made up by the simple apprehension of unity between incompatible items.

Hurtado deals with the division of beings of reason in only one brief paragraph. The standard three-member division applies only to foundational beings of reason (which are not in fact beings of reason as opposed to real beings). The proper ('formal') beings of reason are divided into "whatever figments the created intellect may take the trouble to make up."[61] Thus:

> H2D2: Beings of reason can be divided arbitrarily.

This is a natural consequence of Hurtado's Fallibilism: It makes no sense to divide beings of reason, understood as false propositions, into negations, privations, and relations.

C. Evaluation of Hurtado's Fallibilism

After providing a comprehensive exegesis of Hurtado's treatise on beings of reason,[62] let me summarize his theory. I begin with an overview of the original edition. Concerning the nature of beings of reason, Hurtado claims:

H1N1: In order for something to be a being of reason it is not sufficient that it is an extrinsic denomination.

H1N2: A being of reason is what has merely objective being in the intellect.

H1N3: A being of reason is a (false) proposition that is judged to be true.

H1N4: There are beings of reason.

H1N5: Beings of reason are totally dependent on *actual* mental acts.

H1N6: Some beings of reason can be actualized in reality.

H1N7: Self-contradictory beings are not beings of reason.

H1N8: True judgments about self-contradictory beings necessarily presuppose false judgments in virtue of which they are made up.

H1N9-A: Self-contradictory beings are pure nothing.

H1N9-B: Self-contradictory beings have a peculiar sort of real being, namely, fictitious being.

H1N10: Beings of reason can be destroyed by true judgment.

Concerning the causes and the division he says:

H1C1: Beings of reason are made up only by false mental acts.

H1C2: Beings of reason are made up both by necessarily and contingently false judgments.

H1C3: Simple apprehension of the subject or the predicate is not capable of making up a being of reason.

H1C4: The senses and the will cannot make up beings of reason.

H1CG1: God does not make up his "own" beings of reason.

H1CG2: God knows beings of reason as made up by us.

H1D1: Beings of reason are divided into privations, negations, and relations.

Now let us summarize Hurtado's theory from the revised edition of his work. Concerning the nature, Hurtado claims:

H2N1: The expression 'being of reason' can be used in four senses: (a) effective and subjective; (b) denominative; (c) foundational; and (d) proper.

H2N2: Only beings of reason in the proper sense are nonreal.

H2N3: In order for something to be a being of reason in the *proper sense* it is not sufficient that it is an extrinsic denomination.

H2N4: A being of reason is what posits nothing intrinsic into *any* one thing.

H2N5: There are no beings of reason with a foundation in reality.

H2N6: There is no analogy between real beings and beings of reason.

Hurtado's views on the causes and the division:

H2C1: Beings of reason have no causes in the *physical* sense.

H2C2: Beings of reason may have a material and a formal causes in the a *fictitious* sense.

H2C3: The *intentional* efficient cause of beings of reason is the intellect.

H2C4: Beings of reason have a *nondirect* final cause.

H2C5: Beings of reason are made up by false acts by which we claim that something exists or can exist that in fact cannot, or vice versa.

H2C6: Beings of reason are made up by necessarily false mental acts.

H2C7: It is a verbal issue whether the result of a contingently false judgment should be called 'being of reason'.

H2C8: Beings of reason are not made up by abstraction.

H2C9: Beings of reason can be made up by the simple apprehension of unity between incompatible items.

H2D1: Negations and privations are not beings of reason.

H2D2: Beings of reason can be divided arbitrarily.

We see that in the revised edition Hurtado explicitly adopts H1N2- H1N5, H1N10, H1C1 and H1C4, H1CG1–H1CG2. Hence, the core teaching on nature and on God is held in both editions. There are, however, some doctrinal changes with respect to the status of self-contradictory beings H1N6–N9 and revisions and expansions of the teaching on causes (especially that H1C2 is dropped and that H2C1–H2C5 and H2C8–H2C9 is added). The revised edition contains important additions to the teaching on nature (H2N1–H2N6), therefore providing a broader framework to the original edition, which is, however, compatible with what Hurtado says in the first edition. The views on division (about which, in contrast to Suárez, Hurtado says almost nothing) is also modified (H2D1–H2D2).

More important than the inner development of Hurtado's views, however, is the fact that in spite of some superficial similarities, Hurtado's theory essentially differs from Suárez's: Only propositional beings of reason are admitted (H1N3) and there are no beings of reason with a foundation in reality (H2N5). In the first edition Hurtado uses Suárez's definition of being of reason as 'what has merely objective being in the intellect' (H1N2). However, Hurtado gives it a very different meaning. It is only by mistakes and errors that a being of reason is produced. Its existence is an unfortunate by-product of our fallibility. In contrast, Suárez considers merely objective beings in the intellect to be something *useful*, because in virtue of these beings we can think of nonbeings (privations and negations) and we can think of logical relations. At its core, Fallibilism holds that:

Beings of reasons can be actualized in reality.
Beings of reason are false propositions judged to be true.
Beings of reason are made up by a judgment (at least) typically.

Suárezians are committed to the rejection of all three claims. Even though Hurtado occasionally claims that he has taken over his theory from Suárez, in reality his theory radically differs from it. It is hard to believe that Hurtado would overlook this radical difference, so he might be simply hiding his novel views behind the authority of Suárez. On the other hand, there is an element in Suárez's theory that might be an "inspiration" for Hurtado, namely, Suárez's claim that a being of reason is what has no being in itself but is conceived in the manner of a being (SN7). Based on such definition we could say that a being of reason is thought of otherwise than it is and hence that it is a false proposition that is judged to be true (H1N3). However, Hurtado takes this element of Suárez's theory out of context and transforms it into something wholly different.

The general lesson of this chapter for historians of Baroque scholasticism is that we may not rely on what many Jesuit authors themselves say about

Suárez. Hurtado, who is traditionally considered to be a Suárezian, is in no way a Suárezian with respect to beings of reason.[63] Suárez seems to have become an official authority for them, so that they do not criticize him openly. In reality, however, they often hold views radically different from his. Unless we truly know what a given author teaches we cannot call post-Suárezian authors "Suárezians" in spite of their verbal deference to Suárez. Contrariwise, in the next chapter, we will discuss a *Scotistic* theory of beings of reason which turns out to be a version of *Suárez*'s Objectualism.

7

Mastri/Belluto's Modified Objectualism

In this chapter, I deal with the theory of beings of reason of Bartolomeo Mastri (1602–73) and Bonaventura Belluto (1600–76). Mastri and Belluto (henceforth Mastri/Belluto) were two Italian Franciscan Conventuals and self-professed Scotists. Mastri/Belluto take up beings of reason at two occasions, first in their *Disputations of Organon* (1628) and then again in *Disputations of Metaphysics* (1646). In this chapter I deal only with their theory as it was presented in the former work. The chapter is divided into three parts. First, I discuss Mastri/Belluto's views about the existence and actuality of beings of reason (section A). Second, I discuss their views about the "formality," i.e., the nature, of beings of reason (B). Third, I summarize and evaluate their views and compare them with those of Suárez (C). We shall see that Mastri/Belluto develop a version of Objectualism that in many ways improves on Suárez's. (This might come as a surprise: The two Scotists develop Suárez-like Objectualism, while Suárez's own Jesuit colleague Hurtado rejects it.)[1]

A. Existence and Actuality of Beings of Reason

This section is divided into three parts. In the first I describe the *status quaestionis* as Mastri/Belluto see it; in the second and the third parts, I deal with their views on the existence and actuality of beings of reason, respectively.

1. *Status quaestionis*

As we have seen in the instances of Suárez and Hurtado, Baroque scholastics routinely distinguish among several senses of the term 'being of reason', of which the most proper is (as they say) "what is merely objectively in the intellect." Mastri/Belluto are no exception:

Something may [objectively] depend on reason in two ways: *either it has being,* even if it is not an object of the intellect, such as fire (which is hot

138

even if it is not known by us to be hot), *or it does not have being* if it is not an object of the intellect. [Being of reason in this last sense] has being only insofar as it is known by the intellect. [Thus,] if the act of knowing ceases, such being of reason immediately disappears: For instance, an angel is not a nice boy unless he is conceived so by the intellect. This is the sort of being of reason that is said to be "merely objectively in the intellect."[2]

In this passage we may discern three claims:

MBN1: The expression 'being of reason' means "what is an object of the intellect and nothing else."

MBN2: There are beings of reason.

MBN3: Beings of reason "emerge" only when *actually* thought of (= their being is *completely* mind-dependent, both existentially and essentially).

For most Baroque scholastics, MBN1 and MBN2 as such were not very controversial (only the arguments concerning them were). It is MBN3 that was hotly debated. With respect to the question whether beings of reason are totally mind-dependent, Mastri/Belluto identify three positions:

So far not everybody agrees [on] ... what being is to be attributed to beings of reason. [1] Some authors ... bestow some beings of reason with formal and actual being before any activity of the intellect. ... [2] Other authors assert that every being of reason has its essence independently of the operation of the intellect, although they confess that beings of reason completely depend on the intellect with respect to their existence; accordingly, the essences of beings or reason can be said to have possible-being-in-intellect, much as the essences of real beings have possible-being-outside-of-intellect. [3] Finally, some authors say that beings of reason are utterly dependent on the intellect with respect to all their being, not only existential but also essential.[3]

According to the first view (1), (at least some) beings of reason are mind-independent; according to the second (2) (which I call Potentialism) they are only existentially mind-independent but not essentially; and according to the third (3), they are totally mind-dependent. The first view had some followers before Suárez; its appeal stemmed from the identification of (some) beings of reason with extrinsic denominations.[4] Since extrinsic denominations were usually (with the exception of John of St. Thomas) regarded as real, there followed a highly counterintuitive conclusion that (some) beings of reason are completely mind-independent. This rather naïve or perhaps even absurd view, however, lost its appeal after Suárez, and so we can dismiss it. The real philosophical puzzle concerns the second and the third view. For if the second view is right, then besides the spaciotemporal world of mind-independent entities there is also a world of mind-independent essences: Some can become full-blown entities outside-of-our-minds, while others can become only entities in-our-minds. Mastri/Belluto defend the third view, i.e., the traditional Aristotelianism that denies the extra-world of shadowy mind-independent essences of beings of reason (MBN3).

In the following sections of the present chapter we take a closer look at Mastri/Belluto's arguments concerning MBN2 and MBN3. Mastri/Belluto address these questions in *quaestio* 1 (Whether there is being of reason and, if so, in what sense of 'being'). The *quaestio* is divided into two parts, dealing with the existence and total dependence of beings of reason, respectively.

2. Existence of Beings of Reason

The existence of beings of reason seems to have been acknowledged by almost every scholastic philosopher from the Middle Ages until Caramuel.[5] The justification of this thesis is based on authority (Aristotle, Aquinas, Scotus), on commonsense "scholastic experience," and on the alleged impossibility of the denial of this thesis. All these arguments were standard (see chapter 3, section C.2.2), and so I need not report Mastri/Belluto's particular phrasing of them. This would add nothing new to what Suárez has already said. Mastri/Belluto, however, present and answer several interesting objections against the existence of beings of reason; Suárez does not. First, there is an objection against self-contradictory beings of reason (section A.2.1). Then, there comes the main series of seven objections (A.2.2) of which I discuss here the first, third, and fifth.

2.1. AN OBJECTION AGAINST SELF-CONTRADICTORY
BEINGS OF REASON

The first objection that Mastri/Belluto raise against the existence of beings of reason concerns not so much beings of reason as such, but rather self-contradictory, sometimes also called "chimerical," beings of reason:

> Those who deny beings of reason reply that when the intellect conceives a rational horse, a corporeal angel, and other similar [objects], it does not by this act conceive something fictitious and apparent, which is to be called 'being of reason', but it conceives true and real rationality, true and real corporeality . . . and it connects these two [items] with a horse or an angel. Thus there is never any being of reason that would correspond to the act of fiction from the side of the object.[6]

The objection is that the alleged beings of reason consist of real components; hence, to speak strictly, there are no genuine beings of reason. To this objection Mastri/Belluto reply:

> Arriaga refutes this solution very well, . . . for when the intellect asserts of a horse that it is rational and of an angel that it is corporeal, it clearly does not predicate rationality that belongs to individual human beings nor corporeality that is derived from material things, but some *other* similar rationality, which is contrived by the intellect over and above possible rationalities. . . . Consequently, since . . . this other rationality, distinct from all the rationalities of human individuals, . . . is not real but fictitious and chimerical, a being of reason is truly conceived while we conceive a rational horse or a corporeal angel.[7]

Items such as a rational horse do not consist of a real rationality and a real corporeity but of a fictitious rationality and a fictitious corporeity, according to Arriaga and Mastri/Belluto. Thus, some sui generis fictitious component (which is the desired being of reason) must be postulated. Furthermore, even if we concede that, for instance, a rational horse is composed of a real rationality and a real horse, there is a nonreal unity or at least a nonreal application of the unity:

> Moreover, even if we yield to the objection, beings of reason are not avoided. For even if the rationality applied to a horse were real, the unity of this rationality with the horse would be quite fictitious and of reason.

And if you press further that the intellect applies to the "extremes" [i.e., for instance, to a horse and a rationality] a true unity, . . . a being of reason is still not avoided, for at least the application of this unity will be of reason—it is applied to things that cannot be united.[8]

Hence, it seems necessary that something or other is a being of reason: the rational horse, the rationality of such a horse, the unity of the rationality and the horse, or the application of unity to the rationality and the horse.[9]

2.2. OTHER OBJECTIONS

Mastri/Belluto identify seven other objections against the existence of beings of reason (q1n6–7), of which I mention three (first, third, and fifth, by Mastri/Belluto's counting).

One might argue that there are no beings of reason because no cause can be assigned to them (=Mastri/Belluto's first objection). It cannot be the intellect (to take the most plausible candidate), for it is a real entity and hence it is not supposed to produce nonreal effects. Mastri/Belluto reply that the intellect is capable of producing nonreal beings of reason, even though it itself is real.[10] (See also section C.1 below.)

Another objection against beings of reason goes as follows (=Mastri/Belluto's third objection):

[If there were beings of reason], there would be objects of the intellect that are not first knowable before they are known, which is a contradiction. For clearly what is *known* in the second "instant-act" presupposes that it is *knowable* in the first "instant-act."[11]

The objection assumes MBN3 (actualism) and draws an apparently absurd consequence from it: Suppose beings of reason are totally dependent on actual mental acts. Then there is nothing potentially knowable about them before they are actually known. For if there were something potentially knowable about them before they are actually being known, they would not be totally but only partially dependent on their being known. Then, however, beings of reason would be a peculiar sort of object, for their possibility/ potency to exist would not precede their actual existence. Hence, MBN3 seems to imply the denial of this principle:

PA: In order for something to become actual at t_2 it needs to be potential at an earlier t_1.

Since giving up this principle appears to be too high an ontological price for beings of reason, the conclusion (of the objection) is that there cannot be any beings of reason.

A simple way out would be to reject MBN3, which amounts to yielding to Potentialism, i.e., to the view that beings of reason are only partially (to be more precise, existentially) mind-dependent. But this is precisely what Mastri/Belluto do not want to do:

> It is true that beings of reason do not actually and formally have *being* [that is] *knowable* before they have their *being known*. . . . This, however, does not mean that they are in absolutely no way knowable before they are known, . . . for at least in their causes it can be said that they are first knowable before they are known, or even, in a certain sense, it can be said [of them] formally and actually—but not . . . as such . . . because to be actually known belongs to the essence of beings of reason, and if actuality belongs to the essence of something . . . then the potency does not precede its actuality. This is the reason why God's potency to exist is not said . . . to precede God's act of existence.[12]

As we see, Mastri/Belluto want to hold both MBN3 (beings of reason totally depend on actual mental acts) and PA (their being knowable in some sense precedes their being actually known). They qualify, however, the sense in which beings of reason satisfy PA and also restrict the validity of PA. The former they do in terms of the distinction between "virtual in its causes" potentiality and "formally actual as such" potentiality. Hence, although it is not true that beings of reason are formally potential objects before they are actual objects of the intellect, it is true that:

MBN4: Beings of reason are virtually potential objects before they are actual objects of the intellect.

In addition, Mastri/Belluto point out that the validity of PA is restricted, for it holds only for entities that are not essentially actual, and so it does not apply to God or to beings of reason. (For more on the compatibility of MBN3 and PA, see section A.3 below.)

Finally, one could object to MBN2 as follows (=Mastri/Belluto's fifth objection): Suppose there is some fictitious unity that corresponds, for instance, to the unity of an angel and a corporeity. In that case, the act whereby I think of a corporeal angel is true, for there really is some fictitious unity that corresponds to this act. But if this act is true, then I am not making up anything fictitious. So suppose that the act of thinking of a corporeal angel asserts a true real unity. Then, there is nothing fictitious about the object of this act, for there is only the real angel, corporeity, and unity. Either way, we dispense with postulating the category of beings of reason.[13]

To this objection Mastri/Belluto first reply that it assumes what it refutes, the existence of some fictitious unity.[14] Then they present their own view of how we become aware of the existence of beings of reason. The process has two phases: First we make an act directed toward the fictitious unity. This act, however, takes this unity as real. Thus, the act directed to this fictitious unity is false (or at least inadequate, for, to speak strictly, truth-values are applicable only to judgments). Then we make another (reflective) act whereby we figure out that the unity toward which the first act was directed is not real but fictitious. This reflective act is true.[15]

Having dealt with the objections against the existence of beings of reason (MBN2), Mastri/Belluto take up the question of whether they are essentially actual (MBN3).

3. Actuality of Beings of Reason

Actualism, the view that beings of reason are essentially actual, is a scholastic "default" view. It is common sense to hold that beings of reason are purely mind-dependent and that if nobody actually thinks of them, they do not exist. Thus, Mastri/Belluto do not feel the need to directly argue for this view but only to answer objections to it. Several of these objections are worth our attention:

> It is contrariwise argued against the second part of our thesis [MBN3] that . . . at least some beings of reason are actually there before the operation of the intellect. [1] First, because even without any operation of the intellect there *is* blindness in the eye . . . and other similar "things," which certainly do not import something positively real but of-reason. [2] Second, because beings of reason [must] first have *being knowable* before they have *being known* and first *possible being* before *actual being*— for,

before they *are* conceived as entities, they *can be* so conceived. . . . [3] Third, beings of reason [must] "exist" before the cognitive act by which they are known, . . . for every cognitive potency presupposes its object . . . and does not create it. For instance, the eyes presuppose colors and do not make them by seeing. . . . [4] . . . [5] Fifth, there are essential propositions of eternal truth about beings of reason, much as there are about real beings. Hence, much as it is argued that the truth [of these propositions] is [based on] real essences (from which actual existence is abstracted), so with beings of reason.[16]

The first objection points out that there are "lacks" in the world, such as blindness. And since these lacks cannot be real beings, they must be beings of reason. But these lacks are mind-independent: A blind person *is* blind no matter what anybody *thinks* of her. Thus, at least some beings of reason are mind-independent. To this objection Mastri/Belluto simply reply that blindness is a "real privation" and that it is neither a real being nor a being of reason.[17]

The second objection concerns again the compatibility of PA and MBN3. Does it belong to the essence of beings of reason that they are *actually* thought of? If so, how to square it with PA? Mastri/Belluto again invoke the distinction between virtual and formal; this time, however, they describe it a bit more. Virtual knowability means that the intellect has the power (*virtus*) to make up beings of reason, based on some foundation (which is a real and mind-independent entity). Virtual potentiality is extrinsic and derived from the intellect.[18] How are we to understand these claims? I take them to mean that the intellect creates beings of reason, so to speak, ex nihilo, not out of pre-given essences. But since the intellect has the power to do so, there is a sense in which these beings of reason could be said to be potential even before they are actualized. To speak strictly, however, there are no potential beings of reason. There are only people with the intellectual power to make up beings of reason based on some constrains "imposed" by mind-independent reality (a foundation).

The third objection argues from analogy with sense perception and cognition: Objects of our perceptive and cognitive acts exist prior to actual perception and cognition. Hence, MBN3 is false, for it implies that beings of reason do not exist prior to acts of knowing them. Mastri/Belluto reply that the (commonsense) assumption about the precedence of the objects of perception and cognition does not always hold, for intellects (and senses) can "know" things otherwise than they are, and in this case they *create* them.[19] This is also the case with beings of reason.

Finally (having skipped the fourth objection), we come to the objection that links together in an interesting way eternal truths about real beings and truths about beings of reason. It assumes that eternal truths about real beings are founded on some shadowy world of essences and that therefore truths about beings of reason should likewise be founded on it. Mastri/Belluto deny the assumption that propositions about real entities are founded on some essences independent of their (actual) existence; instead, they are founded on their *possibility* to become really existing (if real) or mentally existing (if of reason).[20]

Mastri/Belluto's fight for actualism was not victorious. Soon after the publication of *Disputations of Organon* (1639), a fellow Scotist, although from a different Franciscan order, John Punch, published a penetrating criticism of Mastri/Belluto's actualism. Punch's view, which abandons actualism, is such a radical departure from the "classical" theory that it should be recognized as one of the four fundamental Baroque theories of beings of reason (Potentialism). Given the intricacy and extent of Punch's discussion and of his exchange with Mastri/Belluto, I need to leave the investigation of Potentialim for another occasion.[21]

B. "Formality" of Beings of Reason

In the second question of Disputation 3, entitled "What beings of reason formally are and what their essence consists in," Mastri/Belluto aim to determine more precisely the nature, or, as they say, the "formality" of beings of reason.[22] This part of my study is divided into four parts. The first describes the *status quaestionis*; the second concerns Mastri/Belluto's arguments against extrinsic-denomination views; the third contains the final "official" description of their views (the five theses); in the fourth I discuss one of the interesting objections that were raised against Mastri/Belluto's view.

1. *Status quaestionis*

Mastri/Belluto identify five basic views on the "formality" of beings of reason:

(V1) EXTRINSIC-DENOMINATION VIEW

We already know this view, or rather family of views, from our discussion of Suárez (chapter 4, section B.2) and Hurtado (chapter 6, section B.1.2). According to it, beings of reason somehow consist in extrinsic denominations. This view comes in at least three varieties. First, the general extrinsic-denomination view claims that beings of reason are constituted by each and every extrinsic denomination. Second, the restricted extrinsic-denomination view claims that beings of reason are constituted only by extrinsic denominations derived from the intellect. Third, the restricted-fallibilist extrinsic-denomination view claims that beings of reason are constituted only by extrinsic denominations derived from false acts of the intellect.[23] For Mastri/Belluto's critical attitude toward these views, see below (section B.2).

(V2) RESULTANT EXTRINSIC-DENOMINATION VIEW

This view, or family of views, was unknown to Suárez, although it was discussed in detail by Hurtado (see chapter 6, section B.1.2). According to this view, beings of reason *result* from (emerge from) extrinsic denominations. Again, this view comes in at least three versions: Some authors say that for the emergence of beings of reason, any sort of extrinsic denomination will do; other authors say that the emergence of beings of reason requires extrinsic denominations from the vital powers; finally, some authors say that for the emergence of beings of reason only extrinsic denominations from the intellect suffice.[24] For Mastri/Belluto's critical attitude toward these all views, see below (section B.2).

(V3) OBJECTUALISM

Above (in A.1) we have already seen that Mastri/Belluto's MBN1 points toward Objectualism. The thesis was so far formulated in linguistic terms; here we get it strengthened by an ontological reformulation:

MBN1': Beings of reason *are* merely objectively in the intellect.

Under the heading of Objectualism, Mastri/Belluto subsume not just the view of Suárez (SN6; chapter 3, section C.2.1) but most ongoing controversies. Mastri/Belluto's characterization of Objectualism is worth quoting in full:

The third view [i.e., Objectualism], pioneered by Suárez and very wide-spread among recent thinkers, teaches that a being of reason is what has merely objective being in the intellect. . . . This is so explained that a being of reason is conceived by the intellect *in the manner of* a being as if it were something, when in fact it is nothing from the side of reality. . . . This explanation is taken from St. Thomas. . . . According to this view, two "aspects" pertain to beings of reason, namely, *nothingness*, which sets them apart from real beings, and *fictitious entitiveness* . . . , which sets them apart from pure nothing. . . . Various doubts and explanations emerge among the proponents of this [third] view. It is doubted [1] first whether this nothingness enters the formality of being of reason or whether it is related to it [just] materially. . . . But in whatever way nothingness is related to beings of reason, it is doubted [2] again what being [*esse*] a being of reason has, whether such that it not only excludes actual existence but also possible existence or whether it is sufficient that it only excludes actual existence . . . (as Hurtado . . . and Arriaga . . . hold). [3] Finally, it is doubted about this *fictitious entitiveness* (i.e., thinking of something in the manner of a real being although it is not) whether it . . . belongs to the concept of being of reason that it is conceived by the intellect otherwise than it is (which is generally held) or . . . whether this is just accidental to it (which is the view of Didacus . . . when he defends the view that it is also possible to make beings of reason when the intellect conceives a thing as it is).[25]

Beings of reason have two components: nothingness, which is the way they are not and which sets them apart from real beings, and fictitiousness, which is the way they are and which sets them apart from pure nothing. With respect to the first we may ask whether it somehow "enters" the "formality" of beings of reason. With respect to the second we may ask (a) whether it excludes just actual or both actual and possible existence, and (b) whether it requires misrepresentation or whether it is possible to think of / make up beings of reason qua beings of reason.[26] We shall see Mastri/Belluto's solution to these problems below (section B.3).[27]

(V4) SYNCRETISM AND (V5) SELF-CONTRADICTORISM

The fourth view consists in some sort of complicated "combination" of the previous views and seems to be somewhat obscure. Mastri/Belluto hesitantly also add a fifth view, self-contradictorism, according to which beings of reason emerge only if a real entity is applied to some other real entity that is incompatible with it.[28]

2. Against Extrinsic-Denomination Views

Mastri/Belluto's criticisms of the extrinsic-denomination views (both V1 and V2) are presented in the first article of *quaestio* 2. The article is entitled "The formality of beings of reason does not consist in an extrinsic denomination derived either from a real form or from an act of reason, whether it expresses a thing as it is or otherwise."[29] Since the rejection of extrinsic-denomination views was, after Suárez, almost universal, I only briefly highlight two points from these discussions, without following the details.[30]

First, there is the following argument for the nonreality of extrinsic denominations, by Smising and John of St. Thomas: In order for some denomination to be real we need a real denominating form, a real denominated thing, and a real unity between the two. Now in the case of an *extrinsic* denomination, the unity with the denominated thing cannot be real. For example, the stone as "seen" cannot be *really* united with its extrinsic form of "being seen." Hence the extrinsic denomination must be a being of reason. Mastri/Belluto reply that there is not just a unity of inherence (*unio per modum inhaesionis*) but also a unity of adherence (*unio per modum adhaesionis*). It is true that an extrinsic denomination does not *inhere* in the denominated thing, but it does really *adhere* to it.[31] Hence, the extrinsic denomination as such is not a being of reason.[32]

Second, Mastri/Belluto (discussing Scotus's *Ordinatio* 1d36) describe an interesting distinction between formal and material beings of reason. I quote the passage not because of the distinction but because it shows that the Scotists were not slavish followers of their master and that occasionally they criticized him:

When the Doctor [=Scotus], ... [speaking of] the being known that creatures have from eternity through the act of the divine intellect, calls it a 'being of reason' ... he does not in fact speak of the diminished being of the creatures but of the relation that is founded in them *toward* God's knowing ... [and] hence it is common in the school of the "subtles" to distinguish material or formal (or, as they say, "made up" or "left behind") being of reason. The former, also called 'actual', has fictitious being from an intellect;, the latter, also called 'potential', is what is capable of having such being from the conceiving or contriving intellect. Thus, extrinsic denominations as such are material beings of reason insofar as they can be conceived [in this way]. . . . Occasionally [even] Scotus himself confuses formal and material being of reason.[33]

Against the resultant extrinsic-denomination view (V2), let it suffice to say that Mastri/Belluto reject it on account of there being nonrelative beings of reason, such as negations/privations. These would be (according to Mastri/Belluto) inexplicable on this view.[34]

3. Five Theses about the Formality of Beings of Reason

In the second article of *quaestio* 2, Mastri/Belluto "identify and declare" the formality of beings of reason. They first divide their solution into five theses; then they deal with objections.

The first thesis is that beings of reason are impossible (i.e., that they cannot exist), or, in other words, that beings of reason are completely distinct from real beings, actual or possible.[35]

MBN5: Beings of reason cannot exist in actual reality.

Matri/Beluto draw several consequences of MBN5 of which I would like to highlight two: (1) The golden mountain is not a being of reason;[36] (2) Hurtado's Fallibilism is false. The first consequence is obvious. (The golden mountain is possible, and hence it cannot be a being of reason in the sense of MBN5.) The second consequence is not surprising either. Mastri/Belluto claim that:

> From [MBN5] it follows that it is false what Hurtado and Arriaga said . . . namely, that in order to form a being of reason it is not necessary for the object to be impossible but it is sufficient that it is not in act as it is represented, although it is otherwise possible. . . . You may insist [with Hurtado/Arriaga] that the proposition *Peter is running*, when in fact he is sleeping or sitting, is something fictitious and it has its complete being only objectively in the intellect, although it is not impossible that Peter is running, ergo, etc. We reply by denying the assumption, namely, that [this alleged] being of reason exists merely objectively in the intellect so

that it neither exists nor can exist outside of it. (Otherwise a rose in winter would be a being of reason since it does not actually exist in reality.) We could also accept the assumption that it is impossible for Peter to run when in fact he is sleeping or sitting, but this is a hypothetical impossibility (as they say) *in sensu composito* (i.e., to run and at the same time not to run) and there needs to be an impossibility as such [*simpliciter*]. . . . The distinction introduced by Arriaga in order to settle this controversy— namely, that there are two sorts of being of reason, namely, chimerical/ impossible and possible—is quite worthless, for possibility destroys the essence of beings of reason.[37]

Mastri/Belluto simply insist that beings of reason must be *ex definitione* (from their essence) impossible-to-exist. It is not sufficient that they cannot exist, given that they do not exist (*in sensu composito*: if ~p then ~◊p); they must be impossible *simpliciter* (~◊p).

The second thesis of Mastri/Belluto is that beings of reason are not pure nothing. The proof is simple: Pure nothing is pure and cannot be admixed with something positive. But beings of reason "contain" always something positive—for instance, blindness is a lack of *sight* and not of *hearing*.[38] Hence, beings of reason are something "in-between" real being and pure nothing.[39]

MBN6: Beings of reason are not pure nothing.

The third thesis appears to claim that the negation of real beings does not enter the formality of beings of reason, for then this formality would be a peculiar positive/negative "mixture." And this is unacceptable for Mastri/ Belluto. But interpreted in this way, the third thesis and the argument for it directly contradict the previous second thesis (MBN6).[40] Hence, I must confess that I do not quite understand the third thesis. Fortunately, the thesis does not seem to play any significant role further on. More illuminating, however, is Mastri/Belluto's comment that they make in passing when discussing the third thesis:

Experience teaches us that we often think of beings of reason without thinking whether they exist in reality or not, . . . for in order to form a being of reason it is sufficient to think of something that does not exist in reality . . . in fact a being of reason would be made up even if the intellect thought that this were a true being, when in fact it is not, and so a being of reason is formed by the very fact that it is an object of the intellect as a being, regardless of whether the intellect knows that it is a being in reality or not; the only difference is that if it knows it, it only makes it up but is not deceived; if it does not know it, it makes it up and at the same time is deceived.[41]

Mastri/Belluto strictly distinguish fiction in the sense of being deceived and in the sense of making up. And this is again a conceptual improvement over Suárez (see chapter 5, section E.2).

The fourth thesis states that beings of reason depend on acts by which something is conceived in the manner of a *true real* being.[42]

> MBN7: Beings of reason are thought of in the manner of true real beings.

No proper defense of MBN7 is made; it is justified by the mere appeal to the authority of both Aquinas and Scotus.

In the paragraph concerning the fourth thesis, Mastri/Belluto make (as if in passing) two further claims. First, they point out that 'being' in 'real being' and 'being of reason' is not meant purely equivocally but by an analogy of attribution—or "perhaps by an analogy of proportionality":

> MBN9: Beings of reason are beings in an analogical sense of 'being'.[43]

Second, they endorse the principle that nothing can be thought of in the manner of a nonbeing.[44] This is an important principle, for, as we have seen, the possibility of thinking "in the manner of a nonbeing" makes Suárez's theory inconsistent (see chapter 5, section E.1).

Finally, in the fifth thesis, Mastri/Belluto present their own view and a sort of "real" definition of being of reason:

> Fifth, from the previous discussions we gather that a being of reason is what is or can be an object of the intellect as if it were in reality when in fact it does not exist and cannot exist. It follows from this that their entire being [*esse*] is objective, mental, and fictitious. Also, they are said to be "shadows" of real beings and their entity is said to be "shadowy" since they are made up by our intellect (which is accustomed to real being) as

if [they were] real. . . . When we acknowledge that its being does not consist in being an extrinsic denomination, we must assert that there is some fictitious being that results in things from the operation of the intellect. Through this being, both the essence and the existence of beings of reason is explained. . . . Insofar as the being of reason is in an act, we say that it is existential being, and insofar as it is considered possible (abstracted from actual being) it is said to be essential being. Hence we deliberately say that a being of reason is what is or can be an object of the intellect as if it were [in reality].[45]

This last thesis repeats previous claims (MBN5 and MBN7), but it also qualifies MBN1′ by modalizing it:

MBN1″: Beings of reason are or *can be* merely objectively in the intellect.

The modalization takes into account the results of the previous debate concerning MBN4 (actualism) and PA (potency precedes actuality; see above, sections A.2.2 and A.3): Beings of reason "virtually" precede their actual existence and so there is an acceptable way to speak about beings of reason that merely *can* become objects of the intellect. By this, Mastri/Belluto do not want to give up total dependence on actual acts (MBN3).

4. Objections

Mastri/Belluto identify four objections against their five theses; I am going to mention only an objection against MBN7 (beings of reason as thought of in the manner of true real beings), because it importantly elucidates Mastri/Belluto's theory.[46] The objection (ascribed to Didacus and Smising) points out that we need to think of beings of reason not just in the manner of real beings but also in the manner of beings of reason. Otherwise we would never know beings of reason as they are, but would forever mistake them for real beings.[47] Mastri/Belluto reply that there are in fact two types of acts of knowing beings of reason: direct and reflexive. In virtue of the first type of act we conceive of beings of reason as they are not (i.e., in the manner of real beings), whereas in virtue of the second type of act we conceive of them as they are. The direct acts give them their (kind of) being, which is already presupposed and "discovered" by the consequent reflexive acts. This reply importantly specifies MBN7:

> MBN7′: Beings of reason are always thought of directly in the manner of real beings (which in fact they are not).

This is compatible with:

> MBN8: Beings of reason are sometimes thought of reflexively in the manner of beings of reason.

Thanks to the reflexive acts, we also get to know that in the previous direct acts we had known beings of reason otherwise than they are.[48]

In passing we might ask: What does it mean to think of something "in the manner of " (*per modum*) something else? Does it mean that whenever I think of a being of reason I make a false judgment that it is a real being? This is certainly one of the possible answers (held, for instance, by Hurtado; see chapter 6) but Mastri/Belluto disagree with it. According to them, to think of something "in the manner of" does not necessarily involve judging. As they say in another context: "It is something quite different to falsely apply one real being to another real being *and* to conceive what is not a real being as similar to a real being (as we hold)."[49] By the term 'in the manner of', Mastri/Belluto mean primarily the product of the first operation of the intellect (of concept formation), although they would also acknowledge beings of reason resulting from the second and the third operation of the intellect.[50]

C. Causes, Attributes, and Division of Beings of Reason

This section is divided into three parts. In the first I describe Mastri/Belluto's view on causes of beings of reason; in the second and the third parts, I deal with their views on the attributes and division of beings of reason, respectively.

1. Causes

According to Suárez, beings of reason have no formal, material, or final cause, but they must have an efficient cause (in an analogical sense of 'cause';

see chapter 4). Against this, Mastri/Belluto, in *quaestio* 3, defend the view that beings of reason need to have all four types of causes, not just the efficient one.

MBC1: Beings of reason have all four types of causes.

This is especially obvious with respect to the final cause, for beings of reason can be useful to us in many ways.[51] It is also obvious that at least some beings of reason (such as chimeras) have a *suo modo* formal and material cause, for they are conceived of as if they were material substances.[52] Here Mastri/Belluto openly point out their disagreement with Suárez.[53] With respect to the objection that a real being (the intellect) cannot via real causality produce nonreal entities, they seem to explicitly acknowledge a sui generis, "metaphorical" sort of causality that is peculiar to the mind.[54] (Suárez tries to avoid this conclusion, which makes his views on causes obscure; see chapter 4, section A, and chapter 5, section E.1.)

MBC2: The causality involved in the production of beings of reason is "metaphorical" (sui generis).

In *quaestio* 4, Mastri/Belluto take up the question of how the intellect and the will make up beings of reason. As usual, Mastri/Belluto start with an overview of the ongoing debates and available positions. The debates concern (a) which faculties (intellect, will, imagination, memory, or external senses) produce beings of reason; (b) which acts (absolute, comparative, direct, or reflexive) produce them; and (c) which operations (first, second, or third) of the intellect.

Mastri/Belluto divide their *quaestio* into two articles. In the first, they claim that no other faculty than the intellect and the will can make up beings of reason.

MBC3: Beings of reason are made up by the intellect and the will only.

This thesis is certainly true about the intellect and probably true about the will.[55] There are two interesting debates in this article, one against Suárez, the other against Arriaga. Against Suárez (who claims that the imagination somehow makes up beings of reason; see 4.B.4), Mastri/Belluto replies that it is false to claim that the imagination would be "powerful" enough to make up (self-contradictory) beings of reason. It only puts together sensible appearances as such that cannot form something self-contradictory. It is, for instance, possible to have an animal look partially like a stag and partially like a goat, but we need an intellect to put together the incompatible *essences* of a goat and of a stag.[56] Thus, Mastri/Belluto disagree with the slogan that "ens imaginabile latius patet quam ens possible" (the concept of imaginable being has wider extension than the concept of possible being), which was widespread among logicians at the time.

Against Arriaga, who argues that even the external senses make up beings of reason, Mastri/Belluto point out that it is not sufficient that we *perceive* something that is not.[57] We would have to perceive something that *cannot be*. And this is impossible. Thus, illusions of color or the bent appearance of a stick in water do not form beings of reason.[58] Moreover, to confirm their view, Mastri/Belluto (in a Cartesian vein) point out that, with respect to the external senses, the intellect can never err if its judgments remain limited to mere appearances. Since beings of reason require that something is conceived of otherwise than it is, perceptual illusions are not enough to make them up.[59]

In the second article of *quaestio* 3, Mastri-Belluto defend two theses: (a) Beings of reason are made up by every type of act (direct, reflexive, etc.),[60] and (b) there are beings of reason resulting from the first, the second, and the third operation of the intellect.[61]

MBC4: Beings of reason are made up by both direct and reflexive acts of the intellect (and the will).

MBC4 seems to disagree with Suárez. Thus, Mastri/Belluto draw a distinction between two senses of 'reflexive', to show that the apparent disagreement is merely verbal. They point out that 'reflexive' may mean that the acts making up beings of reason presuppose some other acts in the past that were directed to real beings. Mastri/Belluto agree here. But there is another, more appropriate sense of 'reflexive', one that refers to acts directed to other acts. In this stronger sense of the word, the act that makes up beings of reason need not be reflexive.[62]

MBC5: Beings of reason are made by the first, second, and third acts of the intellect.

With respect to MBC5, Suárez does not seem to have had a fixed opinion, but there is at least no evidence that he would have rejected it. As we saw in chapter 6, it was Hurtado who rejected MBC5, for in his view only the second operation of the intellect makes mistakes and hence is capable of making up beings of reason.[63] Mastri/Belluto reply that chimeras and other beings of reason may also be made by the first operation of the intellect. Misrepresentation (a result of the first operation) is sufficient to make up beings of reason; we do not need to make false judgments.[64]

In *quaestio* 5, Mastri/Belluto take up the question of whether God can cause beings of reason. This question seems tangential but in fact yields some surprising results and deserves a deeper analysis that cannot be provided here. I merely summarize Mastri/Belluto's theses.

The answer to the question whether God can make up and/or know beings of reason depends on the previous discussions. For those who claim that beings of reason are extrinsic denominations, it makes no sense to deny that God knows them. On the other hand, for those, such as Hurtado, who claim that beings of reason are the results of false judgments, it makes no sense to affirm that God makes them up. Thus, the question is meaningful only within the context of Mastri/Belluto's opinions on the nature (formality) and the formation of beings of reason.[65]

Mastri/Belluto distinguish five views on this question—note the increased complexity of the discussion as compared to what we saw in Suárez (chapter 4, section C) and Hurtado (chapter 6, section A.2). The first view, defended by Vázquez, holds that God does not know beings of reason (not even ours), for to know them would be to make them up, which is incompatible with his perfect essence.[66] The second view, accepted by Arriaga and many others, holds that God both knows and makes up beings of reason, for imperfection applies to them (as objects), not to God (as knower).[67] The third view, represented by Suárez, Rubio, and many others, holds that God does not make up beings of reason but knows them as they are made up by us or can be made up by us.[68] The fourth view, held by Meurisse and perhaps John of St. Thomas, holds that God makes up some beings of reason (relations) while not others (self-contradictory beings).[69] Finally, there is also the fifth view of Didacus, who claims that God can "add" some further objective being to those beings of reason that are made up by us.[70]

Mastri/Belluto's thesis consists of two parts: First, God knows beings of reason made up by us.[71]

MBC-G1: God knows beings of reason made up by us.

In this, they agree with the third view, proposed by Suárez and others. Second, however, Mastri/Belluto claim that it is a matter of equal probability whether God makes up his own beings of reason or not.[72]

MBC-G2: Whether God makes up his own beings of reason is undecidable.

One cannot but be reminded of Kant's antinomies of reason here. Of course, there is a long and twisted way from Mastri/Belluto to Kant, but we observe here the interesting fact that some traditional scholastic authors came to the conclusion that there are well-formed but still rationally intractable problems.

2. Attributes

Quaestio 6 concerns the attributes of beings of reason. In its details it does not seem to be particularly interesting, for if beings of reason are *suo modo* beings, then it is only to be expected that they have *suo modo* attributes.[73]

MBN10: Beings of reason have all the attributes that real beings do.

Nevertheless, the very fact that this *quaestio* is included here indicates two significant facts: First, this question is a novelty introduced by Mastri/Belluto themselves. This observation is confirmed by the fact that Mastri/Belluto do not provide the usual introductory classification of various views. Consequently, in spite of Mastri/Belluto's ardent commitment to Scotus, they can by no means be considered "conservative" repetitors of traditional Scotism. Second, the treatment of the attributes of beings of reason is an implicit acknowledgment that there is a kind of symmetric "mirroring" between real and nonreal entities. Hence, in spite of Mastri/Belluto's unequivocal commitment to realism, to superficial readers the distinction between the science of the real and the "science" of the nonreal might appear blurred.

3. Division

In *quaestio* 7, Mastri/Belluto take up the division of beings of reason. They are aware that the traditional scholastic view divides beings of reason into negation, privation, and relation. It is generally believed that this division comes from Aquinas.[74] Mastri/Belluto, however, point out that this division is plagued with difficulties—first, because negations and privations do not seem to belong to it, since they are real nonbeing(s).[75] Suárez's defense that negations and privations can be taken in two ways—as real (nonbeings) and as beings of reason—fails, as the latter are positive. Hence, there are only positive fictitious entities, no negative ones.[76]

Second, this division is not exhaustive, since there are many species that are not contained in it. This concerns especially self-contradictory beings of reason. We have seen (in chapter 5) that, along the two lines of defense, Suárez presents several arguments in defense of the exhaustivity of this division:

Self-contradictory beings of reason may be subsumed under negations, for they are nonbeings. Mastri/Belluto reply that this defense fails for two reasons: First, the same can be said of relations;[77] second, there is a difference, overlooked by Suárez, between thinking *a non-animal*, that is a human being and a lion, and *an animal* that is a human being and a lion. The former could be perhaps counted as a negation, but not the latter.[78]

Self-contradictory beings of reason are outside of the traditional division, for they have no foundation in reality, and hence there cannot be any science about them. Mastri/Belluto argue that this defense fails for three reasons: First, one can think up all sorts of positive but nonrelative beings of reason, which means that, even if we grant to Suárez the thesis that self-contradictory beings of reason are outside of the traditional three-member division, there remain many other species not included in the traditional division; second, even self-contradictory beings of reason have some foundation in reality, although not proximate but remote (but see below);[79] third, it is not true that self-contradictory beings of reason have nothing to do in science; on the contrary, they are the best examples of the definition of beings of reason in terms of "what is merely objectively in the intellect."[80]

Given all these difficulties, Mastri/Belluto conclude that the traditional division cannot be saved and that one must acknowledge that there are as many categories of beings of reason as there are categories of real beings:[81]

MBD1: Beings of reason are divided into as many categories as there are categories of real beings.

Let me return now to the notion of the *foundation* of beings of reason. In the context of the division of beings of reason, Mastri/Belluto present an interesting discussion of this notion. They claim that (1) the foundation of beings of reason cannot be the imperfection of the intellect, for then all beings of reason would have a foundation, especially those that are considered not to have such a foundation, namely, self-contradictory beings of reason; (2) the foundation of beings of reason cannot be real being in the image of which beings of reason are contrived, for then, again, all beings of reason would have a foundation in reality, even those that are considered to have no such foundation.[82] In Mastri/Belluto's view, the foundation is "the occasion that urges [necessitates] the intellect to form the being of reason."[83] It is not, however, clear to me how Mastri/Belluto's view differs from the 2-view, for the "occasion" is also a real being. (What else could it be?) The difference might perhaps consist in that the real being is a foundation taken in the material sense, whereas the occasion selects the formal aspect of this real being—i.e., it is the foundation from the formal point of view.

One might notice an apparent contradiction in what Mastri/Belluto say: First they claim that all beings of reason even self-contradictory objects, such as chimeras, have a foundation in reality. (This is one of the reasons why they reject Suárez's claim that the traditional three-member division applies only to beings of reason with a foundation in reality.) Here, however, they claim that beings of reason are divided into those with a foundation in reality and those without it. Mastri/Belluto themselves notice this apparent contradiction and draw the following distinction: There is a proximate and a remote foundation in reality. Every being of reason has at least some *remote* foundation in reality, although only some but not every being of reason has a *proximate* foundation in reality.[84]

D. Evaluation of Mastri/Belluto's Objectualism

Let us return now to the results of our exegesis of Mastri/Belluto's first two *quaestiones* about the nature of beings of reason and compare these views with Suárez's.[85] I shall argue that Mastri/Belluto's Objectualism is superior to Suárez's not just concerning the causes, attributes, and division (the thesis that I have defended in section C) but also with respect to the nature of beings of reason. We start with the following set of Mastri/Belluto's claims:

MBN1 ": Beings of reason are or *can be* merely objectively in the intellect.

MBN2: There are beings of reason.

MBN3: Beings of reason "emerge" only when *actually* thought of (= their being is *completely* mind-dependent, both existentially and essentially).

MBN4: Beings of reason are virtually potential objects before they are actual objects of the intellect.

Concerning MBN1", Suárez might be expected to complain that Mastri/ Belluto acknowledge not just actual but also potential beings of reason. However, we need to keep in mind that MBN1" is balanced with MBN3 and explained by MBN4. Hence, to speak strictly, there are only *actual* beings of reason, and only when we speak broadly do we include *potential* beings of reason. Consequently, Mastri/Belluto's MBN1"–MBN4 can be viewed as a legitimate *development* of Suárez's theory with respect to a challenge (namely, how to square actualism with the principle that potency precedes actuality) that did not occur to him.

MBN5: Beings of reason cannot exist in actual reality.

MBN6: Beings of reason are not pure nothing.

MBN7': Beings of reason are always thought of directly in the manner of real beings (which in fact they are not).

MBN8: Beings of reason are sometimes thought of reflexively in the manner of beings of reason.

MBN9: Beings of reason are beings in an analogical sense of 'being'.

Suárez accepts MBN5 but appears to reject MBN6. However, it is only in passing that Suárez makes the claim that beings of reason are nothing, and so it is hard to say how seriously he is committed to this view.[86] At any rate, he does not explicitly say that beings of reason are "pure nothing," so he might have in mind "nothing in extra-mental reality," which is trivial, and which is also acceptable for Mastri/Belluto.

Concerning MBN7, the situation is more complicated. Mastri/Belluto hold the view that beings of reason must be thought of *directly* in the manner of a real being (MBN7), even though they may be thought of *reflexively* in the manner of a being of reason (MBN8). Similarly they would probably have said that a nonbeing must be thought of directly in the manner of a real positive being, even though it may be also thought of reflexively in the manner of a mind-independent lack of being. Such views are consistent with the principle that nothing can be thought of *directly* in the manner of a nonbeing.

But what would Suárez say with respect to MBN7 and MBN8? I believe that he has two stories to tell. According to his "official" story, a nonbeing is indeed thought of only reflexively in the manner of a nonbeing, for the intellect knows directly only beings.[87] Here Suárez would be in complete agreement with Mastri/Belluto. Then, however, he also says something rather different—for instance:

> Blindness ... can be conceived in two ways. First, negatively only—by conceiving that in a certain organ there is no power of sight; in this way there arises no being of reason, since nothing is conceived in the manner of a being, but only in the manner of a nonbeing. Then, however, the intellect [may start to] conceive blindness as a condition affecting an animal or an organ. ... It is now that the intellect conceives of something in the manner of a being, and since it does not conceive a real being, it is properly forming a certain being of reason.[88]

First, we note that Suárez explicitly admits the possibility of thinking of something (for instance, blindness) in the manner of a nonbeing. But is this to be understood as direct or reflexive thinking? Suárez continues:

> Something *similar* can be said about beings of reason founded on extrinsic denominations, such as the relation of being seen. For here *also* ... when the intellect *directly* conceives that the thing is seen ... it does not conceive or form any being of reason.[89]

Here Suárez suggests that just as we can have direct cognition of extrinsic denominations (as they are), we can also have direct cognition of nonbeings (as they are). But even if this interpretation is incorrect, for Suárez there are two equally legitimate ways of thinking about nonbeing: Negations/ privations can be thought of *either* insofar as they are real "removals" of forms *or* insofar as they are beings of reason. Consequently, Suárez carries out a detailed phenomenological comparison of the two types of negations and privations (see chapter 5, section C). Conspicuously, no such procedure can be found in Mastri/Belluto. Why? First, because negations/privations "as they are in reality" are *pure nothing* (although as beings of reason they are *not* pure nothing: MBN6). Hence, it makes no sense to compare two "nothings," in that there is nothing to compare. Second, because the direct act must first *give* being (*esse*) to the being of reason so that eventually another, reflexive act may "discover" that such being is not real. (See above, B.4.) Metaphorically, we could perhaps say that we must somehow "carve out" beings out of nonbeing in order to think of them or compare them with something else. Hence it makes no sense to think of the plurality of negations/privations as they are in reality, for pluralization and quantification indicate that we already take them as beings of reason.

Now Suárez's introduction of real nonbeings next to beings of reason (his "unofficial" story) makes his theory ultimately incoherent (see chapter 5, section E.1). Mastri/Belluto avoid this problem by recognizing as items in their ontology only real beings and beings of reason (perhaps with the addition of pure nothing).

Concerning MBN9 (the analogy between real beings and beings of reason): This analogy is at the core of Suárez's teaching about the nature and existence of beings of reason. In this Suárez agrees with Mastri/Belluto. A difference of opinion might concern the *kind* of analogy between real being and being of reason, but Mastri/Belluto do not take up this issue in Disputation 3, and hence I leave this question open.

To sum up: With respect to the nature of beings of reason, Mastri/Belluto defend a more mature and detailed theory than does Suárez. First, they recognize the challenge of Potentialism and try to avoid it by keeping the commitment to the total dependence of beings of reason on actual acts while acknowledging a weaker (extrinsic) sense in which there are also potential beings of reason. Second, Mastri/Belluto avoid the error that Suárez makes when he introduces real nonbeings and nonbeings of reason as ontological items next to real beings and beings of reason.[90] Mastri/Belluto's treatise on beings of reason is probably the real climax of the scholastic philosophical research on beings of reason. The treatise (nearly thirty-five thousand words) is almost twice as long as the treatise of Suárez.[91] In comparison to Suárez, the authors prudently focus more on foundational issues—namely, on the nature and the causes of beings of reason—and pay less attention to secondary issues concerning various phenomenological details of the division of beings of reason. Although they did not aspire to be "followers of Suárez," their theory of beings of reason is a modified version of Objectualism, to which Suárez also adhered.[92]

8

Caramuel's Linguistic Eliminativism

In this chapter I deal with the theory of beings of reason of Juan Caramuel y Lobkowitz (1606–82). Caramuel was a Luxemburgian-Czech Cistercian, born in Spain, who distanced himself from all established philosophical schools of the Baroque era (he often praised Thomas Aquinas but explicitly denied being a Thomist). Caramuel takes up beings of reason on several occasions, lastly in his essay *Leptotatos* (1681). The chapter is divided into three parts. First, I discuss Caramuel's views on the nature of beings of reason (section A). Second, I turn to his views on other issues, namely the causes and the division of beings of reason (B). Third, I make a brief evaluation of his theory (C). The aim of this chapter is to identify Caramuel's main contribution to the debates about beings of reason. We shall see that Caramuel takes Self-Contradictorism, according to which beings of reason are nothing but self-contradictory items, as a point of departure and then he argues for their complete elimination.[1]

A. Nature of Beings of Reason

My discussion of Caramuel's views on the nature of beings of reason is divided into four sections. First, I say a few words about the main intention of Caramuel's *Leptotatos*, which, unlike the other scholastic writings dealt with in this study, is not an instance of the standard Baroque genre, namely, cursus, but rather an essay. Second, I describe Caramuel's self-contradictorist point of departure. Third, I take up the central issue of Self-contradictorism, which concerns the unity of beings of reason. And fourth, I discuss Caramuel's reply to the "ontological" argument for beings of reason.

1. Caramuel's *Leptotatos*

Leptotatos latine subtilissimus is one of the last of Caramuel's philosophical works, published a year before his death. It is useful to translate its full title, because it nicely describes its purpose:

Leptotatos, which means "The Most Subtle" in Latin, is a new and clever work, indispensable to professors of noble disciplines. It shows that not only gentile philosophers of old, but even Christian Fathers of the Church, both Latin and Greek, [in many places] where they should use proper concepts, stumbled and got altogether stuck and could not express what they wanted due to defective terminology. Thus, in order to apply an appropriate medicine against this widespread disease, this work employs a very easy, concise, and expressive language.[2]

The title indicates Caramuel's central innovation, the idea that one could *construct* an artificial language for metaphysics.[3] Caramuel's language modifies the verb 'to be' (*'esse'* in Latin). This artificial language was first sketched in *Grammatica audax* (1638, 1654), and *Leptotatos* contains its final version. It has three parts, called "dissertations": Metalogical, Philosophical, and Theological. In the first dissertation Caramuel explains his artificial language, and in the following two he applies it to various problems in order to show how useful it is. The second dissertation is divided into three parts: The first deals with negations, the second with beings of reason, and the third with the notion of abstract and contract (*sic*) beings. The third dissertation has only one part dealing with various issues such as the existence of God, his knowledge (ideas), foreknowledge, and omnipotence. The book is dedicated to Aquinas, with the wish to hear from him the words that Jesus Christ addressed to Aquinas: "You have written well of me, John." It might be of historical interest that Leibniz made detailed excerpts of the first and third parts of *Leptotatos* (Sousedík 1990).

Let me briefly describe Caramuel's artificial language. According to the scholastics, all predication involves the verb 'to be'. The meaning of this verb, however, may change from context to context. In Caramuel's view, the confusion between various meanings of 'is' stands behind many metaphysical disputes. His artificial language is to serve as a neutral means of communication between different metaphysical systems. Different meanings of 'to be' express different "modes of being." Caramuel distinguishes among five basic modes of being: 'sare' (conjugation forms: *sam, sas, sat . . .*), 'sere' (*sem, ses, set . . .*), 'syre' (*sym, sys, syt . . .*), 'sore' (*som, sos, sot . . .*), and 'sure' (*sum, sus, sut . . .*). The first mode, 'sare', means, in standard scholastese, "to have essence," "to have quidditative being," "to have essential being." For example, "Human beings *sant* animals," "Paternity *sat* a relation." The second mode, 'sere', means "to have an existence now." For example, "Petrus *set* homo," of an actually existing person. The third mode, 'syre', means "to have simultaneous eternity." For example, "Deus *syt*." The fourth mode, 'sore', applies to the mode of being of prime matter, which is completely dependent for its existence on the existence of the composite. The last mode, 'sure', means "to have some duration," "to exist at some time." For example, "Adam *sut*" (because he was), "you, the reader, *sus*" (because you are), "Antichrist *sut*" (because he will be).

The five basic modes can be further combined. Thus, 'sare' (*habere essentiam*) and 'sere' (*habere existentiam*) can be combined into 'saere', which is (an alleged) intermediate mode of being. It applies to possible entities, since they are possibly existing essences. The basic modes can also by modified by inserting 'i'; this will turn them into "imperfect" modes (*modos essendi imperfectos*). In particular, we should mention here three of these modes: 'saire', which is the mode of existence of beings of reason that can be but actually are not objects of reason; 'seire', which is the mode of existence of beings of reason that are actually objects of reason; and 'syire', which is the mode of existence of the eternally existing (but created) world, if any. Every basic or derived mode of being can be turned into "factitivum" by inserting 'm'. For example, "the Divine Intellect *samit* possible creature" (= God produces possible entities in *what* they are); "an efficient cause *semit* an effect" (= an efficient cause produces an effect in its existence); "God the Father and God the Son *symunt* God the Holy Spirit," etc.

Further details of Caramuel's artificial onto-language need not concern us here. In spite of his claim that his onto-language is indispensable, everything he says can be also easily expressed in ordinary philosophical Latin. In fact, Caramuel himself almost always translates the statements in his artificial language into ordinary Latin in parentheses. His achievement probably does not consist so much in what he constructed (its usefulness is dubious) but rather in the novel idea that one could have a language that is artificial, neutral (avoids commitments of a particular metaphysical system), and rigorous (amends deficiencies of ordinary language). In coming up with this idea he anticipates the ideals of Leibniz's *characteristica universalis*.

2. Self-Contradictorist Point of Departure

Following the standard scholastic habit, Caramuel starts his discussion of beings of reason by distinguishing among the various meanings of the term 'being of reason'. The analysis is presented by means of a diagram:

Meanings of 'Being of Reason'
    Active: (A)
    Passive:
        Real (B)
        Intentional
            Subjective (C)
            Objective
                Impossible (D)
                Possible (E):
                    Logical
                    Physical
                    Psychical
    "Inhaesive" (F)[4]

Let me briefly explain this diagram. The *active* sense of the term 'being of reason' (A) refers to the intellect itself. This sense is dismissed by Caramuel as idiosyncratic. Caramuel also disregards the sense (F), which refers to intelligible species. From the ontological point of view, both (A) and (F) items count as real. Now we come to the *passive* sense of the term 'being of reason', which refers to the "products" of the intellect (B)–(E). These products can be either real (here: extra-mental) (B) or intentional (here: intra-mental) (C), (D), and (E). Examples of (B) include artifacts, which are designed by reason. Examples of (C), characterized as *subjective*, include mental acts, regardless of whether directed to *possible* or *impossible* objects. Both (B) and (C) are, ontologically speaking, real entities.[5] Only (D) and (E) remain. Caramuel dismisses *objective possible* beings of reason (E). Addressing those who admit possible beings of reason, Caramuel says that human reason cannot produce possibility since we cannot "decide" what is possible and what is not. It is the divine intellect that determines the possibilities (and thus "produces" possible entities), and the divine will that gives actuality to some of these possible entities.[6]

Thus we are left with (D)—in the proper sense beings of reason are *objective impossible* entities:

> CN1: The expression 'being of reason' can be used in several senses but in the proper sense it is something objective and impossible (=merely objective).

In order to characterize what this "objective and impossible" means, Caramuel approvingly quotes from *Universalis Philosophia Scholastica* (1654) of Richard Lynch:

> Being of reason is to be distinguished as objective and subjective. The former is commonly defined as *what has merely objective being in the intellect*. This objective being in the intellect means to be an object of the intellect, to be known by it, and to be completely devoid of all [other] being, positive and negative, actual and possible. [1] This is why it is not common to classify possible creatures among [objective] beings of reason, although they are nothing in actuality; to the contrary, because of their possible being, it is common to call them 'real beings'. And this is as it should be. [2] Similarly, lacks, such as shades, are not [objective] beings of reason either, because they have their negative and diminished being even apart from being an object of the intellect and they are known by it. Thus only what cannot exist, even under absolute power, as it is thought, i.e., that what is thoroughly fictitious and known otherwise than it could [ever] be, is objective being of reason. . . . properly and strictly speaking, being of reason is what is completely outside the extension of 'real being'.[7]

Objective being is contrasted here with subjective being. The latter is not controversial (Suárez makes a similar distinction;, see chapter 3, section C.2.1). The status of objective being is more controversial. Lynch agrees with Suárez that possible being is real (1) and then explicitly says what Suárez's text only implied, namely that there is "negative being" (=nonbeing) which is real (2). Caramuel takes the reality of nonbeings so much for granted that he does not even discuss negations in the context of beings of reason—the two issues are quite disjoint for him.

In Caramuel's view beings of reason are something impossible, but in what sense? They are not merely "impossible to exist in actual reality" (as for Suárez; see chapter 3, section B)—they are "the extrinsic or intrinsic union of incompatible things."[8] As we shall see below, Caramuel argues that there can be extrinsically united self-contradictory beings of reason, which, however, are real (since extrinsic denominations are real)—and hence they are not beings of reason in the strict sense—and that there are no intrinsically united beings of reason.[9]

> CN2: A being of reason (if any) is self-contradictory, i.e., it is the extrinsic or intrinsic union of incompatible things.

Caramuel's view very much differs from Suárez's Objectualism according to which self-contradictory beings are only one *kind* of beings of reason. In Suárez's view, although no being of reason can exist in actual reality, only some beings of reason are intrinsically self-contradictory. This is not surprising. What is surprising is that Caramuel does not even consider Suárez's view; self-contradictorism seems to him to be an obvious truism.[10] Both Suárez and Caramuel use the same shibboleths such as "a being of reason is what is merely an object of reason" or "what has merely objective being in the intellect," but their interpretations of these phrases differ dramatically.[11]

3. Central Issue of Self-Contradictorism: Unity of Beings of Reason

If beings of reason consist in the extrinsic or intrinsic unity of incompatible things, the central question becomes: What sort of unity do they have? Caramuel takes up the question of unity in LEP s4n177–81, while evaluating a dispute between Valentín de Herice and Georges de Rhodes and very briefly in LEP s13n203–s14n204, while evaluating a dispute between Arriaga and Lynch.[12]

The starting point of Herice-Rhodes's dispute is Herice's claim that beings of reason are in fact real beings. In Herice's words:

> A being of reason is a quite *real whole*, consisting of *real parts*. Although its parts cannot exist in the way in which they are an object of the intellect, they are united by the cognition [i.e., cognitive act] itself; there is nothing on the part of the object that corresponds to this cognition.[13]

Caramuel interprets Herice's view as a thesis about the ontological status of the *unity* of beings of reason: Their unity is something *actual* (i.e., real) and *extrinsic*, derived from the intellect. Rhodes, in turn, following the consensus of the experts (*communis sententia*), attacks Herice's view as a "bad novelty" and claims that the unity of beings of reason is something *fictitious* and *intrinsic* (*ex parte obiecti*).[14]

After some preliminary clarifications (between: not being intrinsic/not possibly being intrinsic; intrinsic unification/extrinsic unification; unification of concepts or words/unification of the things expressed), Caramuel resolves the dispute in four steps (the fifth is a tangential comment about nominalism, which we leave aside):

STEP 1: AN ATTEMPT IS NOT SUCCESS

> When we make up beings of reason, we conceive of things which are possible as such, although taken together they are incompossible. This is obvious from the fact that whenever we think of a goat-stag we *try* in our apprehension to conceive [together] essences of a goat and a stag, which [otherwise] exist in reality. I use the word 'try' on purpose . . . because our human intellect cannot apprehend [incompatible] essences, but instead apprehends sensible colors and shapes. This is [also] shown in our experience because the painter who depicts a goat stag with his brush expresses it by lines and colors in the picture, similarly as he does by an idea in his intellect.[15]

Caramuel does not believe in the capacity of the human intellect to apprehend two incompatible essences as *united* in one object. Rather, our intellect apprehends the "externals," such as the colors and shapes, for instance, of a goat and a stag and then combines these "externals" into the mental image of a goat stag. Such an "external" combination into a mental image is not impossible. Something quite different would be the unity of two incompatible *essences*, where something would not only *look like* but also be a goat stag. In his view, however, this is never accomplished.[16]

STEP 2: THE POWERS OF LANGUAGE TO UNITE

The intellect cannot unite two incompatible *essences*. What about language? Caramuel says:

> For the unification of the goat-essence and the stag essence *extrinsic* unity is sufficient. To understand this claim, notice that there is a difference between simultaneously conceiving of two natures and conceiving of the

natures as united or identified. For instance, the proposition "Toledo and Seville are royal cities" is true. Nevertheless, the conjunction 'and' does not mean here that these cities are really conjoined—they are quite distant from each other—it means that they are connected in the mind and in speech.[17]

Language enables us to connect words and hence it is language that Caramuel sees as the cause of the extrinsic unification of incompatible predicates (and essences expressed by them):

CC1: The (efficient) cause of extrinsically united self-contradictory objects is language.

Caramuel further recalls the tradition of speculative grammar, where the connection between *things* and *words* is clearly distinguished:

Gerard Joannes Vossius writes in *De Arte Grammatica*: "Conjunction . . . is an expression which conjoins words and sentences. Clearly, to conjoin *things* and *words* is not the same. Disjunctive conjunctions make *things* disjoint but they (and all other conjunctions) make *sentences* connected to other sentences. . . ." Now, in the light of Speculative Grammar I consider our difficulty resolved and settled. When Herice thinks of a goat-stag, he thinks of two natures, namely the goat nature *and* the stag nature. Here the word 'and', which is a conjunction and a unity, has the force of a disjunction, because it does not hold on the side of the object but on the side of the intellect and language; it signifies the two essences, which cannot really be united intrinsically, as really and de facto, although extrinsically, united in the intellect and language.[18]

We see that, according to Caramuel, the alleged impossible entities are united *really* but not *intrinsically*.

CN3: There are no intrinsically united self-contradictory beings of reason.

The unity of beings of reason is extrinsic, which means that it is not on the object side but on the intellect side or, more precisely, on the language side. People often are mislead by the fact that 'and' is a conjunction; we think we are connecting things when in reality we are only connecting sentences.

STEP 3: THERE IS NO SUI GENERIS FICTITIOUS UNITY BUT ONLY A REAL MISPLACED UNITY

At this point Caramuel comes to the core of Herice-Rhodes's dispute: What unity is there between the elements within a being of reason? We have seen that it is extrinsic unity, but is this unity real or nonreal (= fictitious)?

> [1] *I am certain and without doubt that* fictitious unity *as far as the substance and the essence* [quidditas] *is concerned is an incoherent concept. I am so firmly convinced of this thesis that I consider the contradictory thesis improbable.* [2] *But I am not so certain and without doubt that the human being cannot conceive of true and real distinction or unity and to locate it intellectually where there is none.* . . . From this it is clear that *unity* can be called *fictitious* for two reasons [*caput*] [1] First, this name can be understood substantially; such unity, I say, does not make sense. [2] Second, however, this name can be understood [as something real], which is placed [somewhere] instead of something fictitious . . . Now . . . some recent authors [such as Rhodes] take the expression 'fictitious unity' in this latter sense; they claim that fictitious unity is nothing else than true [unity] placed where it cannot be.[19]

Caramuel distinguishes between two views here: (1) The unity is fictitious in the sense of some special, nonreal, type of unity; and (2) the unity is fictitious in the sense of a real misplaced unity (this is Rhodes's view). Caramuel considers the first view absurd. The second view is also rejected—see below, the next step—but more hesitantly and not for clear reasons.

STEP 4: FAREWELL TO (SELF-CONTRADICTORY) BEINGS OF REASON

Finally, Caramuel endorses Herice's view (preferring it to Rhodes's view):

> *The opinion of Herice is smart and plausible: if we explain beings of reason according to it, nothing impossible will be said.* The argument is obvious: every entity to which Herice is committed is true and real; [and] their extrinsic unity is [also] true and real: . . . things which cannot be united intrinsically . . . can be conjoined extrinsically (i.e. in mind or language).[20]

The view of Herice and Caramuel gets rid of "genuine" (nonreal) beings of reason:

> CN4: There are extrinsically united self-contradictory "beings of reason."
> CN5: The extrinsically united "beings of reason" are real beings.

We see that Caramuel distinguishes between intrinsically and extrinsically united beings of reason (CN3 and CN4). He even introduces new terminology for them:

> Beings of reason . . . can be reduced to two classes: Although every being of reason necessarily unites two incompatible things, in some [i.e., *paro-entities*] there is an *extrinsic union* of the incompatible things, which consists in the mental act of thinking the things together. In other [i.e., *pseudo-entities*] there is an *intrinsic union* on the part of the object, which consists in . . . real unity grasped by the intellect and placed where it cannot be. . . . The former will be aptly called legitimate πάροντα and the latter illegitimate ψεύδοντα.[21]

Both types of beings of reason are eliminated as a sui generis ontological category, opposed to real being (CN5). The advantage of this view is parsimony; beings of reason are a special case of real beings: Two real entities are extrinsically united (= a real unity) in virtue of language/intellect (a real cause).[22]

B. Other Issues

There are other issues concerning beings of reason that Caramuel discusses in *Leptotatos*. In this section I briefly discuss two such issues. First, there is an obstacle that Eliminativism must face, namely, the "ontological argument" for beings of reason. Caramuel needs to deal with it. Second, there is the question of the causes of beings of reason.

Suárez and other Baroque scholastic authors commonly employ an argument for the existence of beings of reason which might be called "ontological" (see chapter 3, section C.2.2). According to this argument beings of reason must exist; otherwise we could not even assert that they do not exist. Caramuel addresses the issue in the following passage:

"Titius denies beings of reason; and he knows *what* he denies (he does not think that he can deny beings of reason blindly); thus he knows them and consequently he also makes them up, because in this matter it is the same to know and to make up." This argument is weak. . . . I concede that Titius knows what beings of reason would be *if* they existed, but not what they are, since they do not exist. And I deny that the one who knows what they would be makes them up; in order to make them up it is required to understand what they are. The one who conceives of a circular triangle, makes up a being of reason; but not the one who conceives of a circle, if *per impossible*, it were a triangle.[23]

The point is clear: If I deny the existence of beings of reason, let us say of a circular triangle, I do not *first* make up a circular-triangle and *then* deny the (intra-mental) existence of it. This would be a contradictory procedure. The correct analysis of the denial is that I *first* think of a circle and *then* I assert that *if* this circle *were* a triangle, it would be a being of reason. But the antecedent is false. Thus there are no beings of reason. We see how Caramuel's Russellian strategy enables him to get rid of ontological commitments to beings of reason.

Concerning the causes, Caramuel does not have much to say (the discussion is contained in LEP s7n189–s8n196). The question for him divides into two questions. First, what is the cause of beings of reason in the legitimate sense, i.e., as the extrinsic unity of real beings which is itself real (πάροντα)? Second, supposing that beings of reason existed in the illegitimate sense too (ψεύδοντα), i.e., as the intrinsic fictitious unity of real beings, would they have a cause? The first question has been already answered above: It is language (CC1). The second question is answered positively: Illegitimate beings of reason, if they existed, would need some cause.[24] First of all, they would need an efficient cause.[25] Here Caramuel distinguishes between the cause of the (imperfect) existence of beings of reason, their "seire," where the cause is language,[26] and the cause of the (imperfect) essence of beings of reason, their "saire," where the cause is God.[27]

cc2: The efficient cause of the "existence" of intrinsically united beings of reason (if there were any) would be language.

cc3: The efficient cause of the "essence" of intrinsically united beings of reason (if there were any) would be God.

In a dialogue with Antonio Bernaldo de Quirós, Caramuel briefly argues that illegitimate beings of reason (if they existed) would have no material cause, but they would have an exemplar cause and a final cause.[28] Later on he argues that they would have no formal cause.[29]

> CC4: Intrinsically united beings of reason (if there were any) would have no material and formal cause but they would have an exemplar and final cause.

Concerning the question whether God makes up and/or knows beings of reason, Caramuel has more to say in Article II. Here are the main results of this article:[30]

> CCG1: God does not make up but knows extrinsically united beings of reason as made up by humans.
>
> CCG2: God would know intrinsically united beings of reason if they were indeed made up by humans, similarly as he knows human errors.

Caramuel says virtually nothing about the division of beings of reason. In his view, negations/privations have nothing to do with beings of reason, hence are treated elsewhere, and second intentions are real, hence are also excluded from treatment in the context of beings of reason.[31]

C. Evaluation of Caramuel's Eliminativism

Let me summarize and briefly evaluate Caramuel's contribution to the Baroque debates over beings of reason. Concerning the nature, Caramuel holds that:

> CN1: The expression 'being of reason' can be used in several senses but in the proper sense it is something objective and impossible (=merely objective).
>
> CN2: A being of reason (if any) is self-contradictory, i.e., it is the extrinsic or intrinsic union of incompatible things.
>
> CN3: There are no intrinsically united self-contradictory beings of reason.
>
> CN4: There are extrinsically united self-contradictory "beings of reason."
>
> CN5: The extrinsically united "beings of reason" are real beings.

Caramuel distinguishes between intrinsically and extrinsically united beings of reason (ψεύδοντα and πάροντα). Caramuel denies the existence of intrinsically united beings of reason—or rather, to be more precise, he declares the very term of 'intrinsically united beings of reason' to be meaningless.[32] He acknowledges the existence of extrinsically united beings of reason, but in the sense of real existence—beings of reason are just two words joined together, such as 'square circle', that otherwise cannot be applied together to anything. Beings of reason in the traditional scholastic sense, as something nonreal, are eliminated.

Is it true that we cannot think of intrinsically united self-contradictory objects, as Caramuel claims? Let's consider, for instance, a mathematician trying to disprove (or to prove indirectly) Goldbach's conjecture. She starts by assuming the existence of an even number n, such that it is not the sum of any primes. If the conjecture is true, the number n is impossible. Is this not an instance of thinking an impossible object? However, if it is possible to think of a nonobviously self-contradictory number, why should it be impossible to think of an obviously self-contradictory object? We may feel some *psychological* repugnance at thinking obvious impossibilities but that does not mean we cannot think them.

Caramuel might object that when we try to *think* of self-contradictory objects we only succeed in visualizing nonexisting objects that are not genuinely self-contradictory. The famous Dutch painter Maurits C. Escher, for instance, might try to depict a square circle by arranging "sensible colors and shapes" in a way that might lead one to exclaim, "That's a square circle!" But, of course, it would not *be* a square circle. It would just look like one. To this argument I would reply the following: There is no problem in *defining* an object x such that it has the properties P and Q, where P is the property of being a circle and Q the property of being a square. Such an object x would not only *look like* but truly *be* a contradictory object. And we are capable of thinking of it, even if it cannot exist in reality but only in thought. Hence, Caramuel's elimination of intrinsically united self-contradictory objects is not warranted.

Concerning the causes of beings of reason Caramuel holds the following theses:

CC1: The (efficient) cause of extrinsically united self-contradictory objects is language.

CC2: The efficient cause of the "existence" of intrinsically united beings of reason (if there were any) would be language.

CC3: The efficient cause of the "essence" of intrinsically united beings of reason (if there were any) would be God.

CC4: Intrinsically united beings of reason (if there were any) would have no material and formal cause but they would have an exemplar and final cause.

CCG1: God does not make up but knows extrinsically united beings of reason as made up by humans.

CCG2: God would know intrinsically united beings of reason if they were indeed made up by humans, similarly as he knows human errors.

Caramuel again divides the discussion into the causes of intrinsically and extrinsically united beings of reason. The latter are created by language. The former would be caused also by language insofar as their existence goes and by God insofar as their essence goes. This interesting idea of a joint efficient cause does not seem to have been elaborated by Caramuel, and so it is hard to evaluate it. Even more underdeveloped are Caramuel's considerations of the division of beings of reason. In fact, Caramuel says nothing explicit about it; however, the fact that he divides the discussion of nonbeing and of being of reason into two separate treatises is significant enough: We have seen the problems introduced by Suárez when he acknowledged real nonbeings and negative beings of reason. The traditional scholastic view (Objectualism) was that we cannot think of nonbeing and hence we substitute negative beings of reason for it. The continuation of this tradition is represented by Mastri/Belluto. The other possibility is to acknowledge the possibility of thinking of real nonbeings but then the negative beings of reason become superfluous—hence, we get rid of them. The continuation of this line is represented by Caramuel. This line of thought seems to have been prevalent toward the end of the seventeenth century.[33]

Cautious elimination of beings of reason as nonreal items of our ontology had already occurred among the Jesuits before Caramuel. Still, the Jesuits at least preserved overt loyalty to the *expression* 'being of reason'. It is Caramuel who is probably the first mainstream post-Suarezian philosopher who openly ridicules the whole traditional preoccupation with beings of reason. This is the opening passage of *Philosophical Dissertation*, part 2:

We ask, Whether those very recent metaphysicians who say that they can . . . conceive of a nonbeing as a being and . . . that in this way they make up a being of reason, in consequence [also] say that they can conceive of a being as a nonbeing and thus form a nonbeing of reason or a nothing of reason? . . . Since in my opinion it is altogether impossible to conceive of a nonbeing as a being, I also . . . hold that it is similarly impossible to think of a being as nonbeing. In other words, if I were to acknowledge that beings of reason are possible, in consequence I would need to be induced or seduced to asserting that it is possible to conceive of . . . nothings of reason.[34]

Caramuel's argument is clear: If one insists that there are nonexisting entities that we treat *as if* they existed, then one should also accept existing entities which we treat *as if* they did not exist. And since the consequent is absurd, so is the antecedent.[35]

Caramuel always tackles philosophical problems via the analysis of language. Not only that, he even claims that language has peculiar powers which exceed mental/intentional powers as such. Accordingly, beings of reason turn out to be beings of language:

We have argued in *Metalogica* that neither the imagination, nor the intellect, nor the will can make up such entities [i.e., beings of reason]. In spite of this we claim that they can be made up *by language*. We have introduced into scholasticism 'beings of language', a term not known or heard of before. We have defined it as what consists of two incompatible formalities, which can be put together neither by God nor intentionally by humans; . . . but they can be in reality put together by words. Examples of such monsters of language include *irrational human being, square triangle*, and *shimmering shade*.[36]

Caramuel's preoccupation with language and its tricks seems to have been unique to him among seventeenth century scholastic thinkers. In the emphasis on the power of language, Caramuel anticipates the linguistic turn of twentieth-century analytic philosophy.

With Caramuel we have reached the end of my reconstruction of some of the Baroque scholastic debates about beings of reason. Caramuel is by no means the last scholastic philosopher worthy of scholarly attention; he provides, however, an important insight into the character of later Baroque debates about beings of reason. The debates got technically more and more advanced but became increasingly preoccupied with rather insignificant aspects of the issue. In Suárez beings of reason were supposed to address big issues involving nonbeing and intentional being; in Caramuel and many later Jesuit authors the focus had narrowed down to rather marginal questions concerning the ontological status of self-contradictory objects.

Conclusion: Lessons from the History of Philosophy

During the Middle Ages, beings of reason were discussed in various contexts: logical (second intentions), epistemological and metaphysical (universals), natural (privation as a principle of change), ethical (evil), and theological (God's relation to creatures). These discussions were normally affected by their contexts and prompted by concerns with other philosophical problems. Until the publication Suárez's Disputation 54 (1597), there seems to have been no attempt to treat beings of reason comprehensively, within a unified theory.[1] Suarez's theory of beings of reason promised to give a definitive solution to the issues of mind-dependency, nonbeing, impossibility, fictions, and relations, among others. Unfortunately, solving all these problems proved to be too many birds for one shot. Various objections were raised against Suárez's theory during the seventeenth century, competing theories of beings of reason emerged, and eventually Suárez's theory was discarded—we may notice, for instance, that beings of reason were a significant category in ontology at the beginning of the seventeenth century but became marginalized toward its end.[2]

The aim of my study was to reconstruct at least in part the dialectics behind this dramatic shift of opinion on beings of reason in scholasticism between 1600 and 1680. I have argued that Suárez's theory of beings of reason is beset by various philosophical problems and that Suárez stands at the beginning and not at the end of a series of first-rate scholastic philosophers of the Baroque era. Hence, in view of the philosophical diversity in the Baroque era, it is not anymore acceptable to claim that Suárez was "the main channel by which scholasticism came to be known by modern classical philosophers."[3]

As I have said in chapter 1, there are various reasons for historians of philosophy to undertake serious research into Baroque scholasticism—little work has been done in this area, and any investigation of this period helps to fill an important historiographical gap.[4] It would not be warranted to dismiss Baroque scholasticism as an outgrowth of medieval scholasticism, just as it would not be warranted to dismiss Baroque art as an outgrowth of Gothic art.[5] Furthermore, the thought of famous early modern philosophers such as Descartes, Locke, Leibniz, Kant, and Brentano did not arise out of nothing but rather developed within the broader philosophical context existing at that time. Without knowledge of this context, one cannot properly evaluate these modern philosophers and see their true accomplishments (or shortcomings). But perhaps the reasons to do research on Baroque scholasticism are not just historical but also systematic. As I have pointed out in chapter 2, there are several topics related to beings of reason in contemporary philosophy, such as negative truth-makers, holes, fictions, the ontological status of logical and mathematical entities, predication, etc. Could a comparison with well-developed historical views prove inspiring for, or challenging to, this contemporary work? Anthony Kenny in the second volume of his *New History of Western Philosophy* writes:

> I am by profession a philosopher, not a historian, but I believe that the history of philosophy is of great importance to the study of philosophy itself. It is an illusion to believe that the current state of philosophy represents the highest point of philosophical endeavour yet reached. These volumes are written with the purpose of showing that in many respects the philosophy of the great dead philosophers has not dated, and that one may gain philosophical illumination today by a careful reading of the great works that we have been privileged to inherit. (Kenny 2005, xi)

When I started to work on this project, I wanted not just to fill a historiographical gap and to vindicate the historical value of Baroque scholasticism but also to show that from Baroque scholastic culture one can "gain philosophical illumination" even today. The more I worked on this project, the less feasible it became to carry out the systematic part of it. It became increasingly clear to me that there is too much material in the Baroque era that should be taken into account. Thus, it is not sufficient to read Suárez and then assume that other Jesuit authors are "Suárezians" holding similar views. It is necessary to read other Jesuit authors as well because, contrary to popular clichés, they are epigones neither of their medieval colleagues nor of Suárez nor of each other. (And besides the Jesuits there are also many Baroque Scotists, Thomists, and other thinkers.) In addition, I have realized that there is also another problem: The category of beings of reason is rather heterogeneous and fluid.[6] As I started to unravel the skein of issues with which they are linked, it became apparent that there are many threads that should be followed. The Baroque heading 'being of reason' covers too many disparate problems from the contemporary point of view, and so to bring contemporary and Baroque philosophical culture into dialog is more difficult than I expected.

Given the extent of work needed to understand even the basic flow of argumentation in the Baroque debates, I eventually limited the focus of my project to history. I hope to have shown beyond reasonable doubt that post-Suárezian debates were no "pointless subtleties" and that post-Suárezian works were no mere "summaries of scholastic philosophy." When we pay closer attention to Baroque scholasticism we see that much lively and rigorous research was carried out. Even though Baroque authors were inspired by medieval authors, and paid little attention to the modern non-scholastic philosophy of their time, their research was by no means simple "epigonism" (*pace* Jansen 1936a, 28). The Baroque debates are exciting once their deep dialectics is understood. It is only to be hoped that other studies are produced that relate the knowledge of the Baroque debates to the work of the early modern non-scholastic philosophers and also to concerns that are more contemporary.[7]

In this book I have analyzed just one topic that any complete Baroque philosophical system was obliged to deal with. Given the absence of research on Baroque scholasticism, this kind of piecemeal analytical approach is at this stage necessary. We first need to get hold of the subtleties of Baroque philosophical culture. However, eventually the demand for studies that are more synthetic should grow. The strength of Baroque scholasticism may lie precisely in its bold attempts to develop comprehensive philosophical and theological visions. Thus, to see Baroque achievements adequately—against the background of various shortcomings—investigations into Baroque systems as such, taken as wholes, will be needed.

Baroque philosophical culture put emphasis on collaborative effort. It would be beyond the capacity of any one philosopher to produce single-handedly such a monumental body of arguments and views that any full-fledged Baroque philosophical and theological system consists of. Consequently, however, it is now beyond the capacity of any one historian to carefully read, analyze, and reconstruct the flow of argumentation among competing Baroque philosophical and theological systems. For their proper investigation, besides single-author studies such as this, the need for collective research and the use of computerized information tools is especially urgent.

Progress in philosophy can be more obviously noticed not in the answers that are being suggested but rather in the detailed treatment of problems that are thrown into fuller relief. First we see in a dim mirror, then more clearly. The so-called 'being of reason' is a term that has been lost to contemporary metaphysics—unlike some "perennial" Western philosophical words, such as 'being', 'essence', 'identity', or 'cause'—but the cluster of issues that the term 'being of reason' once veiled is still present, although in various mutations and under different names. Today no less than in the times of Parmenides.[8]

APPENDIX: OUTLINES OF THE TREATISES

A. Suárez's Metaphysical Disputation 54

Note: The division and the descriptive titles that follow are based on the original titles and the division of Suárez's Disputation 54, but I have often modified them to lend them greater lucidity and organization. The Disputation is about eighteen thousand words.

INTRODUCTION

Why do we deal with beings of reason at the end of this book on metaphysics? (n1–2)

THE NATURE OF BEINGS OF REASON (S1)

The first view: There are no beings of reason (n2)

The second view: Beings of reason are real beings (n3)

The true view: Beings of reason "must be granted" but they have "merely objective being in the intellect"—the first conclusion (n4–7)

Why we make up beings of reason—the second conclusion (n8)

Beings of reason are called 'beings' in an analogical sense—the third conclusion (n9–10)

THE CAUSES OF BEINGS OF REASON (S2)

Beings of reason have no formal, material or final cause (n1)

The first view: Beings of reason have no efficient cause (n2)

The true view:

Beings of reason have an efficient cause in an analogical sense—the first conclusion (n3)

B. Hurtado's Metaphysical Disputation 19

Note: There are two versions of Metaphysical Disputation 19. The original 1615 version only has about five thousand words and it has three sections. What is a being of reason? (s1) Does God know beings of reason? (s2) Some clarifications (s3). The 1624 version, at thirteen thousand words, is much longer.

C. Mastri/Belluto's Logical Disputation 3

Note: Mastri/Belluto deal with beings of reason in logic. Their third logical disputation is entitled "On Being of Reason and Second Intentions." It is about thirty-five thousand words.

Solution to the question about the act by which beings of reason are made (a2)

Whether any intellect can effect beings of reason (q5)

THE ATTRIBUTES OF BEINGS OF REASON (Q6)

Whether beings of reason have their proper attributes and what they would be (q6)

THE DIVISION OF BEINGS OF REASON (Q7–8)

What kinds of beings of reason there are (q7)

On the particular species of being of reason which is called 'second intention' (q8)

What is second intention, how it is made, and how it differs from the first intention (a1)

Here second intentions are compared with the first and also among themselves (a2)

D. Caramuel's Philosophical Dissertation, Part 2

Note: Caramuel's treatment of beings of reason in Leptotatos is highly interesting and readable. Its structure, however, is disorganized. Caramuel often deals with the same or a related topic in more than one passage, without making an attempt to join the passages together or to reference them. He seems to have been writing extremely quickly and without revisions. He probably did only one rereading, only to add occasional inserts indicated in his text by '[*]'. Large portions of the text consist in comments and analyses of long passages quoted from other authors. The descriptive titles of the sections of his text are mine. The Dissertation, Part 2, is about twenty three thousand words.

DISSERTATION 2: PHILOSOPHICA

Part 1: On negations

Part 2: On paro-entities and pseudo-entities which are called in Latin 'entia rationis'

Article 1: Are there beings of reason? What are they? (LEP 168–209).

1. On the importance of linguistic analysis (LEP 170)

2. A linguistic analysis of the concept of being of reason; its division (LEP 171–75)

3. What science studies beings of reason? (LEP 176)

4. Do painters make up beings of reason? On the nature of unity of beings of reason (LEP 177–81)

5. If the unity of beings of reason is extrinsic, the human intellect can make them up, but if the unity is intrinsic, it cannot; on the distinction between "legitimate" beings of reason (paro-entities, united extrinsically) and "illegitimate" being of reason (pseudo-entities, united intrinsically) (LEP 182–83)

6. The "states" of pseudo-entities: quidditative, possible, and existential (Actualism vs. Potentialism) (LEP 184–88)

7. On the causes of beings of reason (LEP 189–91)

8. More on the causes of beings of reason (LEP 192–97)

9. The alleged examples of pseudo-entities are often examples of possible entities (LEP 198)

10. The process of making up beings of reason does not consist in conceiving one thing instead of another (LEP 199–200)

11. The intellect cannot assent to evidently false propositions (LEP 201)

12. Beings of reason cannot be simple (LEP 202)

13. More on the nature of beings of reason (LEP 203)

14. The proponents of beings of reason lack arguments to convince opponents (LEP 204)

15. Arriaga on whether beings of reason exist before an act of the intellect (Actualism vs. Potentialism) (LEP 205)

16. Second intentions are real relations, not beings of reason (LEP 206–7)

17. Pseudo-entities are impossible entities which receive imperfect objective being from the intellect (LEP 208)

18. Beings of reason and the divine intellect (LEP 209)

*Article 2: Whether, supposing that there are paro-entities and
pseudo-entities, God and the angels would understand or
make them up (LEP 210–232)*

1. All possible and intelligible perfections are to be attributed to God
   (LEP 210–11)

2. Two sorts of beings of reason need to be distinguished: paro-entities
   and pseudo-entities (LEP 212)

3. God does not make up paro-entities although he knows them as made
   up by humans (LEP 212)

4. Whether angels know paro-entities made up by humans (LEP 213)

5. Neither humans nor God nor angels make up pseudo-entities (LEP
   214)

6. If pseudo-entities existed, God would know them (LEP 215)

7. Are human beings the first causes of beings of reason? (LEP 216)

8. More on whether God makes up paro-entities (Lalemandet, Rubio)
   (LEP 217–19)

9. More on whether God makes up pseudo-entities (LEP 220–32)

Preface

1. "It would be useful to have a detailed study of the history of non-existent objects, but I am sure that this would be the culmination of a life's work if done well. . . . One must be aware of the dangers which await one who enters the treacherous waters between the Scylla of ignorance of the history of philosophy and the Charybdis of simplistic formulations of that history" (Pershyk 1993, 68).

2. The papers are based on "Suárez and Meinong on Beings of Reason and Non-existent Objects" (1999), Canteñs's PhD dissertation. Since Meinong is famous within the analytic tradition for his discussion of non-existing objects, it seems natural to see whether there are some historical scholastic influences on Meinong. Canteñs in his dissertation made a comparison but did not try to track actual influences of scholastic authors on Meinong. There are attempts to show that Brentano was a link between medieval or postmedieval scholasticism on the one hand and Meinong on the other. See Boccaccini (2010).

3. At this point I should mention Christopher Shields's paper "Shadows of Being: Francisco Suárez's *Entia Rationis*" (2012), which appeared in the final stages of the preparation of the manuscript of this book into print. Shields has developed an interpretation according to which "*ens rationis* is a non-existent subject of an existing extrinsic denomination, or, more precisely, that to which an extrinsic denomination would attach if there were something really existing as a subject for that extrinsic denomination. On this approach, which we may term the *tethered counterfactual account*—*tethered* because *entia rationis* are perforce tied to acts of intellection and *counterfactual* because these acts treat them as if they existed though they do not—*entia rationis*, despite their non-existence, may be implicated in the cause nexus." Shield's paper ingeniously challenges the standard interpretation of Suárez; and there are indeed a few passages in which Suárez writes in a way which is compatible with Shield's account. However, Suárez's treatise as a whole seems to make little sense unless we assume the traditional scholastic view that beings of reason have a special mode of mind-dependent (purely objective) existence/being.

4. Thus, we should stop using epithets such as "the last original scholastic philosopher" (Ross 1962, 736). Suárez just happens at the moment to be the

only known representative (together with John of St. Thomas) of a vigorous Baroque philosophical culture. I agree, however, that Suárez could be called the "Father of Baroque Philosophy" given that his comprehensive philosophical synthesis was chronologically the first in a series of other similarly ambitious syntheses. See Pereira and Fastiggi (2006) and Pereira (2007).

5. In order to make complex scholastic theories more transparent and their discussion more rigorous, starting with chapter 3, I shall assign names to the theses drawn from a given passage. The system of abbreviations used for these names will be explained with the first occurrence of a thesis in chapter 3, section A.

6. I have followed American aesthetic "feelings" in including commas and periods into double quotes; my single quotes, however, since they are used strictly for reference to linguistic expressions, follow logic and leave commas and periods outside.

7. I have adopted a free attitude both with respect to existing translations and to Latin originals. I try to let Baroque authors speak for themselves in today's idiom (hence also my profuse use of quotes). That I do not use existing translations should not be understood as a criticism of them. It just means that I have other priorities. John P. Doyle, for instance, adopted a more literalist approach: "[Suárez's] writing style, like that of most Latin scholastics, is dull, matter-of-fact, and repetitious to a fault. His sentences frequently run on and his paragraphs often seem interminable. Nevertheless, I have tried to translate his text as faithfully as possible. . . . Although I was often tempted, I did not restructure any of his often too long paragraphs" (1597/1995, 55).

1. Scholasticism of the Baroque Era

1. An earlier version of this chapter appeared as "In Defense of Baroque Scholasticism" (Novotný 2009). I have corrected some mistakes, updated bibliography, and made small additions in the endnotes.

2. For Ukrainian scholasticism, see Symchych (2009, forthcoming). From among the Baroque scholastics who entered into intellectual dialogue with the Far East, the famous Italian Jesuit Matteo Ricci merits mention (1552–1610; see Ricci et al. 1603/1985). Other important authors include Ippolito Desideri (1684–1733), known for his encounter with the Tibetan dGe Lugs Pa tradition (Pomplun 2010), and Prosper Intorcetta (1625–96), who finalized translations of classical works attributed to Confucius into Latin (Intorcetta et al. 1687). Martino Martini (1614–61), with the help of Cosma Chu, is said to have begun translation of Suárez's *Metaphysical Disputations* into Chinese, but the translation remained incomplete and was never published. See Bertuccioli (1998, 518). Baroque authors published several systematic surveys and analyses of Chinese philosophy, one of the less known being published in Prague by the Belgian Jesuit François Noël (1651–1729); see Kolmaš (2008).

For a general account of the encounter between China and the West, see Mungello (2009).

3. It was Richard Popkin, among others, who has shown convincingly the inadequacy of the "two-party view" of seventeenth-century philosophy by identifying the equally strong "third force,"—namely, a combination of science, theosophy, and millenarianism (Popkin 1992, 91–119). Unfortunately, Popkin underestimates the sociological and intellectual importance of seventeenth-century scholasticism, which could in fact be called the "first force" of seventeenth-century thought.

4. It needs to be said, however, that the interest of Anglo-American scholars in seventeenth-century scholasticism seems to be growing. José Pereira, for example, has recently published two books manifesting the extent and value of Baroque philosophical and theological culture (Pereira and Fastiggi 2006, Pereira 2007). John P. Doyle is also to be mentioned in light of his continued record of publications dealing with Baroque authors (Salas and Doyle 2010, Salas, forthcoming). With respect to Suárez, the situation is even more exciting, with the appearance of several new works dealing with his thought—see Scarbi (2010), Schwartz (2012), Hill and Lagerlund (2012), and Salas and Fastiggi (forthcoming). There are also some excellent works dealing with scholastic natural philosophy, such as Des Chene (1996, 2000), and Hellyer (2005).

5. For a similar list of labels in use, see Forlivesi (2006, 106–10). Forlivesi prefers the label 'Academic philosophy'. This label is appropriate on its own but it does not delimit the period/culture chronologically. It is close in meaning to "scholasticism," and if we apply it we could speak of 'Renaissance' or 'Baroque Academic philosophy'.

6. The vagueness of concepts applied to culture and its history is not surprising. Even though cultural periods do have a "distinct physiognomy" (Kristeller 1979, 17), there are countless respects in which a thinker of one culture may be compared to a thinker of another culture. What makes Augustine (354–50) more similar to Aquinas (1225–74) than to Proclus (411–85)? What makes Suárez more similar to Ockham than to Descartes? One could find countless similarities and dissimilarities, and it is futile to search for the *single* key property.

7. "The 'modern' period in the history of philosophy is conventionally supposed to begin in the seventeenth century, with the *Novum organon* (1620) of Sir Francis Bacon (c. 1561–1626) and the *Discourse on the Method* (1637) of René Descartes (1596–1650). Bacon and Descartes were not isolated thinkers, and their writings are everywhere influenced by the work of their predecessors and contemporaries. Nevertheless, it is not arbitrary to credit them with initiating modern philosophy, since between them they destroyed the assumptions, the methods, and the language which had been the common property of philosophers since the early Middle Ages." (Scruton 1995, 442).

8. According to Kristeller the Renaissance ends by 1600 (1979, 18). According to Kuhn (2005), in 1648, and, according to Schmitt (1983) and Lohr (1988b), by the mid-seventeenth century.

9. Kenny, for instance, writes: "The writings of the classical philosophers of the seventeenth and eighteenth centuries in Europe form a continuous and coherent chapter in the history of philosophy. Despite the many differences of doctrine between them, the major philosophers between the time of Descartes and the time of Kant address a broadly similar agenda by broadly similar methods. When Descartes wrote, the Aristotelian tradition had come to the end of the productive development of the Middle Ages; after Kant's death, European history began to fragment into schools that barely communicated with each other. But in the period between Descartes and Kant the differences between 'empiricist' philosophers in Britain and 'rationalist' philosophers on the Continent were minor in comparison to their shared presuppositions and goals" (1994, 107). Kenny is right in claiming that modern philosophy has a certain kind of gestalt; however, it is a mistake to say that "when Descartes wrote, the Aristotelian tradition had come to the end of productive development."

10. For Le Grand, see Easton (2001/2008). Le Grand engaged another relatively well-known Baroque author, the anti-Cartesian and anti-Lockean Catholic Aristotelian polemicist John Sergeant (1623–1707). For Sergeant (though without mention of the controversy with Le Grand), see Krook (1993). For Izquierdo's empiricist leanings (with further bibliography), see Novotný (forthcoming-b). There were many other "nonstandard" scholastics. For instance, the Italian Capuchin Valerian Magni (1586–1661) considered himself an anti-Aristotelian follower of Augustine and Bonaventure, taking avail of modern experimental methods. Magni was the first to publish the discovery of the vacuum—independently of Toricelli; he was also interested in Galileo's works (Sousedík 1983).

11. According to *Merriam-Webster's Dictionary*, 'scholasticism' appeared in English around 1782 and means "a philosophical movement dominant in western Christian civilization from the 9th until 17th century and combining religious dogma with the mystical and intuitional tradition of patristic theology, especially of St. Augustine, and later with Aristotelianism." The related noun 'scholastic' appears in 1644, the adjective in 1596. These words came into English from the Latin "*doctores scholastici*," which, since the ninth century, was applied to those who taught the seven liberal arts or theology. The Latin word comes ultimately from the Greek 'σχολάζειν', which means "to have leisure for something (such as study)." For a thorough study of the history of this term, see Quinto (2001). Unfortunately, Quinto does not take into account the reality of Renaissance and Baroque scholasticism or recent attempts at decontextualization of this term (Cabezón 1998).

12. Timothy Noone (2003, 55) lists three "overarching traits" of scholastic thinkers: rigorous argumentation (*ratio*), dialogue with Aristotle and other predecessors (*auctoritas*), and the coordination of philosophy with faith (*concordia*). Cabezón (1998, 5–6) lists eight traits: a strong sense of tradition, a concern with language, proliferativity ("the tendency to textual and analytical inclusivity rather than exclusivity"), completeness and compactness ("the belief that the tradition overlooks nothing and contains nothing that is unessential"), the epistemological accessibility of the world, systematicity, rationalism, and self-reflexivity.

13. Other Baroque scholastic authors famous for their non-Aristotelian views include Juan Caramuel y Lobkowitz, Athanasius Kircher (1602–80) and Honoré Fabri (1607–88). For Kircher, see, e.g., Godwin (1979); for Fabri, see, e.g., Elazar (2011). In a still broader sense one may apply the term 'scholasticism' even beyond the context of Western Catholicism to Protestantism (van Asselt and Dekker 2001) and Greek Orthodoxy and, in fact, to other religious traditions as well. First of all the term is applicable to some forms of Islamic culture (Magdisi 1981), but we may speak of varieties of other scholasticisms, such as Buddhist, Neo-Confucian, Hindu, and even Daoist. See Cabezón (1998).

14. Another possibility is to make the term 'Aristotelian' so flexible that it accommodates almost all thinkers of the time: "Until well into the seventeenth century, Scholastic Aristotelianism was the very fiber of higher education. Hence even deviant Aristotelians and vitriolic anti-Aristotelians were Scholastically trained and developed their theories in response to the Scholastic philosophy they were taught. In its highly developed form Scholastic Aristotelianism was no longer identifiable with a single set of fundamental doctrines, but, rather like analytic philosophy today, consisted in an amorphous collection of fluid methods and approaches which formed the basis of every intellectual's philosophical vocabulary. Hence to identify oneself as an Aristotelian at this time was akin to identifying oneself as an analytic philosopher in America today. Scholastic Aristotelians worked in fields as diverse as theology and applied mathematics. Therefore, one cannot assume that every intellectual writing in the Scholastic tradition knew of or even cared about the subtle debates of medieval theologians like St. Thomas Aquinas, John Duns Scotus, and William of Ockham." (Hattab 2009, 224).

15. For a detailed account of Suárez's influence in the Reformed Netherlands, see Goudriaan (1999, 2002, 2006).

16. One speaks also of the *Third scholastic* at the turn of the last century. The Third scholastic stops far short of the qualities of the Second, let alone the First scholastic. However, besides many insignificant authors of the Third scholastic, there are also some who stand out, such as Urráburu (1908) and Gredt (1899/1961).

17. For similar considerations, see Forlivesi (2006, 106–10).

18. See also Lüthy (2000) for Baroque natural philosophy. Historically oriented overviews of Baroque philosophy in English and German include Werner (1889/1962), Grabmann (1926), Eschweiler (1928), Lewalter (1935/1967), Jansen (1933, 1936a, 1936b, 1938, 1951), Wundt (1939), Leinsle (1988), Blum (1998), Pereira and Fastiggi (2006), Schmutz (2000, 2002), and Franklin (forthcoming). These overviews are of various lengths, quality, and geographical focus, but all (perhaps with the exception of Werner) can be read with much profit. See also the Ueberweg series: Schobinger et al. (1988, 1993, 1998) and Holzhey and Schmidt-Biggemann (2001). For an evaluation of this series, see Lüthy (2000, 186–91). Standard historians of philosophy, such as Anthony Kenny (1994), divide the history of Western philosophy between Socrates and Kant into Ancient, Medieval, and Modern; the Renaissance and Baroque scholasticism does not fit into this division and is left out. Exceptions to this rule include Risse (1970) and Ashworth (1974) in the history of logic, Grant (1981) in the history of the notions of space and the vacuum, Kobush (1987) in the history of the ontology of language, Spruit (1995) in the history of the notion of *species intelligibilis*, and Franklin (2002) in the history of the notion of probability. Jacob Schmutz (online: Scholasticon) maintains an impressive database of bio-bibliographical information on hundreds of Renaissance and Baroque authors. An excellent survey of philosophy in the Czech lands (Bohemia, Moravia, and Salesia) with a special emphasis on the rich and diverse regional Baroque philosophical culture was published by Stanislav Sousedík (1997/2009). A model of the history of a Baroque university, namely the University of Dillingen, from its beginning in 1555 until 1648 was published by Leinsle (2006). A model for the history of a Baroque author, namely the Jesuit superior general Thyrso Gonzales y Santalla (1624–1705) was published by Knebel (2010).

19. In English I have noticed the term 'Baroque scholasticism' only in McCool (2000). As far as I know the term was first coined by Eschweiler (1928, 307).

20. Non-Hispanic initiators of the Dominican revival of Thomism include Hervaeus Natalis (1260–1323), Johannes Capreolus (d. 1444), and Peter Crockaert (1465–1514) in France; Dominicus de Flandria (ca. 1425–79), Chrisotomus Javellus (ca. 1470–1538) and Cajetan in Italy; and Petrus Niger (1434–83) in Germany.

21. See Gracia (2000, 70–87). By 'antichristian humanism' I mean a certain kind of humanism, not that humanism as such is anti-Christian. See Kristeller (1955/1961).

22. For instance: Domingo de Soto (1494–1560) advanced the Thomistic synthesis by commenting on several works that Aquinas did not (*Summulae* of Peter of Spain, Porphyry's *Isagoge*, Aristotle's *Categories*). In his commentary on Aristotle's *Physics*, Soto anticipated Galileo's discovery of the uniform acceleration of material objects. Domingo Bañez (1528–1604), known today mainly for his involvement in the controversy over grace and freedom,

published some outstanding commentaries on Aquinas's *Summa*. Diego Más (1553–1608) composed a systematic work in metaphysics, *Metaphysica disputatio de ente et eius proprietatibus* (Masius 1587), ten years before Suárez's *Metaphysical Disputations*. It is not as comprehensive and influential as Suárez's work, but strictly speaking it is Más who could be credited with publishing "the first large treatise on metaphysics composed in the West that is not a commentary on Aristotle's *Metaphysics*." The list of brilliant Spanish Dominicans could go on. See Andrés (1976–77, passim) and Plans (2000).

23. See Farell (1970) and also Hellyer (2005).

24. Jansen (1936a), Grajewski (1946), and Bak (1956); see also Schmutz (2002). The influence of Scotism on Descartes was noticed by, e.g., Roger Ariew (1999, 39–57). It is, however, dubious that there was any direct Scotistic influence on Descartes. Scotistic ideas influenced non-scholastic authors indirectly via the Jesuits; see, e.g., Clemenson (2007, 7–14).

25. Martini also published independently of Timpler. This suggests an interesting question: What brought about the remarkable interest in systematic metaphysics in three confessional groups at around the same time? The emergence of Protestant scholasticism independently from Suárez is defended by Wundt (1939) against Eschweiler (1928). See also Lewalter (1935).

26. The Jesuits made many significant contributions to timekeeping, calculation, geography, mathematics, linguistics, astronomic observation, instrument construction, measurement, calendar theory, etc. In general, however, they did not do research in medicine and biology, although some other scholastic authors did. An instance is Joannes Marcus Marci (1595–1667), one of the most important Catholic intellectuals in the seventeenth century in Bohemia. Marci died a Jesuit, but he spent his life as a married layman. After 1620 he became a professor of medicine in Prague. Apart from medicine and biology, he published works in physics, philosophy, and theology (Čornejová et al. 1995).

27. Arriaga, for instance, did not make any attempt to introduce mathematical considerations into philosophy, although he edited and published the work of his colleague Gregory of St. Vincent (1584–1667), which Leibniz drew on in his discovery of calculus, see Eschweiler (1931, 278).

28. Reported in Mancosu (1996, ch. 1).

29. Mancosu (1996, 42) reports the French bishop Pierre Daniel Huet (1630–1721) to have used mathematical tools in defending the truth of the gospels. For an excellent overview of (Jesuit) scholastic natural philosophy, partially related to mathematics, in early modern (= Baroque) Germany, see Hellyer (2005). There are also other excellent books dealing with Jesuit natural philosophy—e.g., Feingold (2003) and Des Chene (1996, 2000).

30. For a thorough survey of Renaissance Hispanic scholasticism, with only a brief account of the Baroque, see Solana (1941).

31. True, the Thomists continued to produce solid works but these were, at least from the sociological point of view, not very influential, a widespread

misconception notwithstanding, such as Nuchelmans's: "*Thomism* is undoubtedly the most influential school of thought in late-scholastic philosophy"
(1980, 7). Beside Poinsot and Araújo, the most important Baroque Thomistic
authors were the French Dominican Antoine Goudin (1639–95), the Austrian
Benedictine Ludwig Babenstuber (1660–1726), and the Carmelites in Alcalá
(Complutum) and Salamanca who published a complete philosophical and
theological cursus between 1608 and 1704. See Jansen (1938) and Pereira and
Fastiggi (2006).

32. Interestingly, Scruton's description of contemporary "English" (read: analytic)
philosophy fits Baroque scholastics better than it does early modern non-
scholastic philosophers—the late descendants of the modernists become more
similar to the extinguished scholastic tribe than they are to their forefathers.

33. To be more specific in my criticism of the standard historiography, let me
mention, for instance, *The Cambridge History of Seventeenth-Century
Philosophy*. The book is to be praised for superb articles on non-scholastic
philosophy and for not entirely ignoring the scholastic mainstream. Suárez
even appears on the list of canonical authors worthy of having the titles of
their works abbreviated (xv–xvii). However, no major post-Suárezian
scholastic philosopher is discussed. There is a list of primary literature (pp.
1472–1586), which includes, besides Suárez, *Collegium Complutense* (without
indicating whether Carmelites or Dominicans are meant—they both existed),
Collegium Conimbricense, Punch (without mentioning his main rival Mastri,
a *princeps scotistarum*), John of St. Thomas, Rubio, Śmiglecki, and Vázquez.
The names of Toledo and Fonseca also appear, although the two lived and died
in the sixteenth century. Equally, if not more, important Jesuit thinkers such as
Arriaga, Compton Carleton, Hurtado, Izquierdo, and Oviedo, among others, do
not leave a trace. Most appalling is the absence of Caramuel. And not only is
the primary bibliography deficient, but even the secondary one. Thus, for
instance, even the must-read books of Angelelli (1967) and Hickman (1980) in
English and Kobush (1987) and Blum (1998) in German are not listed, let
alone several important articles and studies in Spanish. The translations of
John of St. Thomas into English are also ignored (even though there is a
French translation in the list). Even more serious complaints could be raised
about other books in the Cambridge History series. Indeed, I am not aware of a
synthetic history of seventeenth-century scholasticism in English that would
go substantially beyond Copleston (1953). The recent German scholarship is in
far better condition, and French, Italian, and Spanish scholarship (though I am
only imperfectly acquainted with it) is certainly much better informed. For
similar criticism see Lüthy (2000, 178–86).

34. Today, the differences between insiders and informed outsiders are no less
apparent than they were in the time of Descartes. For instance, the BBC's
program *In Our Time* announced the results of a popular poll of "the greatest
philosopher" in July 2005 (http://www.bbc.co.uk/radio4/history/inourtime/

greatest_philosopher_vote_result.shtml). The vote was preceded by weeks of presentations by professional scholars on their favorite philosopher, thus the vote was made by an informed public. The results were surprising even to the moderator himself (Melvyn Bragg): Marx (27.93%), Hume (12.67%), Wittgenstein (6.80%), Nietzsche (6.49%), Plato (5.65%), Kant (5.61%), Aquinas (4.83%), Socrates (4.82%), Aristotle (4.52%), and Popper (4.20%). Such results could be hardly expected from contemporary professional philosophers. The results of the representative PhilPapers survey gave the following results (from 2,480 respondents) of "non-living philosophers most identified with": Hume (481), Aristotle (416), Kant (398), Wittgenstein (364), Quine (250), Russell (211), Lewis (200), Frege (196), Rawls (154), Davidson (152). (http://philpapers.org/surveys/demographics.pl).

35. The moderns may have won for sociological reasons. Part of it has to do with their status of being laymen living in a secular environment, existentially independent from ecclesiastic institutions. Also, their works are much shorter, written in a personal style of national languages. It was also unfortunate that Baroque authors bought into various false physical theories, under unfortunate pressure from the Holy See. There were scholastic authors who favored new post-Aristotelian physics and cosmology, but these were rather exceptions and had to deal with various forms of censorship (Grant 1984, Hellyer 2005). When the scholastics definitely lost the new-physics and new-cosmology battle in the eighteenth century, the general impression was that all traditional scholastic philosophy was wrong. See also Leinsle (1995, 336–42) and Knebel (2010, 251–58).

36. Of course, Thomistic convictions as such do not imply biased historiography.

37. Barry Smith (1991) argues that contemporary Anglo-American analytical philosophy is an exceptional philosophical culture in the entire history of thought because it is not *commentary-centered*. In this respect Baroque scholasticism is also similar to contemporary Anglo-American analytical philosophy.

38. Also the mere fact that some philosophy is done within a close-knit community should not taint it. From antiquity we see that communities bound together by some fundamental convictions may produce outstanding results (e.g., Pythagoras's sect, Plato's Academy, Aristotle's Lyceum). See Hadot (2005).

39. For Suárez's life, see especially Scorraille (1912); a popular account is given in Fichter (1940); a first, hagiographical account is given in Sartolo (1693). See also Doyle (2010). For the significance of his philosophy, see, e.g., Pereira (2007).

40. There are several general accounts of various fundamental aspects of Suárez's metaphysics. For instance, Courtine (1990), Darge (2004), Heider (2011). For briefer overviews, see Gracia and Novotny (forthcoming), on transcendentals and categories, and Freddoso (2002) on causes.

41. For a comparison with Suárez's views on the nature of beings of reason and a comprehensive bibliography on Rubio, see Novotný (2008b). For broader context of Latin American scholasticism, see Romero (1988), Beuchot (1996/1998), and Redmond (2004, 2005). A treatise on beings of reason by a minor Jesuit thinker, Juan de Alvarado, who seems to have held views similar to those of Rubio, was published in Knebel (2005).

42. A good, if only brief, summary of Smiglecki's theory of beings of reason can be found in Roncaglia (1995). Against Roncaglia two things need to be stressed. First, it is not true that "Suárez's *Disputationes Metaphysicae* appear to be one of the most important of Smiglecius' sources" (Roncaglia 1995, 36). In fact, Smiglecki deals with several important questions that Suárez passes over (e.g.: Is self-contradictorism true? Does conceiving and making up coincide in beings of reason?). Furthermore, Smiglecki mentions Suárez only once (L d1q6n3), and he avoids Suárez's main novelty, i.e., distinguishing and comparing negations/privations "as they are in reality" and "as they are beings of reason." Second, Roncaglia seems to overlook the ambiguity of the expression 'impossible being'. He says: "In identifying *entia rationis* and impossible entities, the problem remained of how to justify the traditional attribution of the label of *entia rationis* to other kinds of unreal beings . . . especially to logical intentions" (Roncaglia 1995, 39) The identification would become problematic if by 'impossible being' we meant a self-contradictory being, i.e., a being involving contradiction. But Smiglecki explicitly argues against the reduction of beings of reason to self-contradictory beings (L d1q2). When Smiglecki calls beings of reason "impossible beings', he means entities that are "impossible to exist in actual extra-mental reality," which is also what Suárez means. ("Sola entia impossibilia esse entia rationis: quia ens rationis est illud quod in re non potest existere. [L d1q1n5]. . . . Et vero sicuti duplex est impossibilitas, alia simplex, proveniens ex simplici rei essentia, alia fundata in coniunctione duorum a parte rei incompossibilium, ita duplex est ens rationis, simplex et compositum." L d1q2n11). Here, the difference between Smiglecki and Suárez is merely verbal: Suárez reserves the term '*ens impossibile*' for self-contradictory beings "involving contradiction" (such as a square circle), whereas Smiglecki uses the term for all beings of reason.

43. More fully: *General Philosophy: The New Edition . . . Expanded and Enriched by Almost One Third so That It Is Fair to See It as a New Work (Universa philosophia: Nova editio quinque anterioribus tertia fere parte auctior, ab ipso authore ita recognita . . . ut novum opus merito videri queat)*. We see that already in the title Hurtado indicates that the latter work is substantially revised.

44. For his role in the bitter controversy over freedom and predestination between Dominicans, such as Bañez, and Jesuits, such as Molina, see O'Brien (1962).

45. A monograph on Araújo's theory of beings of reason was published in Spanish by Fernández-Rodríguez (1972). For a comparative analysis of his theory of beings of reason with Suárez's theory, see Novotný (forthcoming-a).

46. For instance: Joseph Gredt (1899/1961), Jacques Maritain (1959), Henry Veatch (1970), Stanislav Sousedík (2006), Lukáš Novák (Novák and Dvořák 2007). John Deely argues for the crucial importance of Poinsot's theory of signs; see, e.g., Deely (1985, 1994). Each of the listed authors develops Poinsot's insights in an original and independent way. It shows the potential fertility of postmedieval scholastic thought in a contemporary context.

47. The major difference from Suárez is his insistence on the nonreality of extrinsic denominations. For other, relatively minor differences, see Doyle (1994). For Poinsot's views on possible nonexistents, see Coombs (1994).

48. For Arriaga's life, see Eschweiler (1931). Proceedings from an important conference on Arriaga, organized by Stanislav Sousedík in 1996, can be found in Saxlová and Sousedík (1998). Some basic information on Arriaga's theory of beings of reason was given by Kobush (1998). Kobush, however, does not grasp the essence of Arriaga's theory.

49. For Mastri's life, see Crowley (1948) in English or Forlivesi (2002) in Italian. (The former is a short paper, the latter an authoritative study.) Mastri's views on possible entities are treated in Coombs (1993), Sousedík (1996), and Hoffmann (2002). Proceedings from conference on Mastri, organized by Marco Forlivesi in 2002, can be found in Forlivesi (2006). Some basic information on Mastri/Belluto's theory of beings of reason was already given by Kobush (1987 244–50). See also Heider (2011a, 2011b). General introductions to Scotus's thought include Wolter (1964), Honnefelder (1979), Honnefelder (1990), and Williams (2003).

50. For Punch's life, bibliography and an overview of philosophical teaching, see Grajewski (1946).

51. The standard biography of Caramuel and an overview of his work is in Spanish and can be found in Velarde Lombraña (1986). Proceedings from an international conference on Caramuel's life and work can be found in Dvořák and Schmutz (2008). In Czech, there is a book on Caramuel's logic, with special focus on his discovery of relational logic (Dvořák 2006; in English, see Dvořák 2008). For possible worlds theory in Caramuel, see Dvořák (2000).

2. Problems Posed by Beings of Reason

1. Most of the material in this chapter appears in "Scholastic Debates about Beings of Reason and Contemporary Analytical Metaphysics" (Novotný 2012).

2. Of course, this is an oversimplification. First, there are many different accounts of metaphysics (Gracia 1999; Delfino 2006), and second, the very terms 'real', 'exist', 'being', etc. and their various counterparts in Latin, Arabic, and Ancient

Greek have a quite complicated history, and many distinct concepts are expressed by them (Kahn 1973; Hintikka 1986).

3. What I call "item" Meinong calls "*Gegenstand.*" He then divides it into *Objekt* and *Objektiv.* See Meinong (1904, 6), translated in Chisholm (1960, 80). See also Findlay (1933/1995, 60–69). Meinong's translators render '*Objektiv*' as "the objective" (a count noun). The scholastics do not use this term. Among related terms is '*complex signifiable*' (Nuchelmans 1980). There are two reasons why Meinong's terminology should be preferred. First, it highlights the correlation between objectives and objects, and second, it is neutral with respect to the question whether objectives are mental constructs or something real. (The term '*complex signifiable*' seems to carry with it the assumption that it is something mental.)

4. This world/reality has material and nonmaterial "regions." Angels, for instance, belong to the nonmaterial region, and human beings are peculiar hybrids of the two worlds (they have a nonmaterial "part"). God has a sui generis ontological status: Everything, whether material or nonmaterial, depends on God both for beginning and for continuation of its existence.

5. There are several studies of this question that concern postmedieval scholasticism: Beneš (1926), Doyle (1967), Coombs (1993, 1994), Sousedík (1996), and Hoffmann (2002).

6. Millán-Puelles (1990/1996) does not make the same historical mistake, although for systematic reasons he agrees with Rescher's view that mere possibles are nonreal. Even some contemporary Thomists argue that for systematic reasons the traditional thesis about the reality of the possibles is inconsistent with other tenets of scholastic (Thomistic or Suárezian) ontology, see Clarke (1955, 1960) against Conway (1959).

7. Note that in contemporary usage the words 'objective'/'subjective' are used in exactly the reversed sense. The term 'objective' means real and mind-independent, whereas "subjective" means apparent and mind-dependent. How this reversal of meaning happened is still an untold story of the history of philosophy. For "objective being" in Descartes and Rubio, see Ashworth (1999).

8. Millán-Puelles (1990/1996) calls these "paradoxical quiddities" or "openly paradoxical beings." See also Rovira (2000).

9. Suárez and most other Catholic scholastics that I have dealt with (with the exception of Caramuel y Lobkowitz) did not use diagrams. I do not know why—perhaps to avoid associations with the ex-Catholic Petrus Ramus (1515–72) and his influential movement (Ramism), which was using them extensively. See also Øhrstrøm, Uckelman, and Schärfe (2007).

10. The notion of extrinsic cognoscibility is first mentioned in Doyle (1987b), more extensively explored in Doyle (1990).

11. See Doyle (1998a, 1998b, 2003). The philosophical importance of supertranscendental terms for semiotics is stressed by John Deely (1985). According to Deely the top-node 'item' in my scheme, covering both what is real and what

is nonreal, should be replaced by 'sign'. I find this to be a mistake of levels. The scheme classifies ontological, not linguistic, items, even though some of the items in it are the result of human mental scheme-making operations. (I am aware that more would need to be said here, as Deely's theory is quite sophisticated; see Deely 2009). Deely also assumes that John of St. Thomas was important in the development of the theory of signs. I suspect that, much as we find many Baroque authors writing on beings of reason write treatises that are in various aspects original and interesting, so we would find many such authors writing on signs. There is a danger of overestimating the importance of the two authors (Suárez or John of St. Thomas), who at the moment happen to be relatively well known to the community of Anglo-American historians. See also Conimbricenses (1606/2001).

12. Cf. Klima's distinction between soft and hard ontological commitments in pre-Ockhamist philosophy. For Aquinas, beings of reason are "objects of thought and signification that are required by a certain kind of semantics but undesirable as objects simpliciter in ontology" (Klima 1993, 25).

13. In the latter part of the twentieth century, some analytical philosophers came to defend the distinction as well. For instance, Terence Parsons (1980) constructed a logic distinguishing the existence predicate (E!) from the quantifier (∃). Another way of dealing with the distinction was developed by Graham Priest (2005), who treats 'there is' and 'exists' synonymously but interprets them as ontologically neutral. Still, to acknowledge that existence is a property of individuals as such does not imply that it is a nontrivial property. For instance, Peter van Inwagen (2009, 277–92) argues that existence is a trivial property of individuals (amounting to self-identity). For more on existence "as one of the deep topics in philosophy, if not the deepest" (Vallicella 2002), see also Miller (2002) and McDaniel (2009).

14. The traditional idea of transcendentals is one that does not seem to have emerged so far as a topic in analytical metaphysics—with some exceptions, such as Meixner (2004, 22–29). For an introduction into transcendentals in Suárez, see, e.g., Gracia and Novotný (2012).

15. At this point one might wonder whether there is a distinction between negative objects and nonexistent objects. This question is posed by Meinong (1902, 7ff.). The examples of putative negative objects that Meinong gives include: nothing, immortal, infinite, A without B, not-A. In the end Meinong rejects negative objects as distinct from nonexisting objects. I agree with Meinong insofar as I do not see any difference between negative and nonexistent objects: The apple's non-redness is just the apple's nonexistent redness, the soul's immortality is just the soul's nonexistent capacity-to-die, etc. For Meinong's arguments, see Findlay (1933/1995, 81–89).

16. Richard Routley, for instance, takes up Meinong's ideas to develop a *noneism* that posits that there are nonexistent objects and that these objects have no existence, being, or what-have-you. The principle commitment of noneism,

which amounts to Mally's independence principle, is the so-called Characterization Principle: An object has properties that it is characterized as having
(Routley 1980).

17. We can think of it this way: Let us take, for instance, the proposition/judgment
"The apple is not red." It is true in virtue of the real/mind-independent fact
that the apple is not red. This fact involves a nonexistent object, namely, the
apple's non-redness, which is, however, not real but purely intentional: The
apple's nonexistent redness "exists" only as long as somebody is actually
thinking about it.

18. There were exceptions: John Punch seems to have come close to a version of
the quasi-being view according to which beings of reason have a peculiar type
of (essential) being, which is in some sense mind-independent.

19. Ashworth distinguishes between a literary and a logical definition of 'chimera'
in the late-fifteenth- and early-sixteenth-century scholastics: "References [in
the literary definition] were made to such diverse sources as Ovid, Virgil,
Lucian, and the Koran, and the consensus of opinion was that a chimera is a
monster formed out of parts of other animals having, on one account, the head
of a lion, the torso of a girl, and the tail of a dragon. This was said to be
impossible. . . . [For] chimera was thought of not as a mere hybrid, but as
something which had the essences of all the creatures which entered into it,
and it was for that reason that it was thought to be an impossible object. . . .
One of the important features of this definition of 'chimera' is . . . [that it] is
not thought of as a mere aggregate, a random assemblage of different parts. If
the term 'chimera' is to refer, it must refer to some one thing. . . . The logician's
definition of 'chimera', which stems from Buridan, was considerably less
picturesque . . . for it said merely that a chimera is a being composed of parts
which cannot be put together, or which it is impossible to put together" (1977,
63). What Ashworth calls "logical" definition is in fact a solution to the
"problem of chimeras" given several centuries after Buridan by Caramuel:
There are no self-contradictory objects, for we only unsuccessfully *try* to put
some parts together, which is impossible. See chapter 8.

20. Also, there already is an excellent study of second intentions in postmedieval
authors, namely Hickman (1980).

21. Semantic preoccupations seem to have been much more prominent among
medieval and postmedieval Parisian scholastics, especially nominalists; see
Ashworth (1977) and Roncaglia (1995, 36). Klima (1993) argues that it was the
changes in semantics that caused radical reinterpretation of beings of reason in
the fourteenth century. In his view, beings of reason in Aquinas are "objects of
thought and signification that are required by a certain kind of semantics but
undesirable as objects simpliciter in ontology" (1993, 25). Klima's way of
expressing Aquinas's view can be used for Suárez as well: Suárez's beings of
reason are objects to which we are only "softly" or "non-seriously" ontologically committed. As we shall see throughout chapters 3–5, Suárez does not

speak of beings of reason only counterfactually, as Christopher Shields (2012) argues.

22. Two possible explanations for this strange neglect occur to me: First, Baroque authors may have assumed that literary fiction describes possible entities, so that to treat of possible entities is enough (there is no need to explicitly treat literary fiction). Second, literary fiction may have been treated in the context of the theory of imagination. For this, one would need to investigate scholastic texts about imagination to see whether some discussions of fictions can be found there. For some aspects of Suárez's theory of imagination (unrelated to fiction), see South (2001).

23. In part, these topics have been already treated in the secondary literature; for vacuum, see Grant (1981); for possibility, see Coombs (1993), Sousedík (1996), and Hoffmann (2002); for temporality, see Díaz-Herrera (2006) and Schmutz (2001).

24. Thus I leave out two of the most commonly raised topics linked with contemporary discussions of intentional objects, namely, fictions and mathematical objects. Neither was discussed in the texts that I deal with in this book. Texts concerning fictions would probably be found in the context of discussions about imagination. For mathematical objects the texts would be found under the heading of "quantity" (which is commonly considered to be a real accident). For an attempt to apply discussions of beings of reason to the philosophy of mathematics of Evangelista Torricelli (1608–47), see Palmieri (2009).

25. "[R]espondetur as maiorem praedictam, nimirum omne intelligibile prius est antequam intelligatur, eam distinguendo: prius est quoad esse intelligibile et possible, seu quoad esse essentiae: concedo; prius est quoad esse existentiae, negatur, quia de facto ipsamet entia realia saepius prius intelliguntur quam existant realiter: cur ergo esset necesse quod prius esset ens rationis quoad esse existentiae quam intelligeretur." PCI d1q2n14.

26. "[D]entur etiam actu suo modo existentia quaedam entia rationis, quae non cogitantur ullo modo, ergo non bene describitur ens rationis esse quod cogitatur. Probatur antecedens quia quando aliquis cogitat unum ens rationis et alius simul cogitat aliud ens rationis, illa duo entia rationis habent inter se similitudinem rationis non minus quam quaecunque alia entia realia habent inter se similitudinem realem, etiam si nullus consideret aut cogitaret de illa similitudine, ergo dantur entia rationis actu existential suo modo, etiam cum non cogitantur." PCI d1q1n3. Punch proposes this argument in the context of objections against one of the definitions of being of reason that he rejects ("a being of reason is that which is thought of as a being when it has no being in itself"). He does not accept the conclusion of this argument in the unqualified sense, namely that beings of reason *exist* before they are thought of; he accepts it only in the sense that there *are* essences of beings of reason before existence is "added" to them when we actually think of them. Incidentally, Suárez

discusses a similar argument in Disputation 7 (On Various Kinds of Distinctions): "Possunt autem interdum distingui duo entia rationis, quae non possunt dici proprie realiter distingui, quia entia realia non sunt; tamen neque etiam dici possunt ratione distingui proprie ... quia eo modo quo sunt, non iam ex fictione rationis, sed ex se vere distinguuntur." DM d7s1n7. Suárez replies that the similarity between two beings of reason is "quasi-real." In Disputation 54, the problem does not come up again.

27. Another limitation of this study concerns my decision to avoid attempts to track Baroque doctrines and arguments to preceding medieval or Renaissance sources. The size of this book would grow substantially and require much more time for its completion.

3. Suárez's Objectualism: The Nature of Beings of Reason

1. For Aquinas's account of an Aristotelian-scholastic science, see Schmidt (1966, 9–15); for a detailed and penetrating explanation of Scotus's account, see Novák (2011, 19–86).

2. "Dicendum est ergo ens inquantum ens reale esse obiectum adaequatum huius scientiae." DM d1s1n26. Concerning the interpretative doubts surrounding this claim, see Gracia (1991b) and the ensuing discussion, Gracia (1993) and Wells (1993). Notice that the Latin 'ens' in the expression 'ens inquantum ens reale' is a concrete noun that means "a being." It is not an abstract noun like 'being' (esse or entitas), connoting an abstract property that characterizes every being (ens). 'Inquantum' (insofar) or 'ut sic' (as such) indicates the result of an abstraction from various individual differences, but this abstraction does not indicate "being" (esse) in general. This is similar to what happens in physics, which is the science about beings insofar as they are changing, and in biology, which is about beings insofar as they are living. Although these sciences may eventually yield knowledge of what (abstract) changeability is or what (abstract) life is, that is not their primary object.

3. "Haec autem [entia rationis] excluduntur a consideratione directa huius scientiae.... Et ratio est, quia talia neque vere sunt entia sed fere nomine tantum, neque cum entibus realibus conveniunt in eodem conceptu entis, sed solum per quamdam imperfectam analogiam proportionalitatis." DM d1s1n5.

4. "Neque necesse est omnia quae aliquo modo considerantur in scientia, directe contineri sub adaequato obiecto eius, nam multa considerantur ... ut ... obiectum ipsum magis illustretur.... Sic igitur, quamvis haec scientia multa consideret de entibus rationis, nihilominus merito excluduntur ab obiecto per se et directe intento (nisi quis velit de nomine contendere)..... Entia rationis considerantur ..., non tamen per se, sed propter quamdam proportionalitatem quam habent cum entibus realibus, et ut ab eis distinguantur, et ut melius et clarius concipiatur quid habeat in entibus entitatem et realitatem, quid vero non habeat nisi solam speciem eius." DM d1s1n6.

5. "[1] Quanquam in prima disputatione huius operis dixerimus ens rationis non comprehendi sub proprio et directo obiecto metaphysicae . . . nihilominus ad complementum huius doctrinae, et ad metaphysicum munus pertinere existimo, ea quae communia et generalia sunt entibus rationis tradere. [2] Est enim eorum cognitio et scientia ad humanas doctrinas necessaria; vix enim sine illis loquimur, vel in metaphysica ipsa, vel etiam in philosophia, nedum in logica; et (quod magis est) etiam in theologia. [3a] Nec vero potest hoc munus ad alium, quam ad metaphysicum spectare. [3b] Nam imprimis, cum entia rationis non sint vera entia, sed quasi umbrae entium, non sunt per se intelligibilia, sed per aliquam analogiam et coniunctionem ad vera entia, [3c] et ideo nec etiam sunt per se scibilia, nec datur scientia quae per se primo propter illa solum cognoscenda sit instituta. [3d] Quod enim hoc aliqui tribuunt dialecticae, error dialecticus est; nam finis illius scientiae non est nisi dirigere et ad artem revocare rationales hominis operationes, quae non sunt entia rationis, de quibus nunc agimus, sed entia realia. [3e] Itaque nullus artifex nullave scientia per se primo intendit entium rationis cognitionem, sed haec tradi debet quatenus cum cognitione alicuius entis realis coniuncta est." DM d54Intr.n1.

6. Suárez's claim that beings of reason do not belong to logic is an allusion to the standard scholastic practice to take up beings of reason at the beginning of logic textbooks. The rationale for this practice was the (Thomistic) view that the object of logic is second intension (a subclass of relations of reason), and so in order to understand logic one needs to understand beings of reason. Interestingly, Suárez never published a book on logic, though he mentions his own logical commentaries (the manuscripts, however, have not been identified yet) (Doyle 1988, 60).

7. "[1] Metaphysicae proprium est agere de ente rationis ut sic, et de communi ratione, proprietatibus et divisionibus eius, [2] quia hae rationes suo modo sunt quasi transcendentales et intelligi non possunt nisi per comparationem ad veras et reales rationes entium (vel transcendentales, vel ita communes, ut sint proprie metaphysicae), nam quod fictum est, vel apparens, per comparationem ad id quod vere est, intelligi debet. Quare, licet aliae facultates, ut physica, vel dialectica, aliquando attingant aliqua entia rationis, quae cum suis obiectis coniuncta sunt, ut iam exemplis ostendimus, tamen non possunt ex propriis rationes quasi essentiales eorum exponere. . . . [3] Hoc itaque in praesenti disputatione praestandum a nobis est, in qua prius qualemcumque naturam et causas huius entis declarabimus; deinde, adiuncta divisione, varia genera horum entium indicabimus." DM d54Intr.n2.

8. Duns Scotus seems to have been the first to suggest that metaphysics is the study of transcendentals—see Gracia (1992). For transcendentals in Suárez, see Darge (2004) and Gracia and Novotný (forthcoming).

9. Theses throughout this study are assigned consecutive numbers preceded by one or two letters indicating the author of the thesis ("S" for Suárez, "H1" for Hurtado's earlier views, "H2" for Hurtado's later views, "MB" for Mastri/

Belluto, "C" for Caramuel), and one or two letters indicating the subject matter they concern ("M" for metatheory, "N" for nature, "C" for (human) cause, "C-G" for Divine cause, "D" for division). Occasionaly a thesis gets reformulated, which is indicated by prime: '. If a given author makes statements that are at least prima facie contradictory (so that it is hard to see what his real opinion is), the thesis is subdivided and distinguished by "a" and "b."

10. "Suárez is using two senses of 'real', then, which allows him to say that some properties of being are both real (i.e. non-fictitious) and not real (i.e. neither real [=actual] nor possible) without contradiction" (Gracia 1992, 128).

11. "Ens ergo ... interdum sumitur ut participium verbi sum, et ut sic significat actum essendi ut exercitum, estque idem quod existens actu; interdum vero sumitur ut nomen significans ... essentiam eius rei quae habet vel potest habere esse ... non ut exercitum actu, sed in potentia vel aptitudine." DM d2s4n3.

12. "[C]um essentia sit secundum quam res dicitur seu denominatur ens ... ideo non potest explicari in quo consistat ratio entis realis, nisi intelligatur in quo consistat essentia realis. In quo duo peti possunt, quae illis duabus vocibus indicantur: primum, in quo consistat ratio essentiae; secundum, in quo consistat quod realis sit." DM d2s4n6. In order to properly appreciate the claim that the notion of real being involves the notion of real essence, we need to realize that Latin, unlike English, preserves a close etymological connection between 'ens' (a being) and 'essentia' (an essence)—the former is a participle of 'esse' (to be). Thus, Latin essences may be naturally understood as what makes beings be. In English, the word 'essence' is usually indicative of what the given thing must be in order to be the (kind of) thing it is. Thus, English essences are naturally understood as what makes beings be something.

13. "Primum non potest [essentia] a nobis exponi, nisi vel in ordine ad effectus vel passiones rei, vel in ordine ad nostrum modum concipiendi et loquendi. [1] Primo modo dicimus, essentiam rei esse id quod est primum et radicale, ac intimum principium omnium actionum ac proprietatum quae rei conveniunt, [2] et sub hac ratione dicitur natura uniuscuiusque rei ... [3] Secundo autem modo dicimus essentiam rei esse quae per definitionem explicatur ... [4] et sic etiam dici solet illud esse essentiam rei quod primo concipitur de re; primo (inquam) non ordine originis (sic enim potius solemus conceptionem rei inchoare ab his quae sunt extra essentiam rei), sed ordine notabilitatis potius et primitatis obiecti; [5] nam id est de essentia rei, quod ... primo constitui intrinsece in esse rei ..., [6] et hoc modo etiam vocatur essentia quidditas in ordine ad locutiones nostras, quia est id per quod respondemus ad quaestionem quid sit res." DM d2s4n6.

14. "Quid autem sit essentiam esse realem, possumus aut per negationem aut per affirmationem exponere. Priori modo dicimus essentiam realem esse [1] quae in sese nullam involvit repugnantiam, [2] neque est mere conficta per intellectum. Posteriori autem modo explicari potest, [3] vel a posteriori per hoc quod sit principium vel radix realium operationum vel effectuum ... sic enim

nulla est essentia realis quae non possit habere aliquem effectum vel proprietatem realem. [4] A priori vero potest explicari per causam extrinsecam . . . et sic dicimus essentiam esse realem, quae a Deo realiter produci potest, et constitui in esse entis actualis. [5] Per intrinsecam autem causam non potest proprie haec ratio essentiae explicari, quia ipsa est . . . ratio . . . simplicissima . . . ; unde solum dicere possumus essentiam realem eam esse quae ex se apta est esse, seu realiter existere." DM d2s4n7.

15. In Disputation 30 (On First Being), Suárez deals with the question whether the concepts of repugnance and contradiction imply each other: "Constat autem illud maxime repugnare quod contradictionem involvit. . . . Dices hinc recte colligi id quod involvit contradictionem non esse possible . . . non tamen, e contrario, sequi omne id quod non involvit contradictionem esse possible aut ex se non repugnans; nam possunt esse alii modi repugnantiae praeter contradictionem" DM d30s17n10–11. Surprisingly to me, Suárez explicitly argues for the mutual equivalence of these two notions: "Igitur sola illa est vera repugnantia in re quae contradictionem involvit; ergo, e converso, quod non involvit contradictionem, ex se non est repugnans nec impossibile." DM d30s17n12. However, he trades here on the ambiguity of 'contradiction'." He does not say what 'contradiction' means and he gives no examples of it. As we know from Disputation 54, he cannot mean "self-contradiction," which occurs in square circles or chimeras, for there is no such self-contradiction or self-incompatibility in blindness or nothingness. Suárez's confusion over 'contradiction' in the broad sense ("impossible to exist" for whatever reason) and in the narrow sense ("involving incompatible essences") has been overlooked, e.g., by Doyle (1967), although he notes the distinction in his article on John of St. Thomas: "Aside from the fact that all beings of reason involve conceiving non-being as being, negative beings of reason need not be in any other way self-contradictory" (Doyle 1994, 343).

16. Etymologically, the expression 'contradiction' means "speaking against." Hence, it would be better to reserve this expression for a relation between statements. The type of relation between predicates or parts within a being should rather be called 'incompatibility' or "inconsistency."

17. In the introduction to Disputation 54, Suárez says: "What is fictitious or apparent needs to be understood in comparison to what is truly" (nam quod fictum est, vel apparens, per comparationem ad id quod vere est, intelligi debet). DM d54Intr.n2. Unfortunately, this does not help. Aquinas uses the term 'confingere' in *Summa Theologiae* Iq17a1 (On Falsity) but without mentioning beings of reason. Ockham also uses the term 'fictum' in the context of explaining universals. This, however, does not shed light on what Suárez means.

18. See also: "[S]i ens sumatur . . . in vi nominis . . . eius ratio consistit in hoc quod sit habens essentiam realem, id est non fictam nec chimericam, sed veram et aptam ad realiter existendum." DM d2n4s5.

19. For semantic reasons Suárez does not want to say that potential beings *exist*, only that they *can exist*: "[Verbum] sum . . . absolute dictum actuale esse seu existentiam significat; unde etiam dialectici dicunt in propositione de secundo adiacente (= propositions such as "Adam is"] verbum est numquam absolvi a tempore. Et patet etiam ex communi usu, nam si quis dicat Adam est, significat ipsum existere. . . . (H]aec vox existens numquam potest dici de re quae actu non existat, quia semper retinet vim participii verbi existo." DM d2s4n3. Suárez also uses *'dari'* (is given) for the existentially neutral 'there is', 'there are'.

20. He deals with questions such as: What is a real being, while it does not actually exist? What is actual existence and why do things need it? What is the difference between essence and existence? Suárez anticipated these questions in Disputation 2 but deferred their discussion to Disputation 31: "His ergo modis, potest a nobis communis ratio entis declarari; magis autem exacta huius rei intelligentia pendet ex pluribus quaestionibus. Prima est, qualis sit entitas essentiae realis, quando actu non existit. Secunda, quid sit existentia actualis, et ad quid necessaria sit in rebus. Tertia, quomodo existentia distinguatur ab essentia. Sed quia hae quaestiones propriae fere sunt entis creati, et prolixam requirunt disputationem, ideo eas . . . differimus, contenti pro nunc praedicta entis et essentiae descriptione" DM d2s4n7. For Suárez's general conception of being, see Heider (2007, 2011).

21. Concerning beings of reason, in Disputation 31 Suárez basically repeats what he has said in Disputation 2: "respondetur essentiam possibilem creaturae obiectivam divinae scientiae non esse ens confictum ab intellectu, sed esse ens revera possibile et capax realis existentiae, ideoque non esse ens rationis, sed sub ente reali aliquo modo comprehendi. Iam enim supra declaravi essentiam creaturae, etiam non productam, esse aliquo modo essentiam realem. Et in superioribus tractando de conceptu entis, ostendimus non solum sub illo comprehendi id quod actu est, sed etiam quod aptum est esse." DM d31s2n10.

22. Impossible beings in this narrower sense are also called 'chimeras'. See, e.g.: ". . . intellectus . . . potest ex veris entibus ficta conficere, coniungendo partes quae in re componi non possunt, quomodo fingit chymaeram, aut quid simile, et ita format illa entia rationis, quae vocantur impossibilia, et ab aliquibus dicuntur entia prohibita" (emphasis mine). DM d54s1n8. "Ut quia impossibile est equum esse leonem, ideo illud ens, quod concipitur per modum equi et leonis simul, dicimus esse fictum et chymaeram vel aliquid simile nominamus." DM d54s4n10.

23. For semantic reasons Suárez does not want to apply the word 'existence' to beings of reason. In his view 'existence' retains the force of a participle and hence applies only to presently actual beings (DM d2s4n). We may use 'existence' if we are aware that we use it in the existentially neutral sense of 'there is', which is equivalent to Suárez's 'is given' (*dari*).

24. "Non desunt etiam in hac re sententiae extreme contrariae, saltem in vocibus; nam si auctores earum pressius examinentur, fortasse solum de vocibus contendunt." DM d54s1n1.

25. Examples of real items in Suárez's ontology: (real) nonbeings, (real) extrinsic denominations, components and aggregates of real beings (which should also count as real, although Suárez does not say so explicitly). Extrinsic denominations will be discussed in chapter 4, nonbeings in chapter 5. Concerning the aggregates: Suárez calls them 'beings by accident' (ens per accidens)—not to be confused with accidents—and discusses them in section 3 of Disputation 4 (On Transcendental Unity). There he gives the following examples of them: a house (s3n1), Peter as a musician (s3n1), a gilded silver vase (s3n13), and a drink of oxymel (s3n14). From these examples, we see that beings by accident fail to be "proper" real beings not because they are nonreal (made up) but because they are plural (not properly unified).

26. One such opponent is Ockham: He uses the expression 'ens rationis', but he means by it mental acts, and these are real. Suárez knew Ockham—in the Metaphysical Disputations he refers to him sixty-seven times—but not in the context of beings of reason. For the sake of comparison, let me give the number of references Suárez makes to other authors: Aegidius Romanus (78), Albert the Great (96), Alexander of Aphrodisias (52), Anselm (36), Aristotle (1735), Augustine (334), Peter Aureoli (46), Averroes (179), Avicenna (84), Gariel Biel (86), Boethius (33), Bonaventura (38), Tommaso de Vio (Cajetan) (299), Johannes Capreolus (115), Cicero (20), Conimbricenses (13), John of Damascus (71), Dionysius Ps.-Areopagite (56), Durand of St. Porçain (153), Vincent of Ferrara (124), Pedro da Fonseca (114), Gabriel Biel (86), Henry of Ghent (95), Gregory of Rimini (90), Hervaeus Natalis (77), John of Jandun (23), Chrysostomo Javelli (97), John Major (20), Franciscus Mayronis (13), Marsilius of Inghen (37), Niphus (24), Plato (92), Richard of Middletown (34), Scotus (363), Simplicius (41), Paulus Barbus (Soncinas) (192), Domingo Soto (75), and Thomas Aquinas (1008). See Iturrioz (1949, 63).

27. "Quidam ergo simpliciter negant dari entia rationis, sed omnia, quae de iis dicuntur, posse optime de rebus intelligi et in eis salvari. Hanc sententiam ita conatur defendere, diputandi potius quam asserendi gratia, Mayronis . . . ; et quidam Bernardinus Mirandulanus . . . illam defendit. Fundamentum esse potest, quia [1] aut ens rationis dicitur quia est in ratione subiective, vel quia est factum a ratione; et hoc non, quia inesse et fieri sunt proprietates entium realium; unde constat, actus et species, quae fiunt a ratione, eique insunt, entia esse realia [2] vel dicitur esse ens rationis, quia est fictum a ratione et contradictionem involvit dicere tale ens esse, quia quod solum fingitur, non est. [3] Vel saltem (quod ad rem magis spectat) sequitur talia entia rationis minime esse necessaria, neque ad doctrinas, neque ad res veras concipiendas; nam fictiones intellectus ad hos fines necessariae non sunt." DM d54s1n2. Millán-Puelles in commenting on this passage mistakenly identified Mayronis as

Silvestro Mauro (1619–87), see (1990/1996, 225). Mayronis deals with beings of reason extensively in his Quodlibeta 6 and 7 (Mayronis 2006). Suárez obviously did not read these Quodlibeta first hand.

28. Here, by 'being made by reason' Suárez means acts of reason and intelligible species and these are real. But to be a (mere) object of reason is also in some sense to be made by reason. Hence, the causal objection arises: Can the intellect, which is real, make nonreal beings? This objection is not as trivial as it appears. See chapter 5, section E.1.

29. "Altera sententia extreme contraria est, [1] non solum dari entia rationis, verum etiam unica significatione, atque etiam conceptione contineri sub communi appellatione entis, quanquam secundum analogam convenientiam. [2] Immo non desunt, qui inter nonnulla entia rationis et aliqua realia ponant univocam convenientiam, ut inter relationes, quorum sententiam superius refutavimus. [3] Nec etiam desunt qui entibus rationis attribuant entitatem independentem ab actuali cognitione intellectus, quorum opinio attingit quaestionem de modo quo consurgunt, vel suo modo causantur entia rationis, et ideo melius eam tractabimus sectione sequenti?" Suarez then continues: Fundamentum ergo huius sententiae esse potest, quia entia rationis absolute dicuntur esse, ut caecitas, et similia; ergo conveniunt aliquo modo in ratione entis cum entibus realibus. Item, quia proprietates entis conveninunt entibus rationis, nam ens rationis unum est, vel plura, et est intelligibile, etc. DM d54s1n3.

30. Hence, they do not hold a stronger view that a given being could be both real and of reason. If somebody wanted to divide beings of reason into real and nonreal, Suárez would say that he is concerned only with nonreal ones and that in his sense the alleged real beings of reason are no true beings of reason at all. Mutatis mutandis he would say the same to those (such as Ockham) who divide real beings into of-reason and not-of-reason. "Primo ergo dividi solet relatio in eam quae realis est, vel tantum rationis, quam aliqui ita interpretantur, ut doceant, genus praedicamenti Ad aliquid, utramque relationem sub se continere, ac propterea illam divisionem esse univocam, imo et generis in species. . . . Fundamentum eorum est, quia definitio relativorum, quam Aristoteles tradit, et proprietates omnes quae ad illam consequuntur, aeque conveniunt relationibus rationis, ac realibus." DM d47s3n2.

31. "Nihilominus dicendum est, solas relationes reales pertinere ad constitutionem praedicamenti Ad aliquid . . . Ostendimus enim ens non solum non esse univocum ad ens reale et rationis, verum etiam non habere unum conceptum communem illis, etiam analogum, sed vel esse aequivocum, vel ad summum, analogum analogia proportionalitatis. . . . Et ideo merito Soncinas . . . approbat dictum Hervaei . . . non magis posse ens esse univocum ad ens reale et rationis, quam sit homo ad hominem vivum et mortuum." DM d47s3n3 (see also further n4–5).

32. Suárez assumes here that no being of reason is "independent of the actual knowing of the intellect." Presumably, he would also agree with a stronger

thesis, namely, that no component of beings of reason is mind-independent. Two components could come into question here: essence and existence. However, since according to Suárez these components do not really differ in real beings, they should not differ in nonreal beings either. Hence it is impossible that one part (essence) of beings of reason would be mind-independent and the other (existence) mind-dependent. This issue was explicitly addressed by Mastri/Belluto (see chapter 7, section A3)

33. "Fundamentum ergo huius sententiae esse potest, quia [1] entia rationis absolute dicuntur esse, ut caecitas, et similia; ergo conveniunt aliquo modo in ratione entis cum entibus realibus. Item, [2] quia proprietates entis conveniunt entibus rationis, nam ens rationis unum est, vel plura, et est intelligibile, etc." DM d54s1n3.

34. "Dicendum vero est [1] dari aliqua entia rationis, quae neque sunt vera entia realia, quia non sunt capacia verae et realis existentiae, [2] neque etiam habent veram aliquam similitudinem cum entibus realibus, ratione cuius habeant cum illis communem conceptum entis. Prior pars huius assertionis communis est, ut patet ex communi usu et modo loquendi, tam in theologia, quam in philosophia." DM d54s1n4. Suárez then includes reference to Aristotle's distinction between two kinds of being, real and apprehended-by-mind (*Metaphysics* 5.7.1017a32).

35. Millán-Puelles charges Suárez (and Araújo) with conflating the question of the existence of beings of reason with the question of their genesis (1990/1996, 226). This is a misunderstanding of Suárez's argument: Suárez argues that once we know *what* beings of reason are, it becomes obvious that beings of reason indeed are (*dantur*). There is no conflation here.

36. "Non potest autem ratione confirmari haec pars, nisi prius explicemus quale esse, aut qualem essentiam habeat hoc ens rationis, de quo loquimur. Cum autem ens rationis, ut ipsum nomen prae se fert, habitudinem dicat ad rationem, merito distingui solet multiplex ens rationis, iuxta diversas habitudines. [1] Est enim quoddam ens, quod effective fit a ratione, vera tamen et reali efficiencia; quomodo omnia artificiata possunt entia rationis appellari . . . ; non est tamen in usu haec appelatio. [2] Aliud est habitudo ad rationem ut ad subiectum inhaesionis . . . et ita omnes perfectiones, quae inhaerent intellectui . . . dici possunt entia rationis. Sed nunc non est sermo de illis, quia illa sunt vera entia realia, contenta sub generibus accidentium hactenus declaratis; unde neque illa acceptio entis rationis multum est usitata. [3] Alio ergo modo dicitur aliquid esse in ratione per modum obiecti, nam quia cognitio fit per quamdam assimilationem et quasi attractionem rei cognitae ad cognoscentem, dicitur res cognita esse in cognoscente, non solum inhaesive per suam imaginem, sed etiam obiective secundum seipsam." DM d54s1n5. See also Doyle (1987, 52–53).

37. The distinction between subjective relation to the intellect (characteristic of formal concepts) and objective relation to the intellect (characteristic of objective concepts) comes from Scotus, see Novák (2011, 102–14).

38. "[3a] Id autem, quod . . . est obiective in mente, interdum habet vel potest habere in se verum esse reale . . . , et hoc absolute et simpliciter non est verum ens rationis sed reale, quia hoc esse est quod simpliciter per se convenit, obiici autem rationi est extrinsecum et accidentale. [3b] Aliquid vero interdum obiicitur seu consideratur a ratione, quod non habet in se aliud reale ac positivum esse praeterquam obiici intellectui seu rationi de illo cogitanti." DM d54s1n6. For a reconstruction of Aquinas's account of how something can be (objectively, intentionally) in the mind and (really, naturally) outside of it, see Lisska (1976); for later scholastic views, see Clemenson (2007).

39. "[E]t hoc propriissime vocatur ens rationis. . . . Et ideo recte definiri solet, ens rationis esse illud, [quod habet esse objective tantum in intellectu] seu esse id, [quod a ratione cogitatur ut ens, cum tamen in se entitatem non habeat.]" DM d54s1n6. Millán-Puelles, calling beings of reason "pure objects," tries to express this definition phenomenologically as follows: "what has no other manner of validity than its pure and simple givenness as an object before actually conscious subjectivity" (1990/1996, 207). In Millán-Puelles's view, what the scholastics called beings of reason is a special case of "pure object." See also Fernández-Rodriguez (1994). By 'in se entitatem non habeat' I understand that beings of reason have no real entity in themselves (but they have objective/intentional entity). I acknowledge that this passage could be taken as a support for Shields's tethered counterfactual account.

40. "Ex hac ergo declaratione vocis, quae etiam est definitio rei significatae, quantum hic esse potest, manifeste colligi videtur dari aliquid, quod illo titulo possit ens rationis dici. Nam multa cogitantur ab intellectu nostro, quae in se non habent reale esse, etsi cogitentur ad modum entium, ut patet in exemplis adductis de caecitate, relatione rationis, etc. Item multa cogitantur quae sunt impossibilia, et modo possibilium entium finguntur, ut chymaera, quae non habent aliud esse quam cogitari." DM d54s1n7. Note that Suárez is hesitant to say that his explanation of the term 'being of reason' is a definition. Mastri/Belluto explain why: Only extramental things can be, properly speaking, defined; with respect to beings of reason we can have only a "conceptual definition": "Quamvis ut monet Doctor [Scotus l4d1q2a1] ens rationis proprie definiri non possit refringendo definitionem ad quid proprie dictum extra animam, tamen quia definiri potest eo modo, quo definitio exprimit unum conceptum per se in intellectu . . . ideo in hoc sensu quaeritur in praesenti, quid sit ens rationis ac quaedam eius definition." DOA d3q2n11.

41. "Item, hoc ipsum quod agimus disputando de ente rationis non fit sine aliqua cogitatione eius [. . .]. Nemo ergo, nisi propriam vocem ignoret, negare potest dari aliquid huiusmodi sola cogitatione fictum, nisi forte in aequivoco laboret in usu illius verbi, dari, aut esse. Cum enim dicimus dari aut esse entia rationis, non intelligimus dari aut esse a parte rei secundum veram existentiam; alias repugnantiam in terminis involveremus; unde si hoc solum negare intendunt, qui negant dari entia rationis, nobis non contradicunt, non tamen utuntur illis

verbis iuxta subiectam materiam; dicuntur enim dari aut esse huiusmodi entia non simpliciter, sed secundum quid, iuxta capacitatem eorum, scilicet, tantum obiective in intellectu, et sic est res clara. Modum autem huius existentiae magis declarabimus in sectione sequenti." DM d54s1n7. The expression 'modus . . . existendi' is one piece of evidence against Shields's tethered counter-factual approach—Suárez and other scholastics thought of intentional / purely objective being as of a mode of being (or existence).

42. "Secundo colligitur ex dictis quae sit radix vel occasio fingendi aut excogitandi huiusmodi entia rationis. Triplex enim assignari potest. [1] Prima est cognitio quam intellectus noster consequi conatur de ipsis etiam negationibus et privationibus, quae nihil sunt. Cum enim obiectum adaequatum intellectus sit ens, nihil potest concipere, nisi ad modum entis, et ideo dum privationes aut negationes concipere conatur eas concipit ad modum entium, et ita format entia rationis. Hanc rationem tangit D. Thomas quae non videtur habere locum in relationibus rationis, et ideo [2] addenda est secunda causa proveniens ex imperfectione nostri intellectus; cum enim aliquando non possit cognoscere res prout in se sunt, eas concipit per comparationem unius ad aliam, et ita format relationes rationis, ubi verae relationes non sunt. . . . Atque hi duo modi fundantur aliquo modo in rebus, vel ordinantur ad cognoscendum aliquid, quod vere de rebus ipsis dici potest. [3] Est tamen tertia causa proveniens ex quadam foecunditate intellectus, qui potest ex veris entibus ficta conficere, coniungendo partes quae in re componi non possunt, quomodo fingit chymae-ram, aut quid simile, et ita format illa entia rationis, quae vocantur impossi-bilia, et ab aliquibus dicuntur entia prohibita. In his autem conceptionibus non fallitur intellectus, quia non affirmat ita esse in re, sicut ea concipit conceptu simplici. Et ita satis responsum est argumentis primae sententiae." DM d54s1n8.

43. For Suárez's views on beings of reason and (eternal) truth, see Doyle (1988) and Canteñs (2000); for his general theory of eternal truths, see Wells (1981a, 1981b) and Karofsky (2001).

44. As I have already said, the ontological status of beings of reason is the main focus of Suárez's section 1, into which the discussion of intension and extension is embedded. What do I mean by 'ontological status'? "To determine the ontological status of something or, as it can also be put, to give an ontological characterization of something involves locating the thing in question in, as it were, a map of the most basic categories of reality" (Gracia [1988, 121]). Several issues should be answered here: (a) What being or existence do beings of reason have? (b) What unity— individual, universal, or some other kind—do they have? (c) How are they distinct from the mental act directed to them? Suárez deals explicitly only with (a).

45. "[E]ns rationis, quamvis aliquo modo participet nomen entis, et non mere aequivoce et casu (ut aiunt), sed per aliquam analogiam et proportionalitatem ad verum ens, non tamen posse participare aut convenire cum entibus realibus

in conceptu eius. Prior pars . . . [1] ex dictis constat: ens rationis non est appellatum ens, nisi quia ad modum entis fingitur et cogitatur. . . . [2] Denique, quod secundum nullam habitudinem vel proportionem comparari potest ad verum ens, non potest ens rationis appellari, neque appellationem entis ullo modo participare; ergo non dicitur ens de ente rationis nisi per aliquam analogiam, saltem proportionalitatis." DM d54s1n9.

46. "Communis autem conceptus nullo modo habet hic locum, quia huiusmodi conceptus requirit ut forma significata per nomen vere et intrinsece participe-tur ab inferioribus; esse autem . . . non potest intrinsece participari ab entibus rationis, quia esse obiective tantum in ratione non est esse, sed est cogitari aut fingi. . . . [I]deo nec dici possunt habere essentiam, quia essentia, simpliciter dicta, dicit . . . capacitatem [ad esse]; ens autem rationis tale est, ut ei repugnet esse. . . . Et confirmatur, quia plus distat, in ratione entis, ens rationis ab ente reali, quam homo pictus a vero, nam hic saltem intercedit realis similitudo in aliquo accidente, quae inter ens reale et rationis nulla esse potest." DM d54s1n10.

47. "You may say: By a similar argument one could show that there cannot be an analogy of proportionality here, for beings of reason have no proportion with real beings. The answer is: Although beings of reason as such do not have in themselves a proportion or the foundation for a proportion, for in themselves they are nothing, nevertheless, they are thought of in the manner of having a proportion or a relation, and this is enough to found some analogy." DM d54s1n10. "Dices: simili argumento probaretur non posse hic intervenire analogiam proportionalitatis, quia ens rationis neque proportionem habere potest cum ente reali. Respondetur, quamvis ens rationis ut sic in se non habeat proportionem aut fundamentum proportionis, quia in se nihil est, cogitatur tamen ad modum habentis proportionem vel habitudinem, et hoc satis est ad fundandam aliquam analogiam." DM d54s1n10. By 'in se nihil' I understand that beings of reason are nothing real in themselves (but they are something with objective being). I acknowledge that this passage could be taken as a support for Shields's tethered counterfactual account.

48. For an extensive discussion of this disputation, see Doyle (1969). The disputa-tion deals, among other things, with the similarity (analogy) between created beings (possible and actual) and God. Doyle argues that Suárez's analogy is founded in the "non-contradiction . . . intrinsic to . . . essences . . . [that] has . . . quasi-positive ontological density of its own prior to all existences, even that of God." (1969, 341)

49. "Prior ergo analogia sumitur ex proportione plurium rerum . . . [C]onsistit in hoc quod principale analogatum denominatur tale a sua forma absolute considerata, aliud vero . . . in ordine ad illam servat quamdam proportionem cum habitudine primi analogati ad suam formam; ut homo dicitur ridere a proprio actu ridendi . . . pratum vero dicitur ridere a viriditate sua, non absolute, sed prout servat quamdam proportionem pratum viride ad hominem

ridentem. Et quia haec est proportio inter duas habitudines, ideo solet proportio proportionum seu proportionalitas appellari." DM d28s3n4.

4. Suárez's Objectualism: The Causes of Beings of Reason

1. "Utrum ens rationis habeat causam et quaenam illa sit? . . . – Haec quaestio solum potest intelligi de causa efficiente, nam [1] ens rationis ex se nullam proprie habet finalem causam, quia non est . . . per se intentum a natura, vel ab aliquo agente. [2] Quod si ex parte hominis excogitantis . . . entia rationis finalis aliqua ratio reddi possit, illa magis est finalis ratio ipsius cogitationis hominis, quam ipsius obiecti facti et cogitati et ille finis satis explicatus est in sectione praecedenti." DM d54s2n1.

2. Doyle reports that many seventeenth century scholastics adopt Suárez's claim that beings of reason have no final cause (2001, 63). The view that beings of reason have no final cause, however, was criticized by Mastri (see chapter 7, section D.1), by Araújo see Novotný (forthcoming-a), and recently by Millán-Puelles (1990/1996).

3. "[1] Rursus, cum ipsum ens rationis fingatur per modum cuiusdam forma, ut relationis, non est necessaria alia formalis causa. [2] Ac denique, cum in nulla re sit subiective, sed tantum obiective in intellectu . . . etiam non habet causam materialem, [3] quanquam si res, qui ab ente rationis denominatur, consideretur per modum subiecti, possit dici materia vel quasi materia . . . Et consequenter . . . possit dici habere causam formalem, scilicet, ipsum ens rationis in abstracto sumptum; ut cum homo, verbi gratia, dicitur species . . . materia est homo, forma vero relatio speciei." DM d54s2n1.

4. "Aliqui enim hanc causam simpliciter negant de entibus rationis. Ita sensit Soncinas . . . quamvis non dicat absolute non habere causam, sed non habere causam dantem eis esse, et loquitur aperte de esse existentiae, quo sensu est res clarissima, quia . . . ens rationis non habere esse nisi obiectivum in intellectu. . . . ineptum esset inquirere causam qui per realem efficientiam esse tribuat, sive mediate, sive immediate." DM d54s2n2. Soncinas is also known as Petrus Barbus, O.P. (1458–95). For the best recent bio-bibliographical account, see Jindráček (2009)

5. "Tamen, cum ens rationis non semper sit . . . aliquando vero esse incipiat . . . , non est ineptum quaerere causam huius qualiscunque esse." DM d54s2n2.

6. "Sic ergo dicendum . . . est . . . dari aliquam causam efficientem, a qua habet ens rationis ut suo modo sit, quanquam efficientia eius, ut est realis productio, ad illud non terminetur, ut ad terminum effectionis, sed tantum ut ad obiectum ipsius termini producti. Probatur, [1] quia . . . ens rationis habet . . . esse obiectivum, quod tamen non semper habet; ergo quod nunc illud habeat, et non antea, in aliquam causam aliquo modo efficientem referendum est; alioqui nulla ratio sufficiens illius qualiscunque varietatis reddi posset. [2] Item illud esse obiectivum, quamvis in ipso ente rationis nihil sit, tamen necessario supponit aliquod esse reale, in quo fundetur . . . ; illa ergo causa, quae efficit tale

esse reale, est causa entis rationis. [3] Et hinc facile patet . . . talis causa per realem efficientiam aliquid operatur, ut, verbi gratia, talem cognitionem vel fictionem, quae . . . quippiam reale est; tota vero illa efficientia, ut ad terminum realis productionis terminatur ad formalem conceptum ipsius mentis, et ibi sistit; inde tamen fit, ut illemet conceptus formalis terminetur aliquo modo, ut ad obiectum, ad ipsum ens rationis . . . Atque ita tandem ipsum ens rationis habet esse obiectivum in intellectu." DM d54s2n3. This is one of the passages that Shields (2012) takes as a support for his tethered counterfactual account: "The causation thus ends in the changes effected in the intellect . . . from that point forward, urges Suárez, no further causation is required or possible. To expect more is to inquire, after having allowed that an opaque object has interrupted a ray of light: yes, but after the light is interrupted, what actually causes the shadow?"

7. The foundation of a given being of reason is the real being that helps to "shape" it. Hence it is rather misguided to claim that the cause of the founda- tion is the (sufficient) cause of the corresponding being of reason. There is, for instance, an efficient cause that destroyed Homer's sight (the foundation). But this cause is not the sufficient cause of my making up Homer's blindness (a being of reason).

8. "Dico secundo: intellectus est causa efficiens entium rationis; efficit autem illa, efficiendo solum aliquam cogitationem, vel conceptum . . . ratione cuius dicitur ens rationis habere esse obiectivum in intellectu. Haec satis constat ex praecedenti . . . quia si ens rationis habet esse tantum obiectivum in intellectu, ergo illud habet medio aliquo actu intellectus, cui obiicitur; ergo per efficientiam illius actus habet illud esse; illa ergo appellatur efficientia ipsius entis rationis lato modo. . . . Contra hanc assertionem referri posset opinio asserens omnem extrinsecam denominationem esse ens rationis, etiam ante omnem intellectus considerationem, de qua statim dicam." DM d54s2n4.

9. "Circa hanc enim assertionem occurrunt multa inquirenda et explicanda. [1] Primum est, qui sit illa actio vel cogitatio intellectus, per cuius efficientiam dicitur ens rationis resultare . . . an per quemlibet actum mentis resultet . . . vel solum per certos ac determinatos actus. . . . [2] Deinde, an conficere hoc modo entia rationis sit proprium intellectus, vel conveniat etiam voluntati, aut etiam sensibus, et in universum potentiis habentibus . . . obiecta. [3] Denique, an hoc intelligendum tantum sit de intellectu humano, vel etiam per divinum aut angelicum resultent entia rationis." DM d54s2n5.

10. The extrinsic form is not something linguistic: It is what is expressed or meant by a predicate. Doyle charges Suárez that for him "extrinsic denomination is an ambiguous item. At times, it seems close to, if not synonymous with, a mere naming from the outside. But at other, more frequent, and more important times, it is definitely regarded as a feature of things themselves" (Doyle 1984, 157). This ambiguity is, however, only an innocent case of

mention/use, and from the context one can always decide what Suárez has in mind.

11. Similarly as the notion of beings of reason so the notion of extrinsic denominations was applied by Suárez in many various contexts, see Doyle (1984). For an application to Suárez's theory of transcendentals, see Gracia (1992) and Gracia and Novotný (2012). Sven Knebel argues that the rejection of the notion of (merely) extrinsic denominations is one of the major ontological disagreements between modern and scholastic authors (Knebel 1998).

12. "Est ergo quorumdam opinio, entia rationis nihil aliud esse quam denominationem extrinsecam, qua res cognita denominatur ab actu intellectus secundum aliquam proprietatem, aut conditionem convenientem quatenus cognita est, quae denominatio potest esse multiplex. Prima . . . videtur esse illa, qua dicitur res esse cognita . . . Deinde sunt denominationes sumptae ex variis operationibus intellectus, ut . . . esse universale, . . . affirmari . . . esse antecedens . . . etc. Nam quod haec omnia sint entia rationis, communis omnium consensus est; et patet, quia nihil reale est in rebus sic denominatis, et tamen ita concipitur et dicitur, ac si esset aliquid. . . . Et haec sententia sic explicata tribuitur Durando . . . an vero ita sentiat, postea videbimus." DM d54s2n6.

13. Suárez continues with an interesting but for us tangential explanation of this allegation: "Since he said that creatures from all eternity have been produced by God in being known [*esse cognito*]. . . . They [would] therefore be beings of reason. Although, we must stress that Scotus himself . . . states that this being is not the being of a relation of reason but another "diminished" and absolute being about which he does not state, however, whether it should be called real being or of reason." Latin: ". . . dixit creaturas ex aeternitate esse productas a Deo in esse cognito . . . erit ergo ens rationis. Verum est ipsummet Scotum, in [Ordinatio Id36q1§ad2] declarare, quod illud esse non est esse relationis rationis, sed aliud esse diminutum et absolutum, non tamen declarat an sit dicendum reale, vel rationis." DM s54s2n7. See also Maurer (1950).

14. "Et iuxta hanc sententiam sequitur primo, entia rationis non tantum resultare suo modo in rebus cognitis per intellectum humanum vel creatum, sed etiam per intellectum divinum, quia etiam prout obiiciuntur, denominantur cognitae. Quo fere modo Scotus dixit . . ." DM s54s2n7.

15. "Secundo sequitur . . . non solum per intellectum, sed etiam per voluntatem, immo et per visum, et per alios similes actus resultare entia rationis, quia etiam ex illis denominantur obiecta secundum aliquod esse, quod in eis nihil est, videlicet, esse volitum, aut esse visum." DM d54s2n8.

16. "Tertio infertur . . . non solum dari entia rationis ex vi horum actuum potentiarum vitalium, sed etiam ex aliis rebus vel habitudinibus rerum posse consurgere. . . . Huiusmodi est denominatio, qua columna dicitur dextra vel sinistra animali. . . . Quin potius . . . sequitur, denominationem vestiti a veste, locati a loco . . . esse entia rationis. . . . Nam talis denominatio nihil ponit in re

denominata; ideo enim extrinseca appellatur; ergo . . . ens rationis." DM d54s2n9.

17. "Haec igitur corollaria satis, ut opinor, declarant, illam sententiam non posse esse veram quantum ad hanc generalem regulam, quod denominatio extrinseca ut sic constituat ens rationis. Nam si denominatio sumitur a forma reali, hoc ipso in rebus existit, et consequenter non pertinet ad entia ralionis. Antecedens patet, quia illa forma habet verum esse reale sine dependentia a ratione; ergo etiam denominatio ab illa proveniens, quamvis extrinseca, realis tamen est, et non est tantum obiective in intellectu, aut per negotiationem aut fictionem eius." DM d54s2n10.

18. "Dices: hoc ipso quod est sola denominatio, non potest esse plus quam ens rationis, nam denominatio opus rationis est. Respondetur: si per denominationem quis intelligat impositionem nominis denominativi, illud quidem est opus rationis; sed nunc non agimus de impositione nominum; hoc enim modo etiam denominatio intrinseca . . . est opus rationis; sed agimus de ipsarum rerum unionibus aut habitudinibus, in quibus talia denominativa nomina fundantur, quae non sunt opera rationis, sed in denominatione intrinseca est realis unio vel identitas, aut aliquid simile; in denominatione autem extrinseca quae ex rebus ipsis sumitur, est habitudo realis unius rei ad aliam, ex qua provenit ut illa res, ad quam est habitudo, denominetur per modum termini alterius habitudinis." DM d54s2n10.

19. This is a point of disagreement between Gabriel Vázquez (1549–1604) and Suárez; the nonreality of extrinsic denominations was also held by the Dominican Thomists, such as John of St. Thomas. See Doyle (1984, 133–34).

20. "Quod si illud principium de denominatione extrinseca sumpta ab ente reali, non est universaliter verum, neque etiam applicatum ad actus intellectus . . . potest esse verum. Quia actus intellectus tam est vera forma realis, sicut aliae, et in re ipsa habet habitudinem realem . . . ad obiectum, ex qua provenit ut obiectum denominetur cognitum." DM d54s2n11.

21. "Dices, hoc esse peculiare in denominatione sumpta ab actibus intellectus, quod possit cadere etiam in entibus rationis, et ideo . . . posse appellari ens rationis; sed hoc non satis est, nam inde solum infertur aliquam denominationem extrinsecam posse extendi ad entia rationis, etiamsi . . . a forma reali sumatur, non vero e converso hanc denominationem sufficere ad constituendum ens rationis. Quocirca, ut recte notavit Scotus . . . hae denominationes extrinsecae possunt fundare aliquod ens . . . rationis, si concipiantur tanquam aliquid in re denominata; ipsae tamen praecise sumptae non sunt proprie entia rationis." DM d54s2n11.

22. "Sed dici ulterius potest hoc esse peculiare denominationibus sumptis ab actibus intellectus, ut illud esse quod conferunt, tantum sit obiective in intellectu, quod est proprium entis rationis, ut supra diximus; denominationes vero extrinsecae sumptae ab aliis rebus aut actibus, etsi in hoc conveniant cum denominationibus intellectus, quod nullum esse reale ponunt in rebus

denominatis, in eo tamen differunt, quod non sunt obiective tantum in intellectu, neque pendent ab actuali operatione rationis." DM d54s2n12.

23. "Sed in hac responsione duplex defectus committitur. Primus est, [1] quia vel solum fit vis in nomine entis rationis, vel [2] admittenda erunt alia genera entium, quae nec realia sint, nec rationis. Declaratur hoc, quia [2] si ens illud, quod constituitur per denominationem extrinsecum ab actu rationis, habet propriam quamdam rationem entis condistinctam ab ente reali, ergo etiam ens visum, aut ens amatum, ut sic, et in universum ens extrinsece denominatum, habebit quamdam rationem entis condistinctam ab ente reali. . . . [1] Si autem fiat vis in nomine entis rationis, quod significare videtur peculiarem dependentiam ab actu rationis, facili negotio multiplicare possumus similia . . . nomina, ut ens imaginationis, aut sensus, aut voluntatis, etc., quae omnia erunt condistincta ab ente reali. . . . Quod si . . . ad rem attendamus, cum in illis omnibus sit idem modus entis, convenient in . . . ratione . . . ut significat ens condistinctum ab ente reali, quod potest dici ens extrinsecae denominationis." DM d54s2n12.

24. "Secundo, deficit illa evasio, quia . . . falsum est denominationem sumptam ab actu directo intellectus habere tantum esse obiective in intellectu, nam proprie potius habet esse formale in intellectu quam obiectum. [1] Unde cavenda est aequivocatio, quando agimus de esse cognito. . . . Potest enim vocari esse cognitum, illud esse quod cognoscitur, quodque proprie est obiective in intellectu; vel potest vocari esse cognitum, illudmet esse quod res habere dicitur, ex eo praecise quod cognoscitur, quod . . . non est obiective in intellectu, sed potius est formaliter . . . , [2] obiective autem est in cognitione reflexa, qua intellectus cognoscit se cognoscere, vel potius qua cognoscit rem esse cognitam. [3] Et praeterea, licet respectu talis cognitionis illud esse sit obiective in intellectu, non tamen est tantum obiective, quia forma, a qua est illa denominatio, non est tantum obiective in mente, sed in re ipsa. Sicut quando intellectus cognoscit rem esse amatam, est quidem illud esse amatum obiective in intellectu, non tamen hoc est totum esse illius . . . nam in re ipsa talis actus amoris tendit et terminatur ad talem rem." DM d54s2n13.

25. That is, insofar as he is known by Peter. For Peter does not know everything about Paul and so only a partial aspect of Paul is known by Peter.

26. "Quocirca, si . . . sistamus in denominatione extrinseca proveniente a forma reali, et ab aliqua eius habitudine non ficta sed vera, et in re ipsa existente, non existimo pertinere ad ens rationis, sed comprehendi sub latitudine entis realis. . . . Unde, si intellectus nihil aliud cognoscat quam talem formam, verbi gratia, visionem, habere intrinsecam habitudinem ad tale obiectum . . . et inde tale obiectum extrinsece denominari visum, nullum ens rationis concipit, nam omnia illa revera ita sunt in re, sicut cognoscuntur, scilicet, res denominata, forma denominans, et illa . . . unio complens denominationem quae potius est realis habitudo. Et quoad hoc eadem est ratio de denominatione sumpta ex actu intellectus, ut directe cognoscentis rem, a quo res dicitur cognita. . . . Quae omnia magis ex sequentibus constabunt." DM d54s2n14.

27. Canteñs offers a somewhat diffirent conclusion: "Suárez agrees that beings of reason are extrinsic denominations; but he does not agree that all extrinsic denominations are beings of reason" (Canteñs 1999, 111). "While a being of reason is an extrinsic denomination it does not follow that all extrinsic denominations are beings of reason" (121). Canteñs's formulation, as it stands, allows for some extrinsic denomination to be a sufficient condition of a being of reason. My formulation of Suárez's view excludes this possibility—no extrinsic denomination is a sufficient condition of a being of reason.

28. "Dicendum est ergo, ens rationis proprie fieri per illum actum intellectus, quo per modum entis concipitur id, quod in re non habet entitatem. [1] Haec assertio sumitur ex dictis in sectione prima. . . . [2] Secundo probatur ex dictis contra praecedentem sententiam, quia si sola denominatio extrinseca non sufficit, nullus alius superest modus explicandi hanc causalitatem entium rationis. [3] Tertio declaratur ex re ipsa, et quasi inductione quadam, nam caecitas, verbi gratia . . . dupliciter concipi potest, primo negative tantum, concipiendo in tali organo non esse potentiam visivam, et tunc nullum insurgit ens rationis, quia nihil concipitur per modum entis, sed solum per modum non entis; inde vero fit, ut ad formandum conceptum simplicem ipsius caecitatis, intellectus concipiat illam ut affectionem animalis seu organi . . . tunc ergo concipit aliquid per modum entis; cumque non concipiat ens reale, tunc proprie format tale ens rationis." DM d54s2n15.

29. "Simile quid considerare licet in entibus rationis, quae in extrinsecis denominationibus fundamentum habent, ut est relatio visi, cogniti, etc., nam etiam hae denominationes possunt esse duplices, scilicet, [1] aut tantum denominationes extrinsecae, et sic dum intellectus directe cognoscit rem esse visam . . . nullum ens rationis format aut cognoscit. [2] Alio modo . . . respective, quia intellectus noster . . . concipit . . . aliquid per modum entis respectivi in re sic denominata." DM d54s2n15.

30. "Dico secundo: actus intellectus, quo ens rationis consurgit, est aliquo modo comparativus, vel reflexivus, praesertim quando ens rationis fundatur in actu intellectus. Probatur et declaratur, quia ille actus, quo ens rationis suo modo fabricatur et consurgit, . . . supponit alium conceptum realis entis, ad cuius proportionem seu imitationem concipitur seu formatur ens rationis; ut in privatione, verbi gratia, in tenebris, supponitur aliqua cognitio lucis, ut remotio vel negatio eius concipiatur per modum oppositae affectionis. . . . Sic . . . dici potest fabricatio entis rationis fieri per reflexam cognitionem, extendendo nomen reflexionis ad cognitionem omnem supponentem aliam, et quasi fundatam in illa . . . hanc reflexionem posse esse multiplicem . . . sed quamprimum concipitur per modum entis quod vere non est ens iam intelligitur fabricatum ens rationis." DM d54s2n16.

31. "Hinc etiam facile est secundam interrogationem expedire. Dicendum est enim neque in sensibus, neque in voluntate . . . formari . . . entia rationis, quia [non] . . . habent hanc vim formandi aut concipiendi per modum entis id quod

vere non est ens. Sensus enim non est reflexivus . . . [et] ens ut ens non sit adaequatum obiectum sensus . . . eadem est ratio de voluntate." DM d54s2n17.

32. "[I]nterdum voluntas humana tendat in id quod in re non est bonum, ac si bonum esset; tamen ipsa non fingit tale bonum, sed supponit apprehensum et repraesentatum per intellectum; unde etiamsi illud computetur inter entia rationis, non est a voluntate fabricatum, sed ab intellectu. Quanquam autem voluntas, sicut et sensus, denominet suum obiectum amatum et desideratum denominatione reali extrinseca . . . tamen ipsa voluntas non ulterius reflectitur vel inquirit quid sit in tali obiecto esse amatum vel desideratum . . . sed hoc spectat ad intellectum. Et quamvis voluntas possit . . . reflecti in suum actum, amando amorem vel desiderium . . . tamen per hanc reflexionem non fingit aliquid per modum entis aut boni, quod in se bonum non sit, sed in unumquodque tendit sicut in se est, vel sicut ab intellectu proponitur." DM d54s2n17.

33. "Ab hac tamen generali regula excipi potest imaginatio humana, quae interdum fingit quaedam entia, quae revera nusquam sunt, vel etiam esse non possunt, componendo illa ex his entibus quae sub sensum cadunt, ut cum fingit montem aureum, qui non est, licet sit possibilis; eodem tamen modo fingere potest rem impossibilem, ut chymaeram. Nam . . . habet vim componendi species simplices, per eas formando idolum; . . . [et] sicut potest componere ea quae non involvunt repugnantiam . . . ita etiam potest fingere compositionem inter ea quae cohaerere repugnat. Unde etiam dialectici dicunt ens imaginabile latius ampliare quam ens possibile. Atque ita sane dicendum est ea entia rationis, quae sunt mere impossibilia et non habent . . . fundamentum in re . . . etiam posse fingi per imaginationem." DM d54s2n18.

34. "[T]amen, quia imaginatio humana in hoc participat aliquo modo vim rationis, et fortasse nunquam id facit nisi cooperante ratione, ideo haec omnia dicuntur entia rationis, et, simpliciter loquendo, etiam hoc munus rationi tribuitur." DM d54s2n18.

35. A similar criticism of Suárez's view on imagination was recently leveled by Millán-Puelles (1990/1996, 789–91). An overview of Millán-Puelles's views on causes can be found in Spanish (Fernández-Rodriguez 1996–97). Another possible explanation for Suárez's confusing remarks might lie in the Renaissance Thomistic dotrine of "physical premotion": the intellect empowers the imagination to do things that are ordinarily beyond its capacities. (For a discussion of this doctrine, see Peroutka 2010).

36. "Multis enim videtur non esse denegandum divino intellectui. . . . Nam intelligere omne intelligibile, perfectionis est; haec autem entia rationis sunt aliquo modo intelligibilia, ergo ad divinam perfectionem pertinet illa etiam intelligere." DM d54s2n19.

37. "Rursus ad perfectionem intelligentis pertinet, ut unumquodque cognoscat sicut est seu quale est; sed haec entia rationis talia sunt, ut in se non sint vera entia, cogitari tamen possint per modum entium . . . nulla igitur imperfectio

erit in divino intellectu, quod hac cognoscat per modum entium, cum entia non sint, sed est, imperfectio ipsius obiecti." DM d54s2n19.

38. "Nihilominus aliunde videtur repugnare perfectioni divini intellectus, ut per illum formentur entia rationis, quia ens rationis non formatur nisi concipiendo per modum entis id quod ens non est; at vero hoc provenit ex imperfectione intellectus." DM d54s2n20. "Unde falsum esse videtur . . . formationem entium rationis non provenire ex imperfecto modo cognoscendi . . . ; nam omnis conceptio rei, quae aliter se habet . . . quam res cognita se habeat, in se est imperfecta et non habet illam conditionem ex vi obiecti, sed ex parte cognoscentis. . . . quia perfectio cognitionis consistit in adaequatione ad rem cognitam, et consequenter in repraesentatione eius sicut in se est." DM d54s2n21.

39. "Et discurrendo per singula obiecta seu entia rationis, id facile constare potest; nam ens absolutum . . . non postulat cognosci per modum relativi; quantumvis enim duae res nobis videantur inter se connexae, si tamen revera non sunt relatae, perfectius cognoscentur prout in se sunt, et cum ea connexione quam vere habent sine ulla relatione vera vel conficta, quam si modo relativo, qui eis extraneus est, cognoscantur. Et simili ratione, . . . ens positivum per modum negativi, quantum est in se, neque e converso negatio per modum positivi. Quanquam hoc ultimum difficilius existimatur, eo quod negatio nihil habeat entitatis quae per cognitionem repraesentari possit, nisi per modum entis fingatur. Sed est considerandum, perfectam cognitionem negationis non consistere in hoc quod ipsa directe et per modum entis repraesentetur, sed in hoc quod, cognoscendo clarissime entia positiva, in eis cognoscatur unum non esse aliud . . . absque alia directa repraesentatione ipsius negationis." DM d54s2n22.

40. "Et hoc modo perfectissime cognoscit Deus negationes ipsas, non quidem sine positivo actu et iudicio, quo Deus, intuendo duas res, simplicissime simul intuetur unum non esse aliam. . . . Praeter hunc actum Deus non habet alium ratione distinctum, quo apprehendat ipsam negationem per modum entis positivi; hic enim conceptus neque Deo est necessarius, neque ad perfectionem spectat. Quod autem Deus dicitur cognoscere ea quae non sunt, tanquam ea quae sunt, non ideo dicitur quia ad cognoscenda ea quae non sunt, . . . necesse sit Deum cognoscere negationem per modum entis positivi, sed quia tam clare et distincte cognoscit ea quae sunt, sicut ea quae non sunt, cognoscendo et iudicando de unoquoque id quod est vel non est. Et praeterea, quia Deus non accipit cognitionem a rebus, neque, ut eas cognoscat, pendet ex existentia illarum, sed aeque cognoscit possibilia sicut existentia, et futura sicut praesentia, unumquodque tamen ita cognoscendo esse sicut est, vel non esse sicut non est." DM d54s2n22.

41. "Haec posterior sententia vera mihi videtur, et maxime consentanea divinae perfectioni. Solum addendum occurrit, quanquam Deus per se et immediate non intelligat formando entia rationis, nihilominus tamen perfectissime

cognoscere ipsa entia rationis, et ea ratione dici posse huiusmodi entia habere aliquod esse ex vi divinae cognitionis. Quia esse eorum est esse obiective in intellectu; si autem a Deo cognoscuntur, sunt obiective in intellectu divino, ergo habent esse sibi proportionatum ex vi divinae intellectionis." DM d54s2n23.

42. "Declararique potest, quia Deus comprehendit omnes actiones humanae imaginationis vel rationis; ergo comprehendit omnes fictiones formales (ut ita dicam) quae in his potentiis esse possunt; ergo etiam cognoscit fictiones obiectivas quae illis actibus mentis correspondent seu obiiciuntur, atque ita cognoscit omnia entia rationis, quae per operationes harum potentiarum quovis modo insurgere possunt." DM d54s2n23.

43. "Dicere . . . potest aliquis, licet Deus . . . cognoscat entia rationis id non satis esse ut illa dicantur actu esse . . . sed solum ut dicantur esse possibilia, vel potius imaginabilia, seu fingibilia per humanam mentem. . . . Quanquam si latius loquamur de quolibet esse obiectivo illorum, sicut actu cognoscuntur per intellectum divinum, ita etiam dici possunt actu esse." DM d54s2n24.

44. For the sake of completeness I report here Suárez's view: angels normally do not make up beings of reason, although they may do so, e.g., in the case of their (imperfect) knowledge of God: "Ex his autem quae diximus de intellectu divino et humano, ferendum est iudicium de intellectu Angelico . . . . Nam quatenus perfecte cognoscunt res prout in se sunt, vel in seipsis, non formant entia rationis. . . . si quae fortasse intelligit imperfecto modo . . . potest aliqua entia rationis formare; ut cognoscendo Deum naturali cognitione, potest illum cognoscere per aliquam habitudinem ad creaturas." DM d54s2n25.

5. Suárez's Objectualism: The Division of Beings of Reason

1. "This division is common enough and has a basis in Aristotle . . . . This division is also taken from St. Thomas . . . and all more recent authors use the same distinction." "Divisio haec satis vulgaris est habetque fundamentum in Aristotele . . . D. Thoma . . . et omnes recentiores eadem distinctione utuntur." DM d54s3n1.

2. "Habet tantum nonnullam difficultatem, tum in sufficientia, tum etiam in distinctione . . . membrorum. . . . Et de priori quidem parte dicemus sectione sequenti. Quoad alteram vero partem, ratio dubitandi . . . esse potest, [1] quia negationes et privationes immerito numerari videntur inter entia rationis, quia non sint aliquid mente confictum, sed vere rebus ipsis conveniunt, nam in re ipsa aer est tenebrosus et carens lumine. . . . [2] Quod si haec dicantur esse entia rationis quatenus per modum entis finguntur, hoc modo omnia entia rationis erunt negationes quaedam; quia omnia sunt non entia realia et vera. . . . [3] Aliunde etiam non apparet cur negatio et privatio ut diversa entia rationis numerentur. . . . [4] Denique etiam negatio et privatio non concipiuntur ut entia rationis sine habitudine ad aliud; non ergo recte distinguuntur a relatione rationis. Antecedens patet, quia privatio, alicuius est privatio." DM d54s3n2.

3. "Sic igitur tam negatio quam privatio, si consideretur praecise quatenus non entia sunt, ut sic, nec sunt entia realia, nec rationis, quia non sunt entia nec considerantur ut entia, sed ut non entia, et hoc modo non sunt aliquid fictum, et dicuntur convenire rebus ipsis, non ponendo in eis aliquid, sed tollendo. . . . Et sic dicimus dari in rebus privationes, ut caecitatem in oculo, tenebras in aere, malum in actionibus humanis; sicque Aristoteles posuit privationem principium generationis naturalis." DM d54s3n3.

4. "Noster intellectus illam [sc., negationem vel remotionem entitatis] attribuit rebus, non solum negando, sed etiam affirmando, [ergo] fit ut haec non solum concipiantur a nobis pure negative, sed etiam per modum entis positivi; sub qua consideratione habent rationem entis, non rei, sed rationis . . . patet, tum quia in hac affirmatione 'Homo est caecus' virtute includitur praedicatio entis; nam verbum 'est' includit participium entis; tum etiam quia noster intellectus non concipit aliquid ut in rebus existens, nisi concipiat illud per modum entis." DM d54s3n4.

5. "in hoc modo conceptionis aut affirmationis non admiscetur falsitas vel deceptio; nam huiusmodi locutiones omnino verae sunt. . . . Ergo non . . . [ponimus] aliquam entitatem in re, ergo . . . ens rationis tantum." DM d54s3n4.

6. "Quod vero relatio sit in illo ordine et latitudine diversum ens rationis ab aliis duobus, constat . . . ex diversitate fundamenti; nam fundamentum, quod habet intellectus ad concipiendam relationem rationis, non est negatio aliqua vel remotio entitatis, sed potius est aliqua positiva entitas, quae a nobis non perfecte concipitur nisi per modum respectus." DM d54s3n5.

7. "Dices: ad concipiendum respectum rationis, semper supponitur in re carentia respectus realis; nam si interveniret respectus realis, non fingeretur relatio rationis. Respondetur: verum est supponi huiusmodi carentiam seu negationem tanquam conditionem necessariam, non tamen ut proprium fundamentum huiusmodi relationis. Unde relatio rationis non fingitur ad concipiendam ipsam negationem seu carentiam relationis per modum entis positivi, sed ad concipiendum aliquid aliud, quod in re positivum est, et absolutum, ita tamen connexum cum alio, ut ea ratione per modum respectivi a nobis concipiatur." DM d54s3n5.

8. "Denique, quod spectat ad distinctionem inter alia duo membra, scilicet, privationem et negationem, non est dubium quin aliquo modo sint distincta; nam privatio dicit carentiam in subiecto apto nato, negatio vero dicit carentiam in subiecto absolute et simpliciter. An vero differentia sit essentialis seu formalis necne, quaestio est parvi momenti, quam in sect. 5 expediemus commodius. Nunc solum adverto . . . negationem dupliciter sumi posse: primo in communi, et sic proprie et adaequate condistingui a relatione rationis, et ulterius dividi in privationem . . . et in negationem pressius sumptam, prout dicit carentiam in subiecto non apto seu inepto. . . . Atque ita illa trimembris

divisio, quam tractamus, duas bimembres continet: prima est entis rationis in positivum . . . et negativum." DM d54s3n8.

9. "Potest tamen de hac divisione dubitari, an sit univoca, an analoga; et si est univoca, an sit generis in species, vel qualis sit; sed haec, quae parvi momenti sunt, legentis disputationi et cogitationi relinquo. Mihi quidem videtur esse univoca, quia nulla est sufficiens ratio analogiae; videtur etiam esse generis in species" DM d54s3n9.

10. "Ratio dubitandi est, quia ens rationis proportionaliter dividi potest per omnia pradicamenta; ergo non satis comprehenditur in illis tribus membris. . . . [Q]uia discurrendo per omnia praedicamenta . . . confinguntur . . . entia rationis . . . quae totidem praedicamenta rationis proportionaliter possunt constituere. Ut in substantia concipitur chymaera, aut similia monstra rationis. . . . In quantitate videtur esse imprimis spatium imaginarium . . . [vel] quantitas etiam illa quam in chymaera . . . concipimus . . . Rursus in qualitate videtur esse magna latitudo entium rationis; nam famam, verbi gratia, et honorem concipimus, ut dispositionem convenientem personae honoratae, seu bonae famae, cum tamen in illa tantum sit ens rationis. . . . Deinde sicut fingimus chymaeram, ita in illa fingere possumus figuram propriam eius, quae ut sic etiam erit quaedam qualitas rationis. . . . Ergo non recte coarctatur partitio entium rationis ad illa tria membra." DM d54s4n1.

11. The first defense of the traditional division is in nn. 2–9 of section 4. The general part of the argument is in nn. 4–6. The particular examples of the alleged positive beings of reason that are not relations are discused in nn. 7–9.

12. This point is overlooked by Doyle (1987, 57).

13. "Duo possunt esse modi explicandi dictam divisionem. Prior est, ut illa divisio non intelligatur dari de ente rationis in tota sua latitudine sumpto, sed tantum de illo, quod in re habet aliquod fundamentum. . . . quaedam sunt entia rationis, quae habent in rebus fundamentum, licet a ratione habeant complementum, ut ratio universalis . . . et . . . negationes et privationes . . . Alia vero sunt entia rationis omnino ficta per intellectum sine fundamento in re, ut chymaera. Divisum ergo illius divisionis esse potest ens rationis, quod in re habet fundamentum. Et ratio reddi potest, quia huiusmodi ens rationis aliquo modo deservit ad scientias, et cognitiones rerum . . . nam aliud ens rationis mere fictum, est omnino per accidens, et in infinitum multiplicari potest. . . . Ac denique iuxta hanc interpretationem concedi poterit, entia rationis, quae mere ficta sunt, vagari per omnia praedicamenta . . . secus vero esse de iis qui in re habent fundamentum." DM d54s4n2.

14. "Sed iuxta hanc sententiam adhuc superest exponendum, cur illa entia rationis, qui in re habent fundamentum . . . non possint saltem per plura praedicamenta accidentium multiplicari. Ut enim in praecedenti sectione dicebam, ens rationis . . . prius dividitur in ens positivum et negativum; ut ergo illa divisio sit adaequata, oportet ut omne ens rationis positivum sit etiam relativum;

huius ergo rei rationem investigamus; nam discursus in principio factus videtur ostendere plura esse entia rationis habentia in re fundamentum, quae excogitantur ad modum aliorum praedicamentorum, prasertim qualitatis . . . et actionis, et passionis." DM d54s4n3.

15. For relation, see also DM d54s6n2, discussed below in chapter 5, section D.

16. "Atque haec quidem interpretatio huius divisionis satis accommodata est, et sufficienter rem declarat. Addere vero possumus modum alium, quo illa divisio adaequata sit de toto ente rationis, comprehendendo sub negatione entia ficta et impossibilia, sive per modum substantiae, sive per modum accidentis fingantur. Cum enim . . . entia ficta simpliciter sint non entia, merito sub negatione comprehenduntur." DM d54s4n10.

17. "[I]mmo interdum ad explicandum quasi per simplicem conceptum complexam et impossibilem negationem, huiusmodi entia impossibilia finguntur. Ut quia impossibile est equum esse leonem, ideo illud ens, quod concipitur per modum equi et leonis simul, dicimus esse fictum, et chymaeram vel aliquid simile nominamus; et ad eumdem modum, ut explicemus hanc negationem esse necessariam, "Bos non potest volare", apprehendimus bovem volantem, ut quid impossibile et ens rationis." DM d54s4n10.

18. Millán-Puelles (1990/1996, 566–74) reports that Araújo and John of St. Thomas also hold that self-contradictory beings are negations. He rejects this view, however. In his view beings of reason are divided into three genera, namely negations, relations of reason, and "padoxical quiddities" (=self-contradictory beings). Since relations of reason are subdivided into those with and those without a foundation in reality, one may also first divide beings of reason into those with and those without a foundation in reality and then sudivide the latter into relations of reason without a foundation in reality and paradoxical quiddities (1990/1996, 571–74). An overview of Millán-Puelles's views on the division of beings of reason can be found in Spanish (Fernández-Rodriguez 1997). Mastri/Belluto also criticize Suárez's claim that self-contradictory beings fall under negations (see in chapter 7, section C.3).

19. "Et hic videtur esse communior sensus huius divisionis, quod, nimirum, haec omnia sub negatione comprehendantur; hoc etiam modo, adiunctis aliis quae in priori interpretatione diximus, facile constat divisionem sufficientem esse . . . nam reliqua omnia, praeter relationes, per modum privationum aut negatio-num confinguntur." DM d54s4n10.

20. "De negatione et privatione agere possumus, vel solum quatenus removent formam seu entitatem positivam, vel quatenus entia rationis sunt; has enim duas rationes superius distinximus, et secundum eas diversae etiam sunt considerationes negationum et privationum." DM d54s5n1.

21. "Si vera sit negatio, nulla est fictio intellectus; sed dum intellectus concipit praecise hominem non esse equum, illud vere concipit quod in re est . . . quia vere et a parte rei unum non est aliud, etiamsi ab homine non consideretur, nec cognoscatur. Dixi autem, si vera sit negatio, quia si negatio falsa sit, ut si quis

concipiat hominem, qui non sit animal, tunc illa negatio etiam sub ratione negationis est mere conficta per intellectum, solumque habet esse obiective in illo, et ideo est ens rationis, vel potius negatio rationis, nam illa etiam negatio praecise concepta in ratione negationis non apprehenditur per modum entis, sed potius per modum non entis, et ita est quaedam negatio per rationem conficta. Aliae vero negationes, quae verae sunt, dici possunt negationes . . . reales, quatenus vere removent formas aut naturas reales." DM d54s5n2.

22. "Omissis autem falsis seu fictis negationibus, quia nec ad prasentem consider-ationem referunt, nec novam expositionem requirunt, praeter ea quae de falsitate dicta sunt in disputatio IX, vera et realis negatio, et privatio, [1] in hoc imprimis conveniunt, quod utraque . . . in sola remotione consistit. . . . [2] Conveniunt secundo, quod utraque est extremum alicuius oppositionis in rebus ipsis aliquo modo inventae, et non fictae per intellectum . . . in obiectis suppo-nunt aliquam oppositionem, quae non est facta per intellectum, sed omnem fictionem eius antecedit, ut supra, disp. 45, declaratum est." DM d54s5n3.

23. This line of reasoning would lead towards the theory that Hurtado develops: beings of reason are mistakes (see chapter 6).

24. These two rather strange references might provide clues for a theory of the development of Suárez's theory.

25. "Tertio conveniunt, quod utraque potest habere fundamentum in re cui tribuitur talis negatio. . . . Fundamentum appellamus non solum subiectum cui negatio vel privatio tribuitur (ut in homine negatio hinnibilis . . . fundatur in intrinseca differentia hominis), sed proximam causam seu radicem, ratione cuius talis negatio vel privatio convenit tali subiecto . . . ut si homo sit caecus, non fundatur illa privatio in praecisa hominis natura, sed in aliqua alia causa, quae removet formam quam negat illa privatio." DM d54s5n4.

26. "Quarto conveniunt, quia tam negatio quam privatio possunt vere et absolute praedicari de re sine ulla fictione intellectus; non dico sine opera-tione intellectus, cum ipsa praedicatio sit quaedam intellectus operatio; sed dico, sine fictione, quia ex parte ipsarum rerum supponatur sufficiens fundamentum, ut intellectus possit unam rem de alia negare, utramque prout in se est concipiendo. Unde, sicut intellectus divinus vel Angelus sine ulla fictione et sine compositione aut divisione cognoscit negationem vel privationem, ita humanus intellectus sine ulla fictione . . . media tamen compositione seu divisione propter suum imperfectum operandi modum. Quo fit ut id etiam non faciat sine indirecta et quasi discursiva cognitione." DM d54s5n5.

27. "Nam hoc etiam commune est privationi et negationi, ut non possint per proprium speciem directe repraesentari; nam, cum sint non entia, non possunt habere huiusmodi propriam speciem; cognoscuntur ergo a nobis per speciem oppositae formae indirecte et medio aliquo discursu, et ideo cognitio privationis necessario supponit cognitionem positivi per quod possit intellectus in cognitionem privationis pervenire." DM d54s5n5.

28. "Est autem considerandum, dupliciter hoc cognosci ab intellectu: primo, per modum divisionis seu negationis; et tunc proprie cognoscitur sicut est . . . secundo, per modum compositionis et affirmationis, ut cum dicimus, homo est caecus, vel est non albus, et tunc iam videtur admisceri quidam improprius modus cognoscendi et concipiendi; nam cum in verbo est, ipsum ens aliquo modo includatur, iam attribuitur per modum entis id, quod revera non est ens. . . . Est autem animadvertendum, quod in his affirmationibus non attribuitur subiecto modus quo praedictum concipitur, ut illo modo subiecto attribuatur, sed solum tribui id quod concipitur, nempe negationem seu privationem ipsam; quare in re illa affirmatio negationi aequivalet quantum ad remotionem praedicati." DM d54s3n6.

29. If "blind" as such could not be a being of reason, we would have to conclude that the first operation of the intellect (concept-formation) is incapable of making up beings of reason. This would lead to Hurtado's Fallibilism: only the second operation of the intellect, when judging falsely, is capable of making up beings of reason (see chapter 6).

30. "Differunt autem . . . quia privatio dicit carentiam formae in subiecto apto nato; negatio vero . . . dicit carentiam sine subiecti aptitudine. . . . Haec autem diversitas non est in propria et formali ratione quam in recto dicit privatio et negatio, sed in connotato; privatio enim ut sic non includit intrinsece subiectum aut aptitudinem eius, alioqui et privatio non distingueretur a subiecto privato, quod est quasi compositum ex subiecto et privatione, et non esset purum non ens reale, sed constans ex realitate potentiae, et negatione actus seu formae, quod est contra rationem privationis. Igitur privatio . . . hoc modo dicitur differre a negatione in obliquo . . . Quod genus discriminis etiam solet inter formas positivas tali modo conceptas . . . reperiri; sic enim saepe Aristoteles ait differre simitatem a curvitate, nam, licet de formali dicant eamdem figuram, tamen simitas significat illam cum habitudine ad talem materiam . . . ita ergo de negatione et privatione sentiendum est." DM d54s5n7.

31. "inter negationem et oppositam affirmationem non datur medium: inter privationem autem et habitum datur medium. [n12] . . . negatio simpliciter removet formam . . . , et nullam peculiarem conditionem in subiecto requirit, et ideo fieri non potest quin vel forma vel negatio formae in subiecto conveniat. At vero in privative oppositis datur medium . . . quia privatio non dicit simpliciter negationem, sed connotando in subiecto aptitudinem, et ideo ex defectu huius connotati dari potest subiectum . . . ut lapis nec est caecus, nec videns, quamvis necessario sit videns aut non videns [n13]." DM d54s5n12–13.

32. "Sed occurrit obiectio, quia etiam inter terminos contradictorie oppositos datur medium per abnegationem, saltem respectu subiecti non existentis, ut chymaera neque est alba, neque est non alba; utraque enim affirmatio est falsa, cum sit de subiecto non supponente. [1] Respondetur primo, negationem non habere medium, si in vi purae negationis sumatur; at si admisceatur aliquid

positivi, ex ea parte poterit habere medium; ut si haec est falsa, chymaera est non videns, ideo est, quia non pure negatur visio, sed affirmatur entitas vel esse. Atque ita ut praedicata contradictorie opposita nunquam habeant medium, etiam dum per modum affirmationis denuntiantur, oportet ut sumantur respectu proprii subiecti, quod sit aliqua res existens, et ita servatur aliqua proportio inter negationem et privationem. [2] Secundo respondetur negando assumptum. Nam ex illis duabus propositionibus, ea, quae est de praedicato negativo, est vera, etiamsi subiectum non existat, praesertim si (ut dialectici dicunt) illa negatio non infinitanter, sed neganter sumatur." DM d54s5n14.

33. The view according to which "a chimera is a chimera" is false, whereas "a chimera is not a chimera" is true is held by Ockham and Buridan (Roncaglia 1995, 34).

34. "Unde etiam colligi potest alia differentia inter privationem et negationem puram, quia privatio non potest attribui nisi veris et realibus entibus; nam . . . privatio dicat carentiam formae in subiecto apto nato . . . [et] aptitudo ad formam non est nisi in ente reali . . . [d54s5n15] At vero negatio non solum veris entibus et existentibus, sed fictis etiam et non existentibus attribui potest . . . ; haec enim propositio . . . vera est, chymera est non ens; nam si est ens fictum, ergo est non ens; . . . quod si est non ens, etiam est non homo, non equus, et quodlibet aliud simile contentum sub non ente." DM d54s5n15–16.

35. "Ratio autem esse potest, quia, licet hae habeant formam affirmationum, tamen in sensu et significatione aequivalent negationibus, ita ut licet illa negatio . . . postponatur copulae, tamen in virtute et quoad sensum cadat in illam." DM d54s5n16.

36. "Vel aliter dici potest illa copula absolvi a tempore, quia, eo modo quo subiectum concipitur ut ens fictum, praedicatum est de intrinseca ratione subiecti, et ideo potest propositio illa non solum vera esse, sed etiam necessaria. Atque haec responsio ac differentia . . . mihi non displicet." DM d54s5n16.

37. "solum adverto, quod dictum est de privationibus, intelligendum esse de veris et realibus privationibus, nam possunt esse etiam aliquae privationes imaginariae et confictae in fictis entibus, ut . . . chymaeram caecam . . . , aut imaginarium spatium . . . tenebrosum . . . ; huiusmodi enim privatio attribui poterit enti ficto in ordine ad copulam . . . ampliantem tale esse fictum. Et eodem modo possunt quibusdam entibus fictis attribui negationes aliorum . . . ; sic enim concipitur chymaera non esse hyrcocervus." DM d54s5n16.

38. "Secundo modo agere possumus de illis formaliter quatenus entia rationis sunt et sic etiam conveniunt in his omnibus quae communia sunt enti rationis ut sic vel enti rationis absoluto (ut sic dicam), id est, ut condistinguitur ab ente rationis, quod est relatio." DM d54s5n20.

39. Privations as qualities: "Itaque recte dictum videtur, privationem in universum, si vera et propria sit, apprehendi seu cogitari per modum qualitatis." DM

d54s5n22; see nn20–22. Negations as various categories: "negatio non semper apprehenditur per modum qualitatis, sed etiam ad instar aliorum praedicamentorum. Diximus enim supra, entia impossibilia, quae ad modum substantiarum finguntur, sub negatione comprehendi." DM d54s5n23.

40. "Ex quo ulterius colligere licet discrimen inter negationem et privationem, nam privatio semper concipitur ut quid adhaerens vel adiunctum alicui subiecto, ut explicatum est; negatio vero non semper, nam ipsum nihil est quaedam negatio, quae nulli rei adhaerere intelligitur, et idem constat ex aliis exemplis supra adductis." DM d54s5n24.

41. Sometimes they differ formally: "Negatio enim, quae concipitur quasi per se, et extra subiectum . . . formaliter differt a privatione, et consequenter etiam ab illa negatione, quae ex se concipitur ut adhaerens alicui, et illud denominans." DM d54s5n25. Sometimes they differ only relatively: "Quando vero privatio et negatio sunt eiusdem formae comparatione diversorum subiectorum, ut negatio visus respectu hominis et Angeli, tunc quidem in ratione entis rationis non videntur essentialiter differre, sed tantum denominatione, aut relatione sumpta ex ordine ad diversa subiecta." DM d54s5n26.

42. "[H]ic loquimur de negatione prout concipitur per modum incomplexae formae; nam si de complexis negationibus sit sermo, sic potest intelligi diversitas essentialis. . . . Haec enim negatio, Angelus non habet visum, aut haec affirmatio, Angelus est non videns, longe diversae sunt ab his, Homo est caecus, aut caret visu; nam illae sunt necessariae propositiones, hae vero contingentes: unde essentialem diversitatem habent. Neque id mirum est, quia respectu complexionis ipsa extrema intrinsece comparantur tanquam illam componentia, et ideo variato altero extremo variatur compositio et habitudo complexionis; secus vero est in ipsa simplici forma secundum se spectata; illa enim intrinsece non includit hoc vel illud subiectum, sed habitudinem ad subiectum quasi adaequatum." DM d54s5n27.

43. However, Suárez's reference to Henry of Ghent (1217–93) might indicate a forerunner of a modern ontology of polyadic relations: "Quaeri vero hic potest an una relatio unum habeat subjectum, et quodnam illud sit. Quod praecipue interrogo propter Henricum, qui Quodlib. 9, q. 3, sentit relationem secundum proprium esse ad, unam et eamdem esse inter duo extrema quae referuntur. Nam relatio secundum propriam rationem est veluti medium quoddam inter extrema relata, et ideo, sicut Aristoteles dixit eamdem esse viam ab Athenis ad Thebas et a Thebis ad Athenas, ita dicit Henricus unam et eamdem esse habitudinem quorumcunque duorum extremorum ad invicem se habentium, scilicet, patris ad filium, et filii ad patrem, vel duorum fratrum, aut similium inter se." (DM 47.6.3). For a criticism of the post-Fregean ontology of relations, see Sousedík (2006).

44. "[O]mnia, quae solent esse necessaria ad relationem realem, qualia sunt: subiectum capax [part of condition 1], fundamentum reale cum debita ratione fundandi [part of condition 3], et realis terminus actu existens cum sufficienti

fundamento reali [part of conditions 1 and 3]." DM d54s6n2. Suárez does not explicitly state the condition 2 here, but it is implied in the examples that follow.

45. "[D]uo videntur ad illam [=relationem rationis] requiri: unum est, ut in ea non concurrant omnia, quae solent esse necessaria ad relationem realem. . . . Aliud est, ut aliquid eorum, quae ad relationem realem concurrunt, fundet aliquo modo . . . relationem rationis, vel potius cogitationem et modum concipiendi, quo relatio rationis confingitur, supplente ipso intellectu id quod in re deest ad verum respectum." DM d54s6n2.

46. "[I]deo relatio rationis . . . definiri potest, esse relationem, quam intellectus fingit per modum formae ordinatae ad aliud, seu referentis unum ad aliud, quod in re ipsa ordinatum aut relatum non est." DM d54s6n1.

47. "Haec ergo dici potest prima divisio relationis rationis, in eam quae omnino est conficta per intellectum absque ullo fundamento ex parte rei . . . [1] In priori membro continentur omnes relationes rationis, quae inter alia entia rationis cogitantur, praesertim si talia entia rationis sint mere conficta, ut est relatio similitudinis inter duas chymaeras, vel dissimilitudinis inter chymaeram et hircocervum, et similes. [2] Huc etiam pertinere possunt relationes rationis inter duas privationes, quo modo unus locus tenebrosus dicitur similis alteri. . . . hae relationes fundatae in privationibus vel negationibus rerum, aliquod maius in rebus ipsis habeant fundamentum, saltem remotum. [3] Tertio, possunt ad hoc membrum reduci relationes rationis inter entia realia possibilia, non tamen existentia, ut est relatio antecessionis Adami ad Antichristum, et similes, quae maius habent in rebus fundamentum, quia extrema earum non sunt omnino entia rationis, quamvis, ut apprehenduntur ut extrema vel subiecta relationum, sint entia rationis." DM d54s6n3.

48. "At vero relationes rationis, quae in rebus existentibus habent aliquod fundamentum, subdistingui ulterius possunt . . . [1] primo constitui possunt relationes illae quae tribuuntur rei existenti respectu termini non existentis, sive illud sit ens possibile, sive fictum, ut relatio prioritatis Petri existentis ad Antichristum futurum, vel diversitatis Petri existentis a chymaera. [DM d54s6n4] [2] Secundo constituuntur sub illo membro relationes quae concipiuntur inter extrema, quae sunt reale quid, tamen in re non habent distinctionem realem vel actualem ex natura rei, sed rationis tantum. . . . Et iuxta diversam distinctionem rationis inter extrema huius relationis, erit etiam diversitas inter huiusmodi relationes. Interdum enim est tantum distinctio rationis ratiocinantis, ut est in relatione identitatis eiusdem ad se ipsum; aliquando vero est distinctio rationis ratiocinatae, qui in re est fundamentalis seu virtualis, ut est relatio distinctionis inter attributa divina et sic de aliis. [DM d54s6n5] [3] Tertio, constituuntur in hoc ordine illae relationes rationis, quae licet versentur inter res distinctas, et alioqui capaces relationum realium praedicamentalium, ex defectu tamen intrinseca fundamenti sunt rationis, vel

in utroque, vel in altero extremo. . . . . Unde ad hoc genus spectant imprimis relationes omnes, quae in utroque extremo fundantur tantum in denominatione extrinseca, ut est relatio signi ad placitum, quae tam in signo, quam in signato est relatio rationis, ... Deinde, eiusdem sunt modi relationis domini et servi inter homines, nam illae non fundantur nisi in quadam extrinseca denominatione sumpta a voluntate; et similes sunt aliae multae, ut omnes illae quae oriuntur ex contractibus et voluntatibus humanis, ut inter maritum et uxorem in ratione coniugum, inter ementem et vendentem ex voluntate contrahendi, et sic de aliis. [DM d54s6n6] [4] Quarto et ultimo possumus aliud membrum constituere earum relationum, in quibus multi ex praedictis defectibus ex necessariis ad relationem realem concurrunt, cum aliquo fundamento remoto ex parte rei, et proximo in aliqua denominatione extrinseca; et huiusmodi videntur esse relationes rationis, quae intentiones logicales appellantur, ut sunt relationes generis, speciei, praedicati, subiecti, et similes." DM d54s6n8. See also Doyle (1987, 63–69).

49. To my knowledge the first overall study of Suárez's theory of beings of reason was published in Spanish by Yela Utrila (1948). In English a more reliable study was written by Canteñs (1999). Neither study is critical of Suárez's theory.

50. The claim that beings of reason belong to metaphysics in the same way as real beings was first made by Clemens Timpler at the beginning of the seventeenth century. See Eschweiler (1928, 292). At the end of the seventeenth century, another Protestant, Johann Clauberg, writes: "Est quaedam scientia, quae contemplatur ens quatenus ens est . . . ea vulgo *Metaphysica*, sed aptius *Ontologia* . . . nominatur. . . . Quod a vulgo res et aliquid, a dialecticis thema, a philosophis etiam ens appellatur, vocibus hisce in latissima significatione sumptis, illud ita describi potest: ens est quicquid quovis modo est, cogitari ac dici potest." (1691/1968, 283). Trevisiani (1993) claims that Clauberg disagrees with Timpler on this point. I have not noticed any disagreement here.

51. For a discussion in the context of the Meinongian tradition, see e.g. Parsons (1979).

52. Doubts about the equivalence of Suárez's various descriptions of beings of reason have also been expressed recently by Millán-Puelles (1990/1996, 521) but without an argument showing that they are nonequivalent.

53. This line was taken by the majority of the Scotists. John Punch, for instance, writes: "Negationes et privationes non sunt entia rationis. Haec est communior Scotistarum contra aliquos Thomistas, quos sequitur Suárez [DM d54s3]. Probatur manifeste ex dictis, quia insunt rebus realibus independenter a consideratione, verum est enim dicere quod caecus nullo intellectu considerante habet privationem visus et brutum negationem rationalitatis, ergo non sunt entia rationis." PCI d1q2n19. See also Mastri/Belluto in chapter 7, section C.3.

54. Pace Doyle who states that Suárez can "with total consistency" say at times that "privation as such is a being of reason" but again that it is "not a fiction" but "a defect of being" (1987, 59). Millán-Puelles also adopts Suarez's view (1990/1996, 585). The problem of how to differentiate between real privations/negations is addressed by Millán-Puelles as follows: "As Aristotle contended '. . . just as there are no differences in nothing, so there can be none in non-being'. But it is such differences which are constitutive of positive quiddities as such. It is evidently impossible to find something, in the makeup of the quiddity of a given absence, that would be positively responsible for its being different from other absences. . . . It is true that absences are not relations, and yet they are inherently related to that of which they are absences. It is in terms of such relations, therefore, that it is possible to render absences specific. . . . Consider, for example, the cases of deafness and blindness. Although it is not possible for the difference specific to hearing to be a formal constituent of the quiddity of deafness, or . . . of blindness, it is nevertheless unquestionable that deafness and blindness are different from each other reductive [sic], since hearing is different from sight." (1990/1996, 589) In my view, Millán-Puelles's point cannot concern real privations/negations but only nonreal ones. (The difference between deafness and blindness is not real but "projected" by our minds.)

55. According to the potentialists, beings of reason are in some sense real. Suárez notes this explicitly in *De anima*: "Certe, si eiusmodi entia rationis existerent etiam quando non cognoscuntur, realia plane essent: non enim medium datur inter esse fictum et reale." DA d9q3n30.

56. "[P]roprio . . . modo dicuntur [entia rationis] actu esse, quando actu finguntur" DM d54s2n24. Other places of Suárez's actualism: DM d3s1n10, d6s7n2, d8s2n20, d25s1n5.

57. "[E]sse aliquam vim, quae finxerit, vel, ut tuo verbo utar, quae fabricata sit hominem," Cic. *Ac.* 2 (in the sense of to form, shape, or make); "animo et cogitatione fingere," Cic. *Tusc.* 5,24,68 (in the sense of to represent mentally or in speech, to imagine, conceive, think, suppose). More narrowly, it may mean "to contrive, devise, invent, or feign something untrue." Hence, 'fictus' means "feigned, fictitious, or false": "in amicitia nihil fictum est, nihil simulatum" Cic. *Lael.* 8, 26.

58. For instance, Suárez has the whole Disputation 9 (On Falsity) without mentioning beings of reason.

59. Although Suárez has long Disputation 5 on individuality, he limits his discussion to real beings. See Suárez (1596/21982). I briefly discuss the issue in Novotný (2011, 45).

60. Some of these questions were noticed by later Baroque authors, such as Mastri/Belluto. For instance, concerning the reidentification of beings of reason, they say: "[O]mnes fateri tenentur, per repetitos actus posse ab eodem intellectu idem ens rationis saepius fieri." DOA d3q4a1n59.

6. Hurtado's Fallibilism

1. An abbreviated version of this chapter is to be published as "The Historical Non-Significance of Suárez's Theory of Beings of Reason: A Lesson From Hurtado" (Novotný forthcoming-c).

2. Hurtado also discusses beings of reason in section 4 of Logical Disputation 1 (On the Object of Logic). The original 1615 version of the section is entitled "An Attack on an Opinion about Being of Reason" ("Impugnatur opinio de ente rationis," DUP-L d1s4n17-24:72–74). The section has about 1,500 words, and the primary targets of the section are those who claim that the object of logic is being of reason. For our purposes nothing noteworthy is said there. The revised version of the section, entitled "Whether Being of Reason is the Object of Logic" ("Utrum ens rationis sit logicae obiectum?" UP-L d1s4n41–80:51–57), is already more substantive. It is about 5,500 words long and it contains an interesting analysis of what the expression 'being of reason' means (d1s1n41–44:51). Hurtado briefly summarizes the results of this analysis at the beginning of the revised Metaphysical Disputation 19.

3. "Quid sit ens rationis [s1n2–19], Utrum Deus cognoscat entia rationis? [s2n20–29] Nonnulla expediuntur [s3n30–33]."

4. "[D]ividitur ens rationis in privationem, negationem, et relationem, id est secundam intentionem. Quod intellige quando haec apprehenduntur diverso modo, quo sunt. . . . Ens rationis dividitur pro universitate mendaciorum . . . quo pacto certis carceribus teneatur, consule Patrem Suárez [d54s4]." DUP-M d19s3n33:606.

5. Hurtado's metatheory of beings of reason agrees with Suárez's in that beings of reason belong to metaphysics rather than logic: "[C]ontrariorum eamdem esse disciplinam, quapropter . . . ens rationis spectare ad metaphysicum, quia opponitur enti reali, cum quo habet veram oppositionem et fictam aliquam affinitatem, de quo late disputat Pater Suarez [DM d54], in cuius initio ait esse dialecticum errorem opinari illius considerationem ad Dialecticam pertinere. Unaquaeque facultas [=disciplina] . . . considerat entia rationis in particulari, suis obiectis . . . opposita: at vero considerare naturam et essentiam [et causas et divisio] entis rationis proprium est metaphysici instituti." DUP-M d19Intr. n1:599.

6. Hurtado does not give the names of the Thomists he has in mind. It could not have been John of St. Thomas (Poinsot), for he published his *Cursus* years later (1631–35).

7. "Commune est Thomistis universis ens rationis esse, quod nihil intrinsecum point in rebus. Unde deducunt secundas intentiones generis, et speciei, subiecti, et praedicati esse ens rationis, quia nihil ponunt in obiecto: item omnes extrinsecae denominationes erunt entia rationis. Huius asserti nullam eorum vidi rationem, sed illud ponunt ut Metaphysicum principium. Quos ita primum arguo: Id, quod a parte rei habet esse physicum, est ens reale, et non rationis . . . [et] extrinseca denominatio est aliquid conceptus realis physice

alicubi existens: ergo habet esse physicum a parte rei: probo antecedens, cognitio v.g. est denominatio extrinseca obiecto, intrinseca autem intellectui: ergo extrinseca denominatio habet esse intrinsecum alicubi." DUP-M 19s1n2:599. The discussion continues in n3–8.

8. "[1] Est ergo ens rationis, quod tantum habet esse obiective in intellectu. . . . [2] Ubi duo reperiuntur, et cognitio, quae rem denominat cognitam et obiective in mente existentem, et res ipsa sive obiectum, quod extrinsece a tali cognitione denominatur. [3] Quando cognitio denominat rem, quae habet illud esse sicut cognoscitur et denominatur, tunc talis res non habet esse obiective tantum in intellectu: sed praeter illam extrinsecam denominationem et existentiam obiectivam in intellectu habet etiam proprium conceptum obiectivum respondentem illi denominationi et conceptui formali. In quo eventu nullum fit ens rationis. [4] Ut cum quis mente affirmat Petrus est homo, identitas inter Petrum et hominem habet esse obiective in intellectu id affirmante . . . [sed] praeter illud esse obiective, habet etiam esse reale identitatis, quia Petrus habet identitatem cum homine etiam extra intellectum Pauli, [ergo] . . . Petrus est homo non habet esse obiective tantum in intellectu. [5] Quando autem cognitio non terminatur ad rem sicuti est, neque illi respondet obiectum . . . tunc fit ens rationis: quia obiectum non est in re, sed tantum in cognitione; tale autem obiectum vocatur ens rationis, quia non habet esse nisi a ratione apprehensum, [6] exempli gratia, ego affirmo quantitas est substantia, quae tamen a parte rei est accidens, ecce in meo intellectu et cognitione quantitas est substantia, idest, iudicatur esse substantia: at vero in se non est substantia; ecce identitas substantiae et quantitatis nullum habet esse nisi obiective in intellectu." DUP-M 19s1n9:600.

9. The scholastics accounted for judging (predication) in terms of "identity." In their view predication is the identification of the predicate and the subject by means of the copula 'is'. A version of this traditional scholastic view has been rigorously formulated and defended within the tradition of contemporary analytic philosophy by Sousedík (2006).

10. "Unde colliges primo, halucinatum esse Vallesium, et cum illo non paucos, negantes entia rationis: nam tam est clarum esse entia rationis, quam apertum eos fuisse deceptos: multa enim affirmamus et negamus, quae non habent esse praeter nostram affirmationem et negationem. Obiecta igitur quae sic denominatur et repraesentatur diverso modo, quo sunt . . . propositione Petrus est lapis, repraesentantur Petrus, lapis, et unio, ea autem unio nullibi habet esse, nisi in cognitione." DUP-M 19s1n10:601.

11. "Colligo secundo . . . quia ens rationis tantum habet esse obiective in intellectu . . . actus, qui facit ens rationis, est falsus necessario: patet consequentia: quia ex parte obiecti non est quod actus repraesentat . . . ergo talis actus est difformis obiecto: ergo falsus . . . Quam explicationem colligo non modo ex Aristotele et D. Thoma . . . verum et ex eodem Patre Suarez, Vazquez, Fonseca, et caeteris agentibus de ente rationis." DUP-M d19s1n11:601.

12. "Colligo tertio: male nonnullos opinari esse ens rationis ante actualem operationem intellectus . . . Quos impugno, quia ens rationis in se non habet esse, neque actuale, neque possibile . . . [1] Dices, posse esse. Contra . . . quia id habet formaliter ab actu falso possibili." DUP-M d19s1n12:601. "Colligo quarto, ens rationis non praecedere ratione actum, quo effingitur . . . [2] Dicunt aliqui, prius est esse, quam cognosci. Contra, quia hoc est verum in rebus habentibus esse distinctum a cognosci: quod si ens rationis consistit in cognosci, quo pacto est prius, quam cognosci?" DUP-M d19s1n13:602-3.

13. "[1] Colligo quinto, ad efformandum ens rationis, non requiri ut obiectum actus sit impossible; sed requiri, ut obiectum non sit sicut repraesentatur per actum; quia in eo solo casu habet esse obiective tantum in intellectu, [2] v.g. Petro non currente ego affirmo Petrus currit; existentia exercita Petri non habet esse nisi obiective in meo intellectu: quia licet habeat esse possibile, id tamen non representatur per illum actum, sed solum esse actuale, ut actuale: actualitas autem illa solum est in meo intelectu. [3] E contra vero si actus conformatur cum obiecto, licet obiectum in se sit chimaera, tamen comparatione illius actus, non est ens rationis, quia habet aliud esse, quam esse per illum actum, verbi gracia, cognosco ego." DUP-M d19s1n14:602.

14. "Petrum decipi meus actus est verus, quia conformatur cum obiecto; et quia ille actus nihil fingit, quare eius obiectum non est obiective tantum in intellectu per illum, sed praeter esse obiectivum per illum, habet aliud esse: nempe esse obiective tantum in intellectu alterius, vel fuisse obiective in eodem intellectu per alium actum." DUP-M d19s1n14:602.

15. "Rogas, utrum per simplicem apprehensionem fiat ens rationis? [1] Respondeo, per solam apprehensionem subiecti vel praedicati non fieri, quia . . . in illis non reperiri falsitatem. [2] Dices, quando apprehenditur chimaera ut subiectum huius propositionis, Chimaera est ens rationis: tunc fit ens rationis, quia chimaera non habet esse nisi obiective in intellectu. [3] Respondeo, ibi nullum fieri ens rationis . . . quia obiectum illi actus non habet esse obiective tantum in intellectu per illum, sed potius habet aliud esse, cui conformatur actus: [4] nec tunc chimaerae tribuitur esse, sed potius negatur: idem est enim dicere, Chimaera est ens rationis, ac Chimaera est aliquid fictum, cui quia negatur esse, actus est verus. Est ergo illa propositio de obiecti sicuti est, [5] ly sicuti est sumpto non pro esse reali, sed pro esse ficto, quod vere convenit chimerae." DUP-M d19s1n15:602-3.

16. "[1] observa, in ente rationis duo considerari: actum fingentem et obiectum fictum. Actus fingens realis est et eius denominatio, qua obiectum est fictum et cognitum, est etiam realis, in quo non differt ab ente reali . . . [2] At obiectum fictum, nihil est et tota denominatio realis ficti et cogniti cadit supra nihil: [3] et ideo est falsa, quia non cadit in obiectum ex parte sui habens id, quod illi dat cognitio: et hoc est esse obiective tantum in intellectu. . . . [4] itaque discrimen est inter obiecta et non inter actus." DUP-M d19s1n19:603.

17. If it seems counterintuitive to consider fictitious being to be a sort of real being, consider this: Mental acts are real; hence, the objects that are immanent (="staying within") to these acts are also real. Hence, the fictitious objects created by our minds are also real, for they are proper parts of real mental acts and every proper part of a real whole is real.

18. We see that 'chimera' means here not a fictional animal but a (necessarily) false proposition.

19. "[1] Itaque ut aliquid sit ens rationis, ita debet esse obiective in intellectu ut per illum non cognoscatur sicuti est: nam si cognoscitur sicuti est, . . . destruitur per intellectum: [2] exempli gratia, ego dico quantitas est substantia. Do esse obiectivum identitati illarum rerum, quod non habent a parte rei et sic facio chimaeram. [3] Cum autem dico chimaera est dicere quantitatem esse substantiam, iste . . . actus non facit ens rationis sed potius destruit et . . . iam factum actu priori; et hic secundus est verus, quia conformatur obiecto, quod habet esse in se distinctum ab esse obiectivo, quod habet in intellectum per secundum actum." DUP-M d19s1n16:602.

20. "Multo minus fit ens rationis . . . per sensus, quia hi neque affirmant aliquid neque negant. . . . [V]oluntas non efficit entia rationis, sed efficta amat aut odit." DUP-M d19s1n18:603.

21. "Primum opinor fide et ratione factum Deum non efficere entia rationis a me explicata: repugnat enim Deo actus falsus." DUP-M d19s3n20:603.

22. "Difficilius sane est dignoscere, noverit ne Deus entia rationis a nobis effecta? Qua in re magnum est dissidium inter P. Franciscum Suarez et Gabrielem Vazquez, quod fateor a me non posse sine difficultate componi. P. Suarez [d54s2n23] affirmat, dubitari non posse entia rationis a Deo cognosci. . . . quia Deus comprehendit actus humanos . . . ergo cognoscit eorumdem obiecta; patet consequentia quia actus non potest comprehendi, quin cognoscatur de quo obiecto fit. . . ." DUP-M d19s3n21:603 "Respondet P. Vazquez: Deum cognoscere extrema realia, quae sunt obiectum illius actus, non tamen unionem fictam." DUP-M d19s3n22:603.

23. "Haec solutio mihi non placet, nam fictio non solum repraesentat extrema realia huius chimaerae, exempli gratia, homo est irrationalis, sed repraesentat identitatem inter haec extrema, immo ea ratione propositio est falsa. [DUP-M d19s3n22:603] Secundo probatur quia licet sit imperfectio fingere chimaeram quia apprehenditur res diverso modo ac est, tamen cognoscere ens ab alio male cognosci . . . est . . . perfectio; sicut est magna perfectio cognoscere aliorum errores." DUP-M d19s3n23:604.

24. In case of human beings the perfection (in some loose sense) is not just the knowledge of the errors of other people but also of one's own past errors: "[P]ostquam quis cognovit suum errorem, potest actu reflexo cognoscere se errasse et obiectum a se fuisse confictum. Hic reflexus actus esset verus . . . ergo confirmatur obiecto, ergo illud repraesentat sicuti est." DUP-M d19s3n25:604.

25. "Vazquez . . . hanc opinionem mordet accerrime . . . quia si Deus mente sua retinet id quod non est, licet non primario sed secundario (primario fictum est ab intellectu humano), re vera format in mente sua figmentum et monstrum illud, quod . . . virtute sui intellectu conservat. . . . Confirmatur . . . si Deus nunc cognoscit ens rationis ab homine factum, ergo illud cognovit ab aeterno, ergo habet ab aeterno aliquod esse obiectivum . . . a solo Deo, ergo fit a Deo ens rationis." DUP-M d19s2n25:604.

26. "Ad probationem: Deus nec retinet aliquid neque conservat monstrum ab homine fictum sed potius illud verissimis suis actibus destruit. . . . Deus non tribuit figmento esse quod illi tribuit humanus intellectus, sed potius illud destruit cognoscendo hominem esse deceptum . . . videt illud ab homine formatum quae visio verissima est quia exprimit obiectum sicuti est." DUP-M d19s2n27:605.

27. "[L]icet [ens rationis] habeat illud esse obiective in Deo, tamen non habet esse obiective tantum in Deo: nam etiam ex parte obiecti est, sicuti est in Deo obiective . . . et non diverso modo . . . in se. Ens autem rationis licet nullum habeat in se esse reale actuale nec possible, habet tamen in se esse fictum in aliqua differentia temporis vel saltem esse fingibile et tale cognoscitur a Deo." DUP-M d19s2n28:605.

28. "Sectio 1: Utrum denominationes extrinsecae sint ens rationis? Subsectio 1: Sententiae affirmantis fundamenta convello; Subsectio 2: Impugnatur haec sententia; Sectio 2: Utrum ens rationis sit aliquid derivatum ex denominatione extrinseca reali; Subsectio 1: Sententia prima; Subsectio 2: Proponitur sententia derivari ens rationis ex omni denominatione extrinseca; Subsectio 3: Impugnatio prima eius sententiae; Subsectio 4: Impugnatio secunda; Subsectio 5: Duo argumenta solvuntur; Subsectio 6: Impugnatio tertia eiusdem sententiae; Sectio 3: Quid sit ens rationis; Sectio 4: Nonnulla corollaria; Sectio 5: De causis entis rationis et divisione; Sectio 6: Utrum Deus cognoscat ens rationis." UP-M d19.

29. "Recognosce quatuor significationes entis rationis. . . . [1] Est enim ens rationis effective et subiective pro actu intellectus quem ratio producit in se. [2] Denominative pro passive denominatione per quem obiecta dicitur cognita. [3] Fundamentaliter pro denominatione extrinseca praebente fundamentum ut a nobis concipiatur ut intrinseca. [4] Propriissime pro ente quod non est a parte rei fingitur tamen esse." UP-M d19Intr.n2:942.

30. "[1] E quibus constat ens rationis esse nomen aequivocum: significat enim plura ut plura, quae . . . in nullo conveniunt: ens enim fictum in nullo convenit cum vero: actus intellectus quid habent commune cum ente ficto? [2] Praesens disputatio non est ad explicandum ens rationis in prima significatione: nam de actibus rationis . . . agit animasticus. Neque agimus de ente rationis in secunda significatione: illa enim spectat ad logicum: tertia autem significatio ex parte spectat ad metaphysicum. [3] Quarta autem propriissime: agimus enim de ente

rationis ut opponitur enti reali. . . . In tribus autem primis significationibus non distinguitur ens rationis ab ente reali ut sic." UP-M d19Intr.n2:942.

31. "Sit secunda sententia, ex omni denominatione extrinseca derivari quoddam ens. . . . Haec sententia non quia nova displicet, nec quod sit sine authore ullo, sed quod sine ullo fundamento asseritur. Quam libet ex instituto proponere et argumentorum inanitatem ostendere." D19s2sb2n29:946.

32. I hope, however, that even my brief report suffices to show that Hurtado's and Suárez's discussions of extrinsic denomination substantially differ, even though they both agree that exstrinsic denominations are real. Hurtado, *pace* Doyle (1987, 75n156), does not provide "an insightful understanding of Suárez on the reality of extrinsic denominations."

33. "Primum argumentum et duae confirmationes quibus nunc probavi denomi-nationes extrinsecas esse reales evincunt aperte ens rationis absolute non posse in illis consistere: nunc autem disquiro utrum ex illis denominationibus extrinsecis aliquid derivetur in obiecta quod vere sit ens rationis nullum habens esse a parte rei, sed obiective in intellectu" (emphasis mine). UP-M d19s2n19:945. I translate 'derivetur' as 'results' in order to avoid equivocation: From extrinsic denominations one can "derive" beings of reason "in objects" (this is what the proponents of the resultant extrinsic-denomination views hold) or one can derive extrinsic denominations from various forms (this is how extrinsic denominations are made).

34. "[A] Communis est inter Thomistas opinio omnem extrinsecam denominatio-nem esse ens rationis. . . . [B] Ostendi tamen . . . eos non esse locutos de ente rationis ut opponitur enti reali ut sic, sed de uno ente extrinseco alicui obiecto, intrinseco tamen aliis. . . . [C] Exempli gratia obiectum esse cognitum dicunt esse ens rationis, quia esse cognitum non est intrinsecum obiecto cognito . . . at vero cognitio qua obiectum dicitur cognitum, quamvis non est intrinseca obiecto, est tamen intrinseca intellectui. . . . [D] Definiunt autem hi authores ens rationis quod nihil intrinsecum ponit in rebus. Quae definitio si intelliga-tur de omnibus rebus est vera; si autem intelligatur de aliquibus rebus solum, est falsa, quia ens intrinsecum alicui rei potest esse aliis extrinsecum." UP-M d19s1n4:943.

35. The same point is repeated later by Hurtado: "Haec sententia [ens rationis consistit in denominatine extrinseca] a multis authoribus docetur non de ente rationis formaliter sed fundamentaliter: in tertia significatione praemissa . . . estque in eo sensu vera. Tamen absolute censendum eiusmodi denominationes a formis realibus non esse absolute entia rationis sed realia. . . . eamque docet P. Suárez [DM d54s2n10] et P. Rubius tractatu de ente rationis." UP-M d19s1sb2n13:944.

36. Hurtado's subsection 1 concludes with a criticism of Rubio's view. I mention this, for in (Novotný 2010) I have argued that Suárez's and Rubio's views of the nature of beings of reason were identical. Hurtado seems to have read in

Rubio the restricted extrinsic-denomination view (which Suárez does not hold), although he points out that Rubio's text is obscure: "P. Rubius in tractatu de ente rationis plane fatetur esse plures denominationes extrinsecas reales ut columnam esse dexteram, obiectum esse visum, et alias. Affirmat tamen esse cognitum formaliter esse ens rationis, quia sic habet praecise esse obiective in intellectu. In explicando hoc esse obiective ille mihi videtur tam obscure versari ut a me quoque percipiatur obscure." UP-M d19s1sb1n10:943. Hurtado tries to understand and criticize Rubio in UP-M d19s1n10-11:943-944. Gilson (1913/1979, 110) quotes Rubio in a passage that also seems to indicate that Rubio held the restricted extrinsic-denomination view.

37. "Nonnulli sunt opinati nihil derivari ex actibus voluntatis aut aliarum potentiarum in obiecta, quod vere sit ens rationis: derivari autem ex actibus intellectus." UP-M d19s2sb1n20:945.

38. "Constat eam sententiam nulla ratione vel leviter probari: nunc impugnanda est a priori et ostendendum id quod fingitur ex denominatione extrinseca derivari non esse ens rationis sed reale." UP-M d19s2sb3n39:948.

39. "Superest ut hi authores confugiant ad entia moralia, quae nec sunt realia nec rationis formaliter: ut dominium, significatio vocum, valor . . . et similia. Quibus uno verbo respondeo omnia entia moralia esse denominationes intrinsecas aut extrinsecas ab aliquo ente reale . . . dominium . . . creatum est denominatio extrinseca a voluntate transferentis ius . . . significatio vocum est denominatio extrinseca a voluntate eas imponentis, sicut valor monetae a voluntate principis. . . . Nullum ergo est ens morale, quod non sit reale." UP-M d19s2sb5n51:950.

40. "[H]ae enim propositiones Deus nunc cognoscitur a me et Deus est cognitus nunc a me, distinguuntur in grammatica, nedum in metaphysica." d19s1sb1n11:944. Again here and at other places: "pueri enim primam orationem activam vertunt per passivam: ego amo Deum, Deus amatur a me: suntque istae propositiones de eodem obiecto et synonymae." UP-M d19s2sb3n42:948.

41. "Non potest commode disputari an sit possible ens rationis nisi eius definitionem explanemus. . . . Philosophi atque theologi asseruerunt ens rationis distinctum ab omni esse reali tam actuali quam possibili, positivo et negativo. Eius autem definitionem adstruxerunt: *Ens rationis est* [1] *cuius totum esse consistit in cognosci, sive* [2] *quod non habet esse nisi obiective in intellectu.* Quam definitionem communem proponit P. Suarez [DM d54s1n6]." UP-M d19s3n64-65:952.

42. Concerning H1N5: If the total being consists in being known then there is no "part" of a being of reason that would precede its actual existence in our minds. Hence, although formulations [1] and H1N5 differ, they are equivalent.

43. "[Q]uam [definitionem] sic explico: habere se obiective in intellectu est cognosci per intellectum: in quo obiecta dicuntur esse quia in illo sunt cognitiones imagines obiectorum . . . immo imago solet dici esse res quam

repraesentat: ut cum videmus Caesaris effigiem, dicimus, hic est Caesar: est Caesar intentionaliter sive repraesentative ... in sui cognitione ut in imagine ... obiectum enim non est proprie in sua imagine, sed per metaphoram, dum imago est repraesentatio rei. Unde concludo omnia obiecta quae cognoscuntur habere in intellectu esse obiective, id est, repraesentari ut obiecta suarum imaginum." UP-M d19s3n65:952.

44. "Est tamen hoc discrimen: multa obiecta habent in se aliud esse distinctum ab esse intentionali ... et repraesentatione sui: ... exempli gratia dico Petrus est homo: hoc obiectum et habet esse intentionaliter et obiective in meo intellectu, et praeterquam representari habet etiam in se id quod dicitur ... : Petrus enim homo est intra et extra meum intellectum: ac propterea est ens reale ... neque habet obiective tantum esse in intellectu. Quapropter ea propositio Petrus est homo ideo est vera, quia Petrus est homo. Idem dixerim de privatione et negatione. Haec enim obiecta Antonius est caecus, lapis non est videns ... non solum sunt obiective intra intellectum, sed etiam extra illum ... perinde ... contingunt independenter a nostro intellectu." UP-M d19s3n66:953

45. "Alia vero obiecta non sunt extra illam propositionem per quam affirmantur aut negantur, exempli gratia Deus non est trinus, homo est brutum: haec obiecta non sunt in se sicut intellectu concipiuntur. Carentia enim Trinitatis non est in Deo ... nec irrationalitas est in homine. ... Ecce haec obiecta habent esse obiective in intellectu per illas propositiones; at nullibi habent aliud esse: habent ergo esse obiective tantum in intellectu. Neque vero illae propositiones repraesentant solum extrema realia quae habent esse extra intellectum. ... Qui enim dicit, homo est brutum non solum concipit hominem et brutum sed etiam utriusque identitatem realem: quae nullibi est nisi in illa representatione. Quae ideo est falsa, quia repraesentat in obiecto esse quod vere non est." UP-M d19s3n67:953.

46. Note also that the quotes clearly indicate Hurtado's mentalism, see also Schmutz (2007). Whereas Suárez has been charged with / praised for being a mentalist, although the evidence is that he is not, Hurtado clearly is one: All we know directly are images and only indirectly we know what they represent (similarly as we directly see the statue of Caesar but only derivatively the real Caesar). See Gracia (1991b, 1993) who argues against Wells (1993) that Suárez was not a mentalist. See also Cronin (1966).

47. "Secundo deduces ... denominationes extrinsecas a forma reali extrinseca non esse ens rationis: quia illae nihil sunt fictum, sed existunt a parte rei. ... illae denominationes sunt sicut affirmantur: quae omnia aliena sunt ab ente rationis, quod est chymaera reddens actum falsum." UP-M d19s4n71:953.

48. "Deduces non effici ens rationis per omnem actum ad illum terminatum ... : exempli gratia fingitur directe chimaera: possum ego habere duos alios actus reflexos: alterum quo reflexe cognosco a me iudicari hominem esse brutum, praescindendo a veritate et falsitate illius iudicii directi. Iste actus reflexus non facit ens rationis: quia licet terminatur ad chimaeram, non tamen illam

affirmando: iudicium enim reflexum verum est affirmans rem sicuti est: ego enim iudicavi hominem esse brutum, ergo actus quo reflexe cognosco me iudicasse, verus est. . . . Secundus actus reflexus potest esse quo affirmetur fictam esse chimaeram per actum directum: hunc actum non dare esse, sed potius adimere." UP-M d19s4n74:954.

49. "Quinto deduces contra Durandum, Valesium, et alios non paucos dari entia rationis. Etenim negari non potest posse a nobis affirmari aliquid impossibile. . . . Preterea dices non respondere in obiecto praeter ens reale. Respondeo . . . respondere etiam aliquid quod non est in obiecto: alioquin iudicium non esset falsum." UP-M d19s4n75-6:954.

50. "Ex hac doctrina haec deducuntur corollaria. Primum, non recte dividi ens rationis in formale actuale et in fundamentale. Nam ens fundamentale non est chimaera neque fingitur, sed in sententia suorum authorum pullulate ex denominationibus extrinsecis independenter ab operatione intellectus." UP-M d19s4n70:953.

51. "Tertio deduces privationem et negationem non esse proprie species entis rationis. Quia omne ens rationis est fictum sine fundamento in rebus proximo vel remoto. . . . privationes et negationes non sunt aliquid fictum. . . . Conveniunt item cum ente reali positivo in independentia a cognosci et in non habere esse obiective tantum in intellectu et in fundanda propositione vera, eius veritati praebito fundamento." UP-M d19s4n72:953.

52. "Tandem deduco ens esse nomen pure aequivocum: quia aptitudo ad existendum et repugnantia ad existendum sunt primo diversa . . . : cum autem ens rationis non habet nisi esse fictum, non potest convenire cum esse vero. Imo neque habet ullam analogiam etiam impropriam qualem in risu habent pratum et homo: pratum enim intrinsecam habet viriditatem per quam hilarescere et ridere videtur: ens autem rationis nihil habet ex parte obiecti quo realis imitetur. Apprehenditur quidem a nobis ac si esset, non tamen propterea est." UP-M d19s4n77:954.

53. "Causas physicas nullas habet quia cum nihil physicum sit, nullam habet physicam dependentiam. Causam materialem fictam potest habere, ut cum apprehenditur habere subiectum aliquod praedicatum accidentarium. . . . Potest item habere causam formalem fictum ut si concipiamus effectum aliquem formalem impossibilem ortum ex aliqua forma. Efficientem habet intellectum ut quod, ut quo vero actum fingentem: haec efficientia est intentionalis et non physica, quia dum cognitio repraesentat quod non est dicitur facere ens rationis. Causam finalem potest habere non quidem directam: nec enim natura per se inclinat ad actum falsum: neque aliquis potest assentiri obiecto nisi appareat esse verum: habet ergo eam causam finalem quam habet actus falsus. Hac de re consule P. Suárez" [DM d54s2]." UP-M d19s5n78:954.

54. "De actibus, quibus fit ens rationis, maior est controversia. Dico primo, ens rationis fieri per actum falsum quo iudicamus existere aut existere posse id

quod reipsa repugnat esse: ut hominem esse brutum. Item cum diximus esse aliquid impossibile quod re ipsa possible est." UP-M d19s5n79:954.

55. "[1] Dubium potest esse, utrum per iudicium falsum repraesentans rem possibilem ut existentem fiat ens rationis quando talis res non existit. Exempli gratia non currente Petro dicat aliquis Petrus currit an ille cursus Petri sit ens rationis vel reale? [2] Respondeo quaestionem esse de nomine. Illud non esse ens rationis videtur ostendi inde, quod ille cursus habet esse possible: ergo non est ens rationis: quia hoc est chymaera; existentia autem cursus Petri non est chymaera. [3] Contra vero illud esse ens rationis suadetur, quia illa existentia ut exercita nullibi habet esse nisi obiective in intellectu. . . . [4] Ad argumentum pro prima sententia respondetur, frequentiora entia rationis esse chymaeras: quo non tollitur fieri alia entia rationis, quando non habent illud esse quod de illis praedicatur, licet illud possint habere. In qua sententia ens rationis ut sic est quod ut affirmatur vel negatur, non habet esse nisi obiective in intellectu. [5] Ad argumentum pro secunda sententia respondetur per accidens esse obiectis carere statu existentiae exercitae: nec enim ex hac suppositione expendenda sunt entia rationi, sed praecise ex absoluta repugnantia ad existendum." UP-M d19s5n80:954.

56. Hurtado could arbitrarily decide not to call contingently false propositions, judged to be true, by the term 'being of reason', but then we may ask, "What are they?"—they can hardly be classified as real beings.

57. "Dico secundo. Intellectio praecisiva non efficit ens rationis." UP-M d19s5n81:955.

58. "Dico tertio per simplicem apprehensionem subiecti et predicati non fieri ens rationis. Probatur aperte quia in illa apprehensione nullam reperiri falsitatem." UP-M d19s5n82:955.

59. "Dico quarto. Apprehensione unionis potest fieri ens rationis incomplexum, sicut falsitas incomplexa. Si enim apprehenditur identitas quantitatis et substantiae, illa tantum habet esse obiective in intellectu per illam apprehensionem." UP-M d19s5n83:955.

60. "Dico quinto. Neque sensus externi neque interni efficiunt ens rationis etiam incomplexum. . . . quia sensus interni aut externi neque affirmant aliquid neque negant. . . . Obiicit P. Suarez facultatem imaginatricem habere vim componendi species obiectorum incompossibilium. . . . Ad argumentum ergo respondeo imaginationem non habere vim ad percipiendam unionem obiectorum incompossibilium." UP-M d19s5n84-5:955.

61. "Ens rationis frequenter dividitur in privationem, negationem, et relationem (haec relatio usurpatur pro denominatione extrinseca secundae intentionis; ab aliis forte usurpabitur pro omni denominatione extrinseca). Haec autem divisio non est entis rationis formaliter, sed fundamentaliter tantum. . . . Ens autem rationis proprie usurpatum dividitur in omnia figmenta, quae intellectus creatus potest moliri." UP-M d19s5n87:955.

62. Although it is comprehensive I have left out some off-hand issues briefly raised but not discussed. For instance, Hurtado points out that two people can think the same being of reason: "Adverte, posse duos homines decipi circa idem obiectum, quod habet esse obiective tantum ab illorum intellectibus . . . nihil enim prohibet duos hominess simul decipi circa idem obiectum." DUP-M d19s3n25:604.

63. Hurtado is still classified as a Suárezian in Eschweiler (1928, 307) and Pereira and Fastiggi (2006, 19–20). Differences between Hurtado and "standard scholasticism" were noted already by Caruso (1975). Hurtado's misinterpretation of Aquinas's views on universals is carefully analyzed by Heider (2010). Given the close links that a theory of beings of reason and a theory of universals has to other issues in scholastic metaphysical systems, it is almost certain that Hurtado's views substantially differ from Suárez's views in other questions as well.

Chapter 7: Mastri/Belluto's Modified Objectualism

1. An abbreviated version of this chapter appeared as "Forty-Two Years after Suárez: Mastri and Belluto's Development of the 'Classical' Theory of Entia Rationis" (Novotný 2008b).

2. "[D]upliciter . . . potest aliquid [obiective] dependere . . . a ratione: vel ita quod haberet . . . esse, etiamsi intellectui non obiiceretur, ut ignis, qui est calidus, licet a nobis non cognosceretur ut calidus, vel ita quod non haberet . . . esse, nisi obiiceretur intellectui, sed intuantum illud habet, inquantum ab intellectu cognoscitur (cuius cognitione cessante statim evanescit, ut angelus, qui non est pulcher iuvenis, nisi quatenus tali modo apprehenditur ab intellectu); et hoc est illud ens rationis, et dicitur habere esse tantum obiective in intellectu." DOA d3q1n1:192.

3. "[S]ed adhuc non omnes conveniunt . . . qualenam esse sit eis [i.e., etibus rationis] tribuendum. [1] Quidam enim quibusdam entibus rationis . . . concedant esse formale et actuale antecedenter ad omnem operationem intellectus, ita . . . Medina . . . et Fonseca . . . ; [2] Alii vero etsi fateantur, omne ens rationis quantum ad existentiam ab intellectu prorsus pendere, adhuc tamen asserunt habere suam essentiam independenter ab eius operatione, secundum quam revera dicitur possibile esse in intellectu, sicut ens reale per suam essentiam dicitur possibile esse extra intellectum; [3] alii demum statuunt ens rationis penitus ab intellectu dependens quoad omne suum esse, non solum existentiae, sed etiam essentiae." DOA d3q1n2:292.

4. Mastri/Belluto report Bartolomé de Medina, O.P. (d. 1528) and Pedro da Fonseca (d. 1599) as the supporters of this view, see the previous note.

5. The only significant dissenters include Mayronis and Ockham (the latter, however, is to my knowledge never mentioned in Baroque discussions of beings of reason), see Mayronis (2006) and Ockham (1974, 113; and 1980, 218–19). Beings of reason exist for Ockham in the sense of subjectively

mind-dependent entities. These are real not just for him but for Suárez as well and in this sense they are not disputed. The relevant sense is with objectively mind-dependent entities and these according to Ockham do not exist. For the discussion, see Klima (1993).

6. "Respondent negantes entia rationis, cum intellectus equum rationalem, angelum corporeum, et similia concipit, non utique per talem actum concipere quid fictum, et apparens, quod dicatur ens rationis, sed concipit veram, et realem rationalitatem, veram et realem corporalitatem . . . et eas intentionaliter connectit cum equo, et angelo, atque ideo numquam dari tale ens rationis, quod ex parte obiecti actui fingenti correspondeat." DOA d3q1n4:293.

7. "Sed hanc solutionem optime confutat Arriaga [CP-M1 d6s2n10] nam quando intellectus asserit equum rationalem, angelum corporeum, plane non praedicat rationalitatem, quae convenire solet individuis humanae naturae, neque corporeitatem [quae] conveniet e rebus materialibus, sed aliam consimilem, quam supra numerum earum, quae sunt possibiles, fingit intellectus . . . ita igitur . . . cum alia rationalitas distincta ab omnibus rationalitatibus humanorum individuorum . . . non sit realis, sed ficta et chymerica, quando concipitur equus rationalis et angelus corporeus, vere efficitur ens rationis." DOA d3q1n2:293.

8. "Accedit, quod etiam admissa ea solutione adhuc non evitatur ens rationis, licet enim rationalitas equo applicata esset realis, adhuc unio rationalitatis cum equo esset omnino ficta, et rationis. Quod si instes, intellectum illis extremis etiam applicare veram unionem . . . non adhuc evitatur ens rationis, quia saltim applicato illa . . . ipsius unionis erit rationis et ficta, quia applicatur rebus inunibilibus." DOA d3q1n2:293.

9. Mastri/Belluto failed to convince subsequent scholastic philosophers that this argument is sound—the debate over whether there are self-contradictory beings of reason continued. The debate became especially important for those scholastics who reduced all beings of reason to self-contradictory beings, such as Caramuel (see 8.A.2). On Caramuel's account, since there are no self-contradictory beings of reason, there are no beings of reason. Hence, Eliminativism is a natural successor of Self-Contradictorism. For Mastri/Belluto's account, however, where self-contradictory being of reason is just one kind, the impact of the discussion would be less dramatic. For even if we give up the claim that there are some self-contradictory beings of reason, there would remain other kinds.

10. "[Ens rationis non datur] quia nulla potest illius assignari causa; haec enim praesertim deberet esse intellectus, at hic est causa realis, et causat media actione reali, ac proinde effectum semper attingit realem." DOA d3q1n6:294. "Respondeo . . . dicendum est in intellectu enim esse causam efficientem entis rationis, non tamen proprie, et in rigore dictum quae est vere, et physice . . . sed sicut est ens secundum quid, et veluti umbra, et similitudo entis realis." DOA d3q1n7:294.

11. "... [I]mplicat obiectum in intellectu quod non prius fit intelligibile, quam intellectum: quia quod intelligitur in actu secundo sane supponitur intelligibile in actu primo." DOA d3q1n6:294.

12. "[V]erum est formaliter, et actualiter ens rationis non prius habere esse intelligibile, quam intellectum ...; sed non dicitur quia absolute loquendo nullo modo sit cognoscibile antequam cognoscatur ... quia saltem virtualiter in suis causis potest dici prius intelligibile, quam intellectum, immo etiam et in aliquo sensu formaliter, et actualiter; sed ... non ... in se ... quia actu cognosci est de essentia entis rationis, et quando actus est de alicuius essentia ... tunc in illo potentia non antecedit actum, qua ratione in Deo potentia ad existendum non absolute dicitur praecedere actum existendi." DOA d3q1n6:295.

13. "[S]i actu affirmanti angelum esse corporeum corresponderet ex parte obiecti unio ficti, esset actus verus, quia affirmaret, quod vere daretur, nam inter angelum, et corporeum datur unio ficta, ergo ut sit falsus, debet inter ea concipi unio realis." DOA d3q1n6:294.

14. This reply, however, overlooks that the objection is an indirect argument (ad absurdum). The correct reply to the objection would be that it contains ambiguity between (a) 'being of reason' as "what is mistaken for something else," and (b) 'being of reason' as "what is made up." Hence from the proposition "the act whereby I think of a corporeal angel is true" it does not follow that "in this act I am not making up anything fictitious." It is consistent to hold that there are truths about fictitious entities similarly as there are falsehoods about real entities.

15. "... [Q]uod [argumentum] aliqui magnifaciunt, ut notat Arriaga ... redargutionem involvit, nam in antecedente concedit illi actui unionem fictam correspondere quam deinde negat in consequente, unde ibi bene retorquet argumentum; correspondet igitur actui unio ficta, sed quia fingitur et concipitur, ac si realis esset, ideo actus est falsus, quando vero intellectus denuo reflectitur attingendo illam unionem ut fictam, tunc actus ille verus est." DOA d3q1n7:295.

16. "[E] contra arguitur contra alteram conclusionis partem ... saltim aliqua entia rationis actu dari citra operationem intellectus. [1] Tum quia nullo operante intellectu dantur a parte rei caecitas in oculo ... et similia, quae profecto quidpiam reale positivam non important, sed rationis. Tum [2] quia entia rationis prius habent esse intelligibile quam intellectum, et prius esse possibile quam actuale, nam antequam ad modum entium concipiantur, possunt sic concipi.... Tum [3] ens rationis est prius cognitione illa per quam cognoscitur ... quia quemlibet potentia cognitiva supponit obiectum ... et non actu suo illud efficit, ut oculus supponit colorem, non vero illum efficit videndo.... [4] ... [5] Tum dantur propositiones essentiales de ente rationis aeternae veritatis ex parte obiecti, non minus quam de ente reali, ergo sicut in ente reali arguunt essentiam realem in qua fundatur talis veritas, praecisa existentia, ita et in ente rationis." DOA d3q1n8:295r–296.

17. "Respondendum ad [1] negando enumerata ibi esse entia rationis formaliter, quamvis enim entia realia non sint, non protinus inferendum est esse entia rationis, sed esse negationes, et privationes reales, ut sunt tenebrae, et caecitas. . . ." DOA d3q1n9:296l. Note that Mastri/Belluto (unlike Suárez) would insist here that real privations are known only reflexively based on direct knowledge of privations of reason. A real privation, insofar as it "is" in reality, is pure nothing and cannot be as such "objectively in the intellect."

18. "[Respondendum] ad [2] entia rationis, antequam intelligantur non sunt intelligibilia formaliter, sed tantum virtualiter; ad hoc . . . sufficit si in re praecedat fundamentum, qualecunque illud fit, et in intellectu potentia et virtus intelligendi; . . . esse intelligibile in entibus rationis non est aliquod intrinsecum ut in entibus realibus, sed potius est mera denominatio extrinseca a potentia intellectiva procedens, quatenus quae non sunt, nec esse possunt, concipere ad modum entis potest." DOA d3q1n9:296l-r. A similar answer is given by John of St. Thomas as reported by Doyle (1994, 350).

19. "[Respondendum] ad [3] negatur assumptum . . . potest intellectus rem dupliciter cognoscere, vel sicut est, vel aliter ac est; cum primo modo cognoscit, tunc utique *praesupponit* obiectum esse, sed dum cognoscit secundo modo, tunc, *efficit* obiectum suum . . . qua tale obiectum non habet aliud esse, nisi quod tunc ei tribuit intellectus; . . . toties intellectus per actum suum sibi efficit obiectum, quoties fallitur iudicando esse id, quod re vera non est, ut ipsa experientia docet" DOA d3q1n9:296.

20. "[Respondendum] ad [5] negatur veritatem propositionum in entibus realibus fundari in aliquo esse essentiae, quod res actualiter habeant ante esse existentiae; sed fundatur in eo, quod ipsa essentia rei sit possibilis, ut actu ponatur in esse existentiae et essentiae . . . potius ergo dicendum est, quod sicut veritates entium realium fundantur super possibilitates eorum ut actu sint et actu ponantur in esse extra intellectum . . . ita etiam veritas propositionum essentialium de entibus rationis fundatur in eo, quod ipsa essentia entis rationis possibilis sit ut actu sit et actu ponatur in esse per intellectum." DOA d3q1n10. For more on Mastri/Belluto's views about possible entities, see Coombs (1993), Sousedík (1996), and Hoffmann (2002).

21. The debate between Mastri and Punch spreads over twenty years and proceeds in two rounds: (1) in 1639 Mastri/Belluto publish *Disputationes in Organum*, and in 1643 Punch publishes *Cursus Integer*; (2) in 1646 Mastri (without Belluto) slightly revises *Disputationes in Organum* and replies to Punch in *Disputationes in . . . libros Metaphysicorum*, and in 1659 Punch publishes *Cursus Integer* with *Additiones* (to q1, 2, 10, 11). Posthumously, Mastri/ Belluto's works were given the title *Philosophiae ad mentem Scoti Cursus integer*. Both Punch and Mastri also wrote commentaries on the Sentences, which might contain some more arguments. Mastri published them in 1655 (book 1), 1659 (book 2), 1661 (books 3 and 4); Punch in 1661 (books 1–4). The debate over actualism was started by the following remark of Punch: "Mastrius

negat ens rationis secundum esse proprium et formale esse prius intelligibile quam intelligatur, licet secundum esse fundamentale suum sit prius intelligibile. Sed contra, quia de illo ipso ente rationis formaliter loquendo, quod intelligitur in hoc instanti, verum erat dicere in instanti antecedenti quod erat intelligibile; et non solum id verum est de fundamento eius ut est manifestum; ergo quoad esse etiam formale prius est intelligibile quam intelligatur." PCI d1q2n13.

22. "[L]icet communis sententia ens rationis admittens concedat illud nullum habere extra animam, sed tantum in anima, et obiectivum, ut ex praecedente questione liquet; adhuc tamen discrepat authores in explicando, quid sit illud, quod habet esse tantum obiective in intellectu, et solum tantum est, quamdiu consideratur, quod est proprium esse entis rationis, qua in re plures existant opiniones, quae praesertim ad quatuor reducuntur." DOA d3q2n11:297.

23. "Prima sententia satis famosa constituit formalitatem entis rationis in denominatione extrinseca, quam [1] aliqui sine ulla limitatione amplectentes affirmant quamlibet denominationem extrinsecam a quacumque forma provenientem esse ens rationis . . . ita sensisse videtur Fonseca . . . et Vazquez. . . . [2] Alii vero eiusdem sententiae authores eam coarctant ad solam denominationem in obiectum derivatam ab actu rationis qualis est denominatio cogniti et intellecti, ita Durandus. . . . Onna . . . et probabilissimam censet Didacus a Iesu. [3] Alii demum recentiores adhuc eandem sententiam magis coarctantes dixerunt non omnem denominationem extrinsecam ab actu intellectus provenientem appellandam esse ens rationis formaliter, sed illam dumtaxat, quae provenit ab actu intellectus concipientis obiectum aliter ac sit. Et in hanc sententiam de extrinsecis denominationibus trahi solet Scotus . . . ita sentit Trombeta." DOA d3q2n11:297–98.

24. "Secunda sententia negat ens rationis esse formaliter ipsam denominationem extrinsecam, sed ait esse relationem rationis ex ipsa denominatione extrinseca, seu ex forma rem extrinsece denominante resultantem; quam opinionem [1] aliqui sine limitatione amplectentes affirmant ens rationis esse relationem resultantem per actum cuiuscunque potentiae attingentis obiectum et per omnem formam extrinsece denominantem aliquod subiectum. . . . [2] Alii vero coarctant hanc sententiam ad solas denominationes ex actibus vitalibus desumptas . . . immo [3] aliqui specificant hanc relationem . . . esse illam praecise quem resultat per actum rationis quo cognoscitur obiectum; hanc autem resultantiam ita intelligere videntur, ut relatio insurgat in obiecto statim ac terminat actum potentiae vitalis absque alia operatione reflexa supra praecedentem operationem . . . ; varie loquuntur et in hac sententia fuisse videtur quamplures Thomistae veteres, ut Soncinas . . . et Scotistae. . . ." DOA d3q2n12:298.

25. "Tertia sententia inter Recentiores receptissima, quibus praeivit Suárez [DM d54s2], docet ens rationis esse illud, quod solum habet esse obiective in intellectu . . . id autem ita explicat, ut ens rationis sit illud, quod cum a parte rei

nihil sit, ab intellectu tamen percipitur per modum entis quasi aliquid esset . . . ; quae explicatio desumitur ex S. Thoma [Summa Theologiae Iq16art3ad2]. . . . At quoniam iuxta hanc sententiam ad ens rationis duo spectare videntur, nihileitas nimirum, qua ab ente reali distinguitur, et entitas ficta . . . , qua ab omnino nihil distinguitur . . . hinc variae dubitationes et varii modi dicendi exoriuntur in explicanda hac sententia. Nam dubitatur [1] primo an illa nihileitas iniret formalitatem entis rationis, an potius materialiter ad eam se habeat. . . . Sed quocunque modo nihileitas se habeat ad ens rationis, dubitatur [2] rursus, qualis esse debeat, an scilicet talis esse debeat, ut non solum excludat actualem existentiam obiecti . . . , verum etiam possibilitatem ad sic existendum . . . ut tenet Hurtado . . . et Arriaga. . . . [3] Deinde dubitatur insuper de illa entitate ficta per modum veri entis cum talis non sit, an ita constituat formalitatem entis rationis, ut sit de conceptu entis rationis, quod quando efformatur ab intellectu, concipiatur aliter quam est, ut communis velle videtur . . . vel an id contingat mere per accidens, ut tenet Didacus . . . ubi defendit ens rationis efformari posse ab intellectu etiam cognoscente rem, sicuti est." DOA d3q2n13:298–299.

26. Didacus a Jesu OCarm (1570–1621) studied in Alcalá and then worked as a professor of theology there. He wrote both theological and philosophical works (Lohr 1988a).

27. Note also Mastri/Belluto's attitude toward Suárez's two definitions of beings of reason, namely in terms of something merely objectively in the intellect (SN6), and in terms of thinking of something in the manner of being when in fact it is not (SN7). I have criticized these definitions as nonequivalent, whereas Mastri/Belluto interpret the latter as an explanation of the former. Mastri/Belluto's approach would be valid if Suárez did not acknowledge the possibility of thinking "in the manner of nonbeing." Once this possibility is introduced, the two definitions are not coextensional anymore.

28. "Quarta demum sententia est Recentiorum quorundam Scotistarum, qui . . . admittunt omnes praefatos modos constituendi ens rationis, et ita late describunt ens rationis, ut eius formalitas convenire possit tum denominationibus extrinsecis, tum relationibus ex illis resultantibus, tum entibus confictis per operationem reflexam ad modum veri entis, ita Meruisse . . . et Smising . . . Posset etiam quinta sententia referri non prorsus improbabilis, quae statuit ens rationis in applicatione unius entitatis realis cum alia incompossibili, de qua erit sermo (art.2.huius quaest.in sol. ad 2)." DOA d3q2n14:299.

29. "Dicendum est primo ens rationis formaliter non consistere in extrinseca denominatione proveniente ab aliqua forma reali, neque ab actu rationis, sive hic exprimat rem sicut est, sive aliter. Conclusio est contra auctores primae sententiae." DOA q30a1n15:299.

30. Mastri/Belluto report only Smising and John of St. Thomas as defenders. In contrast, the extrinsic denomination view is rejected not just by the Scotists but even by "Thomistae ac Neoterici fere omnes." Theodor Smising OFMObs

(1580–1626), lat. Smisingus, was a French Scotistic theologian with extensive knowledge of both classic and patristic literature.

31. "Respondet Smising . . . idem habet Ioannes a S. Thoma p.2.Log.q.2.a.1 ait enim quod licet ratione formae denominantis possi extrinseca denominatio dicit realis, ratione tamen unionis et applicationis ad rem denominatam est rationis quia nihil reale in ea ponit. . . . quod illos viros decepit est quod omnem unionem constituunt per modum inhaesionis, quod falsum est, quia etiam admitti debet unio per modum adhaesionis, ex quo . . . oriuntur denominatio- nes extrinsecae sicut ex priori intrinsecae." DOA q30a1n16:300.

32. I have expressed (in Novotný 2010) agreement with the view of John of St. Thomas that extrinsic denominations are beings of reason, hence rejecting the view of Suárez and Rubio that they are real. Applying Mastri/Belluto's distinction, however, I am not so sure that John of St. Thomas is right. At any rate, note that the reality of extrinsic denomintions does not prevent them from becoming a "material" for beings of reason; if somebody thinks that the given extrinsic denomination inheres in (not just adheres to) the denominated subject, then a being of reason does emerge, even on Mastri/Belluto's view. See DOA q30a1n19:302.

33. "Quando autem Doctor [1d36q1 Concedo] illud esse cognitum quod habent creaturae ab aeterno per actum divini intellectus vocat ens rationis. . . . Scotum revera non vocare ens rationis illud esse diminutum creatuarum sed relatio- nem quondam in ipso fundatam ad Deum cognoscentem . . . hinc communiter et praesertim in scholas subtilium ens rationis in materiale et formale seu ut ipsi loquuntur in ens rationis a ratione fabricatum et a ratione derelictum. Ens rationis formale et fabricatum seu actuale est et habet actu existentiam ab intellectu fictam, ens vero rationis materiale derelictum seu potentiale est illud cui ab intellectu sic concipiente vel fingente existentia talis non repugnat; denominationes igitur extrinsecae secundum se sunt entia rationis materialia quatenus se possunt concipi. . . . interdum solet ipse [Scotus] confundere ens rationis materiale et formale." DOA q3a1n20:302.

34. "[N]eque adhuc adaequate attingat in quo consistat formaliter ens rationis, quia non omne ens rationis est relativum ut existimasse videntur ex veteribus Scotisti quamplures." DOA q3a1n21:303.

35. "Primo igitur statuendum est ens rationis formaliter sumptum omnino distingui ab ente reali sumpto tam pro reali existente quam pro possibili." DOA q3a2n24:305.

36. "[Q]uod possibile est in re . . . cum actu non sit, ut mons aureus, non est ens rationis sed vere ens reale, quia ad rationem essentialem entis realis est per accidens actu existere, sed eius essentia salvatur in hoc, quod sit aptum existere." DOA q30a2n24:305.

37. "Ex quo patet falsum esse quod aiebat Hurtado et Arriaga . . . ad efformandum ens rationis non requiri ut obiectum actus sit impossibile, sed sufficere ut obiectum actu non sit, sicut repraesentatur, etiamsi alias sit possibile." DOA

q30a2n24:305. "Sed instabis . . . haec propositio Petrus currit, ipso dormiente aut sedente, quid fictum est, et ens rationis habens totum suum esse obiective in intellectu et tamen non est impossibile Petrum currere, ergo etc. Responden-dum negando assumptum quia ens rationis sic obiective tantum in intellectu existit, ut extra illum nec actu existat neque existere possit, alioquin rosa in hyeme concepta ens rationis esset, quia actu non extat in rerum natura. Vel si concedatur assumptum dicendum est ibi poni impossibile non simpliciter sed ex suppositione, dum enim Petro dormiente vel sedente enuntiatur Petrus currere, sane hoc est impossibile in sensu (ut aiunt) composito, quod se currat pro eo tempore, quod non currit. . . . Distincto autem illa, quam affert Arriaga n. 23 ad sedandam hanc litem de duplici ente rationis, uno chimerico et impossibili, et altero possibili, prorsus vana est, quia possibilitas destruit essentiam entis rationis." DOA q30a2n25:305.

38. "Secundo statuendum est ens rationis formaliter sumptum distingui etiam a puro nihilo; probatur, quia purum nihil ut sic dicit puram negationem cuiuscunque entis sive in re sive in apprehensione . . . purum nihil dicitur, quod nec habet nec habere potest ullam existentiam sive realem sive obiectivam quia si habere posset secundum se existentiam aliquam iam non esset purum nihil sed admixtum cum entitate; cum ergo ens rationis existentiam habeat obiectivam et fit ens licet a ratione factum . . . utique ponendum est a puro nihilo distinctum." DOA d3q2a2n25:305.

39. ". . . [E]ns rationis esse medium inter ens reale et purum nihil. . . . purum nihil non solum dicit negationem realitatis, sed etiam existentiae obiectivae; concedimus ergo ens rationis non esse ens reale, sed inde non sequitur esse purum nihil, quia est ens mentale et obiectivum." DOA d3q2a2n25:306.

40. ". . . [A]n solum per . . . obiectivam entitatem ens rationis distinguatur ab ente reali, num vero etiam per negationem entis realis . . . non ita facile est resolvere. [Sed] . . . ens rationis in suo conceptu dicat entitatem obiectivam . . . [et] si rursus includit talem negationem, tunc conceptus entis rationis . . . ex positivo et negativo conflatus esset, quod est incoveniens. [DOA d3q2a2n26:306] Quamobrem dicendum est ens rationis non includere in sua formalitate illam negationem. . . ." DOA d3q2a2n27:306.

41. "[E]xperientia docet fieri plerumque entia rationis nihil cogitando an possint esse vel non esse a parte rei . . . nam ad formationem entis rationis sufficit cogitare esse ens quod re vera non est . . . ; immo adhuc efficeretur ens rationis etiamsi intellectus putaret vere esse ens, cum tale non sit, formatur enim ens rationis eo ipso, quod non ens obiicitur intellectu ut ens, sive intellectus sciat re vera illud non esse, sive nesciat; hoc solum interest si id sciat intellectus fingit solum at non decipitur, si nesciat, fingit simul atque decipitur." DOA d3q2a2n27:307.

42. "Quarto statuendum est illud esse imaginativum, quod sibi proprium vendicat ens rationis, necessario pendere ab ea imaginatione, qua concipiatur per modum veri entis . . . Quae doctrina . . . est communis omnibus recentioribus . . .

[et] in hac materia de ente rationis nullam . . . vertere discrepantiam inter Scotum et D. Thomam." DOA d3q2a2n28:307. Note that beings of reason are strangely called "beings of imagination" here.

43. "[E]ns comunissime sumptum esse aequivocum ad ens reale et rationis, non tamen pure aequivocum sed aequivocum analogum. . . . haec analogia fundari nequit nisi in aliquot ordine attributionis inter ens reale et rationis. . . . Potest etiam dici, quod haec sit analogia proportionis." DOA d3q2a2n28:307.

44. "[S]ub ratione non entis (ait Doctor) nihil intelligitur . . . hac ratione ait Aristoteles 4. Met. Ab initio 'non ens esse dicimus, quia nil intelligitur sub ratione non entis.'" DOA d3q2a2n29:308.

45. "Quinto tandem ex his colligitur ens rationis esse illud, quod obiicitur vel potest obiici intellectui ac si esset, cum tamen nec existet in rerum natura nec existere possit; unde sequitur totum esse illius esse obiectivum, mentale, et fictum, et quia ab intellectu nostro veris entibus adsueto fingitur ad instar veri entis, ideo ens ens rationis dicitur umbra entis realis et eius entitas umbrata . . . [N]on admisso ens rationis . . . consistere in aliqua denominatione extrinseca, necessario est asserendum esse aliquod esse fictum resultans in rebus ex operatione intellectus . . . et per hoc esse explicatur tum essentia tum existentia entis rationis . . . [Q]uatenus [enim] actu est, dicitur esse existentiae, quatenus vero considerari potest ut possibilis, abstrahendo actualitate essendi, dicetur esse essentiae, unde consulto diximus ens rationis esse illud, quod obiicitur, vel obiici potest intellectui ac si esset." DOA d3q2a2n30:308.

46. The first insists that we need to know beings of reason qua beings of reason. The second claims that the theory is inapplicable to relations of reason. The third concerns self-contradictorism. The fourth has to do with similarity of real beings and beings of reason.

47. "In contrarium arguunt primo Didacus et Smising . . . ens rationis fit et concipitur non solum fingendo illud per modum veri entis et concipiendo aliter quam est sed etiam concipiendo illud per modum entis rationis et sicut est. . . . Confirmatur, quia si in cognitione et formatione entis rationis opus esset illud concipere aliter ac sit, i.e. per modum veri entis, plane semper intellectus falleretur et numquam cognosci posset sicut est." DOA d3q2a2n31:308–9.

48. "Respondeo duplicem esse cognitionem entis rationis, unum directam, altera quasi reflexam. . . . [P]rima est, qua fingimus ens rationis concipiendo quod non est ac si esset, secunda, qua concipitur ens rationis sicut vere est, et cognosci-mus rem esse cognitam aliter ac sit. . . . [E]ns rationis utroque modo cognosci: in prima cognitione attingitur aliter ac sit, quia per modum entis realis concipitur, cum tale non sit, in secunda concipitur ut est, quia attingitur ut ens rationis et fictum; per primam cognitionem recipit esse, at per secundam non recipit esse, sed supponitur ei." DOA d3q2a2n31:309. The same claim was recently made by Millán-Puelles, drawing on John of St. Thomas: "To know a being of reason is not the same as to produce or form it. In effect, it is possible

retrospectively to know a being of reason that had already been constituted or formed previously, so that the operation by means of which one would return to it would grasp it not as the product of the given act, but as something that had already been fashioned" (1990/1996, 791–95).

49. "[A]liud enim est . . . concipere ens reale falso alteri applicatum, aliud vero concipere quod non est ens reale ad similitudinem entis realis ut nostra asserit opinio." DOA d3q2a2n35:311.

50. Apart from Hurtado, most scholastics would agree here. As Millán-Puelles put it: "One can form a being of reason in an act of conceiving, judging, or reasoning. . . . This doctrine is one of the least controversial issues in the Scholastic account of entia rationis. It is [therefore] remarkable that Suárez did not examine it, perhaps because he took it to be all-too-evident." (1990/1996, 802).

51. "[Entia rationis] habent . . . suo modo causam finalem, nam saepe intellectus format entia rationis ut res recte et sine errore cognoscat." DOA d3q3n40:313.

52. "[Entia rationis] habent . . . suo modo causam materialem et formalem . . . si enim sumuntur velut causae intrinsecae rem componentes sic entia rationis suo modo habere poterunt causam materialem et formalem et erunt huius-modi omnia illa entia rationis quae fingi possunt ad instar substantiae materiae et corporeae, veluti hircocervus, chimera et similia." DOA d3q3n41:314.

53. "Suárez vero, quem multi ex recentioribus sequuntur, . . . concedit quidem ens rationis eo modo, quo est ens, habere causam effectivam sui esse; id tamen de allis causis et maxime de finali concedere inficiatur. . . . Dicendum tamen est ens rationis . . . habere causas . . . in omni genere causae." DOA d3q3n37:312. In accord with Mastri/Belluto, Punch also argues that beings of reason have all four causes: "Ens rationis habet quattuor genera causarum suo modo concur-rentium ad ipsius productionem." PCI d1q6n67.

54. "[I]ntellectus . . . agit . . . [etiam] actione metaphorica et quasi grammaticali, qualis est cognitio per quam ens rationis producitur (siquidem per cogitatio-nem non producit intellectus aliquam entitatem realem, quia non est actus productivus et vera actio . . .) . . . proinde affert tantum esse quoddam obiectivum non reale, unde si in obiecto, quod intelligitur, nullum aliud esse reperitur praeter hoc esse obiectivum, quod ab intellectu recipit, erit ens rationis." DOA d3q3n37:312.

55. "Dicendum est certum esse nullam potentiam vitalem praeter intellectum et voluntatem posse ens rationis efficere et ex his duabus certum esse intellectus efficere posse, de voluntate vero non ita certum, satis tamen probabile." DOA d3q4a1n49:318.

56. "[D]um enim concipimus hircocervum, chimeram, Deum corporeum, et similia, plane, ut passim notant auctores, non ex vi imaginationis uniuntur naturae aut essentiae incompossibiles, quia nec imaginatio nec alius sensus profundat se usque ad substantiam, sed tantum externa accidentia hirci, v.g.,

et cervi, quorum coniunctio certe non repugnat, nam saepius visa sunt monstra ex diversis animalium figuris coniuncta, unio autem naturarum incompossibilium sit a solo intellectu." DOA d3q4a1n51:320.

57. If we identify Millán-Puelles's notion of pure object with Arriaga's notion of being of reason, then Millán-Puelles's view comes close to Arriaga's view, whom Millán-Puelles mentions but does not discuss in depth. See Millán-Puelles (1990/1996, 788). Millán-Puelles uses the scholastic term 'being of reason' more narrowly in the sense of "intelligible irreality;" in this sense it is then not surprising that "anything intelligible that is apodictically non-existent [=a being of reason] is produced . . . by, and only by, the intellective faculty" (Millán-Puelles 1990/1996, 791).

58. "[A]d ens sensibile aequivalens enti rationis non sufficit quod videatur id quod non est, sed quod etiam illud sit impossibile sicut apparet, modo nec colores apparentes in colio columbae, nec remi curvitas et alia huiusmodi apparentia sunt impossibilia, qua ratione convictus Arriaga concedit per sensus externos fieri non posse ens rationis impossibile sed tantum illud quod actu a parte rei non existit, licet sit possibile." DOA d3q4a1n53:321.

59. "[N]eque intellectus ipse aut imaginativa [potentia] falleretur si eius iudicium feratur non supra obiecti essentiam sed supra solam eiusdem apparentiam, quia tunc iudicaret quod vere a parte rei est." DOA d3q4a1n54:321.

60. "Dicimus primo, ens rationis in universum fieri per illum actum intellectus, quo per modum entis concipitur id quod in re non habet entitatem seu (ut etiam actus voluntatis comprehendatur) fieri per illum actum, ex vi cuius ita aliquid existit obiective in ea potentia, cuius est actus, ut extra illam [sc. potentiam] nullum prorsus esse habeat, vel habere possit; hic vero esse potest absolutus vel collativus, directus vel reflexus, iuxta exigentiam entium rationis, quae fiunt." DOA d3q4a2n60:324.

61. "Dicimus secundo, entia rationis . . . fieri posse per tres operationes intellectus distributive, alia nempe per primam, alia per secundam, alia per tertiam." DOA d3q4a2n63:326.

62. "[S]i actum reflexum sumamus pro cognitione quomodocumque aliam priorem supponente, sic dici potest omne ens rationis fieri per actum reflexum (siquidem necessario illi supponitur cognitio entis realis ad cuius instar efformatur) sed si actus reflexus sumatur proprie, pro eo quo intellectus reflectit vel supra cognoscentem vel supra obiectum ut a se cognitum vel supra actum ipsum cognitionis, . . . sic non est opus omne ens rationis per notitiam reflexam fieri." DOA d3q4a2n62:326.

63. "Obiicies probando per primam operationem nullum fieri posse ens rationis, Tum quia in ea nulla datur falsitas, at ens ens rationis fit per actum falsum, quo nimirum concipitur res aliter quam sit, qua ratione contendat Hurtado fieri solum per secundam operationem." DOA d3q4a2n65:327.

64. "Respondendum est . . . quia ad ens rationis praecise sufficit ut obiectum, quod cognoscitur, non habeat esse, nisi in intellectu, quomodocumque id contingat et

hoc utique fieri posse per primam operationem, dicitur autem in formatione
entis rationis concipi res aliter quam sit non quia semper contigat in ea propria
et formalis falsitas, affirmando nimirum de re quod non est, et negando quod
est, sed quia intervenit potius inaedequatio quaedam et improprietas apprehen-
dendo rem non per proprios conceptus sed extraneos et connotativos quod
concipere rem aliter quam sit . . . quomodo etiam illa ipsa entia rationis . . .
secundum se sint incomplexa, quod eo magis asserendum est de chymera et
hircocervo quorum partes incompossibiles intellectus non componit affirmando
unam de alia quae compositio spectat ad secundam operationem, sed apprehen-
dendo illa duo ut unum per simplicem et incomplexam attindentiam unionis
fictae per illa." DOA d3q4a2n66:328.

65. "[N]eque haec disputatio initur cum illis auctoribus qui supra . . . constituebant
entia rationis formaliter in denominationibus extrinsecis cogniti et cogitati, sic
enim certum est Deum formare entia rationis, quemadmodum indubitandum
est seipsum et alia a se cognoscere. . . . Neque est disputatio cum auctoribus
qui . . . asserebant ens rationis formaliter fieri solum per actus falsos, sic enim
tam certum est divinum intelletum ens rationis efficere non posse, quam falli
non posse vel decipi. Igitur sola disputatio est cum eis qui nobiscum conveniunt tam in formalitate quam in formatione entis rationis ut supra explicatum
est." DOA d3q5n69:329.

66. "Prima [sententia] est eorum, qui . . . nedum negarunt divinum intellectum
ens rationis efficere sed etiam ab alio factum cognoscere, cum enim ens rationis
sit cognosci, profecto si cognoscit, facit; sequuntur Vazquez . . ." DOA
d3q5n70:330.

67. "Secunda [sententia] e diametro opposita, utrumque affirmat, et cognoscere et
efficere, eo quia tota illa imperfectio potius se tenet ex parte obiecti intelligibili,
ita Faber . . . sequuntur . . . etiam multi ex Neotericis . . . praesertim . . .
Arriaga." DOA d3q5n70:330.

68. "Tertia [sententia] media valde communis et plausibilis negat divinum
intellectum entia rationis efficere, addit tamen cognoscere a nobis facta vel
factibilia, ita Suárez . . . Ruvius." DOA d3q5n70:330.

69. "Quarta [sententia] distinguit de ente rationis ficto . . . et fundato, quales sunt
intentiones logicales aliae multae relationes, et concedit entia rationis secundi
generis fieri posse ab intellectu divino, quia nulla in eorum formatione
intervenit imperfectio, ita. . . . Meurisse . . . ita etiam loqui videtur Ioannes a S.
Thoma . . . re tamen vera potius est tertiae opinionis." DOA d3q5n70:330.

70. "Quinta [sententia] tandem affirmat posse divinum intellectum ens
quocumque rationis efficere . . . sed non posse directe et immediate, ut facit
intellectus creatus, sed tantum indirecte et mediate, quatenus cognoscendo
entia rationis a nobis facta dat rursus aliud esse obiectivum quasi secundarium,
ita . . . Didacus." DOA d3q5n70:330.

71. "Dicimus primo Divinum intellectum cognoscere entia rationis a nobis facta,
tamen ex vi illius cognitionis illa non facere." DOA d3q5n71:330.

72. "Maior est difficultas an possit Deus entia rationis in se cognoscere absque ordine ad intellectum nostrum, hoc enim admittendo difficile est evadere, quin formet entia rationis. . . ." DOA d3q5n73:331. "Dicimus secundo utrumque esse probabile, quod divinus intellectus facere possit vel non possit ens rationis." DOA d3q5n74:332.

73. "Non quaerimus hic, num entia rationis habeant proprietates quae ab ipsis vere fluant. Sicut enim non sunt proprie entia ita nequeunt habere veras proprietates. . . . Quamadmodum ergo dicuntur entia per solam analogiam ad ens reale, ita quaerimus proprietates, quae tales dicatur per analogiam ad veras proprietates." DOA d3q6n91:336. "Dicimus primo ens rationis habere in suo ordine proprias affectiones." DOA d3q6n91:336. "Dicimus secundo ens rationis in communi habere suo modo omnes illas proprietates, quae conveniunt enti reali in communi ad cuius instar concipitur, et pariter entia rationis in particulari habere proprietates illorum entium ad quorum instar concipiuntur." DOA d3q6n93:337.

74. "Celebris ac in Scholis frequens divisio entis rationis est illa in tres species, relationem, negationem, et privationem, quam asserunt et recipient Recentiores omnes ut traditam a D. Thoma . . . ita Suárez . . . Ruvius . . . Ioannes a S. Thoma (sed bimembrem, scilicet in negationem et relationem rationis quia sub negatione ample sumpta etiam continetur privatio). . . ." DOA d3q7n99:340r–341.

75. "Sed quocumque modo tradatur haec divisio, semper graves passa est difficultates. In primis enim non videtur recte assignari ut species entis rationis negatio et privatio, quia esto non sint entia realia, non proinde inter entia rationis formaliter computanda sunt, cum vere dentur a parte rei, non quidem ut entia realia privativa vel negativa, ut arbitratur Faber . . . et Fuentes . . . cum multis aliis (hunc enim dicendi modum ut valde improprium confutamus in Physica . . .) sed ut amotiones reales entium." DOA d3q7n99:341.

76. "Quod si dicas cum Suárez et aliis, hic non sumi negationem et privationem ut sunt amotiones realium entium (sic enim a parte rei reperiuntur), sed quatenus concipiuntur ad modum formae positivae ut cum intellectus concipit caecitatem in oculo . . . sic enim sunt aliquo modo entia non realia sed rationis. Contra est quia negatio vel privatio ut concipitur per modum formae positivae non est privatio sed forma positiva ficta . . . ergo nullum datur ens rationis negativum sed omne est positivum." DOA d3q7n99:341.

77. "At inquit Suárez [DM d54s4n10] et sequuntur alii omnia haec figmenta sub negatione comprehendi quia sunt simpliciter non entia. Contra est , tum quia hac ratione, ut bene notat Aversa, etiam relationes rationis sub negatione continentur, quia simpliciter sunt non entia." DOA d3q7n100:341.

78. "At inquit Suárez DM d54s4n10 et sequuntur alii omnia haec figmenta sub negatione comprehendi quia sunt simpliciter non entia. Contra est, tum quia hac ratione, ut bene notat Aversa, etiam relationes rationis sub negatione continentur, quia simpliciter sunt non entia, tum quia, ut ait Blanc. Aliud est

concipere negationem animalis quod simul est homo et leo ... aliud vero
concipere animal simul hominem et leonem; quamvis igitur ens rationis primo
modo formatum ad negationem spectare possit, tamen ens rationis secundo
modo fictum est ab ea distinctum." DOA d3q7n100:341.

79. "Ideo alii, ut salvent sufficientiam illius divisionis, inquiunt haec et similia
entia rationis esse ficta sine fundamento et indcirco in ea non includi, quae
solum est entium rationis habentium fundamentum in re, ita Didacus. . . . [et]
[Suárez DM d54s4n2]. Quae solutio nihil prorsus valet, tum quia plura sunt
entia rationis habentia fundamenta in re, quae excogitari possunt in aliis
praedicamentis a relatione, immo illa ipsa, quae finguntur in praedicamento
substantiae chymaera et hyrcocervus non omni prorsus carent fundamento."
DOA d3q7n100:341–42.

80. In this thesis Mastri/Belluto depart from the traditional view of some older
Thomists and Scotists: "Ex hoc veteres quidam Scotistae et Thomistae
deduxerunt sola entia rationis fundata vere et proprie esse entia rationis,
quorum proinde cognition doctrinalis est est et ad scientias deservire potest,
alia vero minime, sed potius dici debere entia fictitia et prohibita. . . . Verum
immerito huiusmodi entia fictitia excluduntur a serie entium rationis, nam si
ens rationis illud est, quod esse repugnat a parte rei et solum habet esse
obiective in intellectu . . . plane fictitia quoque erunt entia rationis, cum non
habeant esse nisi per opus intellectus; immo ut ait Aversa, haec videntur
quodammodo magis participare de ente rationis, utpote magis pendent a
virtute fictitiva intellectus . . . et consequenter magis distant ab ente reali."
DOA d3q7n105:344.

81. "Dicendum igitur est ens rationis data proportione dividi debere sicut ens reale
ad instar cuius concipitur. . . . probatur . . . quia naturam entis rationis, et quid
sit, et quotuplex, omnino investigare debemus ad modum entis realis, quare
sicut ens reale dividitur in substantiam et accidens, et hoc in absolutum et
respectivum, et rursum absolutum in quantitatem et qualitatem, respectivum
vero in intrinsecus et extrinsecus adveniens, sic ens rationis dividitur. . . ."
DOA d3q7n102:342. Punch also rejects the traditional three-member division:
"Doctores communiter dicunt divisionem entis rationis in negationes,
privationes, et relationes, esse divisionem non entis rationis ut sic, sed entis
rationis habentis fundamentum in re; quae tamen divisio, si ita intelligatur, ut
ipsae negationes et privationes sint entia rationis formaliter, omnino mala est,
quia falsum est quod negationes et privationes sint entia rationis." PCI
d1q10n101. First and second intentions are in his view likewise real beings:
"Nec prima nec secunda intention formali aut obiectiva dicit necessario ens
rationis formaliter." PCI d1q11n107.

82. "Rursus ens rationis in tota sua amplitudine divide debet in ens rationis
fundatum in re et non fundatum, sed a nobis mere fictum, quod hac ratione
sibi vendicavit nomen figmenti ut chymera et hyrcocervus. [1] Et quidem per
fundamentum entis rationis non debet accipi in praesenti imperfection nostri

intellectus ac debilis eius concipiendi modus ut quidam volunt, alioquin omnia entia rationis haberent fundamentum et illa praesertim quae dicuntur chymera et fictitia, ista namque praecipue pendent ex actibus chymericis nostri intellectus ea ad libitum fingentis. . . . [2] Neque per fundamentum entis rationis debet accipi aliquid reale, ad cuius instar concipitur eadem ratione, quia nimirum omnia entia rationis haberent fundamentum in re, etiam chymerae et monstra . . . [quia] chymeram ipsam concipit [intellectus noster] ad instar animalis quod ens reale est." DOA d3q7n103:343.

83. "Itaque per fundamentum entis rationis illud intelligimus, quod est specialis quaedam occasio ac veluti motivum urgens intellectum ad excogitanda entia rationis et tali vel tali modo fingenda, ita ut intellectus non temere et mere gratis sed ex ipsis rerum proprietatibus occasione desumpta efficiat entia rationis et haec est communis explicatio Scotistarum. . . . [E]xplicatio expresse traditur a Doctore . . . [qui] universale ponit esse ens fundatum quia aliquid in re extra correspondet a quo movetur intellectus ad causandam talem intentio-nem et non aliam; figmentum vero inquit esse non fundatum, quia nihil tale extra correspondet . . . [S]ine fundamento illa dicuntur , quae fingimus prout volumus, cum nulla sit necessitas vel occasio, quae nos determinet ad hoc potius quam illo modo fingendum" DOA d3q7n104:343–44.

84. "[O]biicitur quod omnia entia rationis sint fundata, quia semper ad illa effingenda occasionem intellectus sumit a rebus, quod etiam in ipsis chymericis experimur, non enim eas ex incompossibilibus partibus constitutus figere possemus, nisi partes illas seiunctim et in diversis repertas intelligeremus. Respondendum . . . esto enim per fundamentum entis rationis intelligmus occasionem unde movetur intellectus ad fingendum, non tamen quamcumque, sed occasionem proximam et urgentem, nam si levis sit et remota, proprie et ex communi modo loquendi non censetur fundamentum." DOA d3q7n110:346.

85. I have not dealt separately with Mastri/Belluto's views on metatheory for Mastri/Belluto would probably agree with all of Suárez's claims: the proper object of metaphysics is real being (SM1), beings of reason are useful in various ways (SM2), investigation of beings of reason involves nature, causes, division and attributes (SM3), and real beings are ontologically and epistemi-cally prior to beings of reason (SM4).

86. "[E]ns rationis ut sic in se . . . nihil est." DM d54s1n10. Out of context this is one of the few passages that would seem to support Shields's "tethered counter-factual view" (Shields 2012).

87. "Cum enim obiectum adaequatum intellectus sit ens, nihil potest concipere, nisi ad modum entis, et ideo dum privationes aut negationes concipere conatur eas concipit ad modum entium, et ita format entia rationis" DM d54s1n8, see chapter 3, section C.3. " [P]erfectam cognitionem negationis non consistere in hoc quod ipsa directe et per modum entis repraesentetur, sed in hoc quod, cognoscendo clarissime entia positiva, in eis cognoscatur unum non esse

aliud, . . . absque alia directa repraesentatione ipsius negationis vel privationis."
DM d54s2n2, see also chapter 4, section C. "[H]umanus intellectus . . .
potest . . . negationem cognoscere . . . [sed] fit ut id . . . non faciat sine indirecta
et quasi discursiva cognitione." DM d54s5n5, see chapter 5, section C.1.1.

88. "[C]aecitas, verbi gratia, . . . dupliciter concipi potest, primo negative tantum,
concipiendo in tali organo non esse potentiam visivam, et tunc nullum insurgit
ens rationis, quia nihil concipitur per modum entis, sed solum per modum non
entis; inde vero fit, ut ad formandum conceptum simplicem ipsius caecitatis,
intellectus concipiat illam ut affectionem animalis seu organi . . . tunc ergo
concipit aliquid per modum entis; cumque non concipiat ens reale, tunc proprie
format tale ens rationis." DM d54s2n15, see also chapter 4, section B.3.

89. "*Simile* quid considerare licet in entibus rationis, quae in extrinsecis denominationibus fundamentum habent, ut est relatio visi . . . nam *etiam* . . . dum
intellectus *directe* cognoscit rem esse visam . . . nullum ens rationis format aut
cognoscit." DM d54s2n15 (italics mine).

90. Mastri/Belluto do not explicitly chastise Suárez on this point. It is another
author, namely the Salamancan Dominican Francisco de Araújo, who explicitly
points out that "Suarez . . . sectione 5 quandam novam et inauditam sequitur
sententiam, nimis diffuse explicatam . . . privationem et negationem posse
comparari prout sunt in re and prout sunt entia rationis." CUAM q1a5n30:339.

91. This concerns *Disputations of Organon*. Later, Mastri carries on his debate
with Punch in *Disputations of Metaphysics*, which is sixteen thousand words
long. (Punch's treatise, including the debate, is twenty-three thousand words
long).

92. Let me also make again the following general observation. For Mastri/Belluto
there is a kind of symmetric "mirror" between real and nonreal entities:
Whatever is true for real entities is in some (analogical) sense true for nonreal
entities. The symmetry might be observed especially with respect to causes,
attributes, and division.

8. Caramuel's Linguistic Eliminatism

1. An abbreviated version of this chapter appeared as "*Ens rationis* in Caramuel's
Leptotatos (1681)" (Novotný 2008a).

2. For the Latin title, see the bibliography.

3. The general idea of constructing an artificial language might come from
Ramon Lull (1232–1315); the specific design of this language, however, seems
to have been Caramuel's own. See also Sousedík (1991).

4. "*Ens rationis: Activum.* Quo nomine significatur ipsemet intellectus, quae est
quaedam operatrix ratio [A]. *Passivum Reale* [B]. *Intentionale* [C]. *Impossibile*
[D]. *Possibile: Logicum, Physicum, Psychicum* [E]. *Inhaesivum* [E] Et tales sunt
species intelligibiles, si ipsae dantur, et tales sunt illuminationes ab extrinseco
immissae." LEP s2n171. Note Caramuel's mistake in writing two occurrences

of 'E'. Unfortunately, there are several other small mistakes in Caramuel's text (LEP s2nn171–74). Since, from the context, it seems clear what Caramuel means, I present a "polished" version of Caramuel's views without explicit notes of what I amend.

5. "[1]: Prima *entis rationis* acceptio, nec communis, nec propria est. . . . [2]: Multa sunt dicta et scripta de viribus imaginationis. Et ad illa respiciens, quia intellectus *ratio* dicitur, effectus reales, siquos habet, poterunt *entia rationis* nominari. [3]: Secunda [sic!] *entis rationis* acceptio iubet, ut intelligamus isto nomine actum mentis, qui secundas intentiones speculatur. Quoniam nomen *ratio* et intellectum et intellectionem (hoc est, potentiam et actum) significat. Accepta et usurpata primo modo, realiter verbum mentis producit: et tunc id poterit *ens rationis* vocari. Secundo, vero modo, accepta, est ipsemet actus intelligendi et circa obiectum possibile aut impossibile intentionaliter versari poterit. [LEP s2n172] [4]: Tertiam *entis rationis* acceptio rem impossibilem, obiectam intellectui concernit: quando, videlicet, non-ens per modum entis mens cognoscit, eo modo quo exponetur inferius. Omissa igitur prima acceptione, quae non videtur in Scholis recepta, dicendum est *ens rationis* esse duplex: alterum subiectivum, alterum obiectivum." LEP s2n173.

6. "[5]: Si rem possibilem mens humana concipiat illam [non?] samit (non essentiat); non enim illi esse quiditativum impertitur; nec praestat, ut possibilis sit. Quoniam Intelligentia simplex Dei, samit, dat creaturis possiblibus illud esse essentiale et quiditativum, quod habent. Unde quia sere, esse existentiale, procedit a Volitione Divina, posse sere, a Divina Voluntate proveniet. Quam ob rem *possibilitas* erit denominatio ab existentia actuali et Divina Voluntate proveniens. Dicitur enim esse *possibilis* alius mundus, quia alius mundi quiditas potest existentiam recipere. Et eam potest recipere, quia Intelectus Divinus, a Divina Voluntate adplicatus, illam potest communicare." LEP s2n174.

7. "P. Richardus Lynceus . . . dicens: 'Ens rationis aliud est obiectivum, aliud subiectivum; illud definiri ab omnibus solet, *quod habet tantum esse obiective in intellectu;* esse autem obiective in intellectu, est praeter ei [sc. intellectui] obiici, ab eoque cognosci, omni prorsus esse destitui, tam positivo, quam negativo, tam actuali, quam possibili; quo fit, ut creaturae possibiles, etsi nihil actu sint, tamen propter esse possibile, non ens rationis obiectivum, sed potius ens reale dici soleant, ac debeant; inde etiam fit carentias v. gr. tenebras haud esse ens rationis obiectivum, quoniam suum habent esse negativum et diminutum, idque quin intellectui obiiciantur, ab eove cognoscantur; solum igitur illud, quod repugnat de potentia absoluta esse sicut cogitatur, quodque est aliquid dumtaxat fictum, cognitumque aliter quam esse posset, ens rationis obiectivum est . . . illud proprie et stricte est ens rationis, utpote quod extra latitudinem totam entis realis.'" Lynch as quoted in LEP s2n172. Richard Lynch (1610–76) was an Irish Jesuit who taught philosophy and theology in Salamanca and in Valladolid.

8. "... [E]ns rationis obiectivum [vocari solet] extrinseca aut intrinseca rerum incomponibilium unio. ..." LEP s2n172.

9. Caramuel ridicules his philosophical colleagues for claiming the ability to think beings of reason (in the sense of intrinsically united self-contradictory objects): "Sane intellectus non potest obiectum impossibile attingere. Sed quia id philosophi peritissimi negant, hoc in loco ex suppositione discurremus dicemusque tunc *ens rationis philosophicum* fieri cum concipiuntur incomponibilia simul." LEP s2n174.

10. Other Jesuits who seem to assume self-contradictorism: Thomas Compton Carleton (1591–1666), Silvestro Mauro (1619–87), André Semery (1630–1717), and Maximilian Wietrowski (1660–1737). See Doyle (2004, 1995).

11. While Caramuel seems to have been unaware of Objectualism, he briefly mentions Fallibilism: In LEP s2n174 he alludes to it but without treating it; in LEP s10n199 he simply and without argument declares it absurd.

12. Valentín de Herice (1572–1636) was a Spanish Jesuit working in Salamanca and Valladolid; Georges de Rhodes (1597–1661) was a French Jesuit. For a similar debate between other Baroque Jesuits, see Doyle (1995).

13. "Ens rationis esse totum omnino reale, consistens in partibus realibus, quae licet existere non possint eo modo, quo intellectui obiiciuntur, eorum tamen unio sit cognitio ipsa, non tamen aliquid ex parte obiecti respondens illi cognition." Herice quoted by Caramuel in LEP s4n178.

14. "Et hanc sententiam ... Rhodesius novam et malam vocitat. ... Unde, quando fit ens rationis (v. gr. cum cogito chimaeram) cognitioni huic correspondet obiectum aliquod reale, videlice naturae bovis, leonis, et caprae, etc. et praeterea unio .... Differt ab Herice Rhodesius, quod illam intellectualium cognitionum unionem, quam non solum esse realem et possibilem, sed revera existentem Herice iudicat, Rhodesius communi opinioni subscribens reiiciat; velitque dari in ente rationis unionem conceptam, quae ex parte obiecti naturas illas intellectas coniungat." LEP s4178b.

15. "Patet, quia cum hircocervum intelligit, essentias hircinam et cervinam, quae existunt in rerum natura, nititur apprehensione concipere. Et consulto illud *nititur* posui ... quia intellectus humanus non apprehendit essentias, sed earum loco colores et figuras sensibiles. Et id experientia demonstrat, quia pictor qualem hircocervum suo penicillo imaginat sicut illum in tabula lineis et coloribus exprimit, sic in sui intellectus idea imaginatur." LEP s4n179.

16. It is unclear whether a goat stag is a self-contradictory object. Does being-a-goat logically imply not-being-a-stag? Or is the composition of the two essences only physically or metaphysically impossible? Caramuel himself has doubts about the appropriateness of this example and offers a theological counterexample: Does God-man involve a contradiction? Christians believe it does not; consequently, they should not be so certain that a goat stag does. LEP s9n198.

17. "Dico secundo. Ad uniendas hircinam et cervinam essentias sufficit unio extrinseca. Ut autem hoc dictum intelligas, adnotato, aliud esse duas naturas

una aut simul concipere, et aliud concipere illas esse unitas et identificatas. Quoniam haec proposition, Toletum et Hispalis sunt urbes Regiae, est vera; et tamen in illa τὸ et, quae est coniunctio, non significat illas duas civitates revera esse coniunctas (per multas enim leucas distant), sed significat illas in mente, et etiam in ipsamet oratione coniungi." LEP s4n179.

18. "Apud Gerardum Ioannem Vossium de Arte Grammatica.libr.1.cap.2 sic lego: Coniunctio . . . est dictio, quae coniungit verba et sententias. Sane aliud est res coiungere, aliud verba. Coniunctiones disiunctivae res disiungunt: at coniunctiones cum disiunctivae tum aliae omnes sententiam sententiae coiungunt. . . . Hoc lucis radio ex grammatica speculativa desumpto iam, ut puto, praesens difficultas manet dissoluta et decisa. Quoniam, quando Herice hircocervum intelligit, naturas hircinam et cervinam intelligit; hoc autem et, quod est unio et coiunctio, habet ibi coniunctionis disiunctivae virtutem: quoniam non se tenet ex parte obiecti sed ex parte intellectus et linguae; significat enim essentias illas, quae intrinsece et realiter uniri non possunt, realiter et de facto extrinsece in intellectu et in lingua coniungi." LEP s4n179. Vossius (1577–1649) was a German Calvinist philosopher, historian, rhetorician, and linguist.

19. "Dico tertio. *Est mihi certum indubiumque unionis, quaod substanctiam et quiditatem, fictae repugnare conceptum. Et huic tam firmiter adhaeresco sententiae, ut oppositam improbabilem iudicem. At mihi non ita certum et indubium est non posse hominem veram et realem distinctionem et unionem concipere et intellectualiter collocare ubi non possit esse.* . . . [1] Hinc patet *unionem* ex duplici capite posse vocari *fictam*. Potest enim indipisci istud nomen, quae ficta sit quoad substantiam, et talem unionem non esse intelligibilem, dico. [2] Et potest sortiri hoc vocabulum, si in loco ficto collocetur . . . Et quidem . . . hac secunda significatione nomen unionis fictae accipi ab aliquibus novitiis authoribus; et illorum sententia nihil aliud esse intelligere unionem fictam quam intelligere veram ubi esse non potest; . . . Rhodesii verba . . ." LEP s4n180.

20. "Dico quarto. Est opinio Hericae ingeniosa et plausibilis: et si ad illam entia explicentur, nihil dicetur impossibile. Patet: quia omnia entia, quae in entis rationis conceptu ab Herice ponuntur, sunt vera et realia. Unio illorum extrinseca est vera et realis. Et res, quae obiective et intrinsece uniri nequeunt, possunt formaliter et extrinsece (puta, in mente, aut in lingua) conjungi." LEP s4n180.

21. "Entia rationis . . . ad duo genera seu classes reduximus: nam, licet in omnibus duae res incomponibiles uniri debeant, in alteris unio est ipsis rebus incomponibilibus extrinseca, et consistit in actu mentis illas simul intelligente: in alteris est intrinseca et se tenet ex parte obiecti et consistit in unione vera et reali intellecta . . . et posita ubi non potest esse Superest ut convenientia adfingemus vocabula, ut unum ab alio distinguamus . . . ens rationis legitimum Graece dicatur παρὸν et illegitimum vocetur ψευδὸν. . . . Invenimus ergo convenientia vocabula, ut illa duo genera entium rationis dispesceremus: apte

enim legitima παρόντα et illegitima ψεύδοντα poterunt nuncupari." LEP s5n183.

22. Caramuel again takes up the question of unity in section 13 and 14 (LEP nn202–4). The context is Arriaga-Lynch's dispute. Lynch seems to have held the view of Rhodes against Arriaga. LEP n204 basically repeats what has been said in section nine (LEP n193).

23. "Entia rationis negat Titius; scit ergo quid neget; non enim est censendus entia rationis coeco modo negare; ergo cognoscit ens rationis, ergo etiam facit ens rationis, nam in hac materia idem est facere ac cognoscere." Est elumbis haec ratio; . . . concedo a Titio cognosci, quid esset ens rationis si daretur, non autem, quid illud sit, quoniam non datur. Et nego facere ens rationis, qui cognoscit quid illud esset, requiritur enim, ut faciat ens rationis, ut intelligat Titius quid illud sit. Faceret ens rationis, qui conciperet circulum triangularem; non autem qui conciperet circulum, si per impossibile esset triangulus. . . ." LEP s9n198.

24. "Entia rationis . . . ψεύδοντα si darentur, haberent suum saire et suum seire (videlicet esse quiditativum imperfectum et esse existentiale imperfectum) et secundum utrumque esse deberent causam habere." LEP s7n189.

25. "Et Primo, agendo de seire (*esse existentiali imperfecto*) probatur clarissime nostra conclusio. Quia quidquid existit et tamen distinguitur a Deo, debet causam efficientem habere. Sed existere entia rationis dicuntur, et ipsa non sunt Deus. Debent igitur, si existent, causam efficientem habere. Preterea. Illud, quod aliquando existit et non existit, necesse est, ut suum esse, aut existere, illud ab aliquo efficiente recipiat. At ens rationis, quando intelligitur habet esse et quando non intelligitur illud non habet. Ergo necesse est, ut (illud seire) illud esse . . . ab aliquo efficiente recipiat." LEP s7n189.

26. "Nos autem, quia similia entia nec ab Imaginativa, nec ab Intellectu, nec a Voluntate posse fieri in Metalogica nostra statuimus; et tamen lingua dici posse affirmamus, entia linguae (prius ignota et inaudita) in scholas induximus, definivimusque ea consistere in duabus incomponibilibus formalitatibus, quae nec realiter divinitus, nec intentionaliter humanitus, sive per imaginativam sive per voluntatem queant coniugi; et tamen verbaliter coniungantur de facto. Et talia lingae monstra sunt homo irrationalis, triangulus sphaericus, tenebrae coruscantes." LEP s7n189.

27. "Et secundo, agendo de saire (esse quiditativo imperfecto) non habere causam efficientem humanam, certum est. Utrum autem rationis entibus impertiatur Deus illud saire, quod habent, inferius decidetur." LEP s7n189.

28. "Supponit primo et bene Bernaldus, ens rationis nec causam materialem, nec subiectum habere. . . . Supponit secundo ens rationis nullam causam exempla-rem habere. . . . [Sed] ens reale esse exemplarem entis rationis causam, nam ens rationis praesefert entis rationis qamdam similitudinem. Supponit tertio ens rationis causam non habere finalem. At hoc negare poterunt universi, qui ens rationis esse logicae obiectum pronuncient. . . . [LEP s7n190] Pergit ulterius . . . an ens rationis causam formalem habeat." LEP s7n191. Bernaldo de Quirós

(1613–68) was a Spanish Jesuit philosopher and theologian who taught in Valladolid.

29. "Rationis entia, si darentur sairent (haberent suum esse fictum) distinctum ab ipsamet intellectione et hoc ipsum eorum saire (esse fictum) ab intellectu humano seimeretur (quasi efficeretur). Corrolarium, Non ergo concurrit intellection in genere causae formalis." LEP s8n194.

30. "Entia rationis praecisiva, Graece πάροντα (1) Homo cognoscendo facit, (2) Deus autem illa cognoscit, (3) sed non facit. [LEP a2s3n212]. . . . Si darentur ψεύδοντα (entia rationis fictitia), tunc Deus ita illa cognosceret, sicut hodie mendatium v.g. cognoscit." LEP a2s9n215.

31. "Etiam si darentur ψεύδοντα (entia rationis fictitia) deberemus dicere secundas intentiones, quas vocant, esse relationes et denominationes quasdam reales et non entia rationis." LEP s16n206.

32. "Non . . . datur tale (saire) esse quiditativum obiectum. Ergo nomen Ens rationis fictitium est vox quaedam similis Blictri et Scyndapsus, quae nihil omnino significant." a2s7n216

33. The same separation of the questions of beings of reason and negation/privations—so much taken for granted that it is sometimes not even justified—occurs, for instance, in works of Tirso Gonzáles de Santalla (Knebel 2010, 360), in Paul Aler's *Conclusiones ex Universa Philosophia* (1692), or in Maximilian Wietrowski's *Philosophia disputata* (1697).

34. ". . . sub initium inquirimus, Utrum novitii metaphysici, qui dicunt se posse et solere concipere non-ens per modum entis et asserunt ens rationis tunc facere, teneantur addere, se posse concipere ens per modum non entis, et tunc non-ens rationis aut nihilum rationis formare? . . . et quia censeo, esse omnino impossibile, quod non ens per modum entis concipiatur, debeo consequenter assere, similiter esse impossibile, ut ens per modum non entis cogitetur. Caeterum si esse possibile ens rationis admitterem, a consequentia ductus aut seductus assererem, posse . . . intelligi . . . nihilum rationis. . . ." LEP s2n168.

35. Caramuel was unaware that Suárez accepts the antecedent (which brings with it its own problems; see chapter 5, section E.1).

36. "Nos autem, quia similia entia nec ab imaginativa, nec ab intellectu, nec a voluntate posse fi eri in Metalogica nostra statuimus; et tamen lingua dici posse affi rmamus, entia linguae (prius ignota et inaudita) in scholas induximus, defi nivimusque ea consistere in duabus incomponibilibus formalitatibus, quae nec realiter divinitus, nec intentionaliter humanitus . . . queant coniungi et tamen verbaliter coniungantur de facto. Et talia linguae monstra sunt *homo irrationalis, triangulus sphaericus, tenebra coruscantes.*" LEP s7n189.

Conclusion: Lessons from the History of Philosophy

1. Although some medieval discussions of beings of reason were already quite extensive and systematic. See, e.g., Lambertini (1989), Mayronis (2006), or Natalis (2008).

2. Here I disagree with Doyle, who says: "From my own research, I can say that . . . beings of reason . . . by the end of the seventeenth century . . . were at the heart of metaphysics and, consequent to that, at the heart of both theoretical and practical philosophy" (Salas and Doyle 2010, 391). Doyle is right that seventeenth-century metaphysics paid great attention to intentionality and objective being. But for non-Objectualists, being of reason (as impossible or even self-contradictory objects) was rather a curious and not very significant ontological category.

3. (Maurer 1962, 365); Eschweiler even claims that Suárezianism was a standard metaphysics both in Protestant and Catholic countries between 1620 and 1680 (1928, 311) and speaks about "an impressive history and a close unity of the scholastic stream led by Suárez" (1928, 319). The reason why so many good historians such as Maurer or Eschweiler were misled to think that seventeenth century Jesuits form a unitary Suárezian school is the verbal reverence that Jesuits paid to Suárez, even if they deeply disagreed with him. More recent historians, such as Doyle, are already aware of the heterogeneity of Baroque scholasticism, though in my view they underestimate it: "There were some remarkable deviations from his doctrine" (Doyle 1990, 57).

4. It has been said that "our histories of Western philosophy pass in virtual silence over an era that they should celebrate," namely, the later medieval period (Passnau 1997:1); the same applies to Renaissance and Baroque scholasticism.

5. "In mancher Hinsicht ähneln die scholastischen Texte der Frühen Neuzeit damit den vielen mittlealterichen Kirchen Roms, deren romanische oder gothische Baukerne mit den Transformationen des Barock nicht beseitigt, aber durch ganz neue Gestaltideen überformt wurden und so als sie selbst nur noch auf den zweiten Blick erkennbar geblieben sind" (Marschler 2007, 3).

6. This may explain its controversial status among Baroque authors and why some authors considered it an important category, while others tried to eliminate it. It is not unusual in the history of ideas that one familiar term covers a muddle of intertwined issues.

7. One such attempt can be found in Millán-Puelles (1990/1996). Millán-Puelles builds up his own systematic account of irreality by drawing also on the work of Francisco Suárez, Francisco de Araújo, the Complutenses, and John of St. Thomas. Unfortunately, the lack of adequate historiographical works about this period does not allow him to tap all the riches of Baroque scholasticism.

8. For an overview of the problem in ancient philosophy, see, e.g., Bakaoukas (2003); for bibliographies, see Corazzon (2011a, 2011b).

BIBLIOGRAPHY

Medieval Sources

John Duns Scotus.

> Ioannis Duns Scoti, Doctoris Subtilis et Mariani, Ordinis Fratrum Minorum. *Opera Omnia ... studio et cura commissionis scotisticae ad fidem codicum edita, praeside P. Carolo Balić*. Multivolume. Civitas Vaticana: Typis Polyglottis Vaticanis, 1950–.

> Ioannis Duns Scoti. 1639. *Opera Omnia: Quae hucusque reperiri potuerunt, collecta, recognita, notis, scholiis et commentariis illustratae*. Lugduni: Sumptibus Laurentii Durand.

Mayronis, Franciscus de. 2006. "Quodlibeti quaestiones VI. et VII. (De entibus rationis)." *Studia Neoaristotelica* 3: 196–239.

Thomas Aquinas. *Opera Omnia*. Edited by Roberto Busa and Enrique Alarcón. http://www.corpusthomisticum.org/.

William of Ockham. 1974. *Summa Logicae*. Edited by Ph. Boehner. St. Bonaventure, N.Y.: Franciscan Institute.

———. 1980. *Quodlibeta septem*. Edited by Joseph C. Wey. St. Bonaventure, N.Y.: Franciscan Institute.

Postmedieval Sources

Aler, Paulus. 1692. *Conclusiones ex Universa Philosophia: Circa Quaestiones maxime controversas Assertae, auctoritate philosophi et Doctoris Angelici roboratae, argumentis a ratione desumptis confirmatae*. Coloniae: apud Haeredes Ioannis Widenfet et Godfridum de Berges.

Araujo, Francisco de. 1617. *Commentariorum in Universam Aristotelis Metaphysicam*. Burgis et Salmanticae: Typis Ioannis Baptistae Varesii et Antoniae Ramitae.

> References: CUAM q1a5n30:339 for "quaestio 1, articulus 5, numerus 30, page 339."

Arriaga, Rodrigo de. 1632/1669. *Cursus Philosophicus: Iam noviter maxima ex parte auctus et illustratus, et a variis obiectionibus liberatus, necnon a mendis expurgatus*. Lugduni: Sumpt. Philip Borde, Laurentii Arnauld, et Petri Borde.

> References: CP-M d7s2sb1n8 for "*Metaphysica*, first edition, disputatio 7, sectio 1, subsectio 1 [if any], numerus 1."

Caramuel y Lobkowitz, Juan. 1681. *Leptotatos latine subtilissimus: est opus ingeniosum et novum, sublimium scientiarum professoribus maxime necessarium. Demonstrat enim, non solum ethnicos priscae aetatis philosophos, sed et christianos Graecae et Latinae ecclesiae patres, ubi debebant proprias et conceptus exprimere, haesisse omnino, nec potuisse voto suo satisfacere terminorum defectu. Et, ut huic generali morbo opportunam medicinam adhibeat, dialectum metaphysicam, brevissimam, facillimam, et significatissimam exhibet.* Viglevani: Typis Episcopalibus apud Camillum Conradam.

References: LEP s2n171 for "sectio 2, numerus 171."

Clauberg, Johann. 1691/1968. *Opera Omnia Philosophica. Ante quidem separatim, nunc vero conjunctim edita, multis partibus auctiora et emendatiora.* Amsterodami: Ex Typographia P. & I. Blaev. Reprint, Hildesheim: Georg Olms, 1968.

Eustachio a Sancto Paulo. 1609/1629. *Summa Philosophiae quadripartita: de rebus dialecticis, moralibus et metaphysicis.* Editio ultima ab authore recognita et illustrata. Coloniae: Sumptibus Haeredum Lazari Zetzneri.

Fonseca, Petrus. 1577–99/1604–13. *Commentariorum in Metaphysicorum Aristotelis Stagiritae libros.* Coloniae: Sumptibus Lazari Zetzneri.

Hurtado de Mendoza, Pedro. 1615, 1619. *Disputationes in universam philosophiam a summulis ad metaphysicam.* Pars prior, posterior. Moguntiae: Typis et Sumptibus Ioannis Albini.

References: DUP–L: 72 for "*Logicae*, disputatio 1, sectio 4, numerus 17 page 72"; DUP–M d19s1n9:606 for "*Metaphysicae*, disputatio 1, sectio 1, numerus 9 page 606."

———. 1624. *Universa Philosophia: Nova editio quinque anterioribus tertia fere parte auctior, ab ipso authore ita recognita . . . ut novum opus merito videri queat.* Sumptibus Ludovici Prost. Haeredis Roville.

References: UP-L d1s4n41:51 for "*Logicae*, disputatio 1, sectio 4, numerus 41, page 51"; UP-M d19s1n9:942 for "*Metaphysicae*, disputatio 19, sectio 1, numerus 9 page 942."

Intorcetta, Prosperus, Christianus Herdtrich, Franciscus Rougemont, and Philippus Couplet. 1687. *Confucius Sinarum Philosophus sive Scientia Sinensis Latine Exposita.* Parisiis: Apud Danielem Horthemels.

Izquierdo, Sebastian. 1659. *Pharus scientiarum ubi quiduid ad cognitionem humanam humanitus acquisibilem pertinet, ubertim iuxta, atque succinte pertractatur.* Lugduni: Sumpt. Claudii Bourgeat.

Johannes a Sancto Thoma (Poinsot). 1631/1930–37. *Cursus philosophicus Thomisticus secundum exactam, veram, genuinam Aristotelis et Doctoris Angelici mentem.* Edited by B. Reiser. Turin: Marietti.

Le Grand, Antonius. 1672/1679. *Institutio Philosophiae secundum Principia D. Renati Descartes: Nova method adornata et explicata cumque indice locupletissimo aucta in usum iuventutis academicae.* Noribergae: Sumptibus Johannis Ziegeri.

Losada, Luis de. 1724–35. *Cursus philosophici regalis Collegii Salmanticensis Societatis Iesu: In tres partes diuisi.* Salmanticae Francisci Garcia.

Lynceus, Richardus. 1654. *Universa Philosophia Scholastica*. Lugduni: Sumpt. Philippi Borde, Laurentii Arnaud, et Claudii Rigaud.

Masius Didacus. 1587. *Metaphysica disputatio de ente et eius proprietatibus quae communi nomine inscribitur de Transcendentibus in quinque libros distributa.* Valentiae: Apud Petri Huete.

Mastrius de Meldula, Bartholomeus. 1646. *Disputationes in XII Aristotelis Stagiritae Libros Metaphysicorum: Quibus ab Adversantibus, tum Veterum, tum Recentiorum iaculis Scoti Metaphysicis vindicantur. Tomus Prior (in quo agitur de ente ut sic, eius principiis atque passionibus).* Venetiis: Typis Marci Ginammi.

> References: DLM d2q9n233 for "disputatio 2, quaestio 9, numerus 233."

Mastrius de Meldula, Bartholomaeus, and Bonaventura Bellutus. 1639/1646. *Disputationes in Organum Aristotelis.* Venetiis: typis Marci Ginamni.

> References: DOA d3q7n103:343 for "disputatio 3, quaestio 7, numerus 103, page 343."

Oviedo, Franciscus de. 1640/1651². *Integer cursus philosophicus ad unum corpus redactus in summulas, logicam, physicam, de coelo, de generatione, de anima, et metaphysicam distributus; Tomus 2: Complectens Libros de Anima et Metaphysicam.* Lugduni: Sumptibus Philippi Borde, Laurentii Arnaud, et Claudii Rigaud.

Pontius, Ioannes. 1642/1659. *Philosophiae ad mentem Scoti cursus integer.* Lugduni: sumpt. Ioannis Antonii Huguetan & Marci Antonii Ravaud.

> References: PCI d1q1n1sn1 for "disputatio 1, quaestio 1, numerus 1, subnumerus 1"; the latter are not indicated in the editions; the abbreviation 'add' indicates 'additio' appended to questions 1, 2, 10, and 11.

Ruvius, Antonius. 1605. *Logica mexicana, sive Commentarii in Universam Aristotelis Logicam.* Coloniae Agrippinae: Sumptibus Arnoldi Mylii Birckmanni. [1603 version was not called 'Logica Mexicana'.]

Smiglecius, Martinus. 1617/1634. *Logica: selectis disputationisbus et quaestionibus illustrata.* Oxonii: Excudebant I. L. Impensis H. Crypps, E. Forrest, & H. Curteyne.

> References: L d1q3n8 for "disputatio 1, quaestio 3, numerus 8."

Soto, Dominicus. 1587. *In Porphyrii Isagogen, Aristotelis Categorias, librosque de Demonstratione.* Venetiis, ex officina Dominici Guerraei. Reprint: Frankfut, Minerva, 1967.

Suárez, Franciscus. 1597/1965. *Opera Omnia.* Editio Nova ed. C. Berton. Tom. XXV, XXVI. Reprinted as *Disputationes Metaphysicae*, 2 vols. (Hildesheim: Georg Olms, 1965).

> References: DM d54s1n3 for "disputatio 54, sectio 1, numerus 3."

———. *Commentaria una cum Quaestionibus in libros Aristotelis "De anima."* Repr. as part of *Opera Omnia*, editio nova ed. D. M. André. Tom. III. The critical edition of Salvador Castellote, http://www.salvadorcastellote.com/index.htm, is substantially different from Vives's edition.

> References: DA d9q3n30 for "disputatio 9, sectio 3, numerus 30."

Toletus, Franciscus. 1561–75/1615. *Opera omnia philosophica: I. Introductio in universam Aristotelis logicam, II. Commentaria in universam Aristotelis logicam, III. Commentaria in tres libros Aristotelis De anima, IV. Commentaria in octo libros Aristotelis De physica ausculatione, V. Commentaria in libros Aristotelis de generatione et corruptione.* Coloniae Agrippinae: In Officina Birckmannica, sumptibus Hermanni Mylii, 1615–16. Introduction by Wilhelm Risse; repr. Hildesheim: Georg Olms, 1985.

Tolomei, Johannes Baptista. 1698. *Philosophia mentis et sensuum: secundum utramque Aristotelis methodum pertractata metaphysice et empirice. Editio post Romanam, prima in Germania multo auctior et emendatior, adiuncta Philosophia Morali seu Ethica.* Augustiae Vindelicorum et Dilingae: Suptibus Joannis Caspari Bencard.

Vazquez, Gabriel. 1598/1621. *Commentariorum ac Disputationum in primam partem Sancti Thomae.* Tomi I, II. Antverpiae: Apud Petrum et Ioannem Belleros.

———. 1598/1610. *Commentariorum ac Disputationum in primam secundae Sancti Thomae.* Tomi I, II. Ingolstati.

———. 1609–15. *Commentariorum ac Disputationum in tertiam partem Sancti Thomae.* Tomi I, II, III, IV. Antverpiae: Apud Petrum et Ioannem Belleros.

Wietrowski, Maximilian. 1697. *Philosophia disputata.* Pragae.

Translations

Caramuel y Lobkowitz, Juan de. 1654/2000 *Gramática Audaz.* Traducción de Pedro Arias; estudio preliminar de Lorenzo Velázquez. Pamplona: Ediciones Universidad de Navarra. [Caramuel's *Gramatica audax* is part of his *Theologia rationalis* (1654–55).]

Conimbricenses. 1606/2001. *Some Questions on Signs.* Translated with Introduction and Notes by John P. Doyle. St. Louis, MO: Marquette University Press.

John of St. Thomas [Poinsot]. 1631/1949. "*Entia Rationis* and Second Intentions," translated by John J. Glanville, G. Donald Hollenhorst, and Yves R. Simon; *The New Scholasticism* 23:395–413.

———. 1631/1955. *Outlines of Formal Logic.* Translation of the first part of *Ars Logica, Prima Pars, De Dialecticis Institutionibus, Quas Summulas Vocant*; translated by Francis C. Wade, Milwaukee: Marquette University Press. [This is a part of Poinsot's *Cursus Philosophicus Thomisticus.*]

———. 1631/1955. *The Material Logic. Basic Treatises.* Translated by Yves R. Simon, John J. Glanville and G. Donald Hollenhorst. Chicago: University of Chicago Press. [This is a part of Poinsot's *Cursus Philosophicus Thomisticus.*]

———. 1631/1985. *Tractatus de signis.* In Deely (1985). [This is a part of Poinsot's *Cursus Philosophicus Thomisticus.*]

Natalis, Hervaeus. 2008. *A Treatise of Master Hervaeus Natalis (D. 1323), the Doctor Perspicacissimus, on Second Intentions.* Translated by John P. Doyle, Milwaukee: Marquette University Press.

Ricci, Mateo, Douglas Lancashire, Kuo-chen Hu, and Edward Malatesta. 1603/1985. *The True Meaning of the Lord of Heaven (*天主實義*, Tianzhu shiyi, Chinese-English*

Edition). St. Louis, MO: The Institute of Jesuit Sources in cooperation with The Ricci Institute Taipei, Taiwan.

Suárez, Francisco. 1597/1982. *Individual Unity and Its Principle* [Metaphysical Disputation V]. Translated from Latin with an introduction, notes, glossary, and bibliography by Jorge J. E. Gracia. Milwaukee: Marquette University Press.

———. 1597/1983. *On the Essence of Finite Being as Such, On the Existence of That Essence and Their Distinction* [Metaphysical Disputation XXXI]. Translated by Norman J. Wells. Milwaukee: Marquette University Press.

———. 1597/1995. *On Beings of Reason. (De Entibus Rationis): Metaphysical Disputation LIV.* Translated by John P. Doyle. Milwaukee: Marquette University Press.

———. 1597/2006. *On Real Relation: Metaphysical Disputation XLVII.* Translated by John P. Doyle. Milwaukee: Marquette University Press.

Works Cited

Andrés, Melquiades. 1976–77. *La teología española en el siglo XVI.* Vols. 1–2. Madrid: Biblioteca de Autores Cristianos.

Angelelli, Ignacio. 1967. *Studies on Gottlog Frege and Traditional Philosophy.* Dordrecht, Holland: D. Reidel.

Ariew, Roger. 1999. *Descartes and the Last Scholastics.* Ithaca, N.Y.: Cornell University Press.

Ashworth, Jennifer E. 1974. *Language and Logic in the Post–medieval Period.* Dordrecht, Holland: D. Reidel.

———. 1977. "Chimeras and Imaginary Object: A Study in the Post–Medieval Theory of Signification." *Vivarium* 15:57–77.

———. 1999. "Antonius Rubius on Objective Being and Analogy: One of the Routes from Early Fourteenth-Century Discussions to Descartes's Third Meditation." In Brown 1999, 43–62.

Bak, Felix. 1956. "Scoti schola numerosior omnibus aliis simul sumptibus." *Franciscan studies* 16:144–65.

Bakaoukas, Michael. 2003. *Nothing exists. A History of the Philosophy of Non–being.* Philadelphia: Xlibris Corporation.

Beneš, Jaroslav. 1927. "Valor 'Possibilium' Apud S. Thomam, Henricum Gandavensem, B. Iacobum de Viterbo." *Divus Thomas (Piac.)* 30:333–55.

Bertuccioli, Giuliano 1998. *Martini, Martino S.J. Opera Omnia. Vol. 1 Lettere e documenti.* Trento: Università degli Studi di Trento.

Beuchot, Mauricio. 1996/1998. *The History of Philosophy in Colonial Mexico.* Translated by Elizabeth Millán. Washington, D.C.: Catholic University of America Press. Spanish original: *Historia de la filosofía en el Mexico Colonial.* Barcelona: Herder, 1996.

Blum, Paul Richard. 1998. *Philosophenphilosophie und Schulphilosophie: Typen des Philosophierens in der Neuzeit.* Stuttgart: Franz Steiner.

Boccaccini, Federico. 2010. "*Quasi umbrae entium:* Suárez e Brentano sull' ens rationis." In Sgarbi 2010, 271–94.

Brower, Jeffrey. 2005/2009. "Medieval Theories of Relations." In *The Stanford Ency-clopedia of Philosophy* (Winter 2010), edited by Edward N. Zalta. http://plato .stanford.edu/archives/fall2005/entries/relations–medieval/.

Brown, Stephen F., ed. 1999. *Meeting of the Minds: The Relations between Medieval and Classical Modern (Acts of the International Colloquium held at Boston College, June 14–16, 1996, organized by SIEPM)*. Turnhout: Brepols.

Burkhardt, Hans, and Barry Smith, eds. 1991. *Handbook of Metaphysics and Ontology.* München: Philosophia Verlag.

Cabezón, José Ignacio. 1998. *Scholasticism: Cross-Cultural and Comparative Perspec-tives.* Albany: SUNY Press.

Canteñs, Bernardo. 1999. *Suárez and Meinong on Beings of Reason and Non–existent Objects.* A dissertation submitted to the Faculty of the University of Miami, Coral Gables, Fla.

———. 2000. "The Relationship between God and Essences and the Notion of Eternal Truths according to Francisco Suárez." *The Modern Schoolman* 72:127–43.

———. 2003. "Suárez on Beings of Reason: What Kind of Being (*entia*) are Beings of Reason, and What Kind of Being (*esse*) Do they Have?" *American Catholic Philo-sophical Quarterly* 77:171–87.

Caruso, Ester. 1979. *Pedro Hurtado de Mendoza e la Rinascita del Nominalismo nella Scolastica del Seicento.* Firenze: La Nuova Italia Editrice.

Chisholm, Roderick M. 1960. *Realism and the Background of Phenomenology.* New York: Free Press.

Clarke, W. Norris. 1955. "What is Really Real?" In *Progress in Philosophy. Philosophi-cal Studies in Honor of Rev. Doctor Charles A. Hart,* edited by James A. McWilliams, 61–90. Milwaukee: Bruce.

———. 1960. "The Possibles Revisited: A Reply." *The New Scholasticism* 34:79–102.

Clemenson, David. 2007. *Descartes' Theory of Ideas.* London: Continuum.

Conway, James. 1959. "The Reality of the Possibles." *New Scholasticism* 33:139–61, 331–53.

Coombs, Jeffrey. 1993. "The Possibility of Created Entities in Seventeenth-Century Scotism." *Philosophical Quarterly* 43:447–59.

———. 1994. "John Poinsot on How to Be, Know, and Love a Non–existent Possible. *American Catholic Philosophical Quarterly* 68, 321–35.

———. 2003. "The Ontological Source of Logical Possibility in Catholic Second Scho-lasticism." In *The Medieval Heritage in Early Modern Metaphysics and Modal Theory, 1400–1700,* edited by Russell L. Friedman and Lauge O. Nielsen, 191–229. Dordrecht, Holland: Kluwer Academic.

Copleston, Frederick. 1953. *A History of Philosophy. Vol. III: Late Medieval and Re-naissance Philosophy.* Westminster, Md.: Newman Press. Other editions carry the subtitle "Volume III: Ockham to Suárez."

Corazzon, Raul. 2011a. "Entia rationis: History of the Theories of Non–Existent Ob-jects." http://www.ontology-2.com/ens-rationis.htm.

————. 2011b. "Selected Bibliography on the History of the Theories of Non-Existent Objects." http://www.ontology-2.com/biblio/ens-rationis-biblio.htm.

Courtine, Jean-François (1990) *Suárez et le système de la métaphysique*. Paris: Presses Universitaires de France.

Cronin, Timothy J. 1966. *Objective Being in Descartes and Suárez*. Rome: Gregorian University.

Crowley, Bonaventure. 1948. "The Life and Works of Bartolomeo Mastri, O.F.M. Conv., 1602–1673." *Franciscan Studies* 8:97–152.

Čornejová, Ivana, et al. 1995. *Jan Marek Marci: Život, dílo, doba*. Lanškroun: Rosa.

Darge, Rolf. 2004. *Suárez' transzendentale Seinsauslegung und die Metaphysiktradition*. Leiden: Brill.

Deely, John. 1985. *Tractatus de signis: The Semiotic of John Poinsot*. Berkeley: University of California Press.

————. 2009. *Purely Objective Being*. Berlin: Mouton de Gruyer.

Delfino, Robert A., ed. 2006. *What Are We to Understand Gracia to Mean: Realist Challenges to Metaphysical Neutralism*. Amsterdam: Rodopi.

Des Chene, Dennis. 1996. *Physiologia: Natural Philosophy in Late Aristotelian and Cartesian Thought*. Ithaca, N.Y.: Cornell University Press.

————. 2000. *Life's Form: Late Aristotelian Conceptions of the Soul*. Ithaca, N.Y.: Cornell University Press.

Díaz–Herrera, Patricia. 2006. "The Notion of Time in Francisco Suárez's *Disputatio L*." *Studia Neoaristotelica* 3:142–59.

Doyle, John P. 1967. "Suárez on the Reality of the Possibles." *Modern Schoolman* 44:29–48. Reprinted in Salas and Doyle 2010, chapter 2.

————. 1969a. "Suárez on the Analogy of Being (First Part)." *Modern Schoolman* 46:219–49. Reprinted in Salas and Doyle 2010, chapter 3.

————. 1969b. "Suárez on the Analogy of Being (Second Part)." *Modern Schoolman* 46:323–41. Reprinted in Salas and Doyle 2010, chapter 3.

————. 1984. "Prolegomena to a Study of Extrinsic Denomination in the Work of Francis Suárez S.J." *Vivarium* 22:121–60. Reprinted in Salas and Doyle 2010, chapter 6.

————. 1987a. "Suárez on Beings of Reason and Truth (First part)." *Vivarium* 25:47–75. Reprinted in Salas and Doyle 2010, chapter 7.

————. 1987b. "Suárez on Truth and Mind–dependent Beings: Implications for a Unified Semiotic." In *Semiotics 1983*, edited by Jonathan Evans and John Deely, 121–33. New York: University Press of America.

————. 1988. "Suárez on Beings of Reason and Truth (Second part)." *Vivarium* 26:51–72. Reprinted in Salas and Doyle 2010, chapter 7.

————. 1990. "Extrinsic Cognoscibility: a Seventeenth Century Supertranscendental Notion." *Modern Schoolman* 68:57–80.

————. 1994. "Poinsot on the Knowability of Beings of Reason." *American Catholic Philosophical Quarterly* 68:337–62.

———. 1995. "Another God, Chimerae, Goat–Stags, and Man–Lions: a Seventeenth Century Debate About Impossible Objects." *Review of Metaphysics* 48:771–808.

———. 1997. "Between Transcendental and Transcendental: The Missing Link?" *Review of Metaphysics* 50:783–815.

———. 1998. "Supertranszendent." In *Historisches Wörterbuch der Philosophie* (Band 10: St–T), edited by Joachim Ritter and Karlfried Gründer, 643–49. Basel: Schwabe.

———. 1999. "Supertranscendental Being: On the Verge of Modern Philosophy." In Brown 1999, 297–315.

———. 2001. "On the Pure Intentionality of Pure Intentionality." *Modern Schoolman* 79:57–78.

———. 2003. "The Borders of Knowability: Thoughts from or Occasioned by Seventeenth-Century Jesuits." In *Die Logik des Transcendentalen*, edited by Martin Pickavé, 643–58. Berlin: Walter de Gruyter.

———. 2004. "Wrestling with a Wraith: André Semery, S.J. (1630–1717), on Aristotle's Goat-Stag and Knowing the Unknowable." In *The Impact of Aristotelianism on Modern Philosophy*, edited by Riccardo Pozzo, 84–112, Washington, DC: Catholic University of America Press.

———. 2006. "Mastri and Some Jesuits on Possible and Impossible Objects of God's Knowledge and Power." In Forlivesi 2006, 439–68.

———. 2010. "Francisco Suárez, His Life, His Works, His Doctrine, and Some of His Influence." In Salas and Doyle 2010, 1–20.

Dvořák, Petr. 2000. "John Caramuel and the Possible Worlds Theory." *Acta Comeniana* 38:87–97.

———. 2006. *Jan Caramuel z Lobkovic: Vybrané aspekty formální a aplikované logiky.* Praha: Oikoymenh.

———. 2008. "Juan Caramuel y Lobkowitz." In *The Handbook of the History of Logic (vol. 2)*, edited by Dov M. Gabbay and John Woods, 645–66. Amsterdam: Elsevier.

Dvořák, Petr, and Jacob Schmutz, eds. 2008. *Juan Caramuel y Lobkowitz: The Last Scholastic Polymath.* Prague: Filosofia.

Easton, Patricia. 2001/2008. "Antoine Le Grand." *In The Stanford Encyclopedia of Philosophy* (Fall 2008), edited by Edward N. Zalta. http://plato.stanford.edu/archives /fall2008/entries/legrand/.

Ebbesen, Sten. 1986. "The Chimera's Diary." In Knuutila and Hintikka 1986, 115–43.

Elazar, Michael. 2011. *Honoré Fabri and the Concept of Impetus: A Bridge Between Conceptual Frameworks.* Dordrecht, Holland: Springer.

Eschweiler, Karl. 1928. "Die Philosophie der spanischen Spätscholastik auf den deutschen Universitäten des siebzehnten Jahrhunderts." In *Gesammelte Aufsätze zur Kulturgeschichte Spaniens I (Spanische Forschungen der Görresgesellschaft)*, 251–325. Münster: Aschendorff.

———. 1931. "Roderigo de Arriaga S.J.: Ein Beitrag zur Geschichte der Barockscholastik." In *Gesammelte Aufsätze zur Kulturgeschichte Spaniens III (Spanische Forschungen der Görresgesellschaft)*, 253–85. Münster: Aschendorff.

Feingold, Mordechai, ed. 2003. *Jesuit science and the Republic of Letter*. Cambridge, Mass.: MIT Press.

Fernández-Rodriguez, José Luis. 1972. *El ente de razón en Francisco de Araújo*. Pamplona: Eunsa.

———. 1994. "El 'Ens Rationis', un caso de objeto puro." *Anuario Filosófico* 27:297–318.

———. 1996–97. "La etiológia del ente de razón." *Philosophica* 19–20:109–20.

———. 1997. "Tipología del Ente de Razón." *Anuario Filosófico* 27:297–318.

Ferrater Mora, José. 1953. "Suárez and the Modern Philosophy." *Journal of the History of Ideas* 14:528–47.

Fichter, Joseph H. 1940. *Francis Suárez: Man of Spain*. New York: Macmillan.

Findlay, John Niemeyer. 1933/1995. *Meinong's Theory of Objects and Values*. Second edition. Aldershot: Gregg Revivals, 1995.

Forlivesi, Marco. 2002. *Scotistarum Princeps: Bartolomeo Mastri (1602–1673) E il suo Tempo*. Padova: Centro Studi Antoniani.

Forlivesi, Marco, ed. 2006. *Rem in seipsa cernere: Saggi sul pensiero filosofico di Bartolomeo Mastri (1602–1673): Atti del Convegno di studi sul pensiero filosofico di . . . Mastri . . . Meldola–Bertinoro, 20–22 settembre 2002*. Padova: Il Poligrafo.

Franklin, James. 2002. *The Science of Conjecture: Evidence and Probability Before Pascal*. Baltimore: Johns Hopkins University Press.

———. Forthcoming, 2012. "Science by Conceptual Analysis: The Genius of the Late Scholastics." *Studia Neoaristotelica* 9, no. 1.

Freddoso, Alfred J. 2002. "Suarez on Metaphysical Inquiry, Efficient Causality, and Divine Action." In *Francisco Suàrez, On Creation, Conservation, and Concurrence: Metaphysical Disputations 20–22*, translated by Alfred J. Freddoso, xi–cxxiii. South Bend, Ind.: St. Augustine's Press.

Friedman, Russell L., and Lauge Olaf Nielsen, eds. 2003. *Medieval Heritage in Early Modern Metaphysics and Modal Theory, 1400–1700*. Dordrecht, Holland: Kluwer Academic.

Garber, Daniel, and Michael Ayers. 1998/2003. *The Cambridge History of Seventeenth-Century Philosophy*. Cambridge: Cambridge University Press.

Giacon, Carlo. 1946. *La seconda scolastica*. Milan: Fratelli Bocca.

Gilson, Étienne. 1913/1979. *Index Scolastico-Cartésien*. Paris: J. Vrin.

Godwin, Joscelyn. 1979. *Athanasius Kircher: A Renaissance Man and the Quest for Lost Knowledge*. London: Thames and Hudson.

Goudriaan, Aza. 1999. *Philosophische Gotteserkenntnis bei Suárez und Descartes im Zusammenhang mit der niederländischen reformierten Theologie und Philosophie des 17. Jahrhunderts*. Leiden: Brill.

———. 2002. *Jacobus Revius: A Theological Examination of Cartesian Theology*. Leiden: Brill.

———. 2006. *Reformed orthodoxy and philosophy, 1625–1750: Gisbertus Voetius, Petrus van Mastricht, and Anthonius Driessen*. Leiden: Brill.

Grabmann, Martin. 1926. "Die *Disputationes Metaphysicae* des Franz Suarez in ihrer methodischen Eigenart und Fortwirkung." In *Mittelalterliches Geistesleben I*, 525–60. München: Max Hubener.

Gracia, Jorge J. E. 1991a. "Francisco Suárez: The Man in History." *American Catholic Philosophical Quarterly* 65: 256–66.

———. 1991b "Suárez's Conception of Metaphysics: A Step in the direction of Mentalism?" *American Catholic Philosophical Quarterly* 65, 287–309.

———. 1992. "Suárez and the Doctrine of the Transcendentals." *Topoi* 11, no. 2: 121–33.

———. 1993. "Suárez and Metaphysical Mentalism: The Last Visit." *American Catholic Philosophical Quarterly* 67, 349–54.

———. 1999. *Metaphysics and Its Task: The Search for the Categorial Foundation of Knowledge*. Albany: SUNY Press.

———. 2000. *Hispanic/Latino Identity: A Philosophical Perspective*. Malden, Mass.: Blackwell Publishers.

———. 2003. "Francisco Suárez, Metaphysical Disputations (1597): From the Middle Ages to Modernity." In Gracia et al. 2003, 204–9.

Gracia, Jorge J. E., and Daniel D. Novotný. 2012. "Fundamentals in Suárez's Metaphysics: Transcendentals and Categories." In *Interpreting Suárez: A Collection of Critical Essays*, edited by Daniel Schwartz (Cambridge: Cambridge University Press).

Gracia, Jorge J. E., and Timothy B. Noone. 2003. *A Companion to Philosophy in the Middle Ages*. Malden, Mass.: Blackwell.

Gracia, Jorge J. E., Gregory M. Reichberg, and Bernard N. Schumacher, eds. 2003. *The Classics of Western Philosophy: A Reader's Guide*, Malden, Mass.: Blackwell.

Grajewski, Maurice. 1946. "John Ponce, Franciscan Scotist of the Seventeenth Century." *Franciscan Studies* 6:54–92.

Grant, Edward. 1981. *Much Ado About Nothing: Theories of Space and Vacuum from the Middle Ages to the Scientific Revolution*. Cambridge: Cambridge University Press.

———. 1984. "Were there Significant Differences between Medieval and Early Modern Scholastic Natural Philosophy?" *Noûs* 18, 5–14.

Gredt, Josephus. 1899/1961. *Elementa philosophiae aristotelico–thomisticae (Ed. 13 recognita et aucta ab Eucharius Zenzen)* Barcelona: Herder.

Hadot, Pierre. 1995. *Philosophy as a Way of Life*. Oxford: Blackwell.

Hattab, Helen. 2009. *Descartes: Forms and Mechanism*. Cambridge: Cambridge University Press.

Heanue, James E. 1991. "Ens Rationis II: From the Medievals to Brentano." In Burkhardt and Smith 1991, 246–48.

Heider, Daniel. 2007. "Is Suárez's Concept of Being Analogical or Univocal?" *American Catholic Philosophical Quarterly* 81:21–41.

———. 2010. "Pedro Hurtado de Mendoza's (Mis)interpretation of Aquinas." In Sgarbi 2010, 105–40.

———. 2011a "Bartholomew Mastrius (1602–1673) and John Punch (1599 or 1603–1661) on the Common Nature and Universal Unity." *Proceedings of ACPQ* 84:145–67.

———. 2011b. "The Role of Trinitarian Theology in Universals Bartolomeo Mastri da Meldola (1602–1673) and Bonaventura Belluto (1600–1676)." In *Herausforderung durch Religion? Begegnungen der Philosophie mit Religionen in Mittelalter und Renaissance*, edited by Gerhard Krieger, 251–67. Würzburg: Verlag Königshausen und Neumann.

———. 2011c. *Suárez a jeho metafyzika. Od pojmu jsoucna přes transcendentální jednotu k druhům transcendentální jednoty*. Praha: Filosofia.

Hellyer, Marcus. 2005. *Catholic Physics. Jesuit Natural Philosophy in Early Modern Germany*. Notre Dame, Ind.: University of Notre Dame Press.

Henninger, Mark G. 1989. *Relations. Medieval Theories 1250–1325*. Oxford: Clarendon Press.

Hickman, Larry. 1980. *Modern Theories of Higher Level Predicates: Second Intentions in the Neuzeit*. München: Philosophia Verlag.

Hill, Benjamin, and Henrik Lagerlund, eds. 2012. *The Philosophy of Francisco Suárez*. Oxford: Oxford University Press.

Hoffmann, Tobias. 2002. *Creatura intellecta: Die Ideen und Possibilien bei Duns Scotus mit Ausblick auf Franz von Mayronis, Poncius und Mastrius*. Münster: Aschendorff.

Holzhey, Helmut, and Wilhelm Schmidt–Biggemann. 2001. *Grundriss der Geschichte der Philosophie, begründet von Friedrich Ueberweg. Die Philosophie des 17. Jahrhunderts: Das Heilige Römische Reich Deutscher Nation, Nord– und Ostmitteleuropa*. Basel: Schwabe.

Honnefelder, Ludger. 1979. *Ens inquantum ens. Der Begriff des Seienden als solchen als Gegenstand der Metaphysik*. Münster: Aschendorff.

———. 1990. *Scientia transcendens. Die formale Bestimmung der Seiendheit und Realität in der Metaphysik der Mittelalters und der Neuzeit*. Hamburg: Felix Meiner.

Honnefelder, Ludger, Rega Wood, and Mechtild Dreyer, eds. 1996. *John Duns Scotus: Metaphysics and Ethics*. Leiden: Brill.

Iriarte, Joaquín. 1948. "La proyección sobre Europa de una gran Metafísica—o—Suárez en la Filosofía de los días del Barroco." *Razón y fe. Revista hispano–americana de cultura* 138:229–63.

Iturrioz, Jesús. 1949. *Estudios Sobre La Metafísica de Francisco Suárez*. Madrid: Facultades de Teología y Filosofía del Colegio Máximo S. I. de Oña.

Jansen, Bernhard. 1933. "Deutsche Jesuiten–Philosophen des 18. Jahrhunderts in ihrer Stellung zur neuzeitlichen Naturauffassung." *Zeitschrift für katholische Theologie* 57:384–410.

———. 1936a "Zur Philosophie der Scotisten des 17. Jahrhunderts." *Franziskanische Studien* 17:25–58 (part 1), 150–75 (part 2).

———. 1936b. "Quellenbeiträge zur Philosophie im Benediktineorden." *Zeitschrift für katholische Theologie* 40:55–98.

———. 1938. "Zur Phänomenologie der Philosophie der Thomisten des 17. und und 18. Jahrhunderts." *Scholastik* 17:49–71.

———. 1951. "Die scholastische Psychologie vom 16. bis 18 Jahrhundert." *Scholastik* 26:342–63.

Jindráček, Efrém. 2009. "Pavel ze Soncina a italský tomismus XV: Století." *Studia Neoaristotelica* 6, 247–64.

Karofsky, Amy D. 2001. "Suárez's Doctrine of Eternal Truths." *Journal of the History of Philosophy* 39, no. 1: 23–47.

Kenny, Anthony. 1994. *The Oxford Illustrated History of Western Philosophy.* Oxford: Oxford University Press.

———. 2005. *A New History of Western Philosophy, Volume II: Medieval Philosophy.* Oxford: Clarendon Press.

Klima, Gyula. 1993. "The Changing Role of Entia Rationis in Mediaeval Semantics and Ontology: A Comparative Study with a Reconstruction." *Synthese* 96:25–58.

Knebel, Sven K. 2005. "Juan de Alvarado (1578–1648): A Treatise on Beings of Reason." In *Philosophia Vitam Alere: Prace dedykowane księdzu profesorowi Romanowi Darowskiemu SJ z okazji 70-lecia urodzin,* edited by Stanisław Zemiański, 213–36. Kraków: Ignatianum-Wam.

———. 1999. "The Early Modern Rollback of Merely Extrinsic Denomination." In Brown 1999, 317–31.

———. 2011. *Suarezismus: Erkenntnistheoretisches Aus Dem Nachlass Des Jesuitengenerals Tirso Gonzáres de Santalla: Abhandlung und Edition.* Amsterdam: B. R. Grüner.

Knuutila, Simo, and Jaako Hintikka, eds. 1986. *The Logic of Being.* Dordrecht, Holland: D. Reidel.

Kobush, Theo. 1987. *Sein und Sprache. Historische Grundlegung einer Ontologie der Sprache.* Leiden: Brill.

———. 1998. "Arriagas Lehre vom Gedankending." In *Rodrigo de Arriaga: Philosoph und Theologe,* edited by Tereza Saxlová and Stanislav Sousedík, 123–40, Prague: Karolinum.

Kolmaš, Josef. 2008. "François Noël (Franciscus Natalis): Philosophica Sinica." *Fragmenta Ioanna Collecta* 8:41–70.

Kretzmann, Norman, et al. 1982/1988. *The Cambridge History of Later Medieval Philosophy: From the Rediscovery of Aristotle to the Disintegration of Scholasticism, 1100–1600.* Cambridge: Cambridge University Press.

Kristeller, Paul Oskar. 1955/1961. *Renaissance Thought: The Classic, Scholastic, and Humanistic Strains.* Revised and enlarged edition, New York: Harper and Brothers, 1961.

———. *Renaissance Thought and Its Sources.* New York: Columbia University Press, 1979.

Krook, Dorothea. 1993. *John Sergeant and His Circle: A Study of Three Seventeenth-Century English Aristotelians*. Leiden: Brill.

Kuhn, Heinrich. 2005. "Aristotelianism in the Renaissance." In *The Stanford Encyclopedia of Philosophy* (Winter 2005), edited by Edward N. Zalta. http://plato.stanford.edu/archives/win2005/entries/aristotelianism–renaissance/.

Lambertini, Roberto. 1989. "Resurgant entia rationis: Matthaeus de Augubio on the object of logic." *Cahiers de l'Institut du moyen-âge grec et latin* 59:3–60.

Lattis, James M. 1995. *Between Copernicus and Galileo: Christoph Clavius and the Collapse of Ptolemaic Cosmology*. Chicago: University of Chicago Press.

Leinsle, Ulrich G. 1988. "Die Scholastik der Neuzeit bis zur Aufklärung." In *Christliche Philosophie im katholischen Denken des 19. und 20. Jahrhunderts*, edited by Emerich Coreth, Walter M. Neidl, and Georg Pfligersdorffer, 54–69. Graz: Verlag Styria.

———. 1995. *Einführung in die scholastische Theologie*. Paderborn: Schöningh.

———. 2006. *Diliganae Disputationes: Der Lehrinhalt der gedruckten Disputationen an der Philosophishen Fakultät der Universität Dilingen, 1555–1648*. Regensburg: Schnell/Steiner.

Lüthy, Christoph. 2000. "What to Do with Seventeenth-Century Natural Philosophy? A Taxonomic Problem." *Perspectives on Science* 8, 164–95.

Maurer, Armand. 1950. "*Ens diminutum*: A Note on its Origin and Meaning." *Medieval Studies* 12:216–22.

O'Brien, Chrysostom. 1962. "La enigma de Francisco de Araújo." *Ciencia tomista* 89:221–35.

Lewalter, Ernst. 1935/1967. *Spanisch–Jesuitische und Deutsch–Lutherische Metaphysik des 17. Jahrhunderts: Ein Beitrag zur Geschichte der Iberisch–Deutschen Kulurbeziehungen und zur Vorgeschichte des Deutschen Idealismus*. Darmstadt: Wissenschaftliche Buchgesellschaft.

Lisska, Anthony. 1976. "Axioms of Intentionality in Aquinas' Theory of Knowledge." *International Philosophical Quarterly* 16, 305–22.

Lohr, Charles H. 1988a. "Latin Aristotle Commentaries: II. Renaissance Authors." Florence: Sismel.

———. 1988b. "Metaphysics." In *The Cambridge History of Renaissance Philosophy*, edited by Charles Schmitt, 537–638. Cambridge: Cambridge University Press.

Magdisi, George. 1981. *The Rise of Colleges: Institutions of Learning in Islam and the West*. Edinburg: Edinburg University Press.

Mancosu, Paolo. 1996. *Philosophy of Mathematics and Mathematical Practice in the Seventeenth Century*. New York: Oxford University Press.

Marchlewitz, Ingrid, and Albert Heinekamp. 1990. *Leibniz' Auseinandersetzung mit Vorgängern und Zeitgenossen*. Stuttgart: Franz Steiner Verlag.

Maritain, Jacques. 1959. *The Degrees of Knowledge*. Translated by Gerald B. Phelan. New York: Charles Scribner's Sons.

Marschler, Thomas. 2007. *Die spekulative Trinitätslehre des Francisco Suárez S.J. in ihrem philosophisch–theologischen Kontext*. Münster: Aschendorff.

Maryks, Robert A. 2010. *The Jesuit Order as a Synagogue of Jews: Jesuits of Jewish Ancestry and Purity-of-Blood Laws in the Early Society of Jesus.* Leiden: Brill.

Maurer, Armand A. 1962. *Medieval Philosophy.* New York: Random House.

McCool, Gerald. 2000. "The Christian Wisdom Tradition and Enlightenment Reason." In *Examining the Catholic Intellectual Tradition*, edited by Anthony J. Cernera and Oliver J. Morgan, 75–102, Fairfield: Sacred Heart University Press.

McDaniel, Kris. 2009. "Ways of Being" In *Metametaphysics: New Essays on the Foundation of Ontology*, edited by David Chalmers, David Manley, and Ryan Wasserman, 290–319. Oxford: Clarendon Press.

Meinong, Alexius. 1902. *Über Annahmen.* Leipzig.

———. 1904. *Untersuchungen zur Gegenstandstheorie und Psychologie.* Leipzig.

Meixner, Uwe. 2004. *Einführung in die Ontologie.* Darmstadt: WBG.

Millán-Puelles, Antonio. 1990/1996. *The Theory of the Pure Object.* Tr. Jorge García–Gómez. Heidelberg: Universitätsverlag C. Winter. Spanish original: *Teoría del objeto puro—Colección Cuestiones Fundamentales.* Madrid: Ediciones RIALP.

Miller, Barry. 2002. *The Fullness of Being: A New Paradigm for Existence.* Notre Dame, Ind.: University of Notre Dame Press.

Mungello, David E. 2009. *The Great Encounter of China and the West, 1500–1800.* Third edition. Lanham, Md.: Rowman and Littlefield.

Noone, Timothy B. 2003. "Scholasticism." In Gracia and Noone 2003, 55–64.

Novák, Lukáš. 2011. *"Scire Deum esse": Scotův důkaz Boží existence jako vrcholný výkon metafyziky jakožto aristotelské vědy.* Praha: Kalich.

Novák, Lukáš, and Petr Dvořák. 2007. *Úvod do logiky aristotelské tradice.* České Budějovice: Jihočeská Univerzita.

Novotný, Daniel D. 2006. "Prolegomena to a Study of Beings of Reason in Post-Suarezian Scholasticism, 1600–1650." *Studia Neoaristotelica* 3:117–41.

———. 2008a. *"Ens Rationis* in Caramuel's *Leptotatos* (1681)." In Dvořák and Schmutz 2006, 71–84.

———. 2008b. "Forty-Two Years after Suárez: Mastri and Belluto's Development of the "Classical" Theory of Entia Rationis" *Quaestio: The Yearbook of the History of Metaphysics* 8:473–98.

———. 2010. "Rubio and Suárez: A Comparative Study on the Nature of Entia Rationis." In *Bohemia Jesuitica 1556–2006*, edited by Petra Čemusová, 477–90. Praha: Karolinum.

———. 2011. "Suárezova teorie pomyslných jsoucen a její recepce." *Filozofia* (Bratislava) 1:35–48.

———. 2012. "Scholastic Debates about Beings of Reason and Contemporary Analytical Metaphysics." In *Metaphysics: Aristotelian, Scholastic, Analytic*, edited by Lukáš Novák, Daniel D. Novotný, Prokop Sousedík, and David Svoboda. Frankfurt: Ontos Verlag.

———. Forthcoming-a. "Twenty Years after Suárez: Francisco de Araújo on the Nature, Existence, and Causes of *Entia rationis.*" In *Festschrift for John P. Doyle*, edited by Victor M. Salas. Leiden: Brill.

———. Forthcoming-b. "Teorie obecnin Sebastiana Izquierdo (1601–1681)." In *Problematika univerzálií v první a druhé scholastice*, edited by Daniel Heider and David Svoboda. *Studia Neoaristotelica.*

———. Forthcoming-c. "The Historical Non-significance of Suárez's Theory of Beings of Reason: A Lesson from Hurtado." In *Metaphysics of Francisco Suárez (1548–1617): "Disputationes Metaphysicae" in their Systematic and Historical Context*, edited by Daniel Heider, Lukáš Novák, and David Svoboda, chapter 9.

———. Forthcoming-d. "Suárez on Beings of Reason." In Brill Companion de Suárez, edited by Victor M. Salas. Leiden: Brill.

Nuchelmans, Gabriel. 1980. *Late Scholastic and Humanist Theories of the Proposition.* Oxford: North Holland Publishing.

Øhrstrøm, Peter, Sara L. Uckelman, and Henrik Schärfe. 2007. "Historical and Conceptual Foundation of Diagrammatical Ontology." In *Conceptual Structures: Knowledge Architectures for Smart Applications*, edited by Uta Priss, Simon Polovina, and Richard Hill, 374–86. Berlin: Springer Verlag.

Oeing–Hanhoff, Ludger. 1974. "Gedankending (ens rationis)." In *Historisches Wörterbuch der Philosophie Bd. 3 (G–H)*, edited by Joachim Ritter, 55–62. Basel: Schwabe.

Palmieri, Paolo. "Radical Mathematical Thomism: Beings of Reason and Divine Decrees in Torricelli's Philosophy of Mathematics." *Studies in History and Philosophy of Science* 40:131–42.

Parsons, Terence. 1980. *Nonexistent Objects.* New Haven: Yale University Press.

Pastine, Dino. 1972. "Caramuel contro Descartes: obiezioni inedite alle Meditazioni." *Rivista critica di storia della filosofia* 27:177–221.

Pereira, José, and Robert Fastiggi. 2006. *The Mystical Theology of the Catholic Reformation: An Overview of Baroque Spirituality.* Lanham: University Press of America.

Pereira, José. 2007. *Suárez: Between Scholasticism and Modernity.* Milwaukee: Marquette University Press.

Peroutka, David. 2010. "Imagination, Intellect and Premotion." *Studia Neoaristotelica* 7:107–14.

Perszyk, Kenneth J. 1993. *Nonexistent Objects: Meinong and Contemporary Philosophy.* Dordrecht, Holland: Kluwer Academic.

Plans, Juan Belda. 2000. *La Escuela de Salamanca y la renovación de la teología en el siglo XVI.* Madrid: Biblotheca de Autores Cristianos.

Pomplun, Terence. 2010. *Jesuit on the Roof of the World: Ippolito Desideri's Mission to Tibet.* Oxford: Oxford University Press.

Popkin, Richard H. 1992. *The Third Force in Seventeenth-Century Thought.* Leiden: Brill.

Priest, Graham. 2005. *Towards Non-Being: The Logic and Metaphysics of Intentionality.* Oxford: Oxford University Press.

Prior, Arthur N. 1971. *Objects of Thought.* Edited by Peter Geach and Anthony Kenny. Oxford: Clarendon Press.

Quine, Willard van Orman. 1948/1980. "On What There Is." In *From a Logical Point of View: Nine Logico-Philosophical Essays*, 2nd edition, 1–19. Cambridge, Mass.: Harvard University Press.

Quinto, Riccardo 2001. *Scholastica. Storia di un concetto.* Padova: Il Poligrafo.

Rayo, Agustín, and Gabriel Uzquiano, eds. 2006. *Absolute Generality.* Oxford: Clarendon Press.

Redmond, Walter. 1998. "Philosophy versus Concern for Indians: A Jesuit's Inner Struggle." *Modern Schoolman* 75:329–36.

———. 2004. "Self-Awareness in Colonial Latin American Philosophy, Part 1." *Jahrbuch für Geschichte Lateinamericas* 41:353–71.

———. 2005. "Self-Awareness in Colonial Latin American Philosophy, Part 2." *Jahrbuch für Geschichte Lateinamericas* 42:209–34.

Redmond, Walter, and Mauricio Beuchot. 1985. "La lógica mexicana en el siglo de oro." Mexico: Universidad Nacional Autónoma de México.

Reichberg, Gregory M. 2003. "De Indis and De Iure belli relectiones (1557): Philosophy Meets War." In Gracia et al. 2003, 197–203.

Reicher, Maria. 2006/2010. "Nonexistent Objects." In *The Stanford Encyclopedia of Philosophy* (Fall 2010), edited by Edward N. Zalta. http://plato.stanford.edu/archives /fall2010/entries/nonexistent–objects/.

Rescher, Nicholas. 2003a. "Nonexistents Then and Now." *Review of Metaphysics* 57:359–81.

———. 2003b. *Imagining Irreality: A Study of Unreal Possibilities.* Chicago: Open Court.

Risse, Wilhelm. 1964. *Die Logik der Neuzeit, Vol. I (1599–1640).* Stuttgart: Friedrich Frommann Verlag.

———. 1970. *Die Logik der Neuzeit, Vol. II (1640–1780).* Stuttgart: Friedrich Frommann Verlag.

Romero, Ignacio Osorio. 1988. *Antonio Rubio en la filosofía novohispana*: Ciudad del Mexico: UNAM.

Roncaglia, Gino. 1995. "Smiglecius on *entia rationis*." *Vivarium* 33:27–49.

Ross, James F. 1962. "Suárez on Universals." *Journal of Philosophy* 59:736–48.

Rothbard, Murray N. 1976. "New Light on the Prehistory of the Austrian School." In *The Foundations of Modern Austrian Economics*, edited by Edwin Dolan, 52–74 (Kansas City: Sheed and Ward).

Routley, Richard. 1980. *Exploring Meinong's Jungle and Beyond.* Canberra: Australian National University.

Rovira, Rogelio. 2000. "Las quiddidades paradójicas: sobre la contribución de Antonio Millán–Puelles a la doctrina clásica del ente de razón." *Pensamiento* 46:265–84.

Russell, Bertrand. 1903/1938. *The Principles of Mathematics.* New York: Norton Paperback. Digital edition: http://fair-use.org/bertrand-russell/the-principles-of -mathematics/.

Salas, Victor M. Forthcoming. *Festschrift for John P. Doyle.* Leiden: Brill.

Salas, Victor M., and John P. Doyle, eds. 2010. *Collected Studies on Francisco Suárez S.J. (1548–1617).* Leuven: Leuven University Press.

Salas, Victor M., and Robert Fastiggi, eds. Fortcoming. *Brill Companion to Francisco Suárez*. Leiden: Brill.

Schwarz, Daniel, ed. 2012. *Interpreting Suárez: Critical Essays*. Cambridge, Mass.: Cambridge University Press.

Saxlová, Tereza, and Stanislav Sousedík. 1998. *Rodrigo de Arriaga: Philosoph und Theologe*. Prag: Carolinum.

Scorraille, Raoul. 1912. *François Suárez de la Campaigne de Jésus*. Paris: P. Lethielleux.

Scruton, Roger. 1994. *Modern Philosophy: An Introduction and Survey*. London: Sinclair-Stevenson.

———. 1995. "Modern Philosophy I: The Rationalists and Kant." In *Philosophy 1: A Guide through the Subject*, edited by Anthony C. Grayling, 440–83. Oxford: Oxford University Press.

Schmidt, Robert W. 1963. "The Translation of Terms Like *Ens rationis*." *Modern Schoolman* 41:73–75.

———. 1966. *The Domain of Logic According to Saint Thomas Aquinas*. The Hague: Martinus Nijhoff.

Schmitt, Charles B. 1983. *Aristotle and the Renaissance*. Cambridge, Mass.: Harvard University Press.

Schmitt, Charles B., et al. 1988/1991. *The Cambridge History of Renaissance Philosophy*. Cambridge: Cambridge University Press.

Schmutz, Jacob. 2000. "Bulletin de scolastique moderne (I)." *Revue Thomiste* 100:270–341.

———. 2001. "Juan Caramuel on the Year 2000: Time and Possible Worlds in Early-Modern Scholasticism." In *The Medieval Concept of Time: The Scholastic Debate and Its Reception in Early Modern Philosophy*, edited by Pasquale Porro, 399–434, Leiden: Brill.

———. 2002. "L'héritage des Subtils, Cartographie du scotisme de l'age classique." *Les Études Philosophiques* Les Etudes philosophiques 1:51–81, 75–77.

———. 2007. "Hurtado et son double. La querelle des images mentales dans la scolastique modern." In *Questions sur l'intentionnalité*, edited by Lambros Couloubaritsis and Antonio Mazzù, 157–232. Bruxelles: Ousia.

Schobinger, Jean-Pierre, et al. 1988. *Grundriss der Geschichte der Philosophie, begründet von Friedrich Ueberweg. Die Philosophie des 17. Jahrhunderts: England, Vols. 3.1 and 3.2*. Basel: Schwabe.

———. 1993. *Grundriss der Geschichte der Philosophie, begründet von Friedrich Ueberweg. Die Philosophie des 17. Jahrhunderts: Frankreich und Niederlande, Vols. 2.1 and 2.2*. Basel: Schwabe.

———. 1998. *Grundriss der Geschichte der Philosophie, begründet von Friedrich Ueberweg. Die Philosophie des 17. Jahrhunderts: Allgemeine Themen, Iberische Halbinsel, Italien, Vols. 1.1 and 1.2*. Basel: Schwabe.

Sgarbi, Marco, ed. 2010. *Francisco Suárez and His Legacy: The Impact of Suárezian Metaphysics and Epistemology on Modern Philosophy*. Milano: Vita e Pensiero.

Shields, Christopher. 2012. "Shadows of Being: Francisco Suárez's *Entia Rationis.*" In Hill and Lagerlund 2012, chapter 3.

Smith, Barry. 1991. "Textual Deference." *American Philosophical Quarterly* 28, 1–13.

Solana, Marcial. 1941. *Historia de la Filosofía Española, Vols. I–III.* Madrid: Real Academia de ciencias exactas.

Sousedík, Stanislav. 1983. *Valerián Magni: Kapitola z kulturních dejin Čech 17. století.* Praha: Vyšehrad.

———. 1990. *Leibniz und Caramuels Leptotatos.* In Marchlewitz and Heinekamp 1990, 191–99.

———. 1991. "Universal Language in the Work of Juan Caramuel." *Acta Comeniana* 33:149–58.

———. 1996. "Der Streit um den wahren Sinn der Scotischen Possibilienlehre." In Honnefelder et al. 1996, 191–204.

———. 1997/2009. *Filosofie v českých zemích mezi středověkem a osvícenstvím.* Praha: Vyšehrad. German edition: *Philosophie der frühen Neuzeit in den böhmischen Ländern.* Stuttgart-Bad Cannstatt: Frommann-Holzboog, 2009.

———. 2004. "Pomyslná jsoucna (*entia rationis*) v aristotelské tradici 17. století." *Filozofický časopis* 52:533–44.

———. 2006. *Identitní teorie predikace.* Praha: Oikoymenh.

South, James B. 2001. "Francisco Suárez on Imagination." *Vivarium* 39: 119–58.

Spade, Paul Vincent. 2004/2009. "Medieval Philosophy." In *The Stanford Encyclopedia of Philosophy* (Winter 2009), edited by Edward N. Zalta. http://plato.stanford.edu/entries/medieval-philosophy/.

Spruit, Leen. 1995. *Species intelligibilis, Vol. II (Renaissance Controversies, Later Scholasticism, and the Elimination of the Intelligible Species in Modern Philosophy).* Leiden: Brill.

Strawson, Peter F. 1959/2005. *Individuals: An Essay in Descriptive Metaphysics.* New York: Routledge.

Symchych, Mykola. 2009. *Philosophia rationalis у Києво-Могилянській академії: Компаративний аналіз могилянських курсів логіки кінця XVII-першої половини XVIII ст.* Вінниця: О.Власюк.

———. Forthcoming. "Jesuit Influences, Modernization and Anti–Modernization in Ukrainian Academic Philosophy from the End of the 16th to the End of the 18th Century." In *Innovazione filosofica e istituzione universitaria tra Cinquecento e primo Novecento,* edited by Marco Forlivesi, Padua.

Theron, Stephen. 1991. "Ens Rationis I: Medieval Theories." In Burkhardt and Barry Smith, 245–46.

Trevisiani, Francesco. 1993. "Johannes Clauberg e l'Aristotele riformato." In *L'interpretazione nei secoli XVI e XVII. Atti del Convegno internazionale di studi Milano (18–20 novembre 1991), Parigi (6–8 dicembre 1991),* edited by Guido Canziani, 103–26. Milano: FrancoAngeli.

Urráburru, Joannes Josephus. 1908. *Institutiones philosophicae*. Volume 1, *Logica*. Vallisoleti, 1908.

Vallicella, William F. 2002. *A Paradigm Theory of Existence*. Dordrecht: Kluwer Academic.

Van Asselt, Willem J., and Dekker, Eef. 2001. *Reformation and Scholasticism: An Ecumenical Enterprise*. Grand Rapids, Mich.: Baker Academic.

Van Inwagen, Peter. 2009. *Metaphysics, Third Edition*. Philadelphia: Westview.

Veatch, Henry B. 1970. *Intentional Logic*. New Haven, Conn.: Archon Books.

Velarde Lombraña, Julián. 1986. *Juan Caramuel: Vida y Obra*. Ovideo: Pentalfa Ediciones.

Wells, Norman J. 1981a. "Suarez on the Eternal Truths: Part I." *Modern Schoolman* 58:73–105.

———. 1981b. "Suàrez on the Eternal Truths: Part II." *Modern Schoolman* 58:159–74.

———. 1993. "Esse cognitum and Suárez Revisited." *American Catholic Philosophical Quarterly* 67:339–48.

Werner, Karl. 1889/1962. *Franz Suárez und die Scholastik der letzten Jahrhunderte*. New York: Burt Franklin [original edition of 1889 published in Regensburg].

Williams, Thomas, ed. 2003. *The Cambridge Companion to Duns Scotus*. Cambridge, Mass.: Cambridge University Press.

Wittgenstein, Ludwig. 1922. Reprinted as *Tractatus Logico-Philosophicus*. New York: Cosimo, 2009.

Wolter, Allan. 1964. *Transcendentals and Their Function in the Metaphysics of John Duns Scotus*. St. Bonaventure, N.Y.: Franciscan Institute.

Wundt, Max. 1939. *Die deutsche Schulmetaphysik des 17. Jahrhunderts*. Tübingen: J. C. B. Mohr.

Yela Utrila, Juan Francisco. 1948. "El ente de razón en Suárez." *Pensamiento* 4:271–303.

Medieval Philosophy
TEXTS AND STUDIES